THE SOUTHERN FRONTIER

1670–1732

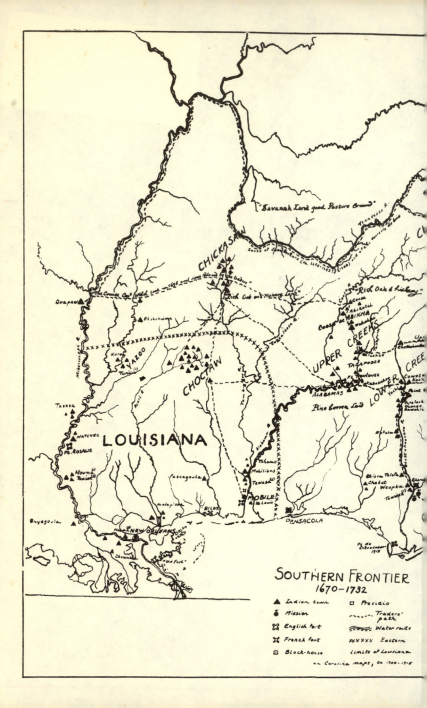

SOUTHERN FRONTIER
1670-1732

▲ Indian town   □ Presidio
🔔 Mission   ∿∿∿ Traders' path
⚔ English fort   ⚓ Water route
⚒ French fort   xxxxx Eastern
◙ Block-house   Limits of Louisiana
                  on Carolina maps, ca. 1700-1715

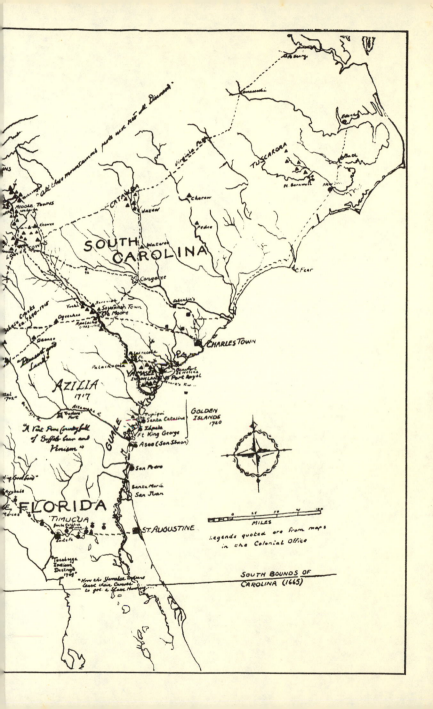

THE SOUTHERN FRONTIER

1670-1732

Verner W. Crane

With a new preface by
Peter H. Wood

W·W· NORTON & COMPANY
New York·London

TO THE MEMORY OF MY FATHER

Library of Congress Cataloging in Publication Data

Crane, Verner Winslow, 1889–1974.
    The Southern frontier, 1670–1732.

    1. Southern States—History—Colonial period,
ca. 1600–1775. 2. Indians of North America—
Southern States—Commerce. 3. Indians of North
America—Southern States—Wars—1600–1750.
I. Title.

F212.C67   1981   975′.02   81–11102
ISBN 0–393–00948–3   AACR2

W. W. Norton & Company, Inc. 500 Fifth Avenue,
New York, N.Y. 10110
W. W. Norton & Company Ltd. 25 New Street Square,
London EC4A 3NT

1 2 3 4 5 6 7 8 9 0

PREFACE TO THE NORTON EDITION

To study colonial American history at Harvard in the early 1960s was to study New England. As an undergraduate in Cambridge I listened attentively to the impressive lectures of Perry Miller, Bernard Bailyn, and Alan Heimert. I heard occasional talks by the legendary Samuel Eliot Morison, and I had contact with such hardworking graduate students as Philip Greven and Pauline Maier. Though they varied greatly in age, outlook, and interest, all these scholars had in common an abiding intellectual commitment to the early Northeast. The West existed as an extension of New England; the South below Virginia scarcely existed at all. Harvard's chair of southern history had long been unoccupied, and a "gut" course on the region, known disparagingly as "Mint Juleps," was taught only intermittently.

Amazingly, I found little reason to question this view from the Hub. Harvard in the Kennedy years was self-confidently defining the country's New Frontiers and appeared fully capable of defining all earlier frontiers as well. I recall hearing Mississippi Governor Ross Barnett, at the height of his struggle to maintain racial segregation, speak in cavernous Sanders Theater, the college's memorial to Civil War dead. The governor's fact-defying proclamation—I remember his exact words—that "there is no hate in the great state of Mississippi" confirmed the local impression that the Deep South somehow had always been, and remained, beyond the pale. When my roommate joined the Mississippi Summer Project to assist in black voter registration, he seemed headed for a foreign land.

In this setting it came as a rude surprise when my history tutor suggested one day that we read a book by Verner W. Crane entitled *The Southern Frontier, 1670–1732*. I had just spent several weeks absorbing the prose of Francis Parkman, and it seemed plausible to extend the study of early imperial expansion and conflict into the southern theater. My tutor allowed that this old book was supposed to be the best—if not the only—study on the subject, and I dutifully settled down to read a copy of the paperback edition, which was still available in those days.

Two things struck me about the book. First of all, its subject matter seemed remote and disorienting, far removed from "mainstream northern" or "antebellum southern" history. After all, here was a study of the South before there was a South, of an eastern frontier complete with cattle herders, Indian traders, and wild buffalo. The cover illustration—a low hazy sun, a tall cypress draped in Spanish moss, a distant log fort—reinforced this sense of remoteness and made a lasting impression on my memory. Secondly I was struck, and at times frankly confused, by the denseness of the book and the thoroughness of its treatment. This was no simple narrative of whites and Indians, but a detailed relation of the interaction between distant European empires and separate Indian nations. The Cherokee, Creek, and Choctaw, like the English, Spanish, and French, all had specific locations and leaders whose names I could not keep straight. Crane had mapped out, in carefully documented detail, the economic and imperial history of a region that my mentors had hardly mentioned and standard textbooks scarcely touched.

Years later I picked up Crane's book again. (By then an interest in the early southern past had entered my bloodstream to stay—in much the manner that malarial fevers once overpowered Carolina settlers.) All at once I realized that it must have been during my brief initial encounter with *The Southern Frontier* that the infecting mosquito of southern history had first bitten me. More than any other volume, Crane's work had shown me that the kind of meticulous historical research so prevalent for the early Northeast could be—and had been—applied to the early Southeast as well. His book, I now understood, had raised a string of unanswered questions in my mind, not only about the substance of colonial southern history but about its relation to the larger fabric of early American culture as a whole.

I found myself asking whether others had been—and still could be—lured by the material touched upon in this unusual book. Where, I wondered, had it come from in the first place? Why, during two generations of scholarly work, had it never been either superseded or even fully absorbed by colonial historians? And why, more than fifty years after its original publication in 1928 by the Duke University Press, was it totally unavailable to those who might wish to follow the winding pathways of the early South that Crane had marked out so carefully?

Seeking answers to these questions has led, I am pleased to say, to the publication of this new Norton edition. We have used the text of the 1956 Ann Arbor paperback in which, according to Crane, "A few errors of names and dates" were corrected. ("I am not aware," he could add in his preface to that reprint, "of any major contributions since 1928 which would greatly alter the narrative or the conclusions," and the same statement might be made again today.) Crane's annotated bibliography, inevitably dated by now, has been omitted, but the small (originally foldout) map that the author himself compiled from contemporary charts has been included.[1] We have restored the preface and appendices from the original edition, and the engraving of the 1730 Cherokee Embassy to England, which Crane selected as a frontispiece for the original edition, appears as the cover illustration.[2]

The Southern Frontier, 1670–1732 was something of an anomaly from the moment of publication. Though obviously a respectable contribution to both colonial and frontier history, it did not fit easily into the prevailing patterns of either category. By the late 1920s historians of early America were already withdrawing from the broad nineteenth-century fascination with European overseas empires to a narrow, if deep, preoccupation with the minds, men, and manners of the early Northeast. Historians of the frontier, hard at work explaining the recently completed "winning of the West," tended with few exceptions to date the beginning of that process from the English acquisi-

---

[1] Regarding references, Crane noted in 1956, "The footnotes remain, to guide those curious in the ways of scholarship to my sources." For maps, see William P. Cumming, *The Southeast in Early Maps* (Chapel Hill, 1958) and J. Ralph Randolph, *British Travelers Among the Southern Indians, 1660–1763* (Norman, Okla., 1973).

[2] This picture is described on p. 297.

tion of the trans-Appalachian region in 1763 or the departure of
Daniel Boone from Hillsborough, North Carolina, to mark out
the "Wilderness Trail" to Kentucky in 1776. A study of the
Deep South before 1732 did not conform to such boundaries of
place and time.

Moreover, *The Southern Frontier* was anomalous even in
personal terms. Its author, Verner Crane, was almost forty
when this first book appeared. Although he maintained a lively
interest in the colonial South throughout his subsequent career,
his writing during the second half of his life turned toward the
North Atlantic region, the Revolutionary era, and the biographical, arts-and-letters approach. By the time of his death
in 1974, at the age of eighty-five, he was known primarily as
an authority on the life of Benjamin Franklin.

More than most lasting studies in American history, therefore, Crane's book seems on first reading to stand apart. It does
not represent the obvious flowering of an old school or the
important founding of a new one. Distinguished scholars of the
early South like Wesley Frank Craven, Richard Beale Davis,
and John R. Alden have benefited indirectly or directly from
Crane's careful overview. But for the most part, *The Southern
Frontier* has remained a monograph too far ahead of its time or
too far off the beaten path to be readily acknowledged and incorporated. For all its uniqueness, however, the book is not
entirely inexplicable. It can be viewed as an interesting hybrid,
reflecting the response of its diligent author to the complex
trends of historical scholarship in the early twentieth century.

Verner Winslow Crane was born in Tecumseh, Michigan, in
1889. His paternal grandfather, a self-taught architect, had
migrated from the Pine Barrens of southern New Jersey in
1837 to establish himself as a prominent builder, assisted in time
by the two eldest of his six children. The second son, Theodore
Horace Crane, shared his New England mother's love of books
but passed up a college education to enter the Union army in
1862 at age eighteen. He was held prisoner briefly in Kentucky
the following year and later saw service recording the oaths of
allegiance of defeated Confederates in Tennessee and Alabama,

the region that would come to fascinate his son.[3] Returning to Tecumseh, Theodore Crane married at the age of forty and worked for years as a patternmaker in a local foundry. One can only speculate as to the ways this shy, bookish craftsman, to whom *The Southern Frontier* is dedicated, may have shaped the interests of his three children. The influence of their mother, Bricena Chadwick Crane, is even more obscure.

The middle child, Verner, expressed an early desire to be an architect. But a family friend from the same village, Claude Van Tyne, had left Tecumseh to become an American historian and was teaching at Ann Arbor, less than twenty-five miles away. Following his older brother Ronald, Verner entered the State University, studied with Van Tyne, and graduated as a member of Phi Beta Kappa in 1911. He spent the next year at Harvard earning a master's degree in history, and then—whether for intellectual or financial reasons, or in response to advice from Van Tyne—he moved to the University of Pennsylvania, where he received his Ph.D. in 1915. After a year's research fellowship at Penn, Crane married a young woman from Tecumseh named Jane Harris and returned to Ann Arbor as an instructor in history. Summoned back to the East in 1920, he spent the next decade teaching at Brown, with two years as a visiting lecturer at Harvard. During this period Crane published a number of essays that reflected not only his doctoral work on the Carolina Indian trade up to 1715 but also the extension of his research interests further into the eighteenth century, in preparation for the publication of *The Southern Frontier*.

In 1930, shortly after publishing *Loyalists in the American Revolution,* Claude Van Tyne died suddenly of cancer at the University of Michigan. Verner Crane was invited to Ann Arbor to take the place of his college mentor. From then on, for nearly

[3] Interestingly enough, another Crane relative also became fascinated with the South. The famous photographer Walker Evans (1903–1975) was the son of Verner Crane's cousin Jessie Beach Crane. He started serious picture-taking in 1928, the same year that this book of his uncle's appeared. During the 1930s he made powerful photographs of southern sharecroppers for the Farm Security Administration, and in 1941 he became well-known for the thirty-one images contributed to James Agee's *Let Us Now Praise Famous Men: Three Tenant Families.*

thirty years, he taught American history at his alma mater. A baldish man with thick glasses and piercing hazel eyes, he was remembered by his students and colleagues as kindly, dignified, and occasionally intimidating, a thorough lecturer and meticulous scholar with "an element of the careful antiquarian befitting a historian whose researches were concentrated in early American history."[4] In 1956, three years before his retirement, the University of Michigan Press honored Crane by issuing a paperback version of *The Southern Frontier,* which went through several printings before it passed out of circulation.

The book's upretentious style and careful documentation have withstood the test of time; it remains a valuable resource for scholars in the field. But beyond the intriguing subject matter itself, what makes this study fascinating for a wider audience interested in the American past is the intuitive way in which Crane balanced two major contemporary trends in historical writing. Most authors of the time felt compelled to choose between an English bias or a nationalist emphasis in analyzing early America. But Crane combined elements of the frontier school associated with the famous graduate of Johns Hopkins University's young doctoral program, Frederick Jackson Turner, and the Anglo-American imperial school epitomized by another distinguished Hopkins graduate, Charles M. Andrews.

Crane's debt to Turner, suggested by the title and acknowledged in the original preface, had a direct and interesting source. In June, 1911, as Crane was receiving his bachelor's degree in the Midwest, Turner ventured out from his new post at Harvard to address the New England Historic Genealogical Society on "The Colonial Frontier about 1700." It marked the first time that Turner, himself a midwesterner, had focused his controversial "thesis" on the eastern seaboard in the early period, and "his tentative explorations into the documents," according to his biographer, "awakened a new interest."[5] It seems inevitable

[4] John R. Alden, *American Historical Review,* LXXXI (June, 1976), 706.

[5] Ray Allen Billington, *Frederick Jackson Turner: Historian, Scholar, Teacher* (New York, 1973), p. 365. On Turner's 1918 conflict with Andrews, see ibid., p. 366. Turner's role in fostering a frontier school of early American history is appraised in Wilbur R. Jacobs, "Colonial Origins of the United States: The Turnerian View," *Pacific Historical Review,* XL (February, 1971), 21–38.

that some of this interest rubbed off on the young M.A. candidate from Ann Arbor who arrived in Cambridge that fall. Judging from subsequent evidence the seminar taken under Turner that year must have challenged him more than anything else to pursue an independent view of frontier history.

A research trip to South Carolina in the spring of 1912 opened Crane's eyes to the existence of a southern equivalent to Turner's New England "frontier about 1700." For almost two decades the early evolution of this frontier absorbed him, and when Frederick L. Paxson's *History of the American Frontier* appeared in 1924, Crane could express wry amusement that anyone could begin the story as late as 1763. In the South by then, as he would show, several generations of provincial explorers and traders, "advance agents of English dominion," had paved the way for a complicated Turnerian sequence of promoters, investors, settlers, and philanthropists. Significantly, when friends arranged a retirement dinner for Frederick Jackson Turner in Cambridge in 1924, the speaker selected to represent his legion of former graduate students was thirty-five-year-old Verner Crane.

But Crane's ties to the separate, and often opposing, imperial school of Anglo-American history are no less clear. Older scholars like Herbert L. Osgood and Charles M. Andrews had been stressing the importance of studying official British documents and of analyzing the English mercantile system as an organic whole, best viewed from the perspective of London. The highlight of Crane's important visit to South Carolina in 1912, therefore, was his discovery in the State Archives at Columbia of the so-called Sainsbury Transcripts, the thirty-six handwritten volumes containing "Records in the British Public Record Office Relating to South Carolina, 1663–1782," which had been compiled in London in 1895 under the direction of W. Noel Sainsbury. Immediately absorbed, Crane extended his stay, and he later recalled with pleasure how the redoubtable archivist A. S. Salley had more than once entrusted him with the keys, instructing him to lock up when he was through. The reliance on official British sources for his work on "Anglo-American origins" in the Southeast continued from then on. The 1920 appearance of *The British Historical Manuscripts Collection* assisted him in his early research on the English origins of the Georgia colony, and in 1927, on sabbatical from Brown, Crane visited London for the first time and was able to check the Colonial Office citations that gave his book its final form.

Linking Andrews and Turner, London and the log house, Crane formulated the history of a strategic frontier within a mercantile empire. "The southern frontier," he wrote in the opening chapter (p. 4), "was but one of many borders, in India, Africa, the West Indies, and North America, where Englishmen of the late seventeenth and eighteenth centuries vied with their rivals . . . for commercial and colonial supremacy." Nor was this border a line to be marked out on a map, "but rather," as he noted in the preface, "a zone, indeed a series of zones, merging into the wilderness." He went on to describe in suggestive detail a striking instance of what Immanuel Wallerstein and the present generation of comparative social scientists would call "the peripheral zone" of the expanding "European world economic system."

Writing about historians of the early South in 1966, Clarence Ver Steeg called Crane's book a "classic" and observed positively that "The eighteenth-century southern frontier will certainly be the center of emerging new interpretations."[6] Such new interpretations have been slow to materialize, and it is possible to feel, reading Crane's optimistic preface and thorough text from 1928, that in some ways our knowledge in this area has actually regressed since the days of Herbert E. Bolton and John R. Swanton. But the groundwork for deeper understanding is currently being laid. In the first place, historical demography has recently come into its own, and it is only a matter of time before we have a detailed picture of the size and distribution of populations throughout the early Southeast and their change over time. It is striking to realize, for example, that for the entire region of the Deep South considered in this book— the area below Virginia and stretching westward from the Carolina coast into East Texas—the total population in 1670 was well over 200,000 persons, of whom fewer than 5,000 were Euro-Americans or Afro-Americans. Over the ensuing two

[6] Clarence L. Ver Steeg, "Historians and the Southern Colonies," in Ray Allen Billington, ed., *The Reinterpretation of Early American History: Essays in Honor of John Edwin Pomfret* (San Marino, Cal., 1966), p. 95.

generations described by Crane, the total population of this region actually declined. By 1730 the Indian population had fallen drastically to roughly 68,000 people, and for the first time these Native Americans were outnumbered by the approximate combined total of whites (42,000) and blacks (31,000) concentrated on the coastal margins of the southeastern domain.[7]

A new generation of anthropologists and historians has become increasingly sensitive to the post-contact Native American cultures of the region. Charles Hudson's recent survey[8] will soon be followed by an encyclopedic tome on Indians of the Southeast in the Smithsonian Institution's new twenty-volume edition of *The Handbook of American Indians,* under the masterly guidance of William C. Sturtevant. Moreover, modern-day concerns have finally led to an enhanced awareness of the early presence of Afro-Americans, whose numbers rose sharply during the very years Crane studied. Historians have started to relate the growth of African slavery to the rise and fall of the considerable trade in Indian slaves which Crane was one of the first to discern. The full scope of this destructive export of Native Americans from the Southeast in the late seventeenth

----

[7] These figures are based on my own research in progress on the intercultural demography of the early South.

[8] Charles Hudson, *The Southeastern Indians* (Knoxville, 1976). Among numerous current monographs, see Gary C. Goodwin, *Cherokees in Transition: A Study of Changing Culture and Environment Prior to 1775* (Chicago, 1977); Gene Waddell, *Indians of the South Carolina Lowcountry, 1562–1751* (Spartanburg, S.C., 1980); and the forthcoming work of Richard White. Historian Daniel Usner of Cornell University has observed to me in a personal communication on *The Southern Frontier:*

Crane argues correctly that the peltry trade produced a social and economic revolution among Indian nations. He concludes hastily, however, that the flow of European goods "bred dependence upon the white man" and eventually led to "the economic and political subjection of the southern tribes." The degree of dependence and subjection varied widely among Indian peoples. The multitude of names that crowd the pages cannot alone reveal the diversity of people they represent. More intense research into political and social groups will show that the different nations of southern Indians made very particular demands on white traders as to what and how they traded. Alterations in Indian social life such as declining household production and rising alcohol consumption occurred at different rates and under various circumstances from place to place. Responses to changes brought on by colonial commerce also ranged from passive adoption to militant rejection of foreign ways of life.

and early eighteenth centuries is only beginning to be understood.[9]

Greater demographic understanding is slowly shifting our
viewpoint in other ways as well. Crane's perspective was con-
sciously Anglocentric, and he took only limited advantage of
the pioneering works by Peter Hamilton and Nancy Surrey
concerning the French Gulf Coast. Marcel Giraud, part of whose
impressive history of French Louisiana was translated into
English in 1974, justly characterized *The Southern Frontier* as
"fundamental for the study of the first phase of the Franco-
British conflict in the Mississippi Basin; [with] important
documentation of English origin, but weaker for the French
part."[10] Through the work of Giraud and others, we now have
greater access to the French side of the story. Recent disserta-
tions by James T. McGowan (1976), Patricia D. Woods
(1978), and Daniel H. Usner, Jr. (1981) on the intercultural
history of the Lower Mississippi Valley in the eighteenth century help to broaden our understanding of this neglected
portion of the southern frontier.

Yet even when all these strands have someday been woven
into a new synthesis, we shall wish to return to *The Southern
Frontier*. Both historically and historiographically, it represents
something of an opening chapter. The work remains a sturdy
landmark of judicious and independent scholarship. Perhaps
this reissue can help spur a new generation of readers and re-
searchers into the unfamiliar but accessible world of the early
South. I hope it will also give pleasure to those who generously
assisted in the preparation of this preface—John Alden, Bernard Bailyn, Ashbel Brice, Theodore Crane, and Dan Usner—
and to John L. Thomas, who first led me to the book.

Peter H. Wood
Duke University

July 1981

[9] See Gary Nash, *Red, White, and Black: The Peoples of Early
America* (Englewood Cliffs, N.J., 1974; revised edition, 1982); William
S. Willis, Jr., "Divide and Rule: Red, White and Black in the Southeast," in Charles M. Hudson, ed., *Red, White, and Black: Symposium
on Indians in the Old South* (Athens, Ga., 1971), pp. 99-115; and
especially J. Leitch Wright, Jr., *The Only Land They Knew: The Tragic
Story of the American Indians in the Old South* (New York, 1981).

[10] Marcel Giraud, *A History of French Louisiana: Volume One, The
Reign of Louis XIV, 1698-1715*, English language edition (Baton Rouge,
1974), p. 383.

PREFACE TO THE 1956 EDITION

This is a book about Anglo-American origins in the great area extending southward from Virginia and the Tennessee Valley to the Gulf of Mexico, and westward to the Mississippi River.

It is a history of the first English settlements on the Carolina coast, and more especially of the rapid advance of their frontiers of trade among the Creek, Cherokee, Choctaw, and Chickasaw Indians; of the triangular contests for empire which ensued with the Spaniards in Florida and the French in Louisiana; of intrigues and wars in the Indian country, and the nearly fatal disaster of the far-flung southern Indian revolt of 1715; of the emerging consciousness among Carolinian promoters of expansion that the ultimate stake in these contests was the dominion of the continent; of their indoctrination of government in Great Britain with imperialist ideas which were then partly assimilated into the earliest British statements of an American western policy; of abortive schemes for new colonies to strengthen the southern frontier against all enemies, promoted in turn by a Welsh planter, a Scottish baronet, and a Swiss wine merchant; and, finally, of the successful launching of the Georgia project. The genesis of Georgia was for the first time traced in full context in this book, in terms both of strategic backgrounds and of the organized philanthropic movement in England—a movement in which the Reverend Thomas Bray and his circle played a significant part, along with that more famous colonizer, James Edward Oglethorpe.

First published nearly thirty years ago, the book has long been unobtainable. A reprint edition is now issued in the hope that it may interest a wider public. This device has prevented extensive revision, which in any case I would be reluctant to attempt, inasmuch as my writing interests have turned to the era of the American Revolution. I am not aware, however, of any major contributions since 1928 which would greatly alter the narrative or the conclusions. In the one instance in which my arguments were seriously challenged—on the institutional relations of the Associates of Dr. Bray with the Trustees of Georgia—I found them confirmed when the long-lost first volume of the minutes of the Associates was recovered.

A few errors of names and dates have been corrected. A few items at the end of the first edition, including the Bibliography, have been omitted. The footnotes remain, to guide those curious in the ways of scholarship to my sources.

Verner W. Crane

Ann Arbor, Michigan
April 17, 1956

PREFACE TO THE FIRST EDITION

The title of this book has its warrant in contemporary usage. For thus was described in many eighteenth-century documents the peculiar situation of South Carolina, prior to the founding of Georgia and even long after, as a border province fronting Florida and Louisiana. But the term had Old World connotations not altogether applicable to the case. No map-maker could define this frontier with certainty as an international boundary. It was never fixed, in fact, until 1763, but was constantly fluctuating, advancing, for the most part, pressed forward by the acquisitiveness of the Anglo-American pioneers. It was no line, but rather a zone, indeed a series of zones, merging into the wilderness. On its hither side it was an area of frontier settlements, at its outer edge a sphere of influence over Indian tribes, in contact and conflict with similar Spanish and French spheres. In reality, then, it was a frontier in a characteristic American sense recognized and defined by Frederick Jackson Turner—but for whose synthetic ideas this book, and many another, could hardly have been written.

Despite the strong lead given by Turner to students of the national period of American history, the English colonial frontiers have been strangely neglected. We have had few investigations of colonial frontier institutions—of the fur trade, for instance—to match a notable series of special studies of provincial society and institutions in the older areas, and of the administration and commercial policy of the Empire. On the side of demography and social history, Turner's own essay on 'The Old West' remains a prospectus for unwritten monographs. And Parkman has been permitted to say almost the last word upon the colonial frontier in its international aspects.

Until recently the least considered of these frontier areas was the South beyond Virginia. When, more than a dozen years ago, the present study was cast into its original form of a thesis on the Indian frontier of South Carolina, 1670-1715 (presented at the University of Pennsylvania for the degree of doctor of philosophy), its bibliography of special studies was brief. The narrative historians of South Carolina had been almost entirely oblivious to the chief differentiating factor in early Carolina history. Logan, to be sure, had brought together a mass of documentary and legendary data upon the upper country and the Indian trade, but without organization or perspective. Writers on Georgia had recognized its border character, but had begun their studies, save for curious glances at the Margravate of Azilia, with the charter of 1732, and so had thrown little light upon Georgia's origins. Stressing Oglethorpe's contests with Florida, they had omitted the more interesting fact that the founding of Georgia was an episode also in the Anglo-French struggle for continental dominion. Parkman had dramatised the sixteenth-century collisions of Spaniards and French 'heretics' in Florida, but had found little space for the historically more significant triangular rivalries of the eighteenth century for the Gulf plains and the lower Mississippi. Justin Winsor, it is true, had assembled some of the materials for a better balanced picture of the colonial contest for the trans-Appalachian West. But it had remained for a French scholar, Pierre Heinrich, to publish the first book—*La Louisiane sous la Compagnie des Indes,* 1908—in which the Carolina traders and agents appeared as protagonists of English expansion in the old Southwest. The meagre printed materials relating to the southern Indian trade were first compiled by McIlwain in a note accompanying his admirable introduction to Wraxall's *Abridgement of the Indian Affairs,* 1915, with its accurate analysis of trade as the basis of Indian politics. Meanwhile, Alvord and Bidgood had resurrected the forgotten Virginians who accomplished the first recorded explorations of the trans-Alleghany region. Batts, Fallam, and Arthur emerged as not unworthy competitors of the French explorers of greater fame, and the frontier society which produced them was admirably described. But, after all, these Virginian activities of the later seventeenth century were isolated episodes, without immediate issue. The Carolinians who continued their work were quite unknown, and the trading expansion which they projected was but vaguely understood.

My own efforts to occupy this field, beginning with an article on 'The Tennessee River as the Road to Carolina,' 1916, and continued in 'The Southern Frontier in Queen Anne's War,'

1919, and other essays, have since been supplemented by important contributions of other investigators. For the Indian background, Swanton's studies have been indispensable. 'A veritable renaissance of interest in the history of the Old Southeast' has been noted by Herbert E. Bolton, who has himself usefully promoted it. In *The Colonization of North America, 1492-1783,* with T. M. Marshall, in 1920, he gave much space to this frontier, as well as to those other Spanish borderlands whose history he has long cultivated with so much zeal and enterprise. In 1925, in collaboration with Mary Ross, he brought out *The Debatable Land,* 'a sketch of the Anglo-Spanish contest for the Georgia country,' presenting new facts from Spanish archival sources. Bolton, moreover, has been stimulating a group of younger historians to explore the wealth of manuscript materials for early Florida history. Although I have drawn upon such Spanish documents as were available in print or transcripts, I have not attempted to duplicate the fruitful work of the Bolton school.

If larger use has been made of French documents, it is because from the close of the seventeenth century the great issue in the South was Anglo-French supremacy. Out of this contest emerged, earlier and more clearly than elsewhere, certain concepts which dominated the international struggle in America to its close in 1763. The *continental* phase of that struggle (the rivalry for the control of the Mississippi valley and its peltry trade) began when the French anticipated the English in the occupation of the lower valley and the adjacent Gulf coast, only to find themselves challenged at every point by the Charles Town traders. Of that English trading advance into the old Southwest and of the parallel development of an Anglo-American sentiment of expansion this book is a survey. The fear of French encirclement was not suddenly aroused in the mid-eighteenth century, when the French undertook to strengthen their line of communications in its middle sector, and when for the first time Virginia and Pennsylvania traders became really active in the West. Before the end of the seventeenth century it was implanted in the minds of a few colonists and officials, especially in the southern colonies; soon after it was translated by the Carolinians into an aggressive policy of expansion. There followed the gradual indoctrination of the colonial authorities, and, at Whitehall, between 1720 and 1730, the definition of a halting but unmistakable British western policy in opposition to the grand French design.

For this point of view may be claimed a considerable degree of novelty. Naturally, since the investigation has traversed a comparatively neglected field, many of the details of the picture are also new. It has been possible to add a whole series of English explorations, border wars, and diplomatic intrigues to the records of wilderness adventure and achievement. For the first time, also, is described, from newly discovered documents, the extraordinary trans-Appalachian settlement project of Price Hughes in 1713. Nowhere has there existed a detailed analysis of the structure and workings of the colonial Indian trade; my discussion, while confined to the South, has therefore not been restricted to the period of the narrative. A special effort has been made to discover the origins, in England as well as in America, both philanthropic and strategic, of the movements which resulted in the establishment of Georgia. New light is also shed upon several familiar episodes. One of these is the Hennepin enigma. The activities of the colonial promoters, Coxe, Montgomery, and especially Purry, are more fully revealed, and placed in their setting of Anglo-French rivalry. Comparison with the neglected Carolina expansionists has compelled a revaluation of the asserted leadership of Alexander Spotswood in the English westward movement.

A special acknowledgement is due to Dean Herman V. Ames, in whose seminary the investigation was begun, for his interest and his patience during its slow fruition. The grant of a Harrison fellowship for research was a material assistance. From librarians and archivists I have received cordial aid: at the Public Record Office, and the Colonial Office Library, Whitehall; at the Library of Congress, the Historical Society of Pennsylvania, the American Philosophical Society, the South Carolina Historical Society, the William L. Clements Library, and elsewhere. Mr. Alexander S. Salley, Jr., secretary of the Historical Commission of South Carolina, was a generous guide to the archives of that state. I have made considerable requisitions upon the pamphlet collections in the John Carter

Brown Library, and upon the bibliographical knowledge and critical acumen of its librarian, Mr. Lawrence C. Wroth. My brother, Professor Ronald S. Crane of the University of Chicago, has made frequent suggestions regarding sources and problems of exposition; and in all the drudgery of the task I have had the constant assistance of my wife, Jane Harris Crane.

VERNER W. CRANE.

CONTENTS

ABBREVIATIONS

AHR: American Historical Review.

BM: British Museum.

CC: *Crown Collection,* compiled by A. B. Hulbert.

CO: Colonial Office Library, Whitehall.

C.O.: Colonial Office papers, Public Record Office.

C.O. Maps: Maps in Colonial Office Library, Whitehall.

CSCHS: Collections of the South Carolina Historical Society.

CSP,AWI: Calendar of State Papers, Colonial Series, America and West Indies.

GHQ: Georgia Historical Quarterly.

HCL: Harvard College Library.

JBT: Journal of the Commissioners for Trade and Plantations (Board of Trade).

JC: Journal of the Council of South Carolina.

JCB: John Carter Brown Library.

JCHA: Journal of the Commons House of Assembly of South Carolina.

JCHA: *idem.,* MS.

JGC: Journal of the Grand Council of South Carolina.

JIC: Journal of the Indian Commissioners of South Carolina.

LC: Library of Congress.

MVHR: Mississippi Valley Historical Review.

SCHGM: South Carolina Historical and Genealogical Magazine.

S.P.: State Papers, Public Record Office.

S.P.G.: Society for the Propagation of the Gospel in Foreign Parts.

WLC: William L. Clements Library.

THE SOUTHERN
FRONTIER

1670–1732

CHAPTER I

First Contacts with the Spanish and the Indians

In April, 1670, some one hundred and fifty colonists from England and Barbados disembarked at the mouth of Ashley River. They were the first permanent settlers of South Carolina, the pioneers in a new zone of English colonial expansion and of international conflict, the southern frontier.

Destined for Port Royal, the little Carolina fleet had been diverted northward, probably by the uncomfortable neighborhood of the Spanish missions, just beyond the Savannah River. Even at Kiawah the new colonists found themselves only two hundred and fifty miles from the presidio of St. Augustine. Twice that distance separated them from the Chesapeake settlements: five hundred miles of coast as yet unoccupied save at Albemarle Sound, a wretched frontier of Virginia, and at Cape Fear, where two recent attempts at planting had met with failure. 'Wee are here setled,' wrote one Carolinian, 'in the very chaps of the Spaniard.'[1]

From the beginning, then, Carolina existed as an exposed border colony against the Spanish of Florida, and against numerous powerful tribes of southern Indians. Westward the wilderness stretched to the Appalachians, southwestward through the Gulf plains to the Mississippi. Who could predict, in 1670, that when a generation had passed, Carolinians would confront Frenchmen on the great river in a contest for the heart of the continent? But even while the first colonists were building the huts and palisades of Old Charles Town, other actors were helping to shape the historic rôle of South Carolina. At Madrid, in May, Lord Godolphin negotiated a treaty in which Spain confirmed the existing possessions of Great Britain in America.[2] In 1669 and 1670, a young Frenchman, Robert Cavelier de la Salle, was attempting to penetrate from

[1] Joseph Dalton to Lord Ashley, September 9, 1670, in *Collections* of the South Carolina Historical Society (hereinafter cited as *CSCHS*), V. 183. This and all other citations from the Shaftesbury papers have been collated with the manuscript originals in the Public Record Office.

[2] *A Treaty for the Composing of Differences . . . between the Crowns of Great Britain and Spain.* London, 1670. Also in Dumont (ed.), *Corps diplomatique,* VII. 138.

Canada into the region south of the Great Lakes. Other French-men, missionaries and *coureurs de bois,* were on the brink of the discovery of the Mississippi. In Virginia, under the patron-age of Sir William Berkeley, plans were being laid for a series of inland explorations which first carried Englishmen to the margin of the trans-Appalachian West. But in the sequel not Virginia but Carolina faced the successors of Marquette and La Salle in the central valley.

The southern frontier was but one of many borders, in India, Africa, the West Indies, and North America, where Eng-lishmen of the late seventeenth and the eighteenth centuries vied with their rivals, notably the French, for commercial and co-lonial supremacy. Only at intervals was this a contest of arms. But always there existed the keenest rivalry for the control of the staples of world trade and of the areas where these could be produced. From Hudson Bay to the Caribbean the competi-tion for sugar, tobacco, indigo, fish, and peltries was waged upon the seas and along a far-flung, imperfectly defined, inter-national border.[3] In the interior of North America rivalry centred in competition for the Indian trade and Indian alliances.

The English advance into the South beyond Virginia was a product of typical forces of the Restoration era, when busi-ness had become a basis for statecraft.[4] The group of courtiers and politicians to whom Charles II, complacently ignoring the rights of Spain, granted in 1663 the great region from 36° to 31° and from sea to sea, included England's boldest and most influential men of affairs. Lord Ashley's 'Carolina business' was but one of the interests which the shrewd promoter-poli-tician shared with his fellow Proprietors and their circle. Members of this group concocted the seizure of New Nether-land. They were the first Englishmen to see the great future of the American fur trade, and organized the Hudson's Bay Company to vie with France for the spoils of the northern forests. From England they directed the penetration of the wilderness west of Virginia and Carolina. Profit from com-merce was their chief aim in colonization. But American real

[3] C. M. Andrews, 'Anglo-French Commercial Rivalry, 1700-1750,' in *American Historical Review* (hereinafter cited as *AHR*), XX. 546.
[4] See C. W. Alvord and Lee Bidgood, *The First Explorations of the Trans-Alleghany Region by the Virginians, 1650-1674,* 1912, pp. 56 *et seq.*

estate—in New Jersey as well as in Carolina—promised further returns. The distresses of the West Indian planters solved the problem of securing settlers for their Carolina estates. In Barbados, especially, the transition to large-scale agriculture had made emigration imperative. And old Barbadians imported with them into Carolina a lively hatred of the Spaniard.

When Lord Ashley, in 1669, took vigorously in hand the promotion of Carolina, it was evident that the earlier struggling settlements at Albemarle and Cape Fear had failed to satisfy any of these businesslike objects. Meanwhile, voyages along the coast had convinced the Proprietors that Port Royal was the best site for settlement. Both Hilton, in 1663, and Sandford, in 1666, had returned glowing descriptions of the soil, climate, and products of this fair country of islands and rivers. 'We could wish,' wrote Hilton and his companions, 'that all they that want a happy settlement, of our English Nation, were well transported thither.'[5]

They had also furnished evidence, these explorers, that the Spanish of Florida still sought to maintain possession of Santa Elena. The spot upon which Ashley and his associates had fixed was the site of one of the early presidios of Florida. For nearly a century, moreover, it had been the scene of persistent missionary efforts, first by Jesuits, later by Franciscans. After ousting the French 'heretics' and founding St. Augustine, Menéndez de Avilés had planted posts and missions all along the Georgia-Carolina coast, 1566-1568. Though San Felipe fort was finally abandoned in 1587, after Drake's descent, missions had been maintained so late as 1655 at San Felipe (Parris Island) and at Chatuache, six leagues to the north.[6] But in 1661 the district of Guale to which these outlying missions were attached had been raided by a fierce northern tribe.[7] Reputed man-eaters, these Indians had come from the borders of Virginia to spread terror in the South. 'Chichumecos' the

[5] William Hilton, *A True Relation of a Voyage upon Discovery* (1664), reprinted in *CSCHS*, V. 24; and in A. S. Salley, Jr. (ed.), *Narratives of Early Carolina, 1650-1708*, 1911, p. 45.

[6] H. E. Bolton and Mary Ross, *The Debatable Land*, 1925, chapters i and ii.

[7] Aranguiz to the King of Spain, September 8, 1662, in J. R. Swanton, *Early History of the Creek Indians and their Neighbors*, 1922, p. 305. See my note in *American Anthropologist*, n.s., XX. 335-6.

Spaniards called them, but they were almost certainly the Ricahecrians who had been expelled from Virginia in 1656, and who, as the Westo, played a great part in early Carolina history. With difficulty Aranguiz, the governor of Florida, had saved Guale. The mission frontier retreated south of the Savannah River.

When Hilton cast anchor in St. Helena Sound he found, therefore, that the Indians used many Spanish words, that several had visited St. Augustine 'but ten days' journey,' and that the Spaniards were accustomed to visit them. Indeed, just at this time, Captain Alanso Argüelles had come from the presidio with soldiers to rescue some castaway English sailors. Both Hilton and Sandford, moreover, noted that 'a fair wooden Crosse, of the Spaniards' ereccon' stood before the town-house of Port Royal. Sandford, however, 'could not observe that the Indians performed any adoration before it,' and in letters to Hilton the Spanish captain had referred to the place as 'this Town of Infidel Indians.' Nevertheless he claimed their allegiance as 'Naturals who had given their obedience to the King our Master.' But in 1666 and again in 1670 they vied with the tribes of Edisto and Kiawah in their prayers that the English colony be planted in their midst, for all the coastal Indians were desperately anxious to secure the protection which the Spanish could not give them against the dreaded Westo.[8]

Among the colonists at Kiawah in 1670 was the young surgeon, Dr. Henry Woodward. Already he had learned much of the country and the Indians and the Spaniards. Woodward's was a career of amazing adventure. The progenitor of a notable line of southern leaders, he was the first settler in South Carolina, the first interpreter and Indian agent, the first Englishman to penetrate the western wilderness beyond the Chattahoochee, the pioneer, in a word, of English expansion in the lower South. In 1666, as a companion of Sandford, Woodward had volunteered to stay at Port Royal to master the Indian tongue. There the chief had shown every honor to his visitor: had placed him on his throne, given him a field of maize, and his own niece to 'tend him and dresse his victualls and be carefull of him.' Before he sailed, Sandford had conveyed to him formal possession of the whole country to hold as tenant-at-will of the Lords Proprietors. Thus Woodward began his apprenticeship as interpreter and explorer. But the Spanish still kept an eye on Santa Elena, and soon appeared to carry him off to St. Augustine. In 1668 he found a chance to escape when the buccaneer Searle raided the town. For a time he sailed the Caribbean as surgeon of a privateer, hoping to get to England to report to the Proprietors. Shipwrecked at Nevis, he took passage thence with the Carolina fleet, to become at once the most useful servant of the Proprietors in Carolina.[9]

Two years at Port Royal and in Florida must have given Woodward a fair notion of how matters stood between the Spaniards and the Indians in that part of the world. On every one of her frontiers in North and South America Spain's Indian policy was based upon the mission.[10] This frontier institution was maintained for religious propaganda, and also for instruction in agriculture and the arts. Along the border, moreover, the missionary, with his soldier guard, upheld the authority of the distant Spanish king. Everywhere efforts were made to convert the barbarous 'infidel' tribes, settle them in villages within sound of mission bells, instruct them in the faith and in settled ways of life. In Florida, during the sixteenth and seventeenth centuries, three mission fields had been developed. Despite periodic revolts, incursions by hostile tribes, and, upon the coast, attacks by buccaneers, these missions of Guale, Timucua, and Apalache survived until the Spanish Indian system, based upon religion and agriculture, came into fatal collision with the English system, based solely upon trade.[11]

[9] J. W. Barnwell, 'Dr. Henry Woodward,' in *South Carolina Historical and Genealogical Magazine* (hereinafter cited as *SCHGM*), VIII. 29-41. *CSCHS*, V. 65, 78 f., 183, 188 note, 190 f. Bolton and Ross, *The Debatable Land*, 1925, pp. 29-32.

[10] H. E. Bolton, 'The Mission as a Frontier Institution in the Spanish-American Colonies,' *AHR*, XXIII. 42-61.

[11] On the Florida missions see J. G. Shea, *History of the Catholic Church in the United States*, I (1886), 100-82; Woodbury Lowery, *The Spanish Settlements within the Present Limits of the United States: Florida, 1562-1574*, 1905; Bolton and Ross, *The Debatable Land*, chapter ii. Special accounts of the Guale missions are J. G. Johnson, *The Spanish Period of Georgia and South Carolina History, 1566-1702* (Bulletin of the University of Georgia, XXIII, number 9b, 1923); J. G. Johnson, 'The Yamassee Revolt of 1597 and the Destruction of the Georgia Missions,' in *Georgia Historical Quarterly* (hereinafter cited as *GHQ*), VII. 44-53; Mary Ross, 'French

Nearest the new English border was the mission district of Guale, which comprised the coast and the sea-islands from St. John's to Port Royal. Since the retreat from Santa Elena, the northern Spanish outpost was at Santa Catalina de Guale, on St. Catherine's Island. At 'Wallie' the English in 1670 found 'brave plantations with a: 100 working Indians' wanting 'nothing in the world.'[12] To meet the new threat to Spanish control a garrison was soon established alongside this mission. On the mainland, a few leagues westward, was the Indian settlement of Tupiqui. On Sapelo Island, north of the Altamaha River, stood the mission of San José de Zápala, with the settlements of Tolemato and Yoa in the hinterland near-by. San Domingo de Talaje occupied St. Simon's Island. Southward, San Buenaventura de Guadalquini on Jekyl Island, or St. Simon's, overlooked the Ospo town, and San Pedro Mocama occupied Cumberland Island. Less successful were the efforts of the friars to convert the barbarous inland Indians of Salchiches, Tulafina, Ocute, Tama. The last was a name broadly applied to the interior region behind the sea-islands and the marshes of Guale, visited occasionally by Spanish missionaries and soldiers whom the lure of riches and the quest of souls still called to the old trails of De Soto, Pardo, and Boyano. But in the hinterland they made no settlements and kept no real sway.[13]

The missions of Guale, already hard-pressed, were naturally the first to feel the force of English expansion. But others were to suffer in their turn. The principal tribe of peninsular Florida was the Timucua. In 1655 the district of Timucua included eighteen missions, stretching eastward and westward from their centre at Santa Fé to link St. Augustine with the populous country of the Apalache.[14] This latter tribe inhabited the very

Intrusions and Indian Uprisings in Georgia and South Carolina (1577-1580),' *GHQ*, VII. 251-81; Mary Ross, 'The French on the Savannah, 1605,' *GHQ*, VIII. 167-94; Mary Ross, 'The Restoration of the Spanish Missions in Georgia, 1598-1606,' *GHQ*, X. 171-99.

[12] *CSCHS*, V. 169.

[13] The English of Charles Town in 1670 knew of four missions 'upon the Spanish keyes' (*CSCHS*, V. 198). On the Indians of Guale and the hinterland see Swanton, *Early History*, pp. 60, 80-109, 174 f., 181 f.

[14] The Timucuan missions appear on an English manuscript map of the early eighteenth century, Colonial Office (hereinafter cited as C.O.) Maps, North American Colonies, General, 7. Swanton, *Early History*, pp. 322 f., prints Spanish lists (1655, 1680) of the missions of Guale, Timucua, and Apalache.

fertile lands along the lower courses of the Ocklocknee (Apalache) and Ocilla Rivers, fronting the northeastern corner of the Gulf of Mexico. In 1655 nine establishments in Apalache were evidence of the success of Franciscan efforts during the two decades since the coming of the friars. There, too, resorted Spanish provision ships, for Apalache had become a granary for St. Augustine and Havana, and at San Luís (Tallahassee) a garrison was maintained to hold the western Florida border against pirates and hostile Indians. Apalache also served as a base for Spanish activities among the Creek Indians and along the Gulf coast westward to Pensacola Bay.[15] With the later advance of the English traders, about 1700 Apalache became the essential point of support for the whole Spanish and French defense of the old Southwest.

Such was the extent of effective Spanish control when the English came to South Carolina. The Carolina charter of 1663, and especially the enlarged grant of 1665 southward to 29°, manifestly prejudiced a great area which was Spanish by right of discovery, exploration and, in the regions described, by continuous occupation.[16] South of the Savannah River the English could have no rights; northward, the title to Port Royal was in some doubt, in view of the recent Spanish retreat. The Godolphin treaty was signed before there could have been any knowledge in Spain or in England of the new settlement at Kiawah. At most it gave the English a quit-claim to the coast as far south as Old Charles Town. But the English seem to have valued article VII of the treaty of Madrid chiefly as a recession from the old Spanish monopoly, rather than as an exact definition of boundaries. Their reliance, throughout the history of this border, was upon the fact of possession.[17]

In Florida, however, the colony at San Jorge (Charles Town) was regarded as a flagrant intrusion, to be driven from Spanish soil. The exit of the Spanish fleets from the Caribbean

---

[15] Bolton and Ross, *The Debatable Land,* pp. 25-27; Shea, *Catholic Church,* I. 165-7, 172, 178.

[16] See Bolton and Ross, *The Debatable Land,* opposite p. 32, for map of the Carolina (1665) and Georgia (1732) grants, superimposed upon a map of the northern Spanish border.

[17] *Arredondo's Historical Proof of Spain's Title to Georgia,* edited by H. E. Bolton (1925), was an elaborate and generally sound refutation of English claims, written in 1742 by the chief-of-staff in the Spanish campaign against Georgia.

through the Bahama Channel was threatened; so too were the most numerous missions north of Mexico. An incident in May, 1670, convinced the Carolinians of the Spaniard's desire 'to cut us off if possibly he can.' A Barbadian sloop, separated by a storm from the fleet, put in by mistake at Santa Catalina de Guale. A landing-party, hunting wood and water, was attacked by the Indians, several men were killed, and two others, including John Rivers, a kinsman of Lord Ashley, sent away prisoners to St. Augustine. Governor Sayle despatched a peremptory demand for their release, but his messengers were also seized at Santa Catalina. The arrest of these colonists and their detention for several years in Florida became a subject of diplomatic remonstrance.[18] Meanwhile, Governor Guerra sent a force from Florida to oust the intruders at Ashley River. Three ships sailed northward, under command of Juan Menéndez Marqués, accompanied by fourteen periagoes of Indians. In mid-August the Carolinians were warned by friendly Indians that the Spanish 'with all the Indians about Ste. Augustine and the Spanish Keyes' were about to attack. Great guns were mounted and defenses hastily improvised. The danger, though exaggerated, was real. Neither the ship *Carolina,* sent to Virginia for provisions, nor the sloop despatched to Bermuda had returned. Starvation already threatened, and now the Spanish fleet blockaded Charles Town bar while the Guale Indians hovered about the Stono inlet. But a storm dragged the Spaniards' anchors, and the ships withdrew without an attempt upon the town. After the *Carolina* returned the Spanish Indians soon melted away. The first crisis had been passed. It had served to demonstrate the friendship of the neighboring tribes and the usefulness of Woodward as Indian agent. 'All the Indians about us,' Lord Ashley was told, 'came with their full Strength to our Ayde.'[19]

At St. Augustine Guerra gave way to Zendoya, and the fortification of the presidio was begun. The new governor still hoped to remove the English, in spite of the inconvenient treaty of 1670, which for at least two years Zendoya omitted to pub-

[18] *CSCHS,* V. 169-71, 173 f., 175, 204, 209. 'Letter from Joseph Baily, [December 12,] 1672,' edited by W. E. Dunn, in *SCHGM,* XVIII. 54-56. Guerra to the King, July 12, 1673, in *The Unwritten History of Old St. Augustine,* compiled by Miss A. M. Brooks, [St. Augustine?], [1909?], pp. 116-20.

[19] *CSCHS,* V. 179, 185, 187, 194 f., 198-200, 288.

lish, that he might be freer to act. The Queen, indeed, authorized him in 1671 to drive the English away from Santa Elena,
but without breaking the articles of peace. While Zendoya
looked for aid to Havana and the Viceroy, the projected San
Jorge campaign slumbered.[20]

In a very real sense the conflict thus begun on the Carolina-
Florida border was a continuation of the old festering dispute
in the Caribbean. The leaders at Charles Town, many of them
Barbadians, were not likely to forget past scores. In September,
1670, Dalton described to Ashley the proximity of the Spaniards, 'whose clandestine actions both domesticke and forraigne
are not unknown to your Ldp nor can be blotted out of the
memoryes of the West India planters.' In the main it was a
hopeful view of the strategic situation of Carolina which he
presented. Others agreed that Spanish prestige was declining
among the tribes of the southern Atlantic coast. 'Since Searle
playd that pranck att St. Augustin,' William Owen declared,
'som of the most Intelligible *(sic)* Indians on this side the Cape
doubted of the verity of the frier's Doctrine and now our settle-
ing here putts the priests our neighbors upon new points.'
Already Owen foresaw expansion southward towards the
Guale missions, and believed that the Spanish would be easily
displaced. The real difficulty was for the English to maintain
their reputation among the friendly tribes without violating the
peace at home. 'Our owne Indians,' he said, 'Looke upon it
somthing strange that we doe not goe to Wallie and shoote as
they call it, that they may come along.'[21]

Old Charles Town was now made strong against Indian
attack. By September, 1670, thirty acres at the point had been
surrounded by a palisade : a thousand Indians, it was believed,
could be withstood. In 1672 the militia was organized into six
companies.[22]

---

[20] Royal instructions, June 20, 1671, and Zendoya to the Crown, March
21, 1672, Brooks transcripts from the Archives of the Indies, Seville, in
Library of Congress. Bolton and Ross, *The Debatable Land,* pp. 34 f. On
defense preparations in Florida, see Brooks (comp.), *Unwritten History,*
pp. 130-35.
[21] *CSCHS,* V. 183, 198, 200.
[22] Ibid., 189, 203, 222, 267, 284, 378 f. *Journal of the Grand Council of
South Carolina* (hereinafter cited *JGC*), edited by A. S. Salley, Jr., 1907,
July 9, 1672. See ibid. under November 11, 1671, January 10, August 24, and
September 9, 1672, regarding desertions to Florida, and fears on this
account.

Sandford's companions had prophesied in 1666 'that this Country may bee more Securely sett[l]ed and cheaply defended from any the attempts of its native Inhabitants than any of those other places which Our Count[r]ymen have refined from the Drosse of Indian Barbarisme.'[23] The hospitable attitude of the coast towns of the Cusabo[24] was due to fear of the Spaniards and their allies of Guale, and especially to their dread of the small but warlike inland tribe of Westo. 'As for them at home we have them in a pound,' Owen assured Lord Ashley, 'for to the Southward they will not goe, fearing the Yamase, a Spanish Comeraro as the Indian terms it. The Westoes are behind them a mortall enemie of theirs . . . of them they are more afraid than the little children of the Bull beggers in England.'[25] When the colonists touched at Port Royal, in March, 1670, they had seen distressing evidence of a recent raid. The Westo, 'a rangeing sort of People,' were then settled together 'in an intier body' on the Savannah River, which the Carolinians consequently first knew as the Westobou, or Westo River. By trade with Virginia these Indians had already obtained arms and ammunition, and had thus become formidable out of all proportion to their numbers in their constant encounters with the bow-and-arrow Indians of Carolina and Guale. For a decade Carolina Indian policy was largely determined by the colonists' relations with this remarkable tribe.[26]

In establishing first contacts with the Indians, and in inland exploration, for fifteen years the chief rôle was played by Henry Woodward. Lord Ashley, with the keen business instinct that made him the first colonial adventurer of his day, was quick to appreciate Woodward's usefulness in his own schemes. On Ashley's motion, in the spring of 1671 the Proprietors voted Woodward a reward of £100 out of the common stock, 'which,' he wrote Sir John Yeamans, 'is not all we intend to do for him.'[27] Woodward had been eager to return

---

[23] *CSCHS*, V. 82.
[24] Swanton, *Early History*, pp. 31-80.
[25] *CSCHS*, V. 200-201.
[26] Ibid., pp. 166-8, 194. On the identity of the Westo see the discussion between J. R. Swanton and myself in *Am. Anthropologist*, n.s., XX. 331-6, XXI. 213-6, 463-5; and also Swanton, *Early History*, pp. 288-91. Cf. chapter ii, note 50.
[27] *CSCHS*, V. 315 f.

to England with the report of a mysterious discovery which he had made in his explorations inland, but the Proprietors thought he could not yet be spared from Carolina. The discovery in question had occurred during his journey, *circa* July, 1670, to 'Chufytachyqj that fruitfull Provence where the Emperour resides.' For a fortnight Woodward had marched 'West and by Northe' until he reached 'a Country soe delitious, pleasant and fruitfull, that were it cultivated doubtless it would prove a second Paradize.' He reported that he had 'contracted a league with the Empr. and all those Petty Cassekas bewixt us and them.' A thousand bowmen, it was said, belonged to the town; and their chief was accounted 'the great Emperor of this p[ar]te of the Indies.' Had Woodward found De Soto's Cofitachique? Though several Indians returned with him, the expected inland trade was not developed until the destruction of the Westo opened a clear path to the Lower Creek country.[28]

A variety of motives led Woodward and other early explorers into the country behind Charles Town. 'If the Porch be so beautifull, what must the Temple be?' wrote Dalton to Ashley.[29] Land, mines, Indian trade, Indian wars, played their part. In the spring of 1671 Thomas Gray, Maurice Mathews, and William Owen visited the upper courses of the Ashley and Cooper Rivers as far as the Kusso town. In 1673, when there was war with the Westo, the Grand Council sent four commissioners to negotiate with the 'Esaughs' or Catawba, who already traded with Virginia, and two other commissioners were despatched southward 'for the better knowledge of the maritime parts' between Ashley River and the Westobou. 'The improvement as well as the safety of this Settlement,' the Council declared, 'consists in the knowledge of the lands and inhabitants contiguous to this place.'[30] But soon conservative colonists, possibly with the early experiences of Virginia in

---

[28] Ibid., pp. 186 f., 191, 194, 201, 218, 220, 249, 262, 316, 327, 334, 338. The first map of Carolina to indicate any of the inland tribes, Gascoyne's Plat, *circa* 1685, based on Mathews' survey (B.M. Add. MSS 5414, roll 24), shows 'Cotuchike' on the Santee River a little distance above the forks, below the 'Esah' (Catawba). I no longer regard as probable the suggested identification of this town with Kasihta, first advanced by Langdon Cheves. See *Mississippi Valley Historical Review* (hereinafter cited as *MVHR*), V. 339, note 2.

[29] *CSCHS*, V. 380.

[30] Ibid., pp. 334-5, *JGC*, October 7, 1673, February 2, 1674.

mind, were advising that 'remote discoveries' be prohibited. 'It may be dangerous,' one remarked, 'to follow the fancies of roveing heads which the English have sufficiently experienced.' Lord Ashley was of the same opinion. In May, 1671, he instructed Sayle to 'bind the peoples' mindes wholy to planting and trade,' their only true interests, and to suppress exciting rumors of treasure in the back-country. Woodward's mysterious journey prompted special precautions against private adventures in that quarter, lest the Spaniards, learning thus of the proximity of the Carolinians, should unite all their forces to cut them off. Conflicts with Florida Ashley was anxious to avoid in the interest of a projected secret trade with St. Augustine.[31]

But the proprietary policy on exploration was not altogether negative. With his servant, Woodward, Ashley arranged a code so that the discovery of gold and silver could be secretly communicated to him![32] At exactly this period, moreover, Sir William Berkeley—a Proprietor of Carolina as well as governor of Virginia—was promoting that noteworthy series of explorations from the James which led to the first recorded discoveries by Englishmen in the trans-Appalachian West.[33] Naturally knowledge of the activities of the German traveler, Lederer, and of the agents of the Virginia Indian trader, Colonel Abraham Wood, soon passed to the Proprietors in England. Lederer accomplished little more than a series of journeys of uncertain extent into the Virginia-North Carolina piedmont and foot-hills. The Blue Ridge defied his attempts. But the book[34] which Sir William Talbot made out of his papers had a real bearing upon Carolinian exploration. Published in London in 1672, it was dedicated to Lord Ashley. The unique advantage of Carolina's location, at the southern end of the great mountain barrier, did not escape Talbot. 'From

[31] *CSCHS*, V. 316, 327-8, 380, 442.

[32] Ashley to Woodward, April 10, 1671: 'Pray call gold alwayes Antimony and Silver Iron by which I shall be able to understand you without any danger if your letters should fall into other hands' (ibid., 316-7).

[33] See Alvord and Bidgood, *First Explorations,* especially pp. 61-90, 131-226.

[34] *The Discoveries of John Lederer, in three several Marches from Virginia, to the West of Carolina, and other parts of the Continent.* Translated from Latin by Sir William Talbot, Baronet. London, 1672. Reprinted in Alvord and Bidgood, *First Explorations,* pp. 135-71.

this discourse' it is clear,' he asserted, 'that the long looked-for discovery of the Indian Sea does nearly approach; and Carolina out of her happy experience of your Lordship's success in great undertakings, presumes that the accomplishment of this glorious Designe is reserved for her. In order to which, the Apalatæan Mountains (though like the prodigious Wall that divides China from Tartary, they deny Virginia passage into the West Continent) stoop to your lordships Dominions, and lay open a Prospect into unlimited Empires.' Lederer's conjectures regarding the land beyond the mountains and the fabled arm of the sea stretching from California to the Appalachians, were wild enough, but he offered pertinent comment upon the Indians and their ways, and upon the proper organization of the trade with the remoter tribes. These pages, and also his 'Instructions to such as shall march upon Discoveries into the North-American Continent,' were doubtless read by Ashley with particular attention. Already, in September, 1671, Colonel Wood had despatched Batts and Fallam upon the journey which led from Fort Henry to one of the sources of the Ohio River. By a coincidence Henry Woodward was in Virginia at that moment upon a secret mission for Sir John Yeamans.[35] In 1673 Wood sent out another party, headed by James Needham, erstwhile companion of Woodward in Carolina.[36] Needham and Gabriel Arthur penetrated to the mountains and visited the Tamahita Indians, neighbors of the Cherokee. They found evidence of a former trade with the Spaniards, now interrupted. Needham returned to Virginia, but on a second attempt to reach the mountains he was murdered by the Occaneechi. His travels and his death were narrated in a letter from Wood to John Richards, who became the Proprietors' business agent. Wood also recounted the extraordinary adventures of the servant, Arthur, who was carried by Tamahita war-parties on marches which perhaps extended to Apalache, the Carolina border, and the headwaters of the Ohio.[37] With the annotations of John Locke this epic of English exploration inevitably found its way to Lord Ashley, now Earl of Shaftesbury.[38]

[35] *CSCHS*, V. 188 note, 329 note, 338, 349, 354, 388, 411.
[36] Ibid., 345, 411, 453. Alvord and Bidgood, *First Explorations*, p. 79 note.
[37] Alvord and Bidgood, p. 81, identify Tamahita with Cherokee. But see Swanton, *Early History*, pp. 184-9, with regard to this mysterious tribe.
[38] *CSCHS*, V. 453.

Though the mountains did indeed 'stoop' to Shaftesbury's western dominions, the time was not ripe for emulating the Virginians. It was not until 1679 that Robert Holden, of Albemarle, was commissioned to undertake discoveries beyond the Appalachians; a similar commission was issued to Woodward in 1682.[39] But Shaftesbury, meanwhile, was bent upon developing the trade with the inland tribes. In 1674 he was busily promoting his abortive project for a seigniory at Edisto, where, free from the interference of the men of small estates who controlled the Ashley River council, he meant to experiment with cattle and crops, develop a clandestine commerce with the Spaniards and a trade with the Indians. Andrew Percival, a kinsman, was his principal agent, but Woodward was employed 'in the management of the trade and treaty of the Indians.' In May, 1674, he was ordered 'to settle a Trade with the Indians for Furs and other Comodities,' with the promise of a one-fifth profit for his pains. 'You are to consider,' Shaftesbury directed, 'whether it be best to make a peace with the Westoes or Cussitaws [Kasihta] which are a more powerfull nation said to have pearle and silver and by whose Assistance the Westoes may be rooted out.'[40] In October Woodward found an opportunity to open the inland trade when ten Westo appeared at St. Giles', Shaftesbury's other plantation near the head of Ashley River. Alone, he returned with them to their town on the Savannah River, a week's journey westward. 'Hickauhauga' (Rickahogo) he described as a palisaded village of long bark houses, on the west bank, almost enclosed by a bend of the stream. There he was greeted by a 'concourse of some hundred of Indians, drest up in their anticke fighting garbe.' It was the village of a warlike tribe: under the steep banks seldom lay fewer 'than one hundred faire canoes ready uppon all occasions.' With their arms from Virginia they had been able not only to terrorize the coastal tribes but even to make war upon the Yuchi, the Cherokee, and the Lower Creeks. The immediate result of Woodward's daring 'Westo voyage' was that trade was opened from St. Giles' plantation for 'deare

[39] Public Record Office, Colonial Office Records (hereinafter cited as C.O.), 286, pp. 131, 207.
[40] *CSCHS,* V. 439-46.

skins, furrs and younge Indian slaves.'[41] From 1674 to 1680 the Westo alliance formed the cornerstone of the South Carolina Indian system. The Westo were supplied with arms and were expected to protect the province by overawing the Spanish Indians and all other potential enemies.

Soon after this event the Spanish became uneasily aware of the expanding English sphere of influence. In 1675 it was known at Apalache from a Chisca (Yuchi) woman who had escaped from slavery in Carolina that Englishmen were teaching the Chichimecos or Westos to attack Florida and destroy Timucua and Apalache. Other rumors reached Apalache that same year of the arrival of four Englishmen from the new colony at an unnamed inland town, five days from the Chatot of the lower Apalachicola River, 'for the purpose of exploring and laying waste the land.'[42] Had Woodward already followed Shaftesbury's instructions to treat with Kasihta? If not in 1675, then probably soon after. The Proprietors in 1677 established a complete monopoly of the trade with the inland tribes 'of the Westoes and Cussatoes [Kasihta], two powerful and warlike nations,' whose countries, they recalled, had been discovered 'at the charge of the Earle of Shaftesbury, . . . and by the Industry and hazard of Dr. Henry Woodward, and a strict peace and Amity made between them' and the Carolinians.[43] In 1680 began a series of Indian incursions into Guale under English incitement. By the Spanish they were attributed to the 'Chichumecoes, Uchizes, and Chiluques,' that is, to the Westo, Lower Creeks, and Cherokee.[44]

Until 1680 the Carolinians were involved in no Indian wars of any consequence, although frequent minor collisions occurred between the settlers and the tribes along the fringe of the colony. Out of these early clashes developed the notorious traffic

[41] Henry Woodward to Shaftesbury, December 31, 1674: 'A Faithful relation of my Westo voiage begun from the head of Ashley River the tenth of Octr. and finished the sixth of Novbr. Following' (ibid., 456-62). See my note in *Am. Anthropologist*, n.s., XX. 332.

[42] 'Plans for the Colonization and Defense of Apalache, 1675' (documents from the Archives of the Indies, Seville, audiencia of Santo Domingo, 58-2-5, translated and edited by Katherine Reding), in *GHQ*, IX. 174 f.

[43] C.O. 5:286, pp. 120 f. Printed in W. J. Rivers, *A Sketch of the History of South Carolina to the Close of the Proprietary Government*, 1856, Appendix, pp. 388-90.

[44] *Documentos históricos de la Florida y la Luisiana, siglos XVI al XVIII*, edited by M[anuel] S[errano] y S[anz], Madrid, 1912, pp. 216-19.

in Indian slaves, in which South Carolina achieved a bad eminence among the English colonies. Encroachments upon Indian lands, unfair treatment in trade, destruction of Indian crops by the settlers' cattle—common incidents of a frontier—provoked Indian reprisals. The colonists, too, often complained of the destruction of their cattle and hogs in Indian hunts. Sometimes Englishmen were murdered, as by Westos in 1673 and Kussos the following year, and unless prompt satisfaction was offered, punitive expeditions were sent out. Spanish intrigue was believed to be an irritant. 'The fryers,' Owen had predicted in 1670, 'will never cease to promote their tragick ends by the Indian whom they instruct onlye to admire the Spanish nation.' In 1671 the Kussos were accused of conspiring with Florida to cut off the colony, and 'open war' was ordained. By its league with the small coast tribes, moreover, the province was obliged to guard them against their enemies. This was the principal cause alleged in 1680 for the breach with the Westo. Friction with the natives was inevitable. But the Proprietors were perhaps not far wrong when they charged that wars were begun under specious pretexts, with the real aim of enslaving the Indians. The first official recognition of the practice came, apparently, at the conclusion of the campaign against the Kusso in 1671, when the Grand Council ordered 'that every company who went out upon that expedition shall secure and maintaine the Indians they have taken till they can transport the said Indians.' In inception, then, Indian slavery was a means to secure volunteers for border defense, and for this purpose it was sanctioned by the Proprietors. But soon it developed into a flourishing business, and, later, into a cruelly efficient engine of encroachment upon the spheres of influence of England's rivals in the South and West.[45]

A decade of frontier expansion had raised up two issues, charged with controversy, between the colonists and the Lords Proprietors. One was Indian slavery. The other was the proprietary monopoly of the inland Indian trade.[46] Both were in-

---

[45] C.O. 5:288, pp. 16-19. *CSCHS,* V. 197. *JGC,* September 27, October 2, 1671; June 1, 18, July 2, 6, 9, 22, September 8, 1672; February 24, March 4, September 3, 16, October 4, 7, 1673; February 2, July 25, August 3, November 10, 1674; December 10, 1675.

[46] See below, pp. 118-9.

volved in the tangle of clashing interests and policies which resulted in the downfall of the Westo.

In spite of Woodward's journey, or perhaps because of the proprietary character of the affair, relations between the colonists and the Westo continued to be disturbed. After all, the Westo alliance was chiefly profitable to the Proprietors and to their agent, Woodward. The order of 1677 affirmed a complete proprietary monopoly of trade with the Westo, Kasihta, and the Spanish Indians beyond Port Royal, confining the planters, among whom were a number of restless commercial spirits, to the trade with the settlement tribes. The Proprietors' insistence that this policy was conceived mainly for the safety of the colony and not 'merely out of a designe of gaine,' was no doubt received with reservations. In 1677, following two murders by the Westo, they were forbidden to enter the settlement beyond the trading-plantations on the border: St. Giles', Walley's plantation, and Sewee. This order was renewed in 1680.[47] But Westo attacks upon the Cusabo continued. Indeed, the Grand Council, which reflected the prejudices of the private Indian traders, charged in June, 1680, that Woodward himself had incited the Westo to these raids.[48] A war against the Westo seems to have been eagerly desired by the private traders and slave-dealers, who were powerful in the Charles Town government. Wars brought slaves, and slaves commanded profits in the West Indies. The sending away of Indians, the Proprietors charged, made the Westo War.[49]

In the spring of 1680, two envoys, both trading-planters and slave-dealers, James Moore and John Boone, were sent by the governor and council to treat with the Westo. Woodward seems to have opposed their mission, suspecting, perhaps, an ulterior motive. Parleys were renewed, in April, at Walley's plantation, but war soon followed. The Grand Council laid an embargo upon all intercourse with the Westo, and Woodward was placed under heavy bonds to refrain from trade. In the ensuing campaigns the Carolinians found allies in the Savannah Indians, a migrating group of Shawnee, recent comers, ap-

[47] *JGC,* July 14, 1677; April 12, 1680.
[48] Ibid., June 4, 23, 24, 1680.
[49] C.O. 5:288, p. 17.

parently, from west of the mountains. By their aid the Westo
were defeated, without 'much Blood shed, or Money spilt,' as
an early chronicler recorded. In 1683 the Proprietors were told
that not fifty Westo remained alive and those in scattered
bodies. A decade later, the remnant, after retiring northward,
settled as a town among the Lower Creeks,[50] but soon vanished
from the maps.

The power of the Westo had been broken before the Proprietors, whose policy in Indian affairs was set at nought,
could intervene. At first they hoped to restore peace,[51] but
when it appeared that the Westo were 'ruined' they urged that
'some other Nation . . . whose Government is lesse An-
archicall' be set up in their place, 'that shall be furnished by us
with Arms and Ammunition . . . which will keep your Neigh-
bours the stricter united to you, and deterr the Northern and
Spanish Indians from dareing to infest you.'[52] At the same
time Shaftesbury, who seems in his disgrace to have contemplated an asylum in Carolina,[53] with Colleton privately instructed Percival and Maurice Mathews to get an act from the
provincial parliament restraining the new trade to themselves
alone.[54] But this attempt to restore the essence of the proprietary monopoly system failed. That system had been forever
destroyed by the Westo War. Thereafter the interest of the
Proprietors in Indian policy, and their influence, steadily
declined. Their complete failure to put down the traffic in Indian
slaves, to which the Westo War gave a notable impetus, was
significant of their failing authority.[55] The downfall and exile
of Shaftesbury removed the most energetic of the Proprietors,
the Englishman of his generation most active in promoting
western adventures. Woodward's commission of 1682 to ex-

[50] *JGC,* April 12, June 1, 4, 23, 24, 1680. John Oldmixon, *The British Empire in America,* 1708, I. 337, reprinted in Salley (ed.), *Narratives,* p. 329.
Letter from Thomas Newe, Charles Town, May, 1680, ibid., p. 183. *Am.
Anthropologist,* n.s., XX. 332, 336.
[51] C.O. 5 :286, pp. 153 f.
[52] Ibid., p. 169, *Calendar of State Papers, Colonial Series, America and
West Indies* (hereinafter cited as *CSP,AWI*), *1681-1685,* pp. 16 f.
[53] Historical Manuscripts Commission, *Calendar of Ormonde MSS,* n.s.,
VI. 154; and *Tenth Report,* Appendix, part IV., p. 173 (Throckmorton
MSS).
[54] Letter dated March 9, 1680/1, in C.O. 5 :286, p. 164.
[55] See below, pp. 139-40.

plore the interior and find a passage over the mountains was one of the last instances of positive proprietary intervention in frontier affairs.

For a time the Savannah Indians became the successors of the Westo. These immigrants soon 'united all their tribes' and seated themselves in a place of great strategic importance at the fall-line on the Westobou, to be called thereafter the Savannah River. For a decade or so the Carolinians regularly supplied them with arms, and purchased slaves taken in their raids upon their enemies: fugitive Westo, Winyahs from the North Carolina border, Appomatox from Virginia, Cherokee from the mountains, and Chatot from near the Gulf of Mexico.[56] But unlike the Westo, the Savannah were unable to hinder the further rapid extension of the English Indian trade into the great southern wilderness. Soon Savannah Town became the entrepôt for a commerce with the Cherokee, the tribes of the Tennessee River, and the Lower Creeks. After 1680 the trading expansion of South Carolina began in earnest.

[56] C.O. 5:288, p. 16. Court of Ordinary Records, 1672-1692 (MSS, Columbia, S. C.), under dates of May 31, October 14, 15, 20, 1681: permits for the exportation of Indian slaves.

CHAPTER II

CAROLINIAN EXPANSION IN THE SEVENTEENTH CENTURY

The two decades from the Westo affair to the outbreak of Queen Anne's War saw but meagre growth in the area of settlement in South Carolina, or in the number of planters. In 1700 the population of the province was a scant five thousand, mostly living within a few miles of Charles Town, though now the Port Royal region was also attracting settlers. The transition from mixed farming and cattle raising to rice culture was just beginning, and with it the development of negro slavery.[1] But in another sort of enterprise this weak border province had revealed forces of expansion without parallel in the English colonies. Neglected by the Proprietors, unsupported by the Crown, the Carolinians had contrived to push the first frontier of the province, the frontier of the Indian trade and of Indian alliances, farther into the wilderness than English traders elsewhere were wont to venture. Before the end of the century, therefore, they were in contact and keen rivalry not only with the Spanish of Florida, but also with the French in the region of the Gulf and the lower Mississippi.

Throughout the colonial period, the Indian trade was the chief instrument of Carolinian expansion. Other forces, to be sure, played a part. In an age of projects this debatable land of the South became the favorite field for colonial promoters. The record of these schemes, from the days of Doncaster and Cardross and Coxe to those of Montgomery and Purry and Oglethorpe, reveals a significant transition from the seventeenth-century era of colonization to that of the eighteenth century, with the westward movement as the new setting. The colony promoters, even those who failed, helped to advertise the South as a land of vast promise, and to awaken the government at home to its special strategic importance. But, meanwhile, the actual penetration of the southern wilderness and the

[1] Edward McCrady, *The History of South Carolina under the Proprietary Government, 1670-1719*, 1897, p. 316. U. B. Phillips, *American Negro Slavery*, 1918, p. 87. On the occupation of the southern border, see below, pp. 162-3.

spread of English influence was accomplished under other auspices, by obscure and often nameless explorers and traders.

More than any other English colony, except possibly New York, South Carolina was favored by geography in the development of a western Indian trade. The mountain ranges, so long an effective obstacle to penetration from Virginia and Maryland and Pennsylvania, were easily avoided by all but the Cherokee traders. Nor did any southern tribes in imitation of the Iroquois maintain the rôle of middlemen in the interior trade, and thus block the advance of the English traders.[2] Yet Carolina was geographically less fortunate than either Florida or Louisiana. The Spanish could reach the Lower Creek towns by the Apalachicola River, and the French, once Mobile was established, had easy water carriage to the Alabama, Talapoosa, and Abikha. The Carolina traders had to convey their goods on the backs of Indian burdeners or on packhorses by overland paths which intersected nearly all the important rivers of southeastern North America. However, even possession of the water-routes, and the finesse which the Latins everywhere displayed in Indian diplomacy, were more than offset by the superiority, as complete in the South as in the North, of English trade. The fundamental reason for the successes of the English in the tortuous politics of the wilderness was pithily expressed by the first provincial Indian agent of South Carolina. In 1708 Thomas Nairne asserted that 'the English trade for Cloath alwayes atracts and maintains the obedience and friendship of the Indians, they Effect them most who sell best cheap.'[3] Moreover, one important and peculiar branch of the Carolina trade, the commerce in Indian slaves, depending as it did upon intertribal wars, was extraordinarily wasteful in its effects, and led to rapid penetration of the interior. Then, too, the South Carolina trade was actively fostered by the provincial government. Indeed, the leaders in the government and in the trade were identical. Charges of monopolistic practises were freely made against the great traders who controlled the council

---

[2] See Wraxall, *An Abridgement of the Indian Affairs, 1678-1751,* 1915, especially the Introduction, pp. xlii, lxii-lxiv; A. H. Buffinton, 'The Policy of Albany and English Westward Expansion,' in *MVHR,* VIII. 327-66; Helen Broshar, 'The First Push Westward of the Albany Traders,' ibid., VII. 228-41.

[3] C.O. 5:382 (11).

and assembly. But the frontier interests of men like Joseph Blake (deputy-governor, 1696-1700) and James Moore (governor, 1700-1702) had a consequence for the colony unrecognized by their critics. At the end of the seventeenth century the Indian trade was weaving a web of alliances among tribes distant many hundreds of miles from Charles Town. Blake and his successor, active promoters of the trade, developed a conception of the destinies of the English in that quarter of America notably in advance of the parochial ideas of Proprietors and provincials alike; in advance, too, of the notions of policy of the imperial government itself.[4]

The crucial event of the seventeenth century on the Carolina-Florida border was the collapse of the Spanish missions of Guale in the face of the English traders' advance. Thus was begun, on this frontier, the long process of dissolution of Spanish authority in North America.

In the main, Spanish Indian policy was benevolent and pacific. Though converted Indians were sometimes employed against unfriendly tribes or against the English, the Spanish were loath to place firearms in the hands of their allies. Both in Guale, and, later, in Apalache, this proved a fatal weakness in view of the aggressive, disintegrating, Indian policy of the English. Very early, Indians in the English league were encouraged to direct their raids against the allies of the Spaniard.[5] In 1680 the first blow fell in Guale. Three hundred Indians, Westo, Cherokee, and Creek, attacked Guadalquini and Santa Catalina, 'cabeca y frontera á estos enemigos.' The raiders were stood off, but the mission Indians in alarm now deserted Santa Catalina, and the garrison was withdrawn to Zápala.[6] The Spanish retreat had begun. From St. Augustine the governor, Salazar, protested vigorously to Charles Town against Dr. Woodward's anti-Spanish intrigues among the 'Chichimecas' and other border Indians, and threatened retaliation.[7] But the ravages of the English Indians continued,

---

[4] *AHR*, XXIV. 380 and note 4.

[5] *GHQ*, IX. 174 f.

[6] Serrano y Sanz (ed.), *Documentos*, pp. 216-9. Brooks (comp.), *Unwritten History*, pp. 137-9; Bolton and Ross, *The Debatable Land*, pp. 36 f.

[7] C.O. 5:286, pp. 165, 166. A Spanish punitive expedition in 1682 was described in a colonist's letter from Charles Town, printed in Salley (ed.), *Narratives*, pp. 185 f.

pirates again descended upon the coast, and from 1680 to 1683 the missions rapidly disintegrated. Though Zápala was strengthened by a *casa fuerte,* hope of reoccupying Santa Catalina was abandoned.[8] Meanwhile, the terrorized mission Indians retired southward, or fled to the woods. It was apparently the ill-judged attempt of Governor Cabrera to remove the Guale Indians in a body to the islands of Santa María and San Juan, out of the range of northern attacks, that precipitated the final revolt of Guale in 1684.[9] Spanish authority was further undermined by direct commercial penetration from the north. Part of the Guale Indians deserted, declared the chronicler Barcía, because the English had 'persuaded them to give them obedience.' The Carolina traders were invading the coast region as well as the back-country.[10]

The Indian exodus from Guale was accomplished in three or four distinct migrations between 1684 and 1703. Most of the frightened or disaffected Indians fled first into the interior, to the Creek towns of Kasihta and Coweta. Only in 1685 did they emerge on the immediate border of Carolina. A small group, however, had already resorted directly to the region of Port Royal sound, led by the chief Altamaha. There they became neighbors of the Scots whom Lord Cardross had brought over in 1684 to establish a Covenanters' refuge in America. Altamaha first settled upon St. Helena Island, then Hilton's Head Island was also assigned him by Cardross 'to be as an Outguard to us.'[11] The Yamasee chief warned Cardross that more Indians would follow; but it was with astonishment and alarm that the Port Royal pioneers viewed the great influx of 1685. Early in January the St. Helena band was joined by revolted mission Indians 'from about St. Augustine,' described as 'Sapello, Soho [Asao], and Sapickay [Tupiqui].' Soon the

[8] Bolton and Ross, *The Debatable Land,* pp. 38 f.

[9] [Andrés González Barcía], *Ensayo cronológico, para la historia general de la Florida,* Madrid, 1723, p. 287. Compare Escudero (1734), cited in Swanton, *Early History,* p. 96; Bolton and Ross, *The Debatable Land,* pp. 39 f.

[10] Barcía, *Ensayo,* p. 287. In 1677 the Proprietors issued a license to Solomon Blackleech to trade 'from Ashley River with the Spaniards or any Indians dwellinge near or amongst them.' C.O. 5:286, p. 130. In 1684 Caleb Westbrooke was established as a trader at St. Helena, near Port Royal (C.O. 5:287, pp. 136, 142). See below, note 28a.

[11] Ibid., p. 142.

main body of the Yamasees appeared on the lower Savannah, on the march from the Lower Creek country to their new habitat in South Carolina. A thousand or more had arrived in February, wrote the trader Westbrooke, and daily more were expected.[12] By this migration and its sequel, the removal of Yewhaws (Yoa) in 1702-1703,[13] northern Florida—seacoast and lower coastal plain—was deserted by practically all of the natives. From Santa Catalina the Spanish mission frontier retreated to Santa María (Amelia Island), and to San Juan (Talbot Island).[14] To the English in consequence soon passed the hegemony of the whole region north of peninsular Florida. The route of their traders into the interior was safeguarded against flank attack from the east.

The bitterness of the Spanish defeat in Guale was enhanced by a new intrusion south of the region guaranteed to England by the treaty of 1670. In 1684, Henry Lord Cardross began his proposed settlement of a border county at Port Royal, under patent from the Lords Proprietors.[15] Intended as an asylum for Covenanters, this short-lived colony belongs in a notable category of seventeenth-century enterprises. The fate of Stuart's Town, extinguished in a Spanish raid of 1686, furnished a striking prologue for the drama of Darien. In border history the episode had a significance of its own.

In 1672 Colonel Lockhart's plan for a colony of Scotch Presbyterians in Carolina had come to nought,[16] but a decade later increasing persecutions revived the scheme. Indeed, two separate projects for southern colonization by Scots were brought forward in 1682. The Lords of Trade frowned upon the petition of James, Earl of Doncaster and Dalkeith, for a great proprietary grant of 'Florida, Cape Florida, and Guiana,' and laid down a policy of opposition to further proprietary

---

[12] Ibid., pp. 136, 142.
[13] See below, p. 76.
[14] Bolton and Ross, *The Debatable Land,* p. 41. In 1699 the castaway Quaker, Jonathan Dickenson, with his party, visited these missions on the way from St. Augustine to Charles Town, and left an account of them in his *God's Protecting Providence* (third edition, London, 1720), pp. 79, 84, *et passim.* Pertinent passages from a later edition are cited in Swanton, *Early History,* pp. 92 f.
[15] G. P. Insh, *Scottish Colonial Schemes, 1620-1686,* Glasgow, 1922, chapter vi, is the best narrative, but ignores the trade rivalry which underlay the controversy with Charles Town.
[16] *Bishop Burnet's History of His Own Time,* 1724, I. 526.

grants. The Spanish, Doncaster had argued, could hardly claim to hold the unoccupied portions of Florida by virtue only of 'two small Castles.'[17] Meanwhile, certain Presbyterian leaders, Cardross, Sir John Cochrane of Ochiltree, and Sir George Campbell, after considering New York as an asylum,[18] were attracted to Carolina by the promise of religious toleration, by the prestige of Shaftesbury, and, perhaps, by the batch of promotion pamphlets which were issued in 1682.[19] From the Proprietors they received a patent to one whole county, remote, by the width of one or two counties, from the existing settlements, with the privilege, later, of taking up another county.[20] In the fall of 1682 commissioners were sent out to explore the best rivers in Carolina.[21] Port Royal, the intended goal of the 1669 expedition, and recently shown in some detail on the Gascoyne map, was now chosen as the site.[22] But the Carolina project, unquestionably a *bona fide* venture, became entangled in the Whig conspiracies which culminated in the Rye House Plot.[23] It was not, therefore, until 1684 that the enterprise was set on foot, and then upon a considerably diminished scale. In

[17] C.O. 1:49, nos. 30, 30(i), 57, 71; *CSP,AWI, 1681-1685,* pp. 278 f., 296, 305. The Lords of Trade reported 'that it is not convenient . . . to constitute any new propriety in America' (ibid., p. 296).

[18] Insh, *Scottish Colonial Schemes,* pp. 193 f.

[19] Ibid., pp. 187-90. In 1682 were printed the following tracts advertising Carolina: T. A[she], *Carolina; or a Description of the Present State of that Country;* R. F., *The Present State of Carolina with Advice to the Setlers;* a broadside abbreviated from the last pamphlet, entitled *A True Description of Carolina,* probably printed to accompany Joel Gascoyne's *A New Map of the Country of Carolina* of the same year; and [Samuel Wilson], *An Account of the Province of Carolina in America.*

[20] *Letters . . . to George, Earl of Aberdeen,* edited by John Dunn, Aberdeen (The Spalding Club), 1851, pp. 58, 59 and note. There is some confusion in the documents as to the number of counties, but Cardross later asserted he had liberty to take up a second. C.O. 5:287, f. 139.

[21] Insh, *Scottish Colonial Schemes,* p. 198.

[22] Sir John Cochrane to the Earl of Aberdeen, June 15, 1683, in *Letters . . . to George, Earl of Aberdeen,* p. 127: 'The account I have received from our pilots, sent their to vieu the country, is so good, that I doubt not but we shall carry on a considerable plantation, to the great advantage of the nation. I have sein a description of the river Port Royal in ane exact map. It seems to be a very desirable place to plant upon.' The reference was probably to the Gascoyne map, on which see W. C. Ford, 'Early Maps of Carolina,' in *Geographical Review,* XVI. 273. On March 4, 1684, the Proprietors directed their governor to permit the Scots to settle at Port Royal (C.O. 5:287, f. 129).

[23] Insh, *Scottish Colonial Schemes,* pp. 190-3, 199-201. Cf. L. F. Stock (ed.), *Proceedings and Debates of the British Parliaments respecting North America,* 1924, I. 451.

July the *Carolina Merchant* sailed from Currock with less than a hundred colonists,[24] among them, however, a few men of real ability. In the more prosperous days following the Revolution Lord Cardross became a Privy Councillor in Scotland, and William Dunlop the Principal of the University of Glasgow.[25] The Scottish refugees were in general folk of a class superior to the old Barbadians and the English and Irish planters and servants who made up the colony at Ashley River. They were therefore promised a separate court of justice for their county, and the Fundamental Constitutions were modified to meet their views.[26] At the Proprietors' bidding, Maurice Mathews had already extinguished the Indian title to the region, and, indeed, to the whole area south of Ashley River, westward to the mountains.[27] Arrived at Port Royal, Cardross built a small settlement at the Spanish Point, which he named Stuart's Town.[28] At home the Proprietors counted confidently upon a rapid emigration from Scotland to this promising colony. They were doomed to disappointment. Bitter controversies arose between Stuart's Town and Charles Town, which checked the growth of the new settlement, and exposed it to Spanish attack. Underlying these untimely disputes was the effort of Cardross to control the expanding Indian trade with the Yamasee and the Creeks.[28a]

[24] Insh, *Scottish Colonial Schemes*, pp. 203 f.
[25] *Dictionary of National Biography*, XVI. 209; XVII. 408.
[26] Letters and instructions of March 4, June 25, 28, 1684, in C.O. 5:287.
[27] South Carolina Assembly, *Report of the Committee, appointed to examine into the Proceedings of the People of Georgia*, 1737, Appendices 2, 2b. Cf. C.O. 5:288, p. 100.
[28] John Erskine, *Journal*, edited by Walter Macleod, *Publications* of the Scottish History Society, XIV., p. 139; *Warrants for Lands in South Carolina, 1680-1692*, 1911, edited by A. S. Salley, Jr., p. 179: head-right warrants to Cardross for 850 acres for himself and sixteen others, to Dunlop for 1150 acres for himself and twenty-two others. See *Warrants for Lands, 1692-1711*, 1915, p. 155 regarding the site; also Gascoyne, 'Plat,' *circa* 1685 (B.M. Add. MSS 5414, roll 24).
[28a] This interpretation, which I set forth briefly in *MVHR*, XII. 23-25, is completely confirmed by an important document which has appeared in the *Scottish Historical Review*, XXV. 100-4, while these pages are in press. It is a letter from Cardross and Dunlop to Sir Peter Colleton, from Stuart's Town, March 27, 1685. It contains an interesting account of the settlement of the Scots' colony, reduced to fifty-one men by sickness at Charles Town, fear of Spanish invasion, and by the persuasions of the Carolinians. 'We discovered likewayes the mouth of the West[o] river, and went up the same a good way, and went near to Saint Catharina, which we hear the Spaniards have desarted on the report of our setling here, and

Even before the coming of the Yamasee, Port Royal had acquired importance in the Charles Town Indian trade. The traders were discovering that the best route to their new western base at Savannah Town was the inland water passage from Ashley River to Yamacraw, and thence up the Savannah River. But this route passed right through the Scots' domain. Late in March, 1685, John Edenburgh, a Charles Town trader on his way to the Yamasees, was, he deposed, haled to Stuart's Town and warned by Lord Cardross 'that noe Englishman should trade from Sta. Helena to the Westoe River for all the Indians was his and that noe Englishman should trade between the Westoe River and St. Katherina for that hee had taken up one County and had liberty to take up another County.'[29] Cardross thus claimed an exclusive trade southward into Guale, where, apparently, he expected to expand his colony now that the friars were in retreat. A few weeks later Henry Woodward was arrested at Yamacraw, on the Savannah route to the interior, though he carried an extraordinary commission from the Lords Proprietors for inland exploration. For a time after the Westo War the adventurous Doctor had fallen under a cloud. He had been fined at Charles Town for his dealings with the Westo, and censured by the Proprietors. But a voyage to England had procured him pardon and complete reinstatement. His commission obtained at that time, was a noteworthy

we desyre this summer to vew it and tak possessione of it in his Majesties name for the behove of the lords proprietors.' If it proved necessary for the Proprietors to secure a new patent from the King to this region as 'formerlie in the Spanish dominions,' the Scots hoped to be remembered. They tempted Colleton further with the prospect of opening a trade thence to New Mexico,—'which if effectuated wold be a matter of vast importance both to you and us. We are in order to this plan laying down a method for correspondence and treade with *Cuita* [Coweta] and *Cussita* [Kasihta] nations of Indians, who leive upon the passages betwixt us and New Mexico, and who have for severall yeirs left off any Comercie with the Spaniards; but, Sir, these our endeevors do already provock the Inevey of severall particular persones, who, meinding their own privat Intrist mor than that of the lords proprietors or good of the province, doe so grudge both at the situation of this place doth give us advantage for trade more than these and that they find us ready to improve that advantage, that they do opres our designe and endevour to render us contemptible in the eyes of the Indians about us.' They alluded to their friendly relations with the Yamasee, 'admited to setle heire within our bounds by the Government of Charlestoun the last year since our contract with you.' To secure Colleton's support for their projected Creek trade they proposed that he 'put in with us for a share.'

[29] C.O. 5:287, p. 139.

document in the history of English exploration. It recited the benefits to the Crown and the Proprietors from having 'the Inlands of our Province of Carolina well discovered and what they doe containe and also a passage over the Apalateans Mountaines found out.'[30] But Cardross, according to the affidavits of Woodward and his companions, refused to honor this paper 'for that it was to encourage trade to which hee had as much right as any of them.'[31] Cardross's interference postponed, but did not long prevent Woodward's great western adventure. Summer found the explorer on the Chattahoochee, challenging Spanish influence among the Creeks.[32]

Cardross inevitably failed in this ambitious attempt to engross the southern Indian trade. His contest with Charles Town in its later stages was obscured by personal recrimination and by disputes over jurisdiction. Meanwhile, coöperation for defense was neglected, and Stuart's Town was exposed to certain Spanish revenge.[33]

By the Spaniards all settlements in Carolina were regarded as intrusions into Florida, but especially those south of Ashley River, for so the Council of the Indies read the meaning of the Treaty of Madrid. Nor were officials like Governor Cabrera accustomed to discriminate nicely between the pirates and the colonists who sheltered them. And now the Spaniards were further wantonly provoked by the reckless Indian policy of the Scots. Yamasee were employed from Port Royal in incursions upon the mission province of Timucua; there is evidence that they were incited by Lord Cardross himself and the trader Westbrooke.[34] Ample precedent might be found in the practices of the Charles Town traders, but in view of the exposed situation of Stuart's Town, Woodward, who was not likely to be squeamish, was justified in condemning the Timucuan raid of 1685 as 'an unadvised project.'[35] The Proprietors, too, for all

[30] C.O. 5:287, pp. 198-202, 207. The pardon was dated May 23, 1682; the commission, May 18.
[31] C.O. 5:287, pp. 137 f.
[32] Bolton and Ross, *The Debatable Land*, p. 48.
[33] Insh, *Scottish Colonial Schemes*, pp. 206-8. Documents relating to the controversies between the Scots and Charles Town, and attempts to arrest Cardross and other leaders, are in C.O. 5:287, ff. 136, 140, 141; C.O. 5:288, pp. 71, 73. See also Rivers, *Sketch*, Appendix, pp. 407 f.
[34] C.O. 5:287, p. 143.
[35] Ibid.

their sympathy with Cardross, were convinced that this affair provoked the Spanish attack in the next year.[36] Several Indians who took part in the destruction of Santa Catalina de Afuica were examined on their return by Henry Woodward. They declared that the Scots had armed and incited them, and that they had 'burnt severall Towns and in particuler the Said Chappell and the Fryers house and killed Fifty of the Timechoes and brought away Two and twenty Prisoners which the[y] delivered to the Scotts as slaves.'[37]

In August, 1686, Cabrera took his revenge. In three small vessels—a galley and two pirogues—one hundred Spaniards, with an auxiliary force of Indians and mulattoes, descended upon the Carolina coast. They struck first at Port Royal. Sickness, it is said, had left not more than twenty-five defenders fit to bear arms. These were routed with some casualties, Stuart's Town was burned, and the infant Scotch settlement destroyed. Thence the raiders ranged northward to the Edisto, where more plantations were plundered; among others, the houses of Governor Morton and of the secretary, Paul Grimball, were put to the torch. But a hurricane frustrated the attack on Charles Town. Two of the Spanish craft were wrecked. In one perished the commander, Tomás de León; in the other, by English account, the governor's brother-in-law, a captive in irons, was burned to death when the vessel with its plunder was set on fire by the retreating Spaniards. The whole country was now alarmed, and the raiders retired with the remnant of their booty and their captured slaves to the presidio of St. Augustine.[38]

Though little love was lost between the Scots and the English, and the latter were, perhaps, not sorry that an obstacle to their trading expansion was removed, the colony was in a flame at the Spanish invasion in time of peace, with its alleged atrocities. Parliament was hastily summoned, and an act was

[36] C.O. 5 :288, pp. 121, 160; *CSP,AWI, 1685-1688*, pp. 451f.
[37] C.O. 5 :287, p. 140; *Arredondo's Historical Proof*, p. 157; Brooks (comp.), *Unwritten History*, p. 144; Bolton and Ross, *The Debatable Land*, p. 40, citing other Spanish archival sources.
[38] C.O. 1 :61, no. 18; C.O. 5 :288, p. 106; C.O. 38 :2, p. 109; C.O. 323 :3, E2; *CSP,AWI, 1685-1688*, pp. 295, 336; *Historical Collections of South Carolina*, edited by B. R. Carroll, 1836, II. 350 f.; Rivers, *Sketch*, Appendix, pp. 425, 443 f.; *Historical Magazine*, III. 298 f.; Bolton and Ross, *The Debatable Land*, pp. 41f.

passed to impress men and ships 'to persue, attacque and (by God's grace) to vanquish' the enemy wherever they might be found.[39] Two French privateers were soon fitting out, so the governor of Bermuda reported,[40] with crews of Carolinians and privateersmen. There was reason, apparently, for a clause in the act forbidding the use of the vessels for any other purpose than an attack on the Spanish. But a new governor, Landgrave James Colleton, arrived at the height of the excitement and put an end to the expedition. He threatened, indeed, to hang anyone who set out against Florida.[41] At the same time he approved legitimate measures for defense: a store of powder, galleys, and warning beacons on the coast as far as the Savannah.[42] Colleton's caution was endorsed by the Proprietors, who were not easily convinced that Spanish officials were actually responsible for the invasion, and who threw much blame on the provocative conduct of their colonists. Instead of making war on the subjects of an ally, the Carolinians were admonished to negotiate for the return of their property and the redress of injuries.[43] Cardross was commiserated on his losses: 'in fitting time' the Proprietors promised to apply to the King for reparation.[44] This pacific policy was borne with ill grace by the Carolinians, among whom was a growing antiproprietary party. In 1699 Edward Randolph, who had an ear attuned to such scandal, said that he had learned the truth which underlay this pusillanimity, that 'there was a design on foot to carry on a Trade with the Spaniards.'[45]

Not only was Cabrera sustained at home, but his successor, Quiroga, was charged in 1688 'to continue the operations begun by him until you succeed in dislodging the enemies, Scotch, English and Yamassees.'[46] But Quiroga apparently understood that the time had passed for a successful campaign to recover

[39] *Statutes at Large of South Carolina,* edited by Thomas Cooper, II. 15-18 (act of October 15, 1686).

[40] C.O. 1:61, no. 18; C.O. 38:2, p. 109; *CSP,AWI, 1685-1688,* p. 295.

[41] Ibid., pp. 451f. C.O. 5:288, pp. 121-123. Rivers, *Sketch,* Appendix, pp. 425, 444.

[42] Cooper (ed.), *Statutes,* II. 20 f., 23-25.

[43] C.O. 5:288, pp. 106-7, 121; *CSP,AWI, 1685-1688,* pp. 336 f., 451 f.

[44] C.O. 5:288, p. 109.

[45] Rivers, *Sketch,* Appendix, p. 444; and see charge in address to Sothell, ibid., p. 425.

[46] *Arredondo's Historical Proof,* p. 345, note 52.

Guale and Santa Elena. He now turned to negotiation. About a year after the raid, Bernardo de Medina, an officer of the garrison, accompanied by a friar, appeared at Charles Town. The negotiations that ensued were typical of a long series of futile border parleys.[47] The Spanish denied that the late expedition had been commissioned to attack the English king's subjects in Carolina, and complained of the bad conduct of the Carolinians. In reply, Colleton had first to deny complicity in the pirate raids into Guale; he also disclaimed responsibility for the actions of the Yamasee, 'a people who live within our bounds after their own manner taking no notice of our Government.' He demanded the return of the slaves and plunder carried off in 1686, and proposed the regular delivery in the future of the fugitive slaves and servants, 'who run dayly into your towns.' With the development of the plantation régime in Carolina this grievance became increasingly serious, and furnished the theme of recurring protests to the Spaniards. Apparently the friar had instructions to persuade the Yamasee to return to Florida. A demand that they be sent back Colleton refused. Only war, he declared, could accomplish this, as they were confederated with a larger nation, the Lower Creeks.

With this inconclusive diplomatic exchange, the conflict in the coastal region came, temporarily, to an end. The Spanish governor continued to assert the inclusive Spanish claims, and reported to Charles Town his orders from Spain 'not to lett the English come south of St. Georges.'[48] But his hands were tied by the Anglo-Spanish partnership in the Grand Alliance, and even more by the weakness of Florida.[49] English traders continued to win over the Indian allies of the Spanish, or to reduce them to slavery. Meanwhile, the scene of active conflict shifted to another segment of the Carolina-Florida border.

From an early period the Carolinians had been aware of the existence of the great Creek confederation, or at any rate of the two leading towns of the Lower Creeks, Coweta and Kasihta. Several times before 1681 they had established con-

---

[47] *Historical Magazine*, III. 298 f.: James Colleton to Quiroga, 1687 or 1688, original in Archives of the Indies, Seville; Brooks (comp.), *Unwritten History*, p. 145: royal orders regarding runaway slaves.

[48] C.O. 5:288, p. 160.

[49] Brooks (comp.), *Unwritten History*, pp. 144 f.

tacts with them. But it was not until the Westo barrier was removed that the Lower Creek trade could develop. In the midst of the Westo War the Lords Proprietors had instructed Percival and Mathews to reopen the trade, if unsafe with the Westos, with the 'Chiscah [Yuchi], Sevanaes, or the Cowitaws.' Soon the Lower Creek country became the centre of the Carolinian trading régime.[50]

The Lower Creeks, called Apalachicola by the Spaniards, controlled the whole interior region from the borders of Guale and of Carolina northward to the headwaters of the Savannah, and westward to the Chattahoochee. Several times in the course of the international struggle for the Indian trade in the South they changed their village sites. At this epoch their towns were located on the middle Chattahoochee, near the falls, within easy distance of the Spanish presidio of San Luís and the missions of Apalache. From Apalache, indeed, the Spaniards were now engaged in a series of efforts to convert the Apalachicola to the faith, and thus translate the nominal sovereignty of Spain into a real dominion. In 1679 the first attempt to establish a mission at Sábacola was frustrated by the head chief of Coweta, whose great influence, wielded for many years, won him the title of Emperor both in Florida and in Carolina. In 1681 the Franciscans again appeared, accompanied by soldiers. But again they were forced to withdraw. This time, however, they were followed by their converts, and the mission of Santa Cruz de Sábacola was established further south, at the junction of the Chattahoochee and the Flint.[51]

The Spanish suspected that English intrigue had checked their penetration into Apalachicola. In the summer of 1685, indeed, the Carolinians appeared in person upon the Chattahoochee. Woodward, in spite of Cardross's interference, had made his way, the accredited proprietary explorer of the West, to the 'court' of Coweta. Both at Coweta, the 'war town,' and Kasihta, the 'peace town,' the English with their trading goods

[50] C.O. 5:286, p. 164. See my note on the 'Origin of the Name of the Creek Indians,' in MVHR, V. 339-42. The Gascoyne Plat, circa 1685 (cited above, note 28), has on the extreme western margin, northwest of Savannah Town, an almost illegible statement that 'here begins the Chiscah country.' The Savannah River is still called the Westo on this map.
[51] Bolton and Ross, The Debatable Land, pp. 46-48; Swanton, Early History, p. 130.

were now cordially welcomed.[52] In the Anglo-Spanish conflict which ensued these towns became the strongholds of English influence. They were the leaders, too, in the resulting migration of the Lower Creeks eastward to the Ocmulgee River, nearer to the source of the English trade.

In Apalache Lieutenant Antonio Matheos was in command. At word of Woodward's mission he led a force of Spaniards and two hundred and fifty Christian Indians to arrest the mischief-maker and to punish the Indians who had welcomed him. Englishmen and recreant Indians fled at his approach. Woodward, however, left a letter which stated the objects of his proprietary commission in challenging terms:

I am very sorry that I came with so small a following that I cannot await your arrival. Be informed that I came to get acquainted with the country, its mountains, the seacoast, and Apalache. I trust in God that I shall meet you gentlemen later when I have a larger following. September 2, 1685. *Vale.*[53]

A stockade which was building under English direction, above the falls, Matheos burned, but he retired without achieving his real purpose. Soon the Englishmen were back in the Creek villages. Meanwhile, Cabrera had reinforced the Apalache garrison. In December, 1685, Matheos was despatched with a larger force to demand the surrender of the Carolinians, on pain of the destruction of the Indian towns. Again he failed to lay hands on the traders, though he seized peltry and trading goods in a blockhouse near Coweta. At Coweta, Matheos managed to impose submission upon eight towns. The Indians of Coweta, Kasihta, Tuskegee, and Kolomi were still recalcitrant, and in punishment their villages were burned. Under this blow the two latter towns professed a short-lived repentance. But Kasihta and Coweta held out, and spies brought rumors that they intended to desert their Chattahoochee settlements. Soon the Charles Town traders were busy again along the Chattahoochee. Woodward, ill, made the dangerous journey back to Charles Town in a litter, followed by one hundred and fifty burdeners laden with peltry. This enterprising explorer re-

[52] W. E. Dunn, 'Spanish and French Rivalry in the Gulf Region of the United States, 1678-1702,' in *University of Texas Bulletin*, no. 1705, p. 71; Bolton and Ross, *The Debatable Land*, pp. 48 f.
[53] Ibid., p. 50.

turned no more to the Chattahoochee. But he had laid the foundations of English trade and alliance in the old Southwest. In 1687 other traders appeared in the Creek towns. The struggle had only begun. Quiroga in the next two years was no more successful than Cabrera in ousting the Carolinians. In 1689, after futile negotiations, he sent soldiers under Captain Primo de Rivera to build a Spanish fort in the heart of the old Apalachicola country.[54]

From 1689 to 1691 the Spanish colors waved over the *casa fuerte* of Apalachicola—symbol of an authority which became more and more unreal. Mission and presidio had failed to sustain Spanish dominion in Guale. What prospect that among the Creeks, the shrewdest Indian politicians of the South, force or persuasion could long withstand the pushing Charles Town traders with their desirable goods? What actually occurred, as in Guale, was the wholesale desertion of the old towns on the northwestern border of Florida. From the Chattahoochee the Lower Creeks migrated eastward, by 1690, to the upper waters of the Altamaha.[55] They placed most of their new towns along the upper Ocmulgee, known to the English as Ochese Creek. There they began the cultivation of the broad fields which, long after these in turn were abandoned, were the marvel of the botanist Bartram. Among the Ochese Creek Indians, or the Creeks, as they were soon called by abbreviation, the Carolinians maintained for a quarter-century a great trading centre.[56] Goods were transferred at Savannah Town from periagoes to pack-horses or Indian burdeners, and carried by two paths which branched near the Ogeechee River. One led to Coweta Town, the other—the Lower Path—to the settlements of the Okmulgee and Hichiti.

Until 1715 English influence was paramount among the Lower Creeks. 'These people,' declared an official report of the

[54] Ibid., pp. 50-54 (plan of fort opposite p. 48); Serrano y Sanz (ed.), *Documentos*, pp. 193-8 (report of Matheos, 1686, misdated 1606); also pp. 219-21, 250.

[55] See Iberville (1702), in Margry (ed.), *Découvertes*, IV. 594 f. This migration was first clearly established by Bolton in his 'Spanish Resistance to the Carolina Traders in Western Georgia (1680-1704),' *GHQ*, IX. 115-30; see also Bolton and Ross, *The Debatable Land*, pp. 54 f. Bolton has misread my meaning in *AHR*, XXIV. 381. Kasihta and Coweta were Ochese towns; I identified neither with Oconee.

[56] *MVHR*, V. 339-42.

early eighteenth century, 'are Great Hunters and Warriours and consume great quantity of English Goods.'[57] With keen realization of their importance, the Carolina authorities from the first sought to preserve and exploit the Lower Creek alliance. In 1693 the Commons House became alarmed at the report that some of the Westo had settled among the Tuskegee, and that others planned to join the Coweta and Kasihta. All possible means, they urged, should be used to prevent these old enemies from corrupting 'our friends.'[58] The Ochese country soon became a base for the further extension of trade. From the Ocmulgee were sent out many of those slave-taking expeditions against Florida, and, later, against Louisiana, which provided an outlet for the warlike energies of the Indians, enriched the traders, and served to weaken the defenses of the rival colonial establishments in the South.

Creek depredations in Florida added another lively subject of dispute between St. Augustine and Charles Town. Don Laureano de Torres Ayala protested vigorously to 'San Jorje.'[59] But Joseph Blake, a notable proponent of southwestern expansion, merely replied with a blanket claim of English sovereignty over these Indians.[60] Meanwhile, Torres had sent out a punitive expedition of four hundred Indians, headed by seven Spaniards, against the Indians whom he chose to describe as 'disobedient vassals' of Spain. Fifty captives were taken in one town, but elsewhere the Indians had burned their villages and fled.[61] This, apparently, was the 'Difference with [i.e., between] the Cursitaws &c. & the King of Spaines Subjects' of which Blake gave an account to the Lords Proprietors. The Proprietors counselled peace, and admonished the new Governor, John Archdale, that 'wee give no offence to that Crowne that is in league with us, but treat the Subjects with all tenderness Imaginable.'[62]

[57] C.O. 5 :1264, P 82.
[58] *Journal of the Commons House of Assembly* (hereinafter cited as *JCHA,* or JCHA when references are to manuscript journals), January 13, 14, 1692/3.
[59] Serrano y Sanz (ed.), *Documentos,* p. 224.
[60] Ibid., p. 225.
[61] Ibid. See Swanton, *Early History,* p. 221, and Bolton and Ross, *The Debatable Land,* p. 56, note 2, for conflicting statements regarding date of this expedition. Swanton's assumption that it occurred in 1685 (rather than 1684) seems to be confirmed by a letter of Torres to Archdale, January 24, 1695/6, in Archdale MSS, Library of Congress.
[62] C.O. 5 :289, p. 28.

Governor Archdale was a Proprietor, and a Quaker as well, and so disposed to conciliate the Spanish, but not to the point of yielding any substantial English interest. Moreover, he commissioned Joseph Blake, neither a Quaker nor a pacifist, deputy-governor and commander of the militia;[63] with Blake's expansionist aims he later professed sympathy.[64] Archdale, to be sure, tried to discourage the Indian slave-trade, and returned to Florida four mission Indians captured by the Yamasee near Santa María.[65] Torres thanked him in January, 1696, and promised reciprocal restitution, but renewed his complaints as to 'the Townes of Apalachicola w[h]ich belong to this Government and has always Live[d] under our obeissance and since a Time have Revolted from it and Live in their wickednesse and Rebellion committing abundance of ill and murther in the Province of Apalache having Dispeopled 2 or three Townes.' This, he said, had occasioned the late punitive expedition and would lead to further chastisement. 'For all that you are not to believe that I will break peace with you because those nations as I have told you above are neither vassals nor Subjects to your Government.' But Torres asked that an order issue to draw back from Apalachicola the traders who incited all this mischief.[66] Two months later the Spanish governor repeated his charges and his threats, specifying a recent raid upon the Chacatos.[67] In Archdale's reply,[68] for all its diplomatic tone, was a firm counter-assertion of English mastery in the disputed region, and a warning against Spanish intervention. He had sent an express to the Okmulgees, he said, to forbid hostilities against the vassals of Florida, and expected a like order from Torres. Despite the revengeful character of the Indian, he counted on 'their ready obedience to our Commands to prevent it for the future.' But if the Indians nevertheless continued their wars, 'I desire you not to send any more white persons

[63] Secretary's record of commissions and instructions (MSS, Columbia, S. C.), p. 124.
[64] John Archdale, *A New Description of Carolina*, 1707, p. 31, reprinted in Carroll (ed.), *Collections*, II. 119.
[65] Ibid., pp. 106 f.
[66] Archdale MSS.
[67] Ibid. Torres to Archdale, March 21, 1696.
[68] Ibid. Archdale to Torres, April 4, 1696. Cf. Archdale, *Description*, pp. 20 f., reprinted in Carroll (ed.), *Collections*, II. 107. Archdale also demanded payment of damages for the raids of the preceding decade.

against our Indians least you hereby make the quarrel nationall, and lay me under the necessity of doing the like: pray consider the Circumstances of our European Masters and Kings and lett nott small sparks here begett differences at home betwixt our so amiable soveraines.' Apparently this belligerent rejoinder from the Quaker governor closed the debate. The traders, at all events, were not withdrawn from the Lower Creeks.

In the later years of the seventeenth century, indeed, the Carolinians were penetrating deeper and deeper into the mystery of the West. Beyond the Appalachians, in the valleys of the Tennessee and the lower Mississippi and on the broad plains of the Gulf, they were pioneers of English enterprise, matching in audacity the Canadian *coureurs de bois*. In western exploration they had as yet no real rivals among the English of Virginia or the North, save for isolated adventurers whose wanderings had no significant sequel. To be sure the Spaniards, De Soto, Pardo, Boyano, De Luna, and Villafañe, had long preceded them, but Spanish dominion, despite inflated claims, had never really been maintained beyond the coastal mission provinces. La Salle, too, had dreamed, and struggled, and miserably perished. But till Ponchartrain and Iberville revived La Salle's great project, Tonti's establishment in the Illinois country, and for a short time his Arkansas seigniory, marked the effective limits of the French southward advance. When, at the century's close, Frenchmen returned to the Mississippi under Iberville, and the missionary priests drifted down the great river, everywhere they found disturbing evidences of the presence of the Charles Town traders. Two main routes to the West were followed by these forgotten English explorers. One led north-westward into the mountain country of the Cherokee, where the head streams of the Savannah interlace with the 'western waters' of the Tennessee system. The other consisted of the overland paths from Ochese Creek to the Coosa and Talapoosa, and thence to the land of the Chickasaws and to their neighbors along the Mississippi. Few traces were left by the traders of their activities, save the trails which their successors followed through many decades. Only now and then did they emerge briefly into the light of history, much as when their caravans chanced to pass from the gloom of the vast southern pine forests into some sunny upland savannah.

Traders from Virginia continued to follow the Occaneechi path as far as the Carolina piedmont. But after the period of Col. Abraham Wood there is no clear evidence for many years that they traded with the mountain tribes. Certainly they had no part in the great expansion of English trade westward from the mountains to the Mississippi.[69] The beginnings of Charles Town's contacts with the Cherokee are also obscure. In 1681 a permit was issued for the exportation of several 'Seraquii' slaves, probably Cherokee captured by the Savannah Indians.[70] An important manuscript map of South Carolina, prepared about 1685 from official data, showed a path running up the right bank of the Savannah River from 'the Oldfort,' opposite 'Savana town and fort,' nearly as far as the forks.[71] Thus early, perhaps, this river route had been followed to the Cherokee towns. Certainly by 1690 the Cherokee trade had begun; this was clearly indicated in Sothell's restrictive act of the following year.[72] A pioneer in exploiting the Cherokee trade was the ambitious and impecunious planter, James Moore, who was to play so great a rôle in the creation of the southern frontier and of provincial western policy. 'He is a generous man and lives well,' was the character given him by the Proprietors to palliate his neglect to pay quit-rents.[73] With Maurice Mathews he engaged in slave-trading and other speculative money-making schemes, including a project to exploit the trade and the mines of the southern Appalachians. In 1690 Moore made a journey 'over the Apalathean Mountains,' 'as well out of curiosity to see what sort of Country we might have in Land as to find out and make new and further discovery of Indian Trade.' But Moore wrote that he was prevented from penetrating 'to the place which I had gon to see' by 'a difference about

[69] V. W. Crane, 'The Tennessee River as the Road to Carolina,' in *MVHR*, III. 9 f., and notes 22, 23, 26.

[70] Court of Ordinary Records, 1672-1692 (MSS, Columbia, S. C.), under date October 15, 1681.

[71] Joel Gascoyne, Plat, B.M. Add. MSS 5414, roll 24.

[72] Cooper (ed.), *Statutes*, II, 64.

[73] C.O. 5:288, p. 228.

Trade . . . between those Indians and me.'[74] In a letter of May, 1691, the Proprietors expressed alarm that 'without any war first proclaimed,' certain Carolinians had 'fallen upon the Cherokee Indians in a hostile manner and murdered several of them.'[75] No doubt they had heard from Moore's enemies, who were disturbed by Mathews's secret mission to England to procure an assay of several specimens of ore from the mountains. In April, 1692, Moore was forbidden by the council to leave the settlement to trade with any remote Indians except by permission of governor and council, and ordered to deliver all papers relating to Mathews's English journey.[76] For a number of years, apparently, such trade as developed in this mountain area was intermittent; and the Cherokee long occupied a subordinate position in the Carolina Indian system. Thus in 1693 the Commons House refused to sanction the punishment of the Savannah for a raid against the mountaineers.[77] Indeed, as late as 1708 the Cherokee were officially described as 'a Numerous People but very Lasey,' and their trade as inconsiderable in comparison with the flourishing southern and western trade, 'they being but ordinary hunters and less Warriours.'[78] However, as competition developed with the French in the West, the strategic location of the Cherokee gave them increasing importance.

Vague rumors, no doubt exaggerated, of English penetration into the Cherokee country and even as far as the Tennessee valley were current among the French as early as the epoch of La Salle's explorations. But by reason of the Iroquois hegemony south of the Great Lakes, the French, apparently, had no first-hand knowledge, even at the end of that period, of the great central region of the Ohio and its southern affluents. Such information as they possessed probably came from the Indians, principally from the Shawnee, who were rapidly disintegrating under the assaults of the Iroquois. The maps which

[74] James Moore to Edward Randolph, *circa* 1699, in C.O. 5:1258, C 19; ibid., C 20 (Moore to Cutler, April 3, 1699), gave the date 1691, but the earlier date seems to be confirmed by the Proprietors' letter of May 13, 1691, in C.O. 5:288, p. 176.
[75] Ibid.
[76] *Journal of the Grand Council of South Carolina* (hereinafter cited as *JGC*), April 14, 1692; see also entry of May 28, 1692.
[77] *JCHA*, January 14, 1692/3.
[78] C.O. 5:1264, P 82.

purported to record the results of Marquette's and Joliet's explorations, though exceedingly vague in depicting this section, showed the approximate position of the 'Kaskinonka' Indians, from whom the Tennessee River took its early name. In the great manuscript map by Franquelin recording La Salle's discoveries, the 'Casquinampogamou' appeared as the most important tributary of the Ohio, and the location of the Cherokee on its upper waters was clearly indicated. From 'les Kaskinampo,' on an island in the mid-course of the river, Franquelin showed a path leading to Florida by which these and other Indians 'vont traiter aux Espagnols.' Such was the extent of French information of the Tennessee when La Salle's labors in the Mississippi Valley were completed, and for a decade and a half thereafter. Already the importance of the Tennessee as a route from the English frontier had been recognised, and also the necessity for its control by the French. La Salle himself had feared that the English would come from Carolina by a river which took its rise near the boundaries of that province, and would draw off thither a large part of the French trade. Tonti, whose trading privileges in the Illinois country gave him exceptional opportunities for observing the English advance on the southern frontier, urged in 1694 the danger to the western trade as a reason for the completion of La Salle's enterprise. Had he learned, perhaps, from the Indians of the exploits of James Moore when he asserted that Carolinians were even then established upon one of the branches of the Ohio?[79]

The earliest actual contact between the French and English trading frontiers in the South appears to have been made by one of Tonti's men, but a renegade from his service. This obscure explorer, perhaps the first white man to follow the Tennessee to its sources in the Cherokee country, was a certain Jean Couture. A carpenter, born in Rouen, he was known to La Salle in 1684 as a *coureur de bois* of Canada; he was an acquaintance, also, of Hennepin. Two years later he followed Tonti down the Mississippi in the unsuccessful attempt to join La Salle. On the return he was one of those left at Tonti's

<hr>

[79] *MVHR*, III. 3-5. In the W. L. Clements Library, Ann Arbor, Michigan, is a photostatic reproduction of the Franquelin map, 1688, from the Bibliothèque Nationale MS 4040 B, 6 bis.

seigniory at the mouth of the Arkansas to build a stockaded post which Tonti intended to make serve as an intermediate station between the Illinois and La Salle's colony, to maintain the alliance of the Arkansas tribes and to protect them against the Iroquois. As commandant, Couture remained to hold this farthest outpost of New France in the Mississippi valley when, in 1687, the survivors of La Salle's disaster wandered thither. It was from Couture, on his return to Fort St. Louis in April, 1688, that Tonti first learned of the death of his great leader. Couture was at once despatched to the southwest to seek the ill-fated colony, but a hundred leagues from the fort he was shipwrecked, and turned back without accomplishing his mission.[80]

Within a few years, certainly before 1696,[81] Couture deserted from New France and penetrated eastward to the English frontier colony of Carolina. There, at the end of the century, he was known as 'the Greatest Trader and Traveller amongst the Indians for more than Twenty years,' and the master of eight or nine native languages. His route to Carolina was probably the Tennessee, with which on a later occasion he demonstrated his familiarity. His defection, of course, was not unique, for the severe penalties imposed by the French on unlicensed trading prompted numbers of lawless *coureurs de bois* to carry their goods to the English, or even to desert to the English colonies.

In South Carolina, by virtue of his familiarity with the trans-Appalachian region, Couture came in contact with various promoters of western enterprises characteristic of the southern frontier at the end of the seventeenth century. These included a group of prospectors for silver, who, with the backing of William Blathwayt, the Earl of Bridgewater, and others influential in colonial management in England, were seeking riches in the bed of the Savannah River. Through various misadventures, and the opposition of the Proprietors, the original scheme had come to nought. But in May, 1699, at Savannah

[80] Couture's career was first recounted in my article in *MVHR*, III. 3-18. The archival materials are in C.O. 5:1258, C 19 (no. 1), C 20; C.O. 5:1260, F 29, 29 (i), 29 (ii).
[81] *MVHR*, III. 8, note 17. In *Warrants for Lands in South Carolina, 1692-1711*, p. 126, is a warrant dated August 1, 1696, for 200 acres for 'John Cuture.' See ibid., pp. 161, 174.

Town, the prospectors fell in with Jean Couture. He told them an essentially plausible narrative of wanderings west of Carolina with three companions, 'through Several Nations of Indians above a hundred Leagues beyond the Appalatean Mountains,' where he believed 'that no Europeans had ever been before.' His accounts of a considerable quantity of gold which he had taken up 'not far from the branch of a Navigable River,' and of pearls given him by a nation of Indians 'inhabiting by a very Great Lake,' were calculated to fire the cupidity of the treasure-hunters. With them he entered into an agreement, under bond of £500, to return and make good his finds. Two of the prospectors went to England, armed with Couture's memorial, to get the backing of the Board of Trade against the expected opposition of the Proprietors. But the Board refused to intermeddle, and so nothing came of the French renegade's proposal to exploit, for the benefit of the English, the mineral resources of the southern Appalachians. But Couture was yet to play a large part in another and more significant project for English westward expansion. Already he had aroused the fears of Governor Francis Nicholson of Maryland regarding French activities in the West. And in 1700 it was Jean Couture whom Joseph Blake engaged to guide a party of traders by way of the Tennessee to the Mississippi, to claim the great river for Britain and to divert its trade to Carolina.

Northwestward the mountains raised a barrier, partly effective, to exploration. Southwestward a more rapid advance was possible through foot-hills and plains inhabitated by numerous and hospitable tribes, readily assimilated to the English trading régime.

Of Savannah Town, the focus of all the trails to the West, and the entrepôt of the whole inland trade, little is known at this period. An early map showed the path from Charles Town running by way of Goose Creek and the plantations of Percival and Shaftesbury to the ford of the Edisto or Colleton River at the great bend, and thence westward to the Indian town and the adjacent traders' fort. On the opposite bank appeared the location of 'the Oldfort,' apparently another palisaded warehouse.[82] As early as 1691 the Proprietors recognized the im-

[83] B.M. Add. MSS 5414, roll 24.

portance of the place when they instructed Ludwell 'to Incourage all people that will to reside at the Sevanah towne or any other place among the Indians, that the Inland parts of our province and the strength of the severall Nations of the Indians may be fully knowne.'[83]

The reports of Spanish governors and officers, which had revealed so clearly the English intrusions into Guale and Apalachicola, gave meagre indications of their progress further westward, beyond the Chattahoochee. When Torres, in 1693, sent an expedition to reconnoitre the Gulf coast, a Spanish vessel which put in at Mobile Bay found no Indians thereabouts; it was reported that the Mobilians had retired inland to trade with the English.[84] So recently as 1691, when Sothell secured a monopolistic act restraining the freedom of trade with the distant Indians, though the Coweta and Kasihta and the Cherokee Indians were mentioned, and even some of the Tennessee River tribes, nothing was said of the Upper Creeks or their neighbors.[85] Apparently it was around 1692-1696 that the great push westward from Ochese Creek occurred. In 1708 Thomas Nairne asserted that Mobile was established in 1702 in despite of a just English title, 'all the Inhabitants whereof had for 10 years before submitted themselves and Country to the government of Carolina, and then actually Traded with us.'[86] Moreover, Iberville in 1702 referred to the Choctaw-Chickasaw feud, provoked by English traders to furnish Indian slaves, as then of eight to ten years' standing.[87] Certainly when the French took possession of the lower Mississippi and the adjacent coast of the Gulf, in 1699, everywhere they found English traders securely seated among the interior tribes. To Joseph Blake, deputy governor in 1694 and again from 1696-1700, his friend John Archdale later ascribed the development of the great western trading enterprise of the colony.[88]

[83] C.O. 5:288, p. 195.
[84] Dunn, *Spanish and French Rivalry*, p. 170.
[85] Cooper (ed.), *Statutes*, II. 64.
[86] C.O. 5:382 (11). Other English claims were more sweeping. In 1737 Oglethorpe assured Lord Percival that 'ever since the year 1680' the Chickasaw had taken commissions from the governor of Carolina. (Percival, *Diary*, II. 326).
[87] *Découvertes et établissements des Français dans l'ouest et dans le sud de l'Amérique septentrionale*, edited by Pierre Margry, IV. 517.
[88] Archdale, *Description*, p. 31, reprinted in Carroll (ed.), *Collections*, II. 119.

Some years before the century's close the bolder traders had established their factories among the Alabama, Talapoosa, and Abihka, near the forks of the Alabama, and had laid in train that alliance with the Chickasaw, which, more than any other single factor, was destined to thwart the complete attainment of the French design in the lower Mississippi valley. From the villages of the populous Choctaw, near the Tombigbee, and of the Acolapissa, at the mouth of the Pearl, to the country of the Arkansas, west of the great river, and even as far as the Illinois, the Chickasaw, now that they were supplied with arms by the English, became the scourge of the defenseless western tribes.[89]

Foremost among the Chickasaw traders were Thomas Welch and Anthony Dodsworth. The most notable exploit in the early history of Carolinian trade and exploration was the journey of Welch, in 1698, from Charles Town to the Quapaw village at the mouth of the Arkansas River.[90] Within three decades from the planting of the colony the Carolinians had reached and even passed the Mississippi.

[89] V. W. Crane, 'The Southern Frontier in Queen Anne's War,' in *AHR,* XXIV. 382. In an extraordinary memorial to Queen Anne in 1711 John Stewart of Port Royal claimed to have been 'the first discoverer' of the Upper Creek trade. Paris, Archives Nationales, colonies, C[13] C, 2:76.
[90] C.O. Maps, N.A.C. General, 7.

CHAPTER III

THE MISSISSIPPI QUESTION, 1697-1702

The exploits of Thomas Welch and his fellow traders might have passed unnoted outside of Carolina, but for developments in the larger world which gave to Carolinian expansion a special significance in the unfolding of the Anglo-French conflict for the North American continent.

In 1697 came the Peace of Ryswick and a short breathing space in the wars of Louis XIV. Although the Grand Monarch himself was chiefly concerned with European issues, his ministers, and especially Ponchartrain, minister of marine, gave thought once more to America and the completion of La Salle's great plan, stirred to action by reports of English projects and enterprises in the West. Since 1690, when La Salle's brother, the abbé Jean Cavelier, had urged new efforts,[1] advocates of French expansion had showered alarmist memoirs upon the ministry. La Salle had stressed the value of a colony at the mouth of the Mississippi as a curb to Spain, and as a point of attack upon the Spanish mine-country.[2] But in these later memorials, significantly, it was *English* encroachment that was pictured. no doubt with exaggeration, but also with prophetic insight, as the great peril. 'If the English,' declared Cavelier, 'once render themselves masters of the Colbert [Mississippi], for which they are working with all of their power . . . they will also gain the Illinois, the Ottawa, and all the nations with whom the French of New France carry on trade.' In 1693 Tonti gave warning of the progress of the Carolinians.[3] The Canadians, Louvigny and Mantet, urging the continuation of La Salle's project, referred to English efforts among the Iroquois and the menace of Albany to the western trade.[4] In his notable memoir, Sieur Argoud recounted a rumor that Penn had sent explorers to the Ohio, and said that in the South,

[1] Margry (ed.), *Découvertes*, III, 586 ff. See also on the subject of this paragraph C. W. Alvord, *The Illinois Country, 1673-1818,* 1920, pp. 124-7; and Margry (ed.), *Découvertes,* IV, Introduction.
[2] Pierre Heinrich, *La Louisiane sous la Compagnie des Indes, 1717-1731,* Paris, [1908 ?], pp. xxiv, xxviii.
[3] Margry (ed.), *Découvertes,* IV. 3-5.
[4] Ibid., pp. 9-18.

also, the English were seeking to make themselves masters of the Mississippi. Backed by Argoud in France, Rémonville's proposals of 1697 for a colony on the Mississippi made a strong impression of which echoes were soon borne to England.[5] But royal effort, rather than a chartered company, was the means at length approved by the King. Already Louis XIV in his instructions to the commissioners at Ryswick had charged them not to discuss the title to the Mississippi, announcing that shortly he intended to send vessels thither to assure possession for France.[6] It was news from England, finally, of the rival project of Coxe—following all these reports from America of trading aggressions—that hastened the despatch of Iberville in 1698 on his first voyage of reconnaissance. Biloxi was the result: a temporary settlement, but soon transformed into the colony of Louisiana when Louis XIV became convinced of the reality of the English peril and of the French opportunity in the West.

Daniel Coxe, projector of Carolana, was an English doctor of medicine of some distinction, a court physician under Charles II and Queen Anne, and a fellow of the Royal Society. His pioneer experiments to determine the effect of nicotine upon animals and his chemical contributions to the *Philosophical Transactions* are quite forgotten,[7] but the pamphlet compiled by his son from

[5] Ibid., pp. 21-34. Circumstantial accounts of the preparations of the French Louisiana company were printed in London newspapers and periodicals in January, 1698, and were probably known to the English promoter, Coxe. The *Post Man,* January 8-11, reported that M. de Beaujeau, who had 'carried thither some years ago Monsieur *de Salle,'* had been chosen to command the squadron. The *Post Boy* of January 15-18, and also the *Present State of Europe,* IX, no. 1 (January, 1698), pp. 48 f., recounted that 300,000 livres would be raised; and that the King granted the propriety of the country, a fleet to transport the colony, and eight companies of foot. In February, however, the project was said to have vanished (*Post Boy,* February 8-10). We prefer, remarked the writer of a Paris news-letter, that the English should be fooled by the fables of the late Sieur de la Salle and the monk Hennepin! (P.R.O., S.P. 101:23. Paris, 10 Fevrier, 1698). But again in May London was told that Louis XIV had approved 'the new Company, who intend to errect a Colony on both sides the River Mechisippy' (*Post Boy,* May 28-31, 1698). See Margry (ed.), *Découvertes,* IV. 62.
[6] Margry (ed.), *Découvertes,* IV, Introduction, iv.
[7] G. D. Scull, 'Biographical Notice of Dr. Daniel Coxe, of London,' in *Pennsylvania Magazine of History and Biography,* VII. 317-37; *Philosophical Transactions,* IX. 4, 150, 169; B.M. Add. MSS 6194, f. 39. For a somewhat too favorable view of Coxe's credibility as an historian of the early western movement, see F. E. Melvin, 'Dr. Daniel Coxe and Carolana,' in *MVHR,* I. 257-62.

his Carolana memorials remains one of the curiosities of the literature of colonial promotion. For a scientist Coxe was strangely credulous. 'I believe he is an honest gentleman and a very good doctor,' declared Francis Nicholson, 'but I am afraid several people have abused the Doctor's good nature and generosity by telling him of Strange Countries and giving him Mapps thereof.'[8]

Before Coxe developed his grand project of a vast western empire he had been concerned in a variety of typical colonial enterprises, none very successful, for fishing, commerce, mining, the production of naval stores, and for trade with the Indians. These ventures had centered chiefly in the Jersies, where the Doctor had become a great proprietor.[9] Indeed, from 1687 to 1692 he was in sole possession of the government of West Jersey. An inventory of his American estates[10] drawn up *circa* 1688 included a description of his Minnisink Province. It was apparently possession of this tract of three or four hundred thousand acres overlooking the Delaware which first stirred Coxe's interest in the West. Minnisink, he declared, was admirably situated for trade with the distant Indians, 'the upper part being within six dayes easy Journey of the greate Lake whence most of the furres are carried to Canada and brought to New York, Jersey, Pennsylvania and Maryland. I have been att great Expence,' he boasted, 'to make friendshipp with the Indians, discover the passages to the Lakes and open'd a way for a vast trade thereunto.' Though the elder Coxe never saw America, in imagination he stood tiptoe upon his Jersey hills and strained his eyes westward. From this period he collected all the accounts, maps, and traditions that he could meet with of travels into the trans-Appalachian region. As early as 1687 he was in possession of a copy of the Fallam journal.[11] Did Coxe, through his agents in West Jersey, actually emulate those Virginian pioneers whose deeds he so often recalled? His own unsubstantiated claims as a promoter of western explora-

[8] C.O. 5:1312, E 16; *CSP,AWI, 1700*, p. 497.

[9] C. M. Andrews, *Colonial Self-Government*, pp. 123 f. See Rawlinson MSS C, 379.

[10] *Pa. Mag. of Hist. and Biog.*, VII. 331.

[11] Alvord and Bidgood, *First Explorations*, p. 183 note. In April, 1693, Coxe wrote to Sir Hans Sloane to borrow the seventh and eighth *Decades* of Herrera (B. M. Sloane MSS 4036, f. 147).

tion were made when he was seeking to sell his Jersey holdings, or later when he was asking royal support for his Carolana enterprise. In one memorial he gave a circumstantial account of a journey of three of his tenants by way of the Schuylkill, Susquehanna, and Ohio rivers to the Mississippi and beyond. At just this period, it is true, the Albanians, spurred by the aggressive Dongan, were challenging the French upon the Great Lakes.[12] Arnout Viele, who returned to Albany in the summer of 1694 from a two years' exploration as far as the Wabash, had followed in the main the route described by Coxe, and had made Minnisink his base.

Before Coxe other Englishmen, colonial officials and provincials, had envisaged a West controlled by England in the interest of the fur trade, and eventually, perhaps, of English colonization. But in England Coxe was the first to give currency to this program. By his propaganda he helped to spread a momentous idea: that the destiny of the English in America embraced more than the settlement and exploitation of the Atlantic seaboard.

In 1690, Dr. Coxe, still a member of the West Jersey Society, petitioned the King for a grant of an enormous area between 36° 30′ and 46° 30′, stretching westward from Virginia, Pennsylvania, and New York to the South Sea.[13] His schemes of inland trade were taking shape. But the Lords of Trade declined to help him to a monopoly of the furs of the West. Not long after, he acquired possession of the old patent granted by Charles I in 1629 to Sir Robert Heath, and of a later grant to Lord Maltravers.[14] Thus he secured some sort of title to an even vaster western estate: to Norfolk county in Virginia, and by the Heath patent to the province of Carolana which ran from sea to sea between the parallels of 31° and 36°

[12] Helen Broshar, 'The First Push Westward of the Albany Traders,' in *MVHR*, VII. 228-41; C. A. Hanna, *The Wilderness Trail*, 1911, I. 137-43.
[13] C.O. 5:855, no. 87; 1081, no. 160A. *CSP,AWI, 1689-1692*, pp. 251, 761. In the Privy Council's reference of Coxe's petition to the Lords of the Committee there was a recognition that this 'Country being possessed by the English, the Commerce of the French with the Indians will be wholy destroyd.'
[14] Scull says (*doc. cit.*, p. 318) between 1692 and 1698. See above, note 11, and evidence below that Coxe had matured his plan by 1697. On the intermediate history of the Heath patent see H. L. Osgood, *The American Colonies in the Seventeenth Century*, II. 200 f.

Soon Coxe was deep in the business of colonial promotion. To be sure, subsequent charters to the Carolina proprietors had ignored the Carolana grant. Carolana, moreover, embraced a large part of Florida, and of the great central valley which La Salle had named in honor of Louis XIV. What countenance might Coxe expect from the Lords Proprietors? from the mercantilists of the Board of Trade? What sufferance from Madrid or Paris? Where would he find colonists to hold so precarious a frontier for England?

As a matter of fact, when Coxe launched his Carolana scheme there were several circumstances to encourage so sanguine a promoter. With the peace America might, and did briefly, engage the attention of the Crown. From the Continent, from an old companion of La Salle, came a spectacular appeal to William III to take possession for the English of the Mississippi valley, which Coxe knew how to turn to his own uses. In 1683 Father Hennepin's *Description de la Louisiane,* dedicated to Louis XIV, had helped to make La Salle famous.[15] But the imaginative Recollet had quarrelled with his leader; he was now an exile from France in the Low Countries. In 1697 he launched his notorious revision, the *Nouvelle découverte,* with its impossible claim that two years before La Salle the author had descended to the mouth of the Mississippi, as well as explored its upper waters—all in forty-eight days![16] Was it only

[15] See Margry (ed.), *Découvertes,* IV, Introduction, ix; and Alvord, *Illinois Country,* p. 92.

[16] Margry (ed.), *Découvertes,* IV, Introduction, xiv; R. G. Thwaites, introduction to his edition of Hennepin, *A New Discovery,* 1903, I. xxxiv-xxxvi. In defense of Hennepin see J. G. Shea, introduction to his edition of Hennepin, *A Description of Louisiana,* 1880, pp. 31-53. Shea threw the blame for the plagiarisms and impossible claims in Hennepin's later writings upon a suppositious 'ignorant,' or 'careless, irresponsible editor'; and he suggested that the contemporaneous English project furnished a journalistic motive, 'to make the volume bear directly on a question of the day,' that is, the Mississippi question. He did not, however, intimate a definite political motive. The typographical evidence in support of his view has been discredited by Paltsits; and other facts here presented make it almost certain that Hennepin personally supervised the Utrecht publications of 1697. P. Jérome Goyens, in his article in *Archivum Franciscanum historicum,* XVIII (1925), attempted a complete rehabilitation of Hennepin; but he quoted from Froidevaux the French archival evidence which goes far to stamp Hennepin a tool of the English. It was long since established by Sparks and Parkman that Hennepin freely pilfered Membré's journal in Le Clercq's suppressed work. See Parkman, *La Salle and the Discovery of the Great West,* Boston, 1897, pp. 246 f. and note. In this connection it is of interest that a contemporary reviewer of the *Nouvelle découverte* hinted at its de-

vanity that led Hennepin to make this scandalous attack upon the glory of La Salle, whose work others in France were now planning to crown by a colony on the Mississippi? Was there, perhaps, another reason, of policy? At this stage in Hennepin's career his acknowledged patron was William Blathwayt, long secretary of the Privy Council, reputed colonial expert, and now a member of the newly created Board of Trade and Plantations. It was Blathwayt's intercession, at the King's direction, declared Hennepin, that had secured for him from the general-commissary of his order leave to go again as a missionary to America, and meanwhile leisure to reside in the United Provinces and digest his later memoirs; it was Blathwayt who had provided generously for his subsistence, and who had presented him to the King. His new writings he dedicated to William III, voicing the hope that they would prove of advantage 'especially to the English Nation, to whose Service I entirely devote my self.'[17] It is not inconceivable that the whole notorious attack upon the fame of La Salle, and hence upon the current French Mississippi projects, was engineered by William Blathwayt.

In any case Hennepin's writings had the effect of stirring English interest in new colonization, as the French discovered to their chagrin.[18] The *Nouvelle découverte* and its continuation, issued a few weeks later, passed through many editions and translations;[19] the first of these was promptly published in

pendence upon Le Clercq: 'Caeterum obiter maneo, cum historia Dectectonis hujus non inutiliter conferri posse Relationem, quem Pater *Christianus Clericus,* itidem Missionarius Recollector, A. 1691. Paris, in 12. 2 vol. edidit . . . ; *Premier establissement de la foi'* (*Bibliotheca librorum novorum,* Utrecht, I, 94-97, April-May, 1697).

[17] Hennepin, *A New Discovery,* London, 1698 [1697], Preface. Hennepin, *Nouvelle découverte,* Utrecht, 1697, *avis au lecteurs.*

[18] See Margry (ed.), *Découvertes,* IV. 20, for the reaction upon the Rémonville enterprise, involving the withdrawal of mercantile support. See also correspondence of Bonrepaus and Ponchartrain, June and July, 1698, in Archives Nationales, monuments historiques, K. 1349: IX: négociations, Hollande, printed by Henri Froidevaux in 'Une épisode ignoré de la vie du P. Hennepin,' in *Journal de la Société les Américanistes de Paris,* n.s., II (1905), 281-7.

[19] See N. E. Dionne, *Hennepin, ses voyages et ses oeuvres,* Quebec, 1897, and V. H. Paltsits, *Bibliography of the Works of Father L. Hennepin,* 1903. Both these and all other bibliographers of Hennepin seem to have overlooked the important evidence furnished by book advertisements in contemporary journals to establish the dates of issue. All copies of the *Nouveau voyage* which have been described bear the date 1698. But *Bibliotheca librorum novorum* in its issue of June-July, 1697 (I. 265 f.) named this book in its list of 'Libri Novi'; and published a long summary in August-Septem-

London, probably by the initiative of Coxe. In July, 1698, Bonrepaus wrote to Ponchartrain from the Hague that Hennepin had showed him letters from England reciting Coxe's project for an English Mississippi company, and asking for memoirs on the subject.[20] These had already been furnished by the facile father. They were brought together in *A New Discovery of a Vast Country in America,* dated 1698, but actually issued in October, 1697.[21] This fat little book contained a translation of the *Nouvelle découverte* and the *Nouveau voyage.* There were added Marquette's journal and an account of the death of La Salle and at the end an elaborate puff for the Carolana scheme:

So that the Providence of Almighty God seems to have reserv'd this Country for the English, a Patent whereof was granted above Fifty Years ago to the Lords Proprietors of Carolina [i.e., Carolana], who have made great Discoveries, therein, seven hundred

ber, 1697 (I. 341-9). The book was described as a duodecimo of 389 pages, published by Antoine Schouten at Utrecht. The description, except for date, fits one of the 1698 issues. Was this post-dated, or was there an earlier edition of which no copies have survived? Similar questions arise regarding the English translation (see note 21, below).

[20] Bonrepaus-Ponchartrain correspondence, *loc. cit.*

[21] See E. Arber (ed.), *Term Catalogues,* III. 38, under Michaelmas term, 1697, and the *Post Man,* September 14-16, 16-18, and October 5-7, 1697. The latter advertised *A New Discovery* as 'This Day . . . published' by the stationers Bentley, Tonson, Bonwick, Goodwin, and Manship, who published both the so-called 'Bon-' and 'Tonson' editions known to the bibliographers. It seems likely that this was the 'Bon-' edition from the reading 'To which is added' in the full title as advertised. The September advertisements reveal the curious vicissitudes of the translation before it reached the public in the form that we know, and may help to explain the notorious typographical peculiarities of the 'Bon-' edition. The September 14-16 issue of the newspaper announced that 'A Continuation of the new discoveries in the North West parts of *America,* with a description of above 200 different Nations and Reflections upon the Enterprizes of M[o]nsieur *de la Salle* Governor of *Quebec,* upon the Mines of *St. Barbe,* &c. as also of the Advantages of Trading this way to the *South Seas,* to the Land of *Jesso,* to *China,* and *Japan,* with proposals for establishing new Colonies, through that vast Country. Dedicated to King *William,* by *Louis Hennepin,* with a map and other Figures. Translated into English. Will be speedily published by *Edw. Castle* near *Whitehall,* and *Sam. Buckley* in *Fleet-street.*' This was, of course, a translation of the *Nouveau voyage,* which makes most of Part II of *A New Discovery,* and possibly included the Carolana puff. But the publishers were different. Moreover, quite another group was already engaged in bringing out a translation of the *Nouvelle découverte.* The two enterprises were now, it seems, combined; for the next issue of this newspaper, of September 16-18, advertised that the continuation 'will be speedily published. And printed for *Matt. Gilliflower, Wm. Freeman, Matt. Wotton,* and *R. Parker,* for whom the first part is printed, and will be published next week.' Possibly the earlier projects of publication fell through, after the translation of the *Nouvelle découverte* was already in print. Possibly both parts were separately issued and the sheets later acquired by Bentley *et al.*

Miles Westerly from the Mountains, which separate between it Carolina and Virginia, and Six hundred Miles from North to South, from the Gulf of Mexico to the great Inland Lakes, which are situated behind the Mountains of Carolina and Virginia. Besides, they have an Account of all the Coast, from the Cape of Florida to the River Panuco, the Northerly Bounds of the Spaniards on the Gulf of Mexico, together with most of the chief Harbours, Rivers and Islands thereunto appertaining; and are about to establish a very considerable Colony on some part of the Great River, so soon as they have agreed upon the Boundaries, or Limits, with the Lords Proprietors of Carolina, who claim by a Patent procur'd long after that of Carolina [sic]. But there being space enough for both, and the Proprietors generally inclin'd to an amicable Conclusion, the Success of this Undertaking is impatiently expected: For considering the Benignity of the Climate, the Healthfulness of the Country, Fruitfulness of the Soil, Ingenuity and Tractableness of the Inhabitants, Variety of Productions, if prudently manag'd, it cannot, humanely speaking, fail of proving one of the most considerable Colonies on the North-Continent of America, profitable to the Publick and the Undertakers.

Postscript.

I am inform'd a large Map, or Draught, of this Country is preparing, together with a very particular Account of the Natives, their Customs, Religion, Commodities, and Materials for divers sorts of Manufactures, which are by the English procur'd at great Expence from other Countries.

Coxe, indefatigable collector of travels, had also secured in Paris a copy of the suppressed memoir, ascribed to Tonti, the *Dernières découvertes* (Paris, 1697). This also was printed in translation at London, in 1698; and, according to Coxe, from his own copy.[22]

By these publications, and also by numerous contemporary newspaper accounts of the French Mississippi project, public as well as official interest was directed towards America, and towards the Southwest. For colonists to settle Carolana, Coxe turned to the French Huguenot refugees who were now thronging to England and to the Protestant countries of northern Europe. With two of their leaders, the Marquis de la Muce and M. Charles de Sailly, he soon came to terms. To these French-

---

[22] In a memorial of 1719, printed in Alvord and Bidgood, *First Explorations,* p. 234, Coxe wrote: 'The book was called in by the French king, and I could not at Paris procure that book under thirty Livers, which was at first sold for one Liver, which book was translated into English 1698 from my french Copy.' *Post Man,* May 14-17, 1698, advertised *An Account* for sale.

men, and to Sir William Waller, he now transferred 500,000 acres on the west side of 'the River Spirito Sancto [Apalachicola] which empties itself into the Bay of Apalache,' on a deferred quit-rent tenure, with leave to take up an equal amount after seven years. The condition of the conveyance, dated May 2, 1698, was that within two years two hundred Protestant families should be settled in this first colony of Carolana. There were soon issued, probably that same summer, printed *Proposals for Settling a Colony in Florida,* 'whereby those who shall think fit to give a helping hand, shall not barely do an act of Charity, but [one] which shall turn to a publick good, and their own advantage.' An appeal was made for the relief of the 'dispersed Protestant Refugees' in Holland, Germany, etc., as well as in England, now a heavy burden to the princes who had given them sanctuary; from the Huguenots on the Continent, it was said, letters had been received expressing approbation of the scheme. There was also a hint of national benefits in the assertion that 'it is designed to plant near the English [i.e. of Carolina], for mutual defence, and to consult on the best ways and means for the common Safety of the Colony, the promoting of Trade, and the Nations Interest in those parts.' In the same glowing terms as in Coxe's memorials were described the navigability of the chosen river, and the valuable products of that land. Two organizations to promote the enterprise were announced: a 'Company' to colonize, govern, and control all matters of land and trade, and a 'Society' of City merchants to provide on contract ships and transportation. Stock in the 'Company' was offered at £25 a share or 'action' which entitled investors to dividends and 400 acres of land. A quarter-share, with 100 acres, was offered each settler, and also 'Transport, and Dyet free.' A joint-stock for trade was described, and the conditions on the emigrant ships carefully regulated. Meetings of the 'Committee of the Company' were advertised to be held at a tavern near Cheapside and at the residence of the Marquis. The illusion, at least, was conveyed of businesslike activity and a serious purpose of colonization.[23]

[23] The conveyance is in Rawlinson MSS A, 271, f. 26. The *Proposals,* which so far as I am aware have not before been described, were printed on two sides of one sheet, without title-page or date. The only copy that I have seen is in a volume of miscellaneous *Tracts relating to America and the West Indies,* XVIII, in the British Museum (BM 816 m 18).

The French, at any rate, were impressed. News of these procedings was carried to Iberville, who was preparing the French Mississippi expedition at Rochefort. The exact destination of the English long remained in doubt; Coxe's ambition, certainly, did not stop at the Apalachicola. The English-Huguenot expedition, Iberville heard, was rapidly forming; captains had been chosen; the King petitioned for vessels; Hennepin was sent for from Holland. The French ministry, too, was at first much disturbed. During the summer a secret agent was instructed to watch closely the activities of the English company. His reports in the autumn of delays at London, and of a rumor that the promoters were awaiting authorization from Parliament, brought relief.[24] Meanwhile, from the Hague, Bonrepaus advised that the restless Hennepin be permitted to return to Canada from France: not that he could be useful there, but to prevent him from further exciting the English. The King consented, but Hennepin seems to have determined instead upon an Italian voyage, which would serve as well. Apparently the Recollet was embarrassed by his new reputation in England as an expert on the West and a collaborator in the English project.[25] The result, naturally, of all these reports was to hasten the despatch of the French fleet.[26]

The race for the Mississippi was on in earnest. The Spanish, mistaking the French objective, hastened to secure Pensacola Bay, where an outpost against the French had been decreed as early as 1694.[27] In October, 1698, Iberville sailed from Brest, and Arriola from Vera Cruz. The same month saw the despatch from London by the Carolana undertakers of two small armed vessels to undertake a preliminary survey of the Gulf coast. In November the Spaniards, first upon the scene, occupied Pensacola Bay. In March, 1699, Iberville entered the Mississippi.[28] But Captain Bond and his companions prudently wintered at Charles Town, where they learned of the western

---

[24] Archives Nat., Marine, B², 136, ff. 27, 84, 253-254; Margry (ed.), *Découvertes,* IV, Introduction, xv-xvi, 58-62, 80, 82, 88.

[25] Bonrepaus-Ponchartrain correspondence, *loc. cit.*

[26] Margry (ed.), *Découvertes,* IV. 82.

[27] W. E. Dunn, *Spanish and French Rivalry,* pp. 171-84.

[28] Margry (ed.), *Découvertes,* IV. 87-209. At Santo Domingo news was received of Coxe's fleet (p. 88) ; at Pensacola, in January, the Spanish were found in possession (p. 96).

exploits of the provincials and arranged a rendezvous for the next year with the Chickasaw traders on the Mississippi. It was not, indeed, until May, 1699, that their voyage of reconnaissance was resumed, with a province vessel, the *Carolina Galley,* replacing one of the English ships. Coasting along the Gulf from Florida Cape to Rio Panuco the explorers altogether missed the Apalachicola. But the Mississippi they discovered from the sea, August 29, 1699. Captain Bond navigated the *Carolina Galley* a hundred miles up the river. But that was Bond's sole claim to glory. 'Un estourdy peu capable,' Iberville described him from old acquaintance in Hudson Bay. Bienville had little trouble in halting him at the Detour des Anglais and warning him away, although the Frenchman had with him only two canoes, engaged in sounding the river.[29] Bond's threat to return next year with an English colony proved as empty as Iberville predicted. The French, however, determined to establish a post to hold the sea-approaches to the Mississippi. But the real English peril, as Iberville was soon to learn, lurked in another quarter.

While the Carolana expedition was homeward bound with charts and surveys and news of the French intrusion, Dr. Coxe was preparing to despatch his Huguenot colony, and meanwhile defending his own pretensions and the claims of England before the Board of Trade.[30] Reverting to his proposal of 1690 he petitioned the King to add a great tract to the north of Carolana. Later, when it appeared that Carolana did not include the Gulf coast, where he planned to colonize, he asked for a

[29] Ibid., pp. 344, 361, 395-7; Journals of the Board of Trade (hereinafter cited JBT), February 14, 16, 1700; C.O. 5:1259, D 23: 1260, E 1, E 2; 1288, ff. 165 f.; *CSP,AWI, 1699,* p. 526; *1700,* pp. 69-71; Coxe, *Description of Carolana* (1722), preface, pp. [iii]-[iv]. See Alvord and Carter (eds.), *The New Régime,* pp. 415-7, for a letter to Shelburne, October 31, 1766, printed from Lansdowne MSS 48: 263 C, in which Phineas Lyman summarized a portion of 'the Journal of Capt. Bond of the Carolina Galley (whose Original I have now by me).'

[30] JBT, October 12, 13, 20, November 14, 16, December 15, 18, 1699, February 15, 16, 1700. C.O. 5:1259, D 13, D 32, D 32 i; 1260, E 1; 1288, f. 122; S. P. Domestic, Entry Book 238, p. 363; *CSP,AWI, 1699,* pp. 459, 572; *1700,* p. 73. The *Post Boy,* September 19-21, 1699, reported: 'We hear three ships are fitting in the River Thames, in order to go and settle a Colony on the Coast of Florida, on board of which ships several Reformed officers, and French Refugees, will go thither to settle, and so to try their Fortune in that part of the World.'

further southward extension.[31] 'I wish that the Doctor would come into these parts of the World, and run out the bounds of his countries,' commented Nicholson, 'and then I suppose he would have so much of the Continent of America that he would not care to come again.'[32] Coxe's scheme was to transform his propriety into a great stock-company, to be incorporated as the Florida Company. His title was held valid by the Attorney-General;[33] meanwhile, it appears that he had reached an agreement with the Carolina proprietors upon a mutual boundary at the Altamaha River. At the demand of the Board of Trade, Coxe, on November 16, 1699, submitted an abstract of his title, a paper containing 'A Demonstration of the Just Pretensions of His Majesty the King of England unto the Province of *Carolana alias Florida,*' and a further account of the commodities of Carolana.[34] With other memorials these documents of 1699 were incorporated by the younger Coxe into his 1722 pamphlet. They were a curious medley of fact and fable. Interwoven with the undoubted exploits of the Virginians and Carolinians were other more dubious tales. 'The Carolina Traders with the Indians,' he wrote, 'are now and have long been as well acquainted with those parts as most of the English with the Road from London to Yorke and have frequently Travelled to the borders of New Mexico in their trading voyages.'[35] After hearing Coxe in person the Board of Trade

[31] C.O. 5:1259, D 21, D 21 (i); 1288 ff. 129, 139-43; *CSP,AWI, 1699,* pp. 517, 578-80.
[32] C.O. 5:1312, E 16.
[33] C.O. 5:1259, D 32, D 32(i); 1288 ff. 136-139; *CSP,AWI, 1699,* pp. 572, 578. In Rawlinson MSS A 305 f. 2, is a 'Draught of the scheme I drew for Dr Daniel Cox many years since for the settlement of New [blank] which we called the New Empire written by Mr. Spooner.' This dates from the reign of William and Mary, and refers either to Carolana or Coxe's earlier project of 1690. For so 'vastly greate' a grant Spooner suggested the organization of 'the Imperiall Compa.' quite in scale, with a capital stock of £400,000 in £5 shares; 20,000 to be retained by the fourteen original proprietors; 5,000 to be promoters' shares; 20,000 to be sold to raise funds for colonization, 20,000 others to be sold for the profit of the proprietors; 5,000 'mayden shares' were reserved for benefactors. The remaining 10,000 should be distributed among 1,000 'Associates,' to include eminent divines, Anglicans and dissenters, city merchants, and 'some of the most publick leading Gentl[men] & of best interest in every County of England and Wales.' Thus a national interest would be created. A leading object was the transportation of the poor, especially imprisoned debtors—an interesting anticipation of the Bray-Oglethorpe project.
[34] C.O. 5:1259, D 22, D 23, D 24; 1288, pp. 129 f.
[35] C.O. 5:1259, D 23, 24.

drafted its somewhat equivocal representation upon Carolana of December 21, 1699.[36] The promoter's plea that the French must be checked in the West, where they were endeavoring to engross the Indian trade by building forts and trading-houses all the way from Canada to the Mississippi, had made a certain impression. Coxe's doctrine of encirclement, indeed, echoed warnings which the Board was receiving at the moment from all the frontier colonies. But the shrewd mercantilists of White-hall were after all half-hearted 'imperialists'; they found many objections to the scheme. A colony on the Gulf would be diffi-cult to defend; French Huguenots, especially, would be liable to molestation. There was danger, too, of draining population from the southern colonies. In the interest of British trade was it wise to arouse the jealousy of Spain? The Board, moreover, 'was suspicious of stock-jobbery by the Carolana promoters. The multiplicity of plantations was held to promote piracy and illicit trade. Finally, since Coxe's proposals rested 'as much on considerations of State as of Trade,' they were referred with-out further endorsement to the Crown.

How far did the King and Council share these doubts? It is certain that early in 1700, when it was known that the French were in possession of the Mississippi, Coxe was forced, reluctantly, to abandon his efforts to establish the Huguenots on the Gulf. Instead he sought to settle them in Norfolk county, Virginia. Several hundred were sent over; but after various vicissitudes they were seated instead at Manikin Town, in the piedmont.[37] The younger Coxe asserted that William III had promised aid to the original Carolana scheme, and that Lord Lonsdale, the Privy Seal, and other notables had given their patronage, but that the death of Lonsdale, and soon after of the King, with the ensuing war, had frustrated the design. Coxe seems to have revived his proposals early in the War of the Spanish Succession.[38] Again in 1719 he was heard by the Board of Trade, which was seeking substantiation, from any quarter, of the English title to the West, to use in boundary discussions in Paris.[39] But after 1700 his sole significance was

[36] C.O. 5:1288, ff. 139-43. *CSP,AWI, 1699,* pp. 578-80.
[37] C.O. 5:1288, ff. 165-7; 1259, D 35. Alvord and Bidgood, *First Explora-tions,* p. 233 note.
[38] Coxe, *Description of Carolana,* 1722, preface, pp. [iv]-[vii].
[39] See below, pp. 224-6.

as a voice warning England against French encirclement in North America.

Thus in France, in England, and also in the American colonies, the closing years of the seventeenth century had seen a new birth of interest in the trans-Appalachian West. From this epoch the international conflict in America began to assume its continental character; Coxe's failure and the success of Iberville in the race for the Mississippi meant that the brunt of the struggle in the Gulf region and the lower Mississippi valley would be borne by the southern traders. Already the reports of the French intention to colonize on the Gulf and the publication of Hennepin's new books had stirred English officials, from New York to Carolina, to propose counter-schemes of western trade. But it was only in Carolina, where the western trade was already well developed, that these projects had a significant sequel.

As early as 1695, Francis Nicholson, then governor of Maryland, had forecast the dangerous consequences of the completion by the French of La Salle's design. 'I hope they will never be able to do it,' he had written Shrewsbury, 'for if they should, and gain the Indians at the back of us, it may be of fatal consequence to most of these countries.' He advised watchfulness at Jamaica and the Bahamas, and especially the extension of the Indian trade from the southern provinces to prevent the Indians, if the French came, from going over to them in a body.[40] Nicholson was confirmed in these views by an interview with a band of Shawnee (Savannah) Indians from the Carolina border and with their companion: a Frenchman, who, Nicholson reported, not quite accurately, had been with La Salle 'that Journey he was killed.' This, surely, was Jean Couture. One of the Indians with the aid of the *voyageur* drew a rude map of the route to the nearest French settlement, in the Illinois country, and thence by the Mississippi to the Gulf. In his report of the episode to the Board of Trade, in August, 1698,[41] Nicholson said that the draught agreed in

[40] C.O. 5:718, no. 18.
[41] *Archives of Maryland*, XXIII. 500. It is clear from Nicholson's reference to page 250 in Hennepin that he possessed a copy of *A New Discovery*, 1698, in the so-called 'Bon-' edition. On this episode see my essay in *MVHR*, III. 11.

some sort with Hennepin's maps, for he had lately been reading the *New Discovery* fresh from the London press, as well as the alarming reports in the 'monthly Mercurys' of the French Mississippi preparations.[42] He was convinced by the Recollet's book and by his own inquiries 'that if they settle that River, that and the River of Canada will encompass all the English Dominions here.' 'I am afraid,' he added, 'that now please God, there is a peace, the French will be able to doe more dammage to these Countrys, than they were able to doe in the War,' and he urged that orders should issue to all governors to encourage a trade with the Indians westward. Nicholson's scheme involved the chartering of companies of English or colonial undertakers in the interior trade, to undersell the French beyond the mountains. The English, he added, should also make settlements among the Indians as the French had done, 'and build Vessels upon their Lakes.'

Thus Nicholson, also, had envisaged the menace of French encirclement, a conception only vaguely understood for some years to come in England, but one which ultimately shaped British western policy. After a few months he became governor of Virginia, where he anticipated certain features of the well-known expansionist program of Alexander Spotswood. Quite in keeping with Nicholson's proposals to the Board of Trade were the suggestions now brought forward by Colonel Cadwallader Jones. Jones was an old Virginia Indian fighter and trader, formerly commander of the Rappahannock fort. His caravans had followed the Occaneechi path into North Carolina; like Spotswood later, he had searched for a path to the West through the Blue Ridge, 'our Cawcasean Mountains.' Jones returned to Virginia from the Bahamas and England in 1698, and once more embarked upon frontier enterprises. He, too, had read Hennepin's *New Discovery*, 'and imediately fell into a labour of the mind, that from the father Some greate advantage might accrew to this Country.' The result was his interesting essay of January 17, 1699, entitled, 'Louissiania

---

[42] Nicholson alluded to the *Present State of Europe*, IX, no. 1 (January, 1698), pp. 48 f. See *supra*, note 5. On the rest of this paragraph see also *Archives of Maryland*, XXV. 586.

and Virginia Improved.'[43] Jones proposed the creation of a company of gentlemen-adventurers to discover the pass, and then to develop a trade from Virginia to the Great Lakes. His chart accompanying the essay was based upon a sight of Hennepin's map, and upon his own experiences. It showed some acquaintance with the Charles Town trade, for he indicated the presence of Carolinians among the Cherokees on the 'Uge' (Yuchi, or Tennessee) River. Nicholson, naturally, supported Jones's scheme; he presented it to his council in February[44] and to the Burgesses in May.[45] But it failed for lack of subscribers in the colony.[46] Unwilling to accept defeat in this essential policy, Nicholson turned to England. He appealed to the Board of Trade to apprise the London merchants of this opportunity to make a profit and at the same time to prevent the French from engrossing the western trade, 'and further settling to the westward of the English on this Continent.'[47] But the Board replied that they had insufficient information to determine 'whether it be proper for us to intermeddle in the promoting' of the trade in England. As for colonial adventures westward, they cautiously urged that these should not 'interfere with or discourage the planting of Tobacco, which is the maine thing to be pursued in that Colony.'[48] And so the projected Virginian trade offensive languished.[49]

But in any case Nicholson's information of the western country was vague, and Virginia remote from the routes then practicable for the trans-Appalachian trade. From 1698 to 1700, however, Nicholson was in active correspondence, seeking to concert a vigorous western policy, with the governors of the two colonies whose situation and Indian relations fitted them

---

[43] C.O. 5:1310, C 37; printed in *Virginia Magazine of History and Biography*, XXX, 329-34, with the map, accompanying Fairfax Harrison's article on 'Western Explorations in Virginia between Lederer and Spotswood,' pp. 323-40. Documents not cited by Harrison discredit his view that Nicholson was indifferent to Jones's project.

[44] Virginia Council Minutes, MSS, Library of Congress, 1698-1700, p. 12 (February 23, 1698/9).

[45] *Journals of the House of Burgesses*, 1695-1702, pp. 166, 169, 176, 178.

[46] C.O. 5:1310, C 2; *CSP,AWI, 1699*, p. 314.

[47] Ibid.

[48] *Va. Mag. of Hist. and Biog.*, XXII. 40. See also JBT, October 10, 1699.

[49] Harrison points out (*loc. cit.*, p. 336) that the law of 1705, under which later Spotswood's Indian company was organized, followed Jones's plan. See also Virginia Council Minutes, MSS, under February 23, June 22, 1699.

peculiarly for leadership in the new continental phase of the Anglo-French contest: Lord Bellomont of New York, and Joseph Blake of South Carolina. In New York, Robert Livingston had brought forward a scheme of trade[50] with the tribes of the Ohio valley similar to that of Jones. Bellomont was alarmed by the decline of the Iroquois, and by the progress of the French among the western Indians. Subordinating the local interest of Albany to imperial ends, he was eager to secure the coöperation of the governors of Pennsylvania, Maryland, Virginia, and Carolina to bring the Miami, Chippewa, and Ottawa within the English orbit.[51] In the fall of 1699 he proposed to the Board of Trade that those governors should meet with him at Philadelphia during the following summer to promote trade expansion westward.[52] The Board approved the conference, and further suggested the raising of contributions from the colonies to finance Indian presents and frontier forts in New York and elsewhere 'untill some proper and effectual provision can be made here.'[53] Unfortunately this conference miscarried.[54] But from the discussions of these years it was becoming clearer that if the French were to be prevented from linking their settlements in Canada with the Gulf, trade with the distant Indians must be encouraged. Bellomont and Nicholson had fixed their eyes upon the Great Lakes and the Ohio, but the latter had also been alarmed at the French enterprise in the Southwest. Furthermore, it had become apparent that the situation of South Carolina, its extensive trade with the western Indians and its experience in border conflicts with Florida, made it the natural head of English opposition to the French in that quarter of America. Even the Board of Trade showed a vague appreciation of the possibilities of the Carolina Indian system. In December, 1699, they summoned a certain James Boyd, 'a Frenchman lately come from Carolina,' to advise them on 'the expediency of promoting a new Trade with some Indians at the Back of Carolina.' Boyd was able to

[50] *Documents relative to the Colonial History of the State of New York,* edited by E. B. O'Callaghan, IV. 500.
[51] See Bellomont to Nicholson, November 12, 1698, and May 6, 1699, in C.O. 5:1309, C. 24; 1310, C 36; *CSP,AWI, 1699,* pp. 50, 319-20.
[52] *Docs. rel. to Col. Hist. N. Y.,* IV. 590.
[53] Ibid., pp. 632, 699 f.
[54] *Colonial Records of North Carolina,* edited by W. L. Saunders, I. 542.

inform their Lordships that 'the English Indian Traders inhabitating there, had made many Journeys through the Country westward to above 1000 or 1200 miles distance.'[55]

The alarm awakened in England and her colonies by Iberville's expedition of 1698 was keenest in South Carolina. Knowledge of a relatively easy land communication with the Gulf and lower Mississippi aroused fears of a speedy conquest by the French, or by the Spanish and French combined. Edward Randolph reported that the more timid settlers, recalling the Proprietors' neglect during the last war, talked of removal to a safer region should the French intrusion develop, or the death of Charles II unite the two crowns.[56] In November, 1698, when Iberville's fleet was not a month out of Brest, the Commons House of Assembly requested Governor Blake to determine whether the French were settled on the Mississippi, and if so, to consider the best way to remove them.[57]

But the able kinsman of the great Admiral[58] needed neither the clamors of his fellow colonists, nor the freely proffered counsels of Nicholson,[59] to arouse his vigilance. So certain was he of the influence his traders had won over the western tribes, that he assured Nicholson, over-confidently, there would be no difficulty in hindering the French from settling on the Mississippi. An episode of 1698 reported in Florida cast light upon the scope of Blake's ambitions. During the summer an emissary from St. Augustine, Francisco Romo de Uriza, saw at the governor's house in Charles Town several Indians from Espíritu Santo bay, or Pensacola. Blake pointed out the place on

[55] JBT, December 8, 12, 1699.
[56] C.O. 5:1258, C 22 (p. 172).
[57] JCHA, November 18, 1698.
[58] Langdon Cheves, 'Blake of South Carolina,' in SCHGM, I. 153 ff.
[59] C.O. 5:1311, D 56; CSP,AWI, 1700, pp. 326-7. In a letter of September 27, 1699, Nicholson asked Blake whether his traders' accounts agreed with Hennepin's book, which he supposed Blake possessed, but for fear he did not, he sent a copy. Did Blake, one wonders, note Hennepin's references to his own agent for exploration, Jean Couture, 'whom I knew particularly well,' wrote the Recollet, 'when I lived in Canada.' Elsewhere, denying that La Salle ever 'found out the true Mouth of the River Meschasipi, nor Father Anastasius neither, who never was in that Part of the Country,' he added: 'And if the last did luckily light upon it by the help of the Savages that guided him, 'twas owing to the Directions he receiv'd from M. Couture, . . . but it may be he will give us more light into this matter hereafter'. A New Discovery, 1698, 'Continuation,' pp. 44-6; from Nouveau voyage (1698), pp. 97, 99.

a large map. When Romo claimed that it was within the Spanish jurisdiction, Blake replied that he expected to occupy it next year for England![60]

Indeed, while Nicholson and Bellomont were discussing 'a western trade,' Blake had been despatching his traders to the Gulf and the Mississippi. Among his special measures of 1699 was an expedition by way of the Cherokee country and the Tennessee and Ohio rivers to the Mississippi. His party of traders carried presents of ammunition and merchandise for the river tribes, and credentials from the governor claiming the Mississippi country as a dependency of Great Britain. Their guide was perhaps the only man who knew that passage to the West, the renegade servant of Tonti, Jean Couture. In February, 1700, the party reached the mouth of the Arkansas, where Couture had formerly commanded at Tonti's post. Following the usual tactics of the Charles Town traders among the distant tribes, Couture's company stirred up the Quapaw Indians to raid the Chakchiuma for slaves. In May, 1700, Le Sueur, in his voyage to the Sioux, encountered one of these traders at the Quapaw village. The Carolinian shared his provisions with the French explorer, but asserted the English claim to the Mississippi valley, and boasted that by the route which he had followed, the English would yet engross its trade.[61]

On the Tennessee River, indeed, the English were securely in control—so the missionary priests and other French travellers on the Mississippi reported.[62] Already, too, the pioneers of Louisiana had learned that Carolinians had been established for several years among the Chickasaw. And now English traders had appeared in canoes on the water highway from Canada to the new colony. Inevitably the event created a profound sensation in Louisiana. Iberville saw in these adventurers the forerunners of a wave of settlement which would soon

---

[60] Dunn, *Spanish and French Rivalry*, pp. 197-8.

[61] V. W. Crane, 'The Tennessee River as the Road to Carolina,' in *MVHR*, III. 12 f.

[62] *The Jesuit Relations and Allied Documents*, edited by Reuben G. Thwaites, LXV. 114, 117-9; *Early Voyages up and down the Mississippi*, edited by John G. Shea (1861), pp. 60, 69; Bénard de la Harpe [attributed to], Journal historique concernant l'établissement des François à la Louisiane (cited from contemporary transcripts in the American Philosophical Society and the Library of Congress, rather than from the inaccurate New Orleans edition, 1831), August, 1703.

pour over the mountains and possess the heart of the continent. A more immediate danger was that the *coureurs de bois* of Canada, forbidden to bring their beaver down the Mississippi, and cut off from the Montreal market by their misdemeanors, would follow the route now opened by the Ohio and Tennessee Rivers to carry their peltry to the English. It was this fear that led Iberville to urge the concession to Juchereau de St. Denys at the mouth of the Ohio, and to seek to lift the ban on the selling of beaver in Louisiana. As a matter of fact in February, 1701, a party of four *coureurs de bois* actually penetrated to South Carolina. They had followed the route of Couture and his companions, whose exploit was probably well-known to them. Although Bellefeuille and Soton and their companions were rebuffed by the assembly in their overtures of trade, news of their wanderings aroused even greater concern in New France than the events of 1700. 'Pour moy, Monseigneur,' wrote Vaudreuil to the minister, 'je reviens à mon but, c'est qu'ils y *ont esté, et que voilà le chemin ouvert.*'[63]

In 1700 Joseph Blake had died, before he had drafted that comprehensive plan to deal with the French danger which he had assured Nicholson that he meant to send home.[64] By the spring of 1700 Charles Town knew for a certainty from the returning western traders, Welch, Dodsworth and others, that the lower Mississippi was in French hands.[65] It was left to Blake's successor, James Moore, veteran trader and explorer, to formulate a scheme to conquer that region for English trade and English sovereignty.[66]

At last the trading frontiers of France and England had come into sharp collision in one part of the trans-Appalachian West. Previous contacts on the Great Lakes had been momentary and indecisive; in the North it was the Indian of the Long House, rather than the English trader, who extended the commercial interests of England into the western wilderness. It

[63] *MVHR*, III. 13-17; Alvord, *Illinois Country,* pp. 130 f., 133 f. See James Moore and council to Proprietors, April 21, 1701, in Secretary's record of commissions and instructions, 1685-1715, MS, p. 196.

[64] C.O. 5:1311, D 56, nos. 9, 10, 10 (liv); *CSP,AWI, 1700,* pp. 311, 326.

[65] Ibid., pp. 326 f.; *1701,* p. 408; C.O. 5:1311, D 56; 1409, f. 144.

[66] Already in 1699 Moore had assured Edward Randolph that with fifty whites and a hundred Indians he could at small expense discover and explore the Mississippi (C.O. 5:1258, C 22, p. 172).

was therefore in the South that the Anglo-French struggle in its continental phase was first clearly envisaged by men of imperialist imagination, that new policies of aggression and defense were first elaborated by French and Anglo-American leaders.

Iberville had anticipated English opposition, but had quite failed to foresee the direction of the attack. Not Coxe, but Welch and his comrades proved to be the real adversaries. One tribe of Indians after another, as the French made their first contacts with them, were found to be the allies of the Carolinians, or terror-stricken victims of their slave-taking raids. In May, 1699, Bienville visited the Acolapissa on the Pearl River, west of Biloxi. He found them under arms, greatly excited, about to attack his party, for they had mistaken the French for the two 'Anglichy' who had recently come at the head of two hundred Chickasaw to raid their village. The French, Bienville promptly assured them by his interpreter, were enemies of the English and eager for their alliance.[67] Thus were the Louisiana Indians initiated into the politics of Europe. Fathers Davion and Montigny, missionary priests of Quebec who descended the Mississippi that spring, encountered an English trader at the Tunica village. Davion accompanied him on horseback to the Chickasaw, and so learned of the trade which he and his companions carried on by pack-horses from distant Charles Town.[68] More heartening was the news that the Pascagoula brought to Biloxi in the fall, that the Choctaws, a powerful nation of whom they spoke with respect and fear, had quarrelled with the English because the latter bought slaves from other Indians.[69] The French, too, were learning something of politics, the intricate politics of the wilderness that encompassed Louisiana.

Iberville at once perceived the need for a comprehensive French program of resistance to the English trading advance. But in his first measures he underrated the obstacles. His attempt with the support of the ministry to persuade the Span-

[67] Paris, Arch. Nat., Marine, B², 153, f. 666; La Harpe, Journal historique, May 23, 1699. For the location and ethnology of the tribes of Louisiana, see J. R. Swanton, *Indian Tribes of the Lower Mississippi Valley and Adjacent Coast of the Gulf of Mexico*, 1911.
[68] Margry (ed.), *Découvertes*, IV. 362, 398.
[69] Ibid., IV. 456 (Sauvole, Journal).

iards, now ruled by a Bourbon, that only the cession of Pensacola to France could check the progress of the Carolinians towards the mine-country, failed to overcome the jealous regard
of that government for the integrity of their colonial empire.[70]
In default of Pensacola, Mobile was established, in 1702,
avowedly as a point of support for the Indians allied with the
French and Spaniards against the English.[71] Meanwhile, a plan
for the forcible expulsion of the English traders from among
the Chickasaw had proved impossible of execution. Early in
1700 Tonti had been instructed to lure the Charles Town emissaries to the Tunica town on a pretext of trade, to arrest them,
and to send them down to Biloxi. But the Taënsas reported the
Englishmen more numerous than had been supposed, and this
strategem was abandoned.[72] Henceforth the central object of
Iberville's frontier policy was the promotion of a general peace
among the Indians, based on friendship and trade with the
French. Negotiations with the Chickasaw were begun by Tonti
in 1700,[73] but were brought to a head only after two years.
Meanwhile had occurred the crucial event in the frontier history of Louisiana: the conclusion of the French alliance with
the Choctaw.

Prior to 1700 the French apparently had no direct contact
with this numerous inland tribe, the bulwark of Louisiana
throughout its later history. In April, Iberville received a circumstantial account of their great strength, but at the time
spring floods prevented his agents from penetrating to their
country.[74] In May, Sauvole brought in two Choctaw whom he
had met at the Tohome village. These were sent back with an
invitation to their principal chief to come down to Biloxi. 'This
nation,' Iberville now recorded, 'is at war with all the other
nations to the north and east of them, allies of the English,

---

[70] Ibid., pp. 476, 484, 489 f., 543-75; Arch. Nat., Marine, B², 153, f. 666.
See Dunn, *Spanish and French Rivalry*, pp. 206-15.
[71] Margry (ed.), *Découvertes*, IV. 372, 548, 578 f.; *Report concerning
Canadian Archives for the Year 1905*, I. 523.
[72] Margry (ed.), *Découvertes*, IV. 362, 406, 418. It was reported, however,
in a letter from Rochefort of March 30, 1700, printed in the *Present State
of Europe*, XI, no. 8 (August, 1700), p. 291, that Iberville had arrested 'an
Englishman who treated with the Savages our Confederates. He came into
that Country through the Rive *Oye*.'
[73] Margry (ed.), *Découvertes*, IV, pp. 418 f., 430, 479.
[74] Ibid., p. 427.

who were armed with muskets.' [75] In September a delegation of Choctaws arrived with the Mobilians to ask the French to join them in their war against the Chickasaw.[76] The traditional enmity between the Choctaw, the most numerous nation of southwestern Indians, and the Chickasaw, the most aggressive, was clearly the *raison d'être* of the French-Choctaw alliance. In the event, this chronic feud proved fatal to Iberville's program of pacification. But in 1702 the Choctaw and the Chickasaw were reconciled at a notable congress at Mobile. On the eve of the Anglo-French war Iberville's Indian policy seemed crowned with success.

The agent who brought these warring Indians together at Mobile was the devoted Tonti. On February 8, 1702, with ten picked men Tonti set out upon his delicate errand.[77] On March 25 he returned with four Choctaw chiefs and three chiefs and four other principal men of the Chickasaw. The following day presents were distributed, and with Bienville as interpreter, Iberville harangued the Indian council. By his own account, he sought to persuade the two tribes that a general peace was to their own interest. In the eight or ten years that intertribal warfare had continued at the solicitation of the English, the Chickasaw, he declared, had made over five hundred prisoners and killed more than eighteen hundred Choctaw; and the Chickasaw themselves had lost some eight hundred dead in their raids. With the Choctaw they should realise, therefore, that the ultimate aim of the English was to exhaust them by wars in order to seize their lands and send them all slaves into distant countries. The Chickasaw must expel the English traders from their towns or he would have no peace or trade with them, but instead would arm the Choctaw, the Mobilians, the Tohomes, as he had already begun to arm the Natchez and other allies. Instead of restraining Illinois attacks, he would spur them on. But once the English were sent packing Iberville promised to build a post in the Indian country between the

[75] Ibid., pp. 429, 460. See *Louisiana Historical Quarterly*, VIII. 31, regarding French information at this time of the Upper Creeks and the English interest there.

[76] La Harpe, Journal historique, September 16, 1701.

[77] Ibid., March, 1702; Margry (ed.), *Découvertes*, IV. 507. Tonti's route was shown on Delisle's *Carte de la Louisiane et du cours du Mississipi*, 1718.

Choctaw and Chickasaw towns. There the French would offer them trade, not for slaves, but for the skins of deer and buffalo.

It was probably Iberville's promise of trade rather than his eloquent picture of the blessings of peace that brought the Chickasaw to agree to live amicably with the Choctaw and to eject the Carolinians. Iberville then promised to forbid his allies to carry on war against them and to secure the return of captives from the Illinois. In return he demanded that they persuade the Creeks to trade at the French fort and to give no heed to the English, under threat to release the tomahawks of the Apalache, of which he claimed to be master. When Iberville had taken a census of the tribes the congress was dismissed, and the Indians returned to their towns, 'très contens,' Iberville believed, 'et disposés à vivre tous en paix.'[78]

Shortly the truce was extended to other tribes, notably the Illinois and the Alabamas, nearest of the Upper Creek towns. Three Canadians were sent to the Illinois country to arrest the hatchet against the Chickasaw, and also against the Shawnee, whom Iberville, in view of overtures to Bellefeuille, hoped to draw down to the Mississippi or to Mobile.[79] In May, 1702, eight Alabama chiefs came in and took the peace talk at Mobile.[80] To the grand vicar of Quebec at the Tamaroas and to the superior of the Jesuits, Iberville appealed for missionaries to the Choctaw and Chickasaw. At the same time he deputed Father Davion and other priests of the lower Mississippi to spread the news of the peace among the river tribes. As a further measure, already contemplated, he sent a youth, 'le petit Saint-Michel,' to live among the Chickasaw and learn their language.[81] So effective did these measures appear that on his return to France Iberville reported: 'La paix est conclue et a resté entre eux.'[82] And Nicolas de la Salle declared: 'Je puis dire que la colonie naissante a toute l'obligation de cette union à M. d'Iberville et à M. de Tonty, qui ont agi dans cette négociation en hommes bien intentionnés pour la réussite d'un des plus fameux establissements que le Roy ait par la suite.'[83]

[78] Margry (ed.), *Découvertes,* IV. 516-21.
[79] Ibid., p. 520.
[80] La Harpe, Journal historique, May 12, 1702.
[81] Margry (ed.), *Découvertes,* IV. 480, 521.
[82] Ibid., p. 630.
[83] Ibid., pp. 531f.

CHAPTER IV

The Southern Frontier in Queen Anne's War

In America, as in Europe, at the beginning of the eighteenth century a rupture seemed inevitable between England and the Bourbon monarchies. For thirty years Spaniards and Englishmen had been jealous and quarrelsome neighbors in the South, and Spanish dominion had steadily dwindled. But the old conflicts on the Guale border were now subordinated to a greater contest for the hegemony of the interior, in which for some years Florida played a minor rôle. The founding of Louisiana, and the southwestward advance of the Carolinians, had created a new zone of Anglo-French rivalry for the Indian trade. The obscure struggles of Indian traders and their savage partizans on the farthest frontier of the English colonies in North America made but small stir in a world absorbed in the momentous issue of the Spanish Succession. A few men only understood that these incidents foreshadowed a contest for the richest prize of 'imperial' ambition in America : the heart of the continent. It was on the southern frontier that the conflict was first clearly joined for the control of the valley of the Mississippi.

Iberville, for one, had foreseen the impending struggle, and had drawn up a comprehensive frontier policy for Louisiana. In 1702 his scheme of pacification in the Southwest seemed completely successful. But his purpose was not merely defensive. He looked beyond the immediate security of the new colony to the expansion of French interest eastward, 'au côté de Caroline,' and to coöperation with Florida to strike at the flank of the English trading advance. Indeed, the conquest of Carolina, and in the sequel of Virginia, Maryland, and even New York, was already in view. This was the subject of an extraordinary 'Projet sur la Caroline' submitted to the ministry in 1702 with Iberville's approving annotations. Spanish weakness and the successful aggression of the Carolina traders foreshadowed the speedy loss of all Florida. Supreme among the inland tribes, and possibly dominating the Havana passage from the Baye de Carlos (Tampa Bay), the English would menace Louisiana. Franco-Spanish coöperation was therefore imperative: Carolina must be destroyed. A joint expedition by land and sea was proposed. While six hundred Spanish troops from St. Augustine, Havana, and Vera Cruz, joined by three hundred French and one hundred Canadians, attacked Charles Town fort, fifteen hundred Spanish Indians, armed with French guns, should create a diversion on the Carolina frontiers. Success would mean that the Florida boundary would be extended northward to the 'river of Virginia,' but in compensation Pensacola should be ceded to France. Louisiana, too, would profit by the plunder of the English province, sharing the cattle and slaves of the abandoned plantations with their allies. For the English settlers would be returned to England, and the French Huguenots, deprived of their leaders, carried to Mobile and won back to the Catholic faith. The conquest of Carolina, moreover, would pave the way for a French alliance with the Creeks, and for greater victories. By 1704 the new Indian league should be strong enough to make possible a grand encircling movement against the English seaboard colonies, this time a French enterprise solely, for the profit only of France. Nor was it too soon to put the larger project in train. Le Sueur should be sent up the Mississippi to make peace between the Sioux and the Illinois, and to remove the latter to the mouth of the Ohio. (Elsewhere Iberville outlined a grandiose scheme for the rearrangement of the tribes, including the Shawnee and the Cherokee, to expose the southern flank of the English colonies.) Two or three thousand Sioux and Illinois, four thousand Choctaw, Chickasaw, and Mobilians, joined with the converted Upper Creeks (Conchaques) would make a sufficient force of auxiliaries, it was predicted, to enable four or five hundred French and Canadians to carry through the conquest of Virginia. With further aid from the western Indians the frontier invasions might be extended victoriously as far as New York. But the first, essential step was the campaign of 1702 against Carolina.[1]

It was, of course, one thing to predict on paper the successive stages in the subjugation of the southern frontier and of the Atlantic seaboard. It was another thing, beyond the

[1] 'Projet sur la Caroline' in Arch. Nat., col. C¹¹, A 20, f. 224 *et seq.* See also Margry (ed.), *Découvertes,* IV. 520.

powers of persuasion of Iberville and his friends, to win support from the ministry, the complete coöperation of an ally chronically suspicious of all intrusions into the Gulf area, and the conversion of the Indian who had learned to look to Charles Town 'pour avoir les choses qui leur sont nécessaire, et à bon marché.' Nevertheless the *projet* was notable for its clear definition of the ultimate aims of both the major participants in the struggle which was beginning in the old Southwest. The analysis of Carolinian policy could be documented at almost every point from the declarations of Joseph Blake and James Moore. And here, could the Carolinians have read it, was full confirmation of that encircling policy of France in North America which for a generation and more to come was the dread of English provincial leaders in the South, to which they shaped their own western policy and at length the frontier policy of the colonial authorities in England.

Short of this program of encirclement the efforts of Iberville soon awakened apprehensions at Charles Town, and provoked a counter-offensive. In a memoir of June, 1702,[2] Iberville analysed the French advantages for rivalling the English traders among the Creek Indians, notably the ease of water-transport from Mobile. Franco-Spanish rivalry on the eastern Gulf coast, in Iberville's view, must be subordinated to the common task of checking the advance of the Carolinians. Even while engaged in furnishing Ponchartrain with arguments for the cession of Pensacola to France, he recognised the necessity of supporting the feeble establishments of the Bourbon ally. In the next war, he declared, St. Augustine, Apalache, Pensacola would lie at the mercy of the English. He therefore helped to secure supplies for the starving garrison at Pensacola, and sought earnestly to link Florida and Louisiana in effective resistance to English intrusions. To the governor of Pensacola he wrote in January, 1702, strongly advising that the Apalache be engaged to oppose the progress of the English and their allies. Men, provisions, munitions, everything that he had, he offered for this essential service.[3]

Apart from Iberville's preaching of a more aggressive

[2] Ibid., p. 594.
[3] Ibid., pp. 546-7, 551, 579.

border strategy, the Spanish had received ample provocation in recent raids of the Creeks and the Carolina slave-dealers. An incursion into Apalache in 1701, and in May, 1702, the destruction of the Timucuan mission of Santa Fé de Toloco, clamored for revenge.[4] Governor Zuñiga in the summer of 1702 sent out a punitive force of Spanish and Apalache Indians more than eight hundred strong, under the command of Captain Uriza. Iberville had advance knowledge of the campaign and he doubted its success. The Apalache were still bow-and-arrow Indians, the Creeks had firearms from South Carolina. The Frenchman's forebodings were fully justified. Anthony Dodsworth and the other Carolina traders at Coweta learned from the Indians of the Spanish march, marshalled some five hundred Creeks, and advanced at their head to the Flint River. There, by a clever strategem, they completely routed the invaders.[5]

More was involved in this frontier skirmish, the prelude to Queen Anne's War on the southern frontier, than in the familiar broils between South Carolina and Florida. In effect it was the first blow struck by the English for the control of the Mississippi Valley. Certainly no doubt existed in the mind of Governor James Moore of Carolina that the unity of policy which Iberville was seeking to attain was a fact with which the English must henceforth reckon.

By 1702 the first panic at Charles Town over the establishment of Louisiana had somewhat subsided. But the approach of war, and the overtures of Iberville to the Creeks raised new fears. In 1701 Col. Stephen Bull was sent on a special mission to the Talapoosas.[6] In August of that year Governor Moore warned the Commons House that whether there was 'warr or peace we are sure to be always in danger and under the trouble and charge of keeping out guards, even in time of Peace, so long as those French live so near us. To put you in mind of the French of Canada's neighborhood to the Inhabitants of New

[4] Ibid., p. 595; Bolton and Ross, *The Debatable Land*, p. 58.
[5] Ibid., pp. 58-9; Margry (ed.), *Découvertes*, IV. 595; Carroll (ed.), *Collections*, II. 351. C.O. Maps, N.A.C. General, 7, has crossed swords near the Flint River, and the legend, 'Battel in 1702 where 600 Spanish Indians were killed or taken by the Carolinians.'
[6] JCHA, August 16, 27, 1701.

England is to say enough on the subject.'[7] Early in 1702 he urged 'that you think of some way to prevent the Tallabooses and other Indians now our friends their trade and acquaintance with the French till some way be found to secure us from the mischiefs and dangers which that trade and acquaintance will bring us.'[8] Already a conference committee on Indian affairs had defined the normal Indian policy of the province, advising that 'the Tallabooses and other Friendly Indians be not Discourag'd from making warr upon those Indians that are our and their Enemies.'[9] Partly as a result of the French threat, the assembly passed the first act regulating the Indian trade.[10] By measures of this sort, and by the persistent activity of the traders, the Upper Creek Indians were brought in 1703 to an open breach with Louisiana.

Meanwhile, Moore was developing his project for striking at the French through Florida. In August, 1702, on the strength of unofficial intelligence of the outbreak of war in Europe, he urged an immediate offensive against Florida. 'The Takeing of St. Augustine before it be Strengthened with French forses,' he declared to the hesitant assembly, 'opens to us an easie and plaine way to Remove the French (a no less dangerous Enemy in time of peace then Warr) from their Settlement on the South *(sic)* Side of the Bay of Apalatia.' By such exploits 'the fronteere Collony of all her Majesties Plantations on the Maine in America' might hope to win royal aid and protection.[11] The St. Augustine expedition of 1702 had, then, its true setting in the international contest for the region of the Gulf and the Mississippi, a fact which was clearly understood in Louisiana and even in France. Moore's vociferous enemies in Carolina, who stoutly opposed the campaign, later villified it as a miserable plundering and slave-catching adventure. To be sure, the affair and its sequel, the Apalache campaign, were not untouched by scandal. Perhaps it was true that the governor and

[7] Ibid., August 14, 1701.
[8] Ibid., January 14, April 2, 1702.
[9] Ibid., August 15, 1701.
[10] See below, p. 144.
[11] JCHA, August 20, 1702. At this time the declaration of war, though communicated by the Proprietors on May 8, had not, apparently, been received. C.O. 5:289, p. 91; 1290, p. 222; *Commissions and Instructions, 1685-1715,* pp. 153-4.

his officers were wont to dine thereafter off the church plate of St. Augustine, and that Spanish Indians labored on Moore's plantations. Moore was ambitious, needy, the head of a large family, but he was also a typical Anglo-American expansionist.[12]

So late as August 22 the assembly refused to authorize the governor to proclaim the war.[13] But under pressure from Moore an act was passed, September 10, to equip the expedition.[14] Five hundred Carolinians and some three hundred Indians comprised the army which set out in fourteen small ships from Port Royal. Moore commanded, and under him Colonel Robert Daniel. The remaining Spanish missions north of San Juan were soon swept away. The Yoa now migrated northward to the 'Indian Land.' The ruin of Guale was complete. A tight embargo had been imposed to keep news of the invasion from the Spaniards. But one of the smaller vessels lost company, and the presidio had two days' warning. October 27 the fleet arrived at St. Augustine, and two days later Colonel Daniel 'made himself Master of the Towne.' The Carolinians marvelled at the size of the churches and the 'abbey,' 'large enouf to entertaine Seven or Eight hundred men,' but they marvelled more at the unexpected strength of the moated castle. Against this regular bastioned fortification the Carolinian battery of four guns made a pitiful showing. Hope of success lay in starving out the enemy—'one thousand Eaters' were reported in the fort—or in securing ordnance before Spanish aid could come from Havana. But an eight weeks' siege sapped the morale of the undisciplined army of frontiersmen. Mortars and ammunition sought in Jamaica had not come; Colonel Daniel had sailed to New York for aid. Moore was hard put to it to hold his grumbling force together. At this juncture appeared off the bar two Spanish men-of-war, believed to rate thirty or forty guns each, with a brigantine and a sloop bringing relief from Havana. The Carolina fleet of

[12] For hostile criticism of the Florida campaigns see John Ash, *The Present State of Affairs in Carolina* (1706?), p. 30, reprinted in Salley (ed.) *Narratives*, p. 272; and Colleton county representation, in Rivers, *Sketch*, Appendix, p. 456.
[13] JCHA, August 22, 1702.
[14] Cooper (ed.), *Statutes*, II. 189 (act not extant).

eight little vessels, ranging from seventy tons burden to less than fifty, was bottled up. Three days longer the siege was maintained. Then Moore set fire to his ships and to the town and its churches, and retreated overland sixty miles to his periagoes. The failure, Robert Quary was convinced, was due to no lack of troops or of courage, but solely to the want of one or two men-of-war and a few bombs. South Carolina was saddled with a debt of over eight thousand pounds, and entered upon the evil course of paper-money issues. But the casualties had been trifling, and plans were soon discussed with Admiral Whetstone for a second expedition, this time with adequate naval assistance.[15]

In a letter to Whetstone of January 28, 1703,[16] the governor and assembly outlined the larger objects of their program:

If it Pleaseth God to Give us Success, it is a Matter of that Great Consequence that if to that Wee ad the conquest of a small Spanish Town called Pancicola, and a new french Colony. . . Both, Sea Port Towns. . . It will make her Majestie Absolute and Soveraigne Lady of all the Maine as farr as the River Mischisipi, which if effected the Colony of Carolina will be of the Greatest Vallue to the Crown of England of any of her Majesties Plantations on the Maine except Virginia by ading a Great Revenue to the Crown, for one halfe of all the Canadian Trade for furrs and Skinns must necessarily come this way, besides a vast Trade of Furrs and Skinns extended as far as the above mentioned River, Mischisipi, which is now interrupted by those Two little Towns, . . . and the Best Service any of her Majesties Subjects can do the Crowne is to add to Its Dominion and Revenue.

In April, 1703, and again in June, Colonel Robert Quary, whose former residence in South Carolina had familiarized him with the problems and the point of view of the southern frontier, wrote home emphasizing in similar fashion the rela-

[15] The printed accounts of this expedition, contemporary and later, are cited by me in *AHR*, XXIV. 386 note; and by Bolton and Ross in *The Debatable Land,* p. 60 note. The present account is largely based upon Moore and Daniel to the council, November 9, 1702 (C.O. 5:382, no. 8, i); council to [Secretary], November 26, 1702 (ibid., no. 8); Michael Cole, shipmaster, to William Blaythwayt, Charles Town, December 22, 1702 (C.O. 5:306, no. 2); Quary to Board of Trade, December 7, 1702 (C.O. 323:3, E 54); JCHA, 1702-1703, *passim.* For evidences of French alarm, see Arch. Nat., Marine, B², 167, f. 523; 168, f. 63; 177, f. 494.

[16] JCHA, January 28, 1702/3.

tion of the Florida campaign to the larger question of continental dominion. The reduction of Florida would, he believed, 'put a stop to the French designs who are endeavouring from Canada, to secure the Inland parts of the whole Maine.'[17]

To the French, meanwhile, the significance, for them, of these English threats to Florida seemed quite as clear. The French ministry was considering a joint expedition to recapture St. Augustine when the news came that the English had retreated—so Cardinal d'Estrées, ambassador to Spain, was apprised. His despatch from Paris was loud in praise of Zuñiga's valor; he was instructed to support his candidacy for promotion to the governorship of Cartagena, and to back Don Francisco Martin of Pensacola for his place, for Martin had won the confidence of Iberville. Florida, clearly, was regarded in France as the first line of defense for Louisiana.[17a]

Quary and Moore saw farther into the future of the intercolonial conflict than most of their English contemporaries. Moore was discredited by the St. Augustine fiasco; he was succeeded by a capable but unimaginative soldier, whose chief interest in frontier policy was apparently to secure his perquisites in presents from the chiefs. In 1703, however, Sir Nathaniel Johnson secured the assent of the assembly to a blow at the Spanish interest which reaped a larger measure of success than any other purely military measure of the war. Like the St. Augustine expedition, the Apalache campaign was directed against Louisiana as well as Florida.

In 1702 and 1703 French overtures to the Alabama and Talapoosa, and the Franco-Spanish projects for employing the Apalache against the Lower Creeks, awakened anxiety at Charles Town for the stability of the provincial Indian system. A general movement northward of the Creek tribes who formed the bulwark of Carolina seemed impending. How to protect these Indians and confirm them in the places in which they lived repeatedly engaged the attention of the government.[18] Soon after the collapse of the attack upon St. Augustine a party of Creeks and English made an incursion into the Apa-

[17] B.M. Add. MSS 11759, f. 169; *Docs. rel. to Col. Hist. N. Y.*, IV. 1048.
[17a] Arch. Nat., Marine, B², 168, f. 63.
[18] JCHA, January 14, 1702; January 15, 16, 19, 20, February 3, September 2, 1703.

lache country, ravishing the missions of San José de Ocuia, Patali, and San Francisco.[19] With Johnson's support Moore now brought forward a project for the elimination of the Apalache. Early in September Johnson hastily summoned the assembly, with a warning that the Creeks were threatened by a combined Spanish and French offensive. The Commons interrogated the Indian traders, Dodsworth, Welch, William Steed, and others, but, questioning the imminence of the danger, hesitated to do more than send a present to the Creeks. But they were convinced when they heard an eye-witness's account of French colonization in Louisiana. On September 7 the assembly requested Johnson to send Moore 'to the Assistance of the Cowetaw and other our friendly Indians, and to attacque the Appalaches.' The treasury was empty, and the Commons refused funds even to supply the army with horses. Moreover, they laid a serious restriction upon a campaign which must pay its way out of slaves and plunder, when they urged that Moore be instructed 'to endeavour to gain [by] all peaceable means if possible the Appalaches to our interest (as we are inform'd they are thereunto inclined).'[20]

By his own interest, and at his own expense, Moore got together at Okmulgee, in December, an army of fifty whites and a thousand Indians. On January 14, 1704, he fell upon Ayubale, 'the strongest fort in Apalache.' For nine hours Father Miranda and his neophytes put up a vigorous defense. The Creeks, meanwhile, were raiding the plantations, and only a handful took part in the two assaults. 'I never see or hear of a stouter or braver thing done,' wrote Moore, 'than the storming of the fort.' Next day he was attacked in the field by Captain Ruíz Mexía, commander of San Luís fort and lieutenant of Apalache. Mexía had assembled thirty mounted soldiers and four hundred Indians; in his company was the devoted Father Juan de Parga, whose harangue to his charges aroused them to fighting pitch against the heretics. Parga insisted on keeping 'his children' company even to death. But the Spaniards were routed, Parga fell in battle, Mexía was wounded and captured.

[19] Zuñiga to the King, March 30/April 10, 1704 (transcript in New York Historical Society) ; Swanton, *Early History*, p. 122.
[20] JCHA, September 2, 3, 4, 6, 7, 15, 17, 1703.

After this victory Moore was unable to restrain his savage allies, who subjected a number of the prisoners to the tortures of the stake. The invaders thereafter marched through Apalache, taking one fortified village after another, until the rich province with its flourishing missions was almost completely ravaged and subdued. Five towns surrendered unconditionally; and the cacique of Ybithachucu compounded for peace, offering the church plate and provisions. Moore did not attempt the fort of San Luís, and the Indians of one other town made good their escape. Besides many Indians killed in battle, or captured and carried away as slaves (325 men, by Moore's report, and a much greater number of women and children) some three hundred men and a thousand women and children whose chiefs had submitted were removed as free Indians to the neighborhood of Savannah Town, to strengthen the immediate frontier of South Carolina. 'All of which,' Moore boasted to the Proprietors, 'I have done with the loss of 4 whites and 15 Indians, and without one Penny charge to the Publick. Before this Expedition,' he added, 'we were more afraid of the Spaniards of Apalatchee and their Indians in Conjunction with the French of Mississippi, and their Indians, doing us Harm by Land, than of any Forces of the Enemy by Sea. This has wholly disabled them from attempting anything against Us by Land.'[21]

The quantities of slaves and plunder which Moore's army had brought from Apalache tempted other leaders, though 'the whole strength' of the province Moore now reckoned at no more than three hundred Indians. A veteran of these cam-

[21] Moore to Johnson, 'in the woods,' April 16, 1704, in 'Spanish Papers,' MSS, Library of Congress, VI, 892-6: printed, with some omissions and inaccuracies, in *Boston News Letter,* May 1, 1704, and reprinted in Carroll (ed.), *Collections,* II. 574-6; Moore to Proprietors, same date, in 'Spanish Papers,' VI. 888; Zuñiga to the King, March 30/April 10, 1704, and extract, translated, in Swanton, *Early History,* pp. 122 f.; 'Extractos de una informacion fecha en San Agustín,' June 9, 1705 (transcript, New York Historical Society). The French were greatly disturbed by this further evidence of an English push towards Louisiana, and began to entertain projects for destroying Carolina. See Arch. Nat., Marine, B², 177, f. 494; 183, f. 47; and Affaires étrangères, Espagne, 153, f. 97. Bienville's report is summarized in *Canadian Archives Report for 1905,* I. 448; see also Swanton, *Early History,* p. 123; South Carolina assembly report, 1741, in Carroll (ed.), *Collections,* II. 352 f. On the settlement of the Apalache at Savannah Town, see JCHA, April 27, 28, 1704. Quary's enthusiastic estimate of the importance of this campaign is in *Docs. rel. Col. Hist. N. Y.,* IV. 1088 f.

paigns, Thomas Nairne, wrote in 1705: 'We have these two
. . . past years been intirely kniving all the Indian Towns in
Florida which were subject to the Spaniards and have even
accomplished it.'[22] Timucua, harassed since 1685, now shared
the fate of Guale and Apalache. The Timucuan missions, San
Miguel de Assile, San Matheo, San Pedro, Santa Fé, San Francisco and the rest,[23] stretched eastward from Apalache along
the road to St. Augustine. 'Wholly laid waste being destroyed
by the Carolinians, 1706,' was the legend printed across this
region on an early official map. 'Tocobogga Indians, Destroyed
1709' was the similar record of an incursion on the west coast,
south of Apalache.[24] In 1708 John Barnwell again traversed
Timucua, and also ascended the St. John's.[25] That river, indeed, became a usual route for slave-catching raids far into the
interior. The course of 'an Expedition in Florida Neck, by
thirty-three Iamasee Indians Accompany'd by Capt. T. Nairn'
was recorded on Moll's map of 1720.[26] Nairne was probably
the anonymous pamphleteer who wrote in 1710 that 'there remains not now, so much as one Village with ten Houses in it,
in all Florida, that is subject to the Spaniards; nor have they
any Houses or Cattle left, but such as they can protect by the
Guns of their Castle of St. Augustine, that alone being now
in their Hands, and which is continually infested by the perpetual Incursions of the Indians, subject to this Province.'[27]

On the Louisiana border as well as in Florida the aftermath of the Apalache campaign, accurately foreseen by French
leaders, was increased actively by the Carolinians, secure, now,
against inland attack. Already the Charles Town traders had
undermined the weakest prop of Iberville's structure of alliances, the peace with the Alabamas. Since 1701 repeated
efforts had been made to offset French control of the river-route

[22] S.P.G. MSS A, II, no. 156. Of the fidelity of the Apalache to the
Spaniards Nairne wrote that 'nothing but downright force brought them
over to our side.' See also Nairne memorial, July 10, 1708, in C.O. 382 (11).
[23] Swanton, Early History, pp. 322, 339 f.
[24] C.O. Maps, N.A.C. General, 7.
[25] Ibid.
[26] Herman Moll, A New Map of the North Parts of America claimed by
France, 1720; C.O. Maps, Carolina, 3.
[27] A Letter from South Carolina, London, 1710, p. 34. Compare the
Spanish account of these ravages, badly translated, in Brooks (comp.),
Unwritten History, pp. 164-7.

to the Alabama and the other Upper Creek towns. In February, 1703, a Commons House committee 'to secure the South-western Indians and the Yamasees to our Interest' proposed that one or two 'Sensible men' go to the Talapoosas and their neighbors with presents and assurances of aid.[28] The governor reported in April that the 'Tallibuses and Stinking Linguas and Abecas our friends and the most southerly Indians allied to us, as well as the Indians which by reason of their being not far situated from the French settlement' should receive most encouragement, had asked for a drum, a stand of colors, and the right to buy ammunition to use against the French and Spaniards.[29] In May, by a French account, two Alabama chiefs came to Mobile with the false report that the English had retired from their towns and the neighboring settlements. Thereupon Bienville sent one La Brie and four Canadians to purchase grain for the Mobile garrison. But the invitation was a ruse. Only one of the *voyageurs* escaped with a broken head to tell of an ambush in which the rest were slain. 'Voilà le sujet de la guerre que nous fismes aux Alibamons,' wrote the chronicler Pénicaut.[30] For nine years the war continued. Punitive expeditions, such as one that Bienville headed in December, 1703, were of little use. More effective were attacks by French Indians spurred on by liberal offers of rewards for scalps and captives.[31] Meanwhile, the Alabama war greatly facilitated the work of the South Carolina traders, who, on this remote border, advanced hand in hand their own profit and the political interests of their province.

In August, 1705, the alliance between South Carolina and the Creek Indians was ratified in form at a council held at Coweta Town. There a treaty, or, rather, an address to Sir Nathaniel Johnson, was signed with the marks of a dozen 'Kings, Princes, Tuskestanagaes, Istechaugaes, Generals, War Captains,' etc., of Coweta, Okmulgee, Kasihta, Tukabahchee, Okfuskee, Alabama, Kealedji, and other towns of the Upper

[28] JCHA, February 3, 1702/3.
[29] Ibid., April 17, 1703.
[30] Margry (ed.), *Découvertes*, V. 429; La Harpe, Journal historique, May 3, 24, 1703. Compare Nairne memorial, July 10, 1708, C.O. 5:382.
[31] La Harpe, Journal historique, December 22, 1703; November 18, 1704; January 21, 1706; November, 1707. Pénicaut, in Margry (ed.), *Découvertes*, V. 429-32, 435, 483.

and Lower Creeks. They acknowledged not merely their 'Hearty Alliance,' but also their 'Subjection' to the Crown of England, pledging fidelity to the 'High and Mighty Ann, Queen of the English, and to all her Majesties Governours of Carolina.' 'All the English Friends and Allies are in like Manner ours, and all their Enemies are hereby Our declared Enemies. Lastly, We do Assure your Honour, we will with our Utmost Power Assist the English, and Endeavour to give a Total Rout to all their and our declared Enemies, the French and Spaniards, not suffering them to settle themselves hereafter in any of Our Territories or Dominions, nor within reach of our Arms.' This extraordinary document was attested by Daniel Henchman as Johnson's agent; the interpreters were two Indian traders and partizan leaders, Captain John Musgrove and Captain John Jones.[32]

The defection of the Alabama, and the closer alliance between the Creeks and the English, following closely the conquest of Apalache, marked the second serious defeat for French frontier policy as initiated by Iberville. It was soon followed by another: the renewal of the Choctaw-Chickasaw feud. That the infant colony on the Gulf nevertheless withstood the assaults of the Carolinians and their savage confederates seems to have been due almost entirely to the adroit Indian management of Iberville's brother and successor. Bienville, declared the Jesuit, Father Gravier, knew perfectly how to govern the Indians.[33] Through the French youths whom he sent to live among them he kept in touch with the rapidly shifting currents of wilderness politics. By flattery, by 'caresses,' he made good in part the meagerness of French presents and the poverty of French trade. Constantly he was receiving Indian embassies at Mobile. Charmed by his remarkable talent for their languages, and by the tact which placed them at his own table in Fort St. Louis, little wonder that his guests were convinced that the

[32] *The Humble Submission of Several Kings, Princes, Generals, &c., to the Crown of England,* London, 1707 (broadside). One of two copies in the British Museum, a proof sheet with marginal corrections, has a note that it was 'communicated to the Benevolent Society of Chyurgeons, by a Member of Theirs and the Royal Society.' This points towards Dr. Coxe. Five divisions of the Creek towns were named: 'The Ochase, Haritaumau [Altamaha], Talliboose, Holbamah and Abecau Nations.'
[33] Arch. Nat., col., C[13] A 1, f. 575. Cf. mémoire de Duclos, October 25, 1713, ibid., A 3, f. 265 *et seq.*

French nation was the finest in the world. Bienville believed the Indians naturally loved the French, that only necessity and interest drew them to the English. But sentiment alone is rarely an efficient political motive, even in a state of nature. At times Bienville's skill was severely tested. The poverty of Louisiana played into the hands of its enemies. Funds set aside for Indian presents and trade had to be used to maintain the garrisons. 'Trop cher' was the younger Ponchartrain's marginal comment when Bienville's memoirs urged that his Indians should receive a musket for every scalp they lifted from an English Indian. Nor did the minister welcome the suggestion that a party of chiefs be carried to France to enhance their respect for French power.[34] More serious was the neglect to authorize the building of the post promised to the Chickasaw in 1702, and impatiently demanded by the Indians. In this juncture the English, by cultivating a band of Chickasaw settled among the Upper Creeks, and by liberal presents to their kinsmen, were again imperilling the central object of French policy, the pacification of the southwestern tribes.[35]

In 1704 the French learned that several Carolinians, laden with presents, had been treating with the Chickasaw, from whom they bought a dozen Taënsa slaves.[36] Early the next year came more alarming news: the Chickasaw had sold to the English several families of Choctaw, seized when they came in good faith on a visit to a Chickasaw village. The Choctaw matched this treachery a little later when they massacred a band of Chickasaw returning from Mobile under the escort of M. Boisbriant and his Canadians.[37] However, Bienville managed to revive the truce, insisting as a condition that the English traders must go, and in January, 1706, Choctaw and Chickasaw again smoked the calumet together at Mobile.[38] But by March the patched-up peace was definitely broken through

[34] Ibid., A 1, ff. 387-96, 514 *et seq.*; A 2, f. 574; *Canadian Archives Report for 1905*, I. 528.
[35] Arch. Nat., col. C[13] A 1, ff. 387-396, 523, 575; JCHA, February 3, 1703.
[36] La Harpe, Journal historique, October 20, 1704; *Canadian Archives Report for 1905*, I. 448.
[37] La Harpe, Journal historique, February, 1705. Boisbriant was accidentally wounded in the mêlée.
[38] Ibid., April 10, December 9, 1705; January 21, 1706; Arch. Nat., col. C[13] A 1, ff. 574f.

the intervention, there is reason to believe, of Thomas Welch. The Chickasaw, so the French learned, made a night attack upon a Choctaw village, carrying off more than one hundred and fifty prisoners,[39] many of whom probably found their way to the Charles Town slave-market. The Choctaw now demanded arms and ammunition from Mobile. This support they received; though Bienville still strove for a general peace, he could not permit the destruction of that tribe. He thoroughly understood that the English were striving by such attrition to wear down the Indian defenses of Louisiana. 'Les Anglois de la Caroline n'epargnent rien pour faire detruire nos Sauvages par les leurs,' was the constant plaint of the officials of Louisiana.[40]

Though the French for several years retained a party among the Chickasaw, English influence was now paramount. The Chickasaw, with their neighbors the Yazoo, were added to the Talapoosa, the Alabama and the other Creek tribes whom the English had been using with disastrous effect in their assaults upon the allies of the French. Thus in the autumn of 1705 the Choctaw had been raided by a great force of Carolina Indians under white leaders, three or four thousand warriors according to French account. The Choctaw villages and fields were laid waste, and many prisoners carried away.[41] A petition of Thomas Welch to the Lords Proprietors in 1708, for the return of certain Indian slaves seized by Governor Johnson as perquisites of office, revealed the method of organizing such a raid. Under a commission from the governor, Welch deposed, he had 'Lede a party consisting of five English, and 300 Indians, against the Chacta Indians Allies to the French and Enemies to the crown of England.' Welch had 'furnished the said 300 Indians with Ammunition for this Enterprise upon a Contract that if they had Success, they should pay fifteen Slaves' to him; he retained for himself five slaves and

---

[39] La Harpe, Journal historique, March 5, 1706. See JCHA, November 6, 1707, petition of Thomas Welch asking payment 'for the powder and shott he gave to the Checkesaws when the French was for persuading them to come over to their alliance.' The prime costs, £61, were allowed.

[40] Quoted from Bienville, August 20, 1709, in Arch. Nat., col. C¹³ A 2, f. 408, but repeated, with slight variations, by Cadillac, Nicolas La Salle, and others.

[41] La Harpe, Journal historique, January 7, 1706. Arch. Nat., col. C¹³ A 1, f. 509.

each of his five English followers received two in the final distribution.[42] Among the weaker tribes a veritable reign of terror was now instituted. In the east, the assaults of the Creeks compelled many of the Apalache, Tawasa, and Chatot and other Indians settled near the Apalachicola River to seek shelter at Mobile.[43] North of Mobile the Tohome and Mobilians were also exposed to attack.[44] Even on the Mississippi the English made their name a dread. In 1706 the Taënsa and Tunica, French Indians, were forced to remove nearer the mouth of the river.[45] By such tactics the Carolinians prepared for the climax of their offensive. In 1707 Pensacola Town was burned, and an elaborate intrigue was set in motion for the destruction of Mobile and all Louisiana.

Meanwhile the war had been carried home to Charles Town. Since 1670 the King and the Council of the Indies had been repeatedly besought by governors of Florida to remove the intruders from San Jorge. But Guale was lost, then Apalache, and nothing was seriously attempted until Queen Anne's War gave the opportunity for an allied attack by sea. In 1704 Zuñiga's report of Carolinian aggression had inspired orders to his successor Arriola, to prepare a plan in concert with the captain general of Havana for the 'extermination of those enemies and the capture of Carolina.'[46] But the initiative apparently came from the French, who saw as clearly as Moore and Quary that through Florida the English were striking at the French control of the West. As early as 1702 Iberville had endorsed a project for a land attack upon South Carolina; in March, 1703, Jérôme Phélypeaux de Ponchartrain agreed that the St. Augustine expedition menaced Louisiana and that the Carolina settlements must be destroyed. After the Apalache campaign the French ambassador to Spain was instructed to

[42] Thomas Welch, petition to Lords Proprietors, December 4, 1708 (MS in Huntington Library).
[43] Margry (ed.), *Découvertes*, V. 457, 460; Swanton, *Early History*, p. 124.
[44] Arch. Nat., col. C[13] A 2, ff. 95, 407.
[45] La Harpe, Journal historique, August 25, October 20, 1706; Pénicaut, in Margry (ed.), *Découvertes*, V. 483.
[46] See, for instance, instructions of June 20, 1671, and March 10, 1704; also Zendoya to the King, March 21, 1672, in Brooks transcripts, Library of Congress; Arch. Nat., col. C[13] A 1, ff. 445-8; Margry (ed.), *Découvertes*, IV. 622.

secure the necessary Spanish coöperation. In August, 1705, Iberville signed a contract with Louis for the use of certain royal ships.[47] Rumors of the intended attack led Johnson to fortify Charles Town and to secure a new act for the organization of the militia and the hiring of lookouts on the coast.[48] When the blow fell, therefore, in August, 1706, the province was adequately prepared. The enemy fleet was composed of five French privateers, reinforced by Spanish troops from Havana and St. Augustine. The attack was badly managed. Though yellow fever was raging in the colony, the militia and the friendly Indians gave a good account of themselves. The landing parties near Charles Town and Sewee were speedily repulsed, some two hundred and thirty prisoners were taken, and Colonel William Rhett with an improvised fleet drove off the French squadron.[49]

At intervals during the war other alarms of invasion were raised, notably in 1708 and 1709. These led to a further development of the provincial system of defense. Scout-boats cruised from Stono to Port Royal and southward to St. Augustine.[50] Special measures were taken to incorporate the Indians into the military organization. Besides the regular militia, wrote a Carolinian, 'English Officers are appointed over the Indians with whom we are in Friendship, who are order'd, with the utmost Expedition, to draw them down to the Sea-coast, upon the first News of an Allarm. This,' he added, 'is reckon'd a very considerable Part of our Strength.'[51] Nor were these native auxiliaries composed only of the Cusabo and other settlement Indians. In April, 1709, when an attack was feared, prepara-

[47] Arch. Nat., col. C[11] A 20, f. 224; Marine, B[2], 167, f. 523; 182, f. 245; 183, ff. 47, 441; 187, f. 518; B[4], 29, f. 213; Affaires étrangères, Espagne, 153, ff. 97, 365; 154, f. 96; 163, f. 129.
[48] Cooper (ed.), Statutes, II. 227; McCord (ed.), Statutes, IX. 617.
[49] The official account is in C.O. 5:382, no. 10. See narratives in Rivers, Sketch, pp. 210-14, and McCrady, S. C. under the Prop. Gov., pp. 396-401.
[50] An act of July 5, 1707, named Thomas Nairne to appoint two watches southward. Six other watches were provided; all employed whites and Indians. Warning guns were to be set up on Nairne's and other border plantations. By later acts of 1707 and 1710 the watches were increased and then reduced. A law of December 18, 1713, established two scout-boats, one to cruise from Port Royal to St. Augustine, manned by two whites and three Indians; the other to cruise from Stono to Port Royal. See Cooper (ed.), Statutes, II. 300-2, 319, 354-7, 607.
[51] Letter from South Carolina, 1710, pp. 31 f.

tions were made for mobilizing one hundred warriors among the Savannah, Apalache, and Yuchi near Savannah Town, as many more among the Cherokee, one hundred and fifty to two hundred among the Lower Creeks, and fifty among the distant Talapoosas and Alabamas.[52] Here was striking evidence of the extent of the Carolinian sphere of influence.

Hitherto the Indian forces of Carolina had been employed almost solely for raids upon enemy Indians. But after the affair at Charles Town in 1706 a new policy of attack was inaugurated, aimed at the centres of French and Spanish power in the Southwest. Though the results fell short of the goal, there was revealed an aggressive, expansionist spirit in South Carolina not without interest in the rise of Anglo-American imperialism.

In the summer of 1707, Bienville was warned by the Indians that the English were mobilizing all of their tribes, this time 'pour manger un village de blancs.' He learned from prisoners captured by a Tohome scouting party that the immediate objective was Pensacola, but that after that post was destroyed an attack was intended upon Mobile. Bienville undertook to put the governor of Pensacola on his guard, but with little success, for a few days later the Spanish town was suddenly attacked. Led by a few Englishmen, a band of several hundred Talapoosas burned and pillaged the houses right up to the fort, which, indeed, they had actually entered before the Spanish rallied to repel them. Eleven Spaniards were killed, fifteen captured, and a dozen slaves carried away as the enemy retired to their base among the Upper Creeks. Again raiders from Mobile brought in accounts of preparations against Pensacola, excited rumors of a hundred English and Huguenots come on horseback to lead a thousand Indians against the Spanish outpost. In November, indeed, Pensacola was once more invested. But dissensions arose, and three-fourths of the besieging force deserted. When Bienville appeared with relief, December 8, the remnant, thirteen Englishmen and three hundred and fifty Indians, had already retired. Bienville had acted with wonted energy. But from Pensacola he met with reproach for having withdrawn the Indians of that region to Mobile.[53]

[52] JCHA, April 21, 23, 28, 30, 1709.
[53] Arch. Nat., col. C¹³ A 2, ff. 89, 95-99; La Harpe, Journal historique, August 25, November 16, 24, 1707.

Already the Carolinians were aiming at a more difficult prize: at Mobile, the key to the control of the eastern Gulf region and the lower Mississippi. All of Bienville's finesse, all his knowledge of wilderness intrigue, were soon in requisition to preserve Louisiana.

The program for this greater western campaign was adopted by the assembly in the autumn of 1707. It had been formulated by Thomas Welch, the veteran Chickasaw trader, and by Thomas Nairne, the provincial Indian agent.[54] To regulate the abuses of the Indian trade an act had been passed in July, 1707, after long agitation and a sharp conflict between Johnson and the assembly. Nairne was the obvious choice of the assembly for the new Indian agency, for the first time established as a regular provincial office. A planter at St. Helena on the southern border, he was specially qualified by long experience with the neighboring Yamasee and as a partizan leader in the Florida campaigns. Unfortunately, he had won the bitter enmity of the governor by his prominence as a leader of the country party in the controversies of the time over the church act, the appointment of the public receiver, and the regulation of the Indian trade under exclusive control of the assembly.[55]

Though South Carolina was torn by factions in 1707, seemingly there was no difference of opinion as to the 'absolute Necessity' that the French 'should be removed.' These were the words of a resolution of both houses in conference in November.[56] The attack on Charles Town, and now rumors from the West Indies of an impending new invasion with the aid of the French Indians near Mobile,[57] made action imperative. Anticipating an early peace, Johnson favored an immediate assault upon Mobile.[58] But Welch and Nairne counselled the Commons House that first of all the most formidable of the French allies, the Choctaw and the Yazoo, must be won over to the English side, or to neutrality.

Nairne's project was to raise a small force of volunteers among the Indian traders, and to assemble at the Upper Creeks

[54] JCHA, October 23, 28, November 1, 22, 1707.
[55] See below, pp. 145-9.
[56] JCHA, November 7, 1707.
[57] Ibid., October 27, 1707, information from a shipmaster recently from St. Thomas.
[58] Ibid., November 7, 1707.

a much larger army of Indians. Captain Welch and Captain Jones, traders, were designated his lieutenants.[59] 'My design,' Nairne afterwards wrote, 'was to fall down from the Talapoosies against the French with a fleet of Eighty Canoes man'd with 500 Indians and 1000 by land, 15 English on the one part and 36 with the other. With these forces I pretended Either to destroy or remove into our Territory all the Salvages from Mobile to the Mississippi, and up the river to 36 Degrees of Latitude.' Thus he hoped to reduce Fort St. Louis, or in any case to destroy the Indian system of Mobile and thereby its trade. 'I design'd to Invite by fair means all that would accept of our friendship, upon the Terms of Subjecting themselves to our government and removeing into our territory,' he continued, 'and quite to ruine such as wo[u]ld not, soe that the French might never be in a Capacity to raise an Indian Army to Disturb us or our Allies; and that the Lower parts of the Mississipi, being left Desolate, the trade of the uper might fall to this province by means of factories, Setled on Cussate [Tennessee] river.'[60] The location of one such factory Nairne indicated on his map at a 'low riff of rocks,' the Muscle Shoals.[61] The route of Couture and of Bellefeuille would thus become the principal route of English trading expansion into the West, and the French program of encirclement would be defeated.

Nairne was a visionary, perhaps, but he was also a man of action. In the spring of 1708—this was his own boast—he ventured his life and made a peace with the Choctaws.[62] Welch meanwhile summoned a council at the Yazoo of the principal river tribes, Yazoo, Arkansas, Tourima, Taënsa, Natchez, and Koroa, with like results.[63] Welch seems also to have contemplated a mission to the Illinois. The sum of £100 in presents

[59] Ibid., November 7, 22, 1707. The men were 'to have £5 in hand and £15 on return,' the commanders more, but plunder should be equally divided between officers and men.

[60] C.O. 5:382, no. 11 (Nairne's memorial of July 10, 1708).

[61] Crisp, A Compleat Description [1711?], Nairne inset.

[62] Nairne, doc. cit. Cf. Bienville to the minister, October 12, 1708, in Arch. Nat., col. C[13] A 2, ff. 168 et seq., and 177-92.

[63] Ibid. Cf. JCHA, December 10, 1708, for petition of Welch, and order on public receiver to pay him £80 'for making a peace with the Yasaws and Cophtas [Quapaws?] and a further reward promised by the House when he hath Removed them to the Cusawte River.'

for which Nairne had asked had been increased by the assembly to nearly £250.[64] Such liberality had its effect, coupled with English sneers at the French as 'the fugitive remnants of a nation destroyed by the English.' Just how far Nairne and Welch were able to carry the intrigue is not quite certain. Bienville reported to Ponchartrain that the Indians, while admitting the Carolinians with their presents and trading goods, refused either to aid or sanction the attack on Mobile. But immediately he set to work to enlarge the stockade at Mobile as a refuge for the neighboring tribes, and sent Chateaugué to restore peace between the Choctaw and the Chickasaw. He even appealed to Pensacola and to the viceroy of New Spain for powder and trading goods. The commissary, D'Artaguiette, was filled with gloom. 'Les Sauvages,' he reminded Ponchartrain, 'sont à qui plus leur donne.'[65]

Though Bienville's diplomacy had checked the western enterprise, apparently it would have been renewed but for developments in Carolina. If there was fear in Louisiana in the spring of 1708, there was also apprehension in the English colony. Strange portents had been observed. On the Louisiana border, Indians recounted, 'there fell a Shower of Blood, in which they walk'd up to their Ankles.' At Edisto and in the 'Indian Land' near Port Royal had been heard the firing of ghostly guns. Then came an account from Jamaica that the Spanish and French were raising a large force supposedly for a second attempt upon Charles Town. It was this alarm, confirmed by reports from St. Augustine, which 'put a full stop,' Nairne said, to the Mobile expedition. An embargo was laid at Charles Town, and preparations were pressed for defense. The provincial militia was strengthened by a force of negro cattle-hunters, and Nairne's army of fifteen hundred Indians was held in reserve to meet the expected invasion.[66]

[64] Ibid., November 22, 1707.
[65] See references in note 62; and also D'Artaguiette to the minister, August 18 and October 1, 1708, in Arch. Nat., col. C[13] A 2, ff. 328 f., 341-8; Charlevoix, *Histoire et description générale de la Nouvelle France*, Paris, 1744, IV. 41 f.
[66] Nairne, *doc. cit. Boston News Letter*, May 24, 1708; ibid., May 31, 1708, after mention of the Mobile project, quoted from letters from Dorchester, S. C., of April 7, that 'our agent that manages the Indian Trade has sent word that 1400 Indians offer their Service, but it is not yet put in execution.'

Meanwhile, Nairne continued his diplomatic manoeuvres until his arrest, the culmination of his feud with Sir Nathaniel Johnson, brought confusion upon the whole ambitious western campaign. June 23, 1708, the Indian agent was clapped into Charles Town jail upon a mittimus and languished there for over five months. He was charged by Johnson with no less a crime than 'High Treason in Endeavouring to disinherit and Dethrone our Rightfull and Lawfull Sovereigne Lady Queen Ann, and to place in her Room the pretended Prince of Wales.'[67] Nairne spent his imprisonment composing vigorous petitions to the Proprietors, the Secretary of State, and the Crown to prove that he was the victim of a singularly tyrannical persecution on personal and political grounds.[68] The amazing charge of treason was based on no overt act, but upon garbled expressions attributed to Nairne by a couple of rogues in employ of Colonel Broughton, Johnson's son-in-law and a magnate of the Indian trade. Broughton was particularly aggrieved, Nairne asserted, because he, as Indian agent, had interfered with the enslaving of friendly Indians. Nairne's interference with the governor's perquisites in Indian presents was also a factor. The treason charge stopped *habeas corpus* proceedings, nor could Nairne secure his freedom on bail. Late in November he was apparently released to take his oath as a member of the assembly, but at Johnson's insistence he was not allowed to sit.[69] The case was never brought to trial. In December the Lords Proprietors, possibly in view of Nairne's complaints, decided to remove Johnson from office.[70] In 1710 Nairne went to England and was soon taken into the favor of the Proprietors.[71] But meanwhile he had lost his Indian agency, and his great Louisiana project had come to nought.

[67] Mittimus signed by Johnson, June 24, 1708 (photostat from MS in Huntington Library).

[68] C.O. 5:306, no. 4. Also petitions to the Secretary, the Proprietors, and the Queen, accompanied by depositions, petition of sixty-two inhabitants of Colleton county for Nairne's release, etc. (photostats from manuscripts in Huntington Library). See, too, JCHA, November 28, 1707.

[69] See JCHA, November 25, 31, December 3, 9, 10, 11, 1708; and April 27-29, 1709, for Nairne's exclusion, his clash with the assembly over the sending of his map to England, and his discharge as agent.

[70] C.O. 5:292, p. 5; see also ibid., p. 15.

[71] Ibid., pp. 34, 44, 46. Nairne was nominated to the Admiralty as judge-advocate for South Carolina. It was probably at this time that he wrote, or supplied the data for, the tract, *A Letter from South Carolina*, 1710.

Nairne, however, had not surrendered those sanguine hopes of English empire in the Southwest which had been, perhaps, the talk of the camp in 1702 in his first campaign with that other notable Carolinian expansionist, James Moore. From Charles Town jail Nairne sent home to the Secretary of State one of the most remarkable documents in the history of Anglo-American frontier 'imperialism.' By this memorial of July 10, 1708,[72] Nairne sought to create an essential condition for future efforts to extend English continental dominion: the education of the English colonial authorities in the strategy of the southern frontier. Only South Carolina, he insisted, 'by trading and other Management,' could put a check to French aggrandizement at the expense of the English colonies on the one hand, and of New Mexico on the other. 'A Consequence of this is that this province being a frontier, both against the French and the Spaniard, ought not to be Neglected.' But neglected it had been by the Proprietors, and already men of Nairne's stamp were looking toward royal government as the hope of Carolina. His western design was described, and the importance of posts along the Tennessee River trade-route as a means of diverting the fur trade of the Northwest was made clear. This was a full decade before Spotswood's suggestion of a fort on Lake Erie, and two years before the Virginia governor developed his fantastic scheme for projecting settlement westward along the James River. The strategic location of the Cherokee, 'now entirely Subject to us . . . our only defence on the Back parts,' raised the question of their protection against the northern raids. Instructions should go to the governors of Maryland and New York to interpose with the Iroquois. 'All parts of the English Dominions,' he wrote, 'ought mutually to Espouse one another's interest in Everything that relates to the Common defense against the French and their party.' With the memorial Nairne submitted a map[73] based upon his own travels and observations 'to the End your noble Lordship may at one View perceive what part of the Continent

---

[72] C.O. 5:382 (11).

[73] Apparently not extant, though the 'tradition' appears in Moll's map of 1715, and in a large manuscript map belonging to the Board of Trade (C.O. Maps, N.A.C. General, 7). For a reference to Nairne's map in 1728 see C.O. 5:360, C 22. See also London *Daily Journal*, October 14, 1730, for a criticism of Nairne's enumeration of the Cherokee.

we are now possest off, and what not, and procure the Articles of peace, to be formed in such a manner that the English American Empire may not be unreasonably Crampt up.' In the negotiations to come due weight should be given to the western claims of South Carolina, which Nairne, ignoring the charters, confidently based upon her long-established Indian trade. The English should therefore insist at the peace upon the surrender of Mobile.

Among other expedients to strengthen the southern frontier, Nairne discussed colonization in the spacious tone of an explorer who had 'had a personall view of most off those parts.' If England could spare colonists it would be best to strengthen the South Carolina border. But 'if an Inclination to Setle any Place to the Eastward of the Mississipi should prevaile,' he urged that 'the old Country of the Apalachias is the only best.' 'This place,' he added, 'wo[u]ld be proper for the seat of a government to take in the Neck of Florida, and 100 miles to the westward along the Bay.' Another possibility was to settle in force a little way west of the Mississippi, conciliate the Indians, develop the logwood trade with Campeche and an underground Spanish commerce, and perchance at some favorable juncture, strike boldly at the Spanish mine-country.

In this grandiose scheme Nairne's imagination carried him beyond the vision of his generation. But certain elements of his program persisted, to be incorporated (1720-1721) in the first statements of British western policy. The successor of Blake and Moore as the organizer of Carolinian expansion, Nairne was also in some sense the forerunner of Montgomery and of Oglethorpe. Through the agency of his neighbor and friend, John Barnwell, his doctrines at length found a hearing in Whitehall. But in the interval a destructive Indian war, of which Nairne himself was the first victim, had imperilled the results of three decades of western expansion.

The vendetta of Johnson and his group against Nairne had most unfortunate results in the West. The campaign of 1708 collapsed, and for several years the frontier policy of the provincial government lacked the aggressive character that Nairne, like Blake and Moore, had imparted to it. Not until January, 1711, was 'the affair of Mobile' once more made the extraordinary business of the assembly. Then for some weeks an attempt against the French was the subject of debates and conferences. The Commons House, though at first disposed to strike, again postponed the enterprise, at the same time pressing for reform of the Indian trading regulations.[74] In May, the governor also recognized the vital interrelation of these matters when he urged a better regulation in order to secure Indian aid to oust the French from the Southwest.[75] Disgruntled customers of cheating traders made dubious allies against Louisiana. Under the combined strains of maladroit management, the licentious conduct of the traders, and the skillful diplomacy of Bienville, the South Carolina Indian system was beginning to show ominous signs of weakness. The first break occurred in 1712, when the French succeeded in making peace with the Alabama Indians. The mismanagement of his successor, Nairne charged, was the 'true cause of the Alabamas deserting to Mobile.'[76]

But already the Carolinians, alarmed by the 'apparent danger . . . from the conjunction of . . . the Choctaws and Chickisaws,'[77] which Bienville continued to promote, had resumed their western offensive. Although the province was engaged at the time in helping to suppress the troublesome Tuscarora rising in North Carolina, energy remained for the prosecution of the Indian trade and for the vigorous renewal of the partizan warfare which was the characteristic method of the Carolinian advance. In May, 1711, the Choctaw-Chickasaw feud was reopened, 'à l'instigation des anglais,' La Harpe recorded.[78] To forestall further French efforts in that direction in June the assembly prepared an expedition intended to ruin the great Choctaw nation utterly, and so destroy the bulwark of Louisiana. Commissions were issued to Captain Theophilus Hastings, appointed to lead the Creeks, and to the Emperor Brims of Coweta. Thomas Welch was also named a captain to lead a supporting body of Chickasaw. Two thousand Indians were expected to join the expedition. Supplies in the propor-

[74] JCHA, January 26, February 8, 9, 10, 24, 1710/11.
[75] Ibid., May 15, 1711.
[76] Journal of the Indian Commissioners (hereinafter cited as JIC), August 18, 1713.
[77] JCHA, June 20, 21, 1711.
[78] La Harpe, Journal historique, May, 1711.

tion of one pound of shot and two pounds of powder for each gunman were ordered sent up from Savannah Town to the rendezvous at the Alabamas. Actually, Hastings was able in the fall to assemble some thirteen hundred Creeks, three hundred of them bowmen. With Hastings and Brims this army marched through the populous Choctaw towns, burning, killing, taking prisoners. Four hundred 'Houses and Plantations,' it was reported, were put to the torch. The Choctaw, however, had not been taken by surprise; their resistance was feeble, but most escaped. Hastings killed but eighty Choctaw and carried off about one hundred and thirty prisoners. Welch, with only two hundred Chickasaw, was reported to have done equal damage. Had his own Indian allies 'been governable, and not run upon their Enemies at first without command,' Hastings believed the Choctaw would have 'met with a fatal blow.'[79] Even so, the year was one of achievement for the frontier forces of Carolina. Pensacola was again attacked from the north.[80] John Barnwell, reporting the success of his North Carolina expedition in February, 1712, congratulated Governor Craven on the 'hon'r and Glory of virtuous South Carolina whose armies are the same winter gathering Laurells from the Cape Florida and from the Bay of Spiritta Sancta even to the Borders of Virginia.[81] English prestige seemed again in the ascendant; it was significant that the wily Brims, politician-extraordinary among the Creeks, promised soon to wait on the governor at Charles Town 'to acknowledge his Loyalty and Obedience to the British Nation.'[82]

To Bienville it was apparent in the spring of 1712 that another crisis, like that of 1708, had arrived. From an escaped French prisoner he learned that at Charles Town preparations were going forward for war by land and sea. Seven brigantines and an armed ship were reported fitting out; and the colonists boasted that these vessels would capture Mobile and Pensacola. His informant had been closely examined by the Carolinians regarding the loyalty of the French Indians and of the Louisi-

[79] JCHA, June 20, 21, 22, 1711; May 24, 1712. *Boston News Letter*, March 31, 1712.
[80] Bolton and Ross, *The Debatable Land*, pp. 62 f. and note.
[81] *SCHGM*, IX, 36. Heinrich, *La Louisiane*, pp. liv-lv, is certainly in error in ascribing the offensives of 1712 to the initiative of Spotswood.
[82] *Boston News Letter*, March 31, 1712.

ana garrison. A Canadian, moreover, who had been held prisoner among the Alabamas, told of three hundred *pirogues* assembled at their village, but five days' journey to Fort St. Louis. All the English allies were said to be mobilizing at the bidding of the traders; they expected at any moment to receive their presents from the governor of Carolina. Confirmation came with each Indian prisoner brought in from the English border. 'I can only assure your highness,' Bienville reported to the minister in March, 'that I am taking every measure to prevent the success of this enterprise.'[83]

Bienville's essential genius for forest diplomacy was again revealed in this emergency. The Alabama held the key to the Mobile border; the Alabama must be won over to the French. Bienville was equal to the task. 'At the end of the same month [March],' wrote La Harpe, 'M. de Bienville granted peace to the Alabamas, the Abihkas, and to other nations of Carolina, and made peace between them and our allies, so that there was a general peace among the savages.'[84] On the eve of the European settlement Iberville's system was restored in the Southwest.

The peace of 1713, following closely upon this triumph of Bienville in Indian negotiation, disappointed Carolinian hopes that the French 'intrusion' into Louisiana, and with it the menace of encirclement, would be brought to an end. The Lords Proprietors, though they had done nothing to support their colonists in the field, in March, 1712, petitioned the Board of Trade that Spanish and French encroachments might 'be re-mov'd at this Treaty of Peace.'[85] At Utrecht, however, the boundaries in the West were left undefined, except by implication in Article XV of the treaty of peace and friendship between the crowns of France and Great Britain.[86] The French therein promised not to molest the Five Nations, 'soûmis à la Grande Bretagne'; and this pledge extended also to 'les autres Nations de l'Amérique, amies de cette Couronne.' At the same time the English promised to deal peacefully with the Indians

[83] Arch. Nat., col. C[13] A 2, ff. 691-695.
[84] La Harpe, Journal historique, March, 1712.
[85] C.O. 5:292, p. 57.
[86] Dumont (ed.), *Corps diplomatique,* VIII. 341. See Heinrich, *La Louisiane,* p. lv and note.

who were subjects or friends of the French. But which tribes should be attributed to either crown was left for later regulation by commissioners. In the South the events of the next two years revealed that the English colonists would press their claims to the utmost under this article. The French at Mobile found the English of Charles Town quite as uncomfortable neighbors in peace as in war. In vain La Mothe Cadillac invited Governor Craven to coöperate in extending the general peace to the southern Indians, English and French alike, to withdraw his traders from the tribes that had traded first with the French, and to comply with the spirit of the peace by preventing those traders from instigating slave-catching raids among the French allies.[87] After 1713 there was no longer question of an attack upon Mobile, but in Indian politics and in partizan warfare the two years ending in 1715 marked the climax of the first English effort to displace the French in the Mississippi valley.

In Louisiana a bitter quarrel had developed between Bienville and the new governor, Cadillac. Bienville and his friends laid the rift to jealousy of his hold over the Indians and the garrison troops. Cadillac, they asserted, by his hauteur had alienated all of the tribes.[88] Certain it is that fourteen or more of the élite of the garrison soon took the path to Charles Town, and that everywhere the Indians welcomed the Carolinians again to their villages. While factions intrigued at Mobile, factionalism in South Carolina was abated. The new governor, Charles Craven, was popular and energetic. In November, 1712, Thomas Nairne had been restored to the principal Indian agency, and had promptly won the praise of the Indian commissioners for 'capacity and diligence' displayed in negotiations with the western tribes. In 1713 he sent goods among the Choctaw, seeking to renew the relations he had established in 1707 with this all-important tribe.[89] The French countered with a council at Mobile (December, 1713), when many of the Choctaw, it was said, were brought to reject the proposals of the English.[90]

[87] Arch. Nat., col. C¹³, A 3, ff. 489-92, 530.
[88] Ibid., ff. 272, 784 f.; La Harpe, Journal historique, 1713.
[89] JIC., June 10, 1712; July 17, 1713. JCHA, November 27, 1712, December 18, 1713.
[90] La Harpe, Journal historique, December 10, 1713.

It was another than Nairne, however, who was made the active director of the new enterprise for the conversion of all the southern Indians to the English trade and alliance. Recently there had arrived in South Carolina a Welsh gentleman of property and connections in Montgomeryshire, Price Hughes, Esq. He had come over to promote a scheme of Welsh colonization, possibly inspired by the visit to England in 1710 of Thomas Nairne, whom he had described in a letter, prior to emigrating, as his 'good friend.' Certainly Nairne had materially assisted his brother, Valentine Hughes, and the Welsh servants whom he had sent out before him to Carolina. Valentine had died in 1712, and on his own arrival Price Hughes had been disappointed in the lands acquired for the settlement at Port Royal, and had dispersed his servants. In 1714 he received another grant of 3,184 acres in Craven county.[91]

But already his ambition had fixed upon another career than that of a patriarchal tide-water planter. Upon him, as upon Nairne, the great West had cast its spell. 'An English Gent., who had a particular fancy of rambling among the Indians'— such was the character given him by Spotswood of Virginia. By testimony of Cadillac, 'il etoit ingénieur, et géographe,' and, moreover, 'homme d'esprit.'[92] With his adventurous tastes Hughes was soon drawn into the provincial service as a volunteer Indian diplomat. In consequence of his western travels he transformed and expanded his settlement plan into an amazing project for a new British province in the lower Mississippi valley. His assassination in Louisiana in 1715 brought unmerited oblivion to his name and his enterprises. For surely Price Hughes was an authentic prophet of Anglo-American westward expansion.

In the spring of 1713 it was thought that the French had 'a design to tamper with the Cherokees,' and shortly Hughes was in the mountain country, sending down intelligence by the traders to the Indian commissioners.[93] 'Our fears here of the

[91] The will of 'Pryce Hughes of Kavllygan, Montgomery, gent.,' dated February 28, 1711/12, and proved June 27, 1719, is in *SCHGM,* V. 221. See also C.O. 5:398, p. 53 (land grant); and letters of Hughes to Dr. Charles Noble, [n.d.], to Thomas Nairne, [n.d.], and John Jones, [*circa* October, 1713], MSS in possession of Maggs Brothers, London.
[92] Spotswood, *Letters,* II. 331; Arch. Nat., col. C[13] A 4, ff. 521 f.
[93] JIC, May 14, August 19, November 31, 1713.

growing Interest of the French makes us redouble our industry,' he wrote on his return, praising the new governor,
Charles Craven, for his encouragement of all projects for cap-
turing the Indian trade of the West. Such a scheme Hughes
had already concocted. On the Tennessee River, he reported,
he had met two Frenchmen from Canada and Mobile, secured
their release from their Indian captors, supplied them with a
cargo, and with the governor's permission despatched them to
the Illinois and to 'seven numerous nations' on the Missouri
River. 'God knows,' he remarked, 'what the effect of so distant
an embassy will be.'[94] Thus were inaugurated those far-reaching intrigues among the western tribes which in the next year
and a half made the name of 'master You' respected and feared
throughout Louisiana. His goal was the capture of the Mississippi fur trade and the closing of the river highway between
Canada and Louisiana.

This was, of course, in essence the old program of Blake,
of Moore, of Nairne, the logical sequel, moreover, of the policy
preached by Nicholson and Bellomont. Nairne, too, had discussed western planting as a supplement to Carolinian trade.
But it remained for Hughes, who held that colonies in the
interior were essential to primacy in the peltry trade, to elaborate the first concrete British plan of the eighteenth century
for trans-Appalachian settlement.

Hughes was an observing traveller; he returned to Charles
Town from his first inland tour intoxicated by what he had
seen. 'This Summer,' he wrote to his brother-in-law at home,[95]
'I've been a considerable way to the Westwd. upon the
branches of the Mesisipi, where I saw a country as different
from Carolina as the best parts of our country are from the
fens of Lincolnshire.' The natives he described as friendly, the
land as abounding 'with many fine navigable Rivers, pleasant
Savannahs, plenty of coal, lead, iron, lime and freestone wth.
several salt springs; a th[o]rough intermixture of Hills and
Vales and as fine timber as the largest I ever saw in England.'
'There's no land in America now left y'ts worth anything,' he

[94] Hughes to the Duchess of Ormonde, Charles [Town], October 15,
1713, MS in possession of Maggs Brothers.
[95] Hughes to 'Bro. [John] Jones,' [circa October, 1713], MS in possession
of Maggs Brothers.

declared roundly, 'but what's on the Mesisipi.' Thither he was now determined to lead the great numbers of Welshmen who, he believed, would come over to Carolina at his bidding. 'If they refuse,' he charged his correspondent, John Jones, 'tell them I let them starve for timorous drones. It was on their account I and my brother came over.' At first only adults should be sent, especially men able to march overland to the colony. Bristol was named as the port of embarkation. From his friends in Wales he selected leaders to assemble the colonists and advance the funds. But the enterprise, he knew, must be upon a national footing. A ship, tools, supplies were required; permission must be had to transport poor colonists, for Hughes disclaimed an intention to rob the country of others, and at least the tacit support of the Crown in what might be made to appear an intrusion into the French dominions in America.

These requests Hughes incorporated into a petition to be presented to the Queen;[96] and from Charles Town he set hopefully to work to create an interest at court. The Duchess of Powis was his friend; through her Jones was advised to cultivate the Duchess of Ormonde, the wife of that great personage the Captain-General in Flanders,[97] and thus gain access to the Queen. In letters to Jones and the Duchess of Ormonde written in October, 1713,[98] Hughes developed his plan. The Queen, he argued, could not better bestow her charity than in aiding the great numbers of poor in Wales who should begin the settlement. 'But I hope that the secureing so fine and spacious a countrey to her Crown will clearly out ballance so small a Charge, and be a lasting fund for the settling poor Familyes hereafter.' The support furnished by Louis XIV to Louisiana was held up for her emulation. 'The French King has given the utmost encouragement to his Colony at Movile. 'Tis he that sends over settlers thither and in a manner bestows the carriage of all the goods. Besides this (to his immortal memory be it spoken) he maintains Missionaryes.' At the same time he recalled the barbarities of the French 'to the New England men.' To prevent 'the like fate here . . . can be done no other-

---

[96] Apparently not extant; described in letters cited in notes 94, 95.
[97] *Dictionary of National Biography*, VIII. 60-5.
[98] The quotations that follow are from the latter.

wise than by possessing ourselves of those vacant parts of this Province: which they will otherwise so soon be Masters off.'

Herein nothing shall be done that's contrary to the Law of nations & the general rights of Mankind. We'le not encroach upon the acquisitions of the French; but in an industrious way seek an honest Settlement in those parts we've allready fixt upon to that purpose: unless our delays will Suffer them when sensible of our designs to slip in before us, wch otherwise they do not for some time design.

We have several traders on the Mesisipi & its branches; & the settlement which the French have at Movile is ab[ou]t 120 miles to the Eastward of the place we have fixt upon [i.e., Natchez or Yazoo?].[99] A great part of both the Rivers [Alabama and Mississippi] we are allready possest off as we were long before the French settled at the mouths thereof. So that they are but encroachers at best. As to what they pretend of being the first discoverers of those parts I flatly deny it; & can prove what I would otherwise assert w[i]th undeniable Reasons. But if some huffing Memorial like what the Spanish Ambassadour gave King William against the Scots (at Darien) should be offerd: her Majesty I hope will give us leave to argue the matter fairly according to the Law of Nations & we desire no more. But in the mean time let this settlement go on least they Supplant us not only in it but in our Trade.

The French when sensible of our designs will probably send some settlers to our neighborhood from Movile. But probably they'le be little the better for it when we have a precedent title both by claim and possession. If the English think proper to follow their garbe at home: the Britains I believe will not be Subject to their Prescriptions in America, Having as yet some little of our old courage as well as discretion left.

None of the Carolinians had asserted more boldly their western claims, based upon the pioneer exploits of their traders. Hughes apparently expected to dispute with the French the navigation of the Mississippi; though the first settlers should go overland 'to the place designed for a town near the mouth of the Messisipi to erect magazines of corn and provisions,' future colonists would be sent round by sea.[100] Like Nairne

---

[99] In the letter to Jones, Hughes referred to an accompanying map: 'Where the Messisipi divides you see I've markt on the places designd for a town.' Unfortunately this does not appear on Spotswood's copy of the Hughes map (C.O. Maps, N.A.C. Virginia, 2). But from various indications it could not have been farther north than the Yazoo.

[100] Hughes to Jones.

he foresaw expansion west of the great river; he advised that the mines be kept unpatented, 'for such assuredly there are the other side the Mesisipi: the Indians having brought me pieces of oar from two Several mines they discoverd to me.' Her Majesty, too, should 'keep that colony in her own hands & not grant it to any body. It may indeed for some time yet pass under the name & government of Carolina; but with the leave of the Honourable Persons owners of that Province, as well as of the King of France who has styld that part of it Louisania, I'le make bold to give it the worthyer name of A n n a r e a in honour of her Majesty through whose bounty 'twill I hope be settled.'[101]

Though nothing came of this forgotten project of western empire, the scheme was not altogether chimerical. Certainly it was significant of the exuberant 'imperialism' which Hughes had so soon absorbed in Carolina, perhaps from his Port Royal neighbors, John Barnwell, and those other memorialists of frontier expansion, Thomas Nairne and John Stewart.[102] Probably nowhere else in America at the time was there a group comparable to this circle of southern border planters in their aggressive ideas of English western policy.

Expansion of English colonization as well as of English trade supplied, then, a motive for the extraordinary activities of Hughes in the West from 1713 to 1715.[103] As a result of his efforts, in coöperation with the traders, new factories were established, a firmer league was formed with the Chickasaw, and even the Choctaw, except two loyal villages, were persuaded to desert the French alliance. On the Mississippi his intrigue embraced the tribes from the Illinois to the Red River and the Gulf. In November, 1713, the Indian commissioners 'ordered that Mr. Hughs have all possible Incouragement given him in his design'd Journey and that a Letter be writt to the

[101] Hughes to Duchess of Ormond. In this letter Hughes also gave an account of the Cherokee Indians, who 'desr'd me to send that good Woman (for so they styl'd her) [Queen Anne] a present from them viz a large carpet made of mulberry bark for herself to sit on and twelve small ones for her Counsellours.'

[102] Arch. Nat., col. C^{13e}, 1, f. 80; 2, ff. 76, 82.

[103] In June, 1714, when the Commons House planned to revise the Indian act, the bill was referred to Hughes, a non-member, as a sort of special commissioner. He was consulted as to the proper amount of a present to a delegation of Chickasaw Indians; and in the matter of Francis Riall, a French deserter among the Alabamas (JCHA, June 8, 12, 1714, et passim).

Agent accordingly.'[104] Soon the French were aware that a new energy had been infused into the Carolinian policy. In April, 1714, led by a dozen Englishmen, a great army of Indians, reported to be two thousand fighting men—Alabamas, Abihkas, Talapoosas, and Chickasaws—descended upon the Choctaw, not, as in 1711, to destroy them, but to impose peace and trade with South Carolina. Four pack-horses, declared Cadillac, staggered under the weight of their presents. Only two towns, Conchaqué and Tchicachaé, dared, or cared, to hold out, and these loyalists were forced to flee their stockade in the night to the shelter of Fort St. Louis. Of the Mississippi River Indians, the Yazoo had long inclined towards the English, and now the Natchez as well admitted Carolina traders to their villages, and joined in raids upon the weaker tribes downstream. Cadillac, complaining to Governor Craven in July, 1714, of a recent Natchez attack upon the Chawasha, wrote in horror of 'ces anglois trafiquants de chair humaine.' While the Cherokee were endeavouring to convert the Illinois to the English trade, Hughes and the Carolinians on the Mississippi were intriguing with the French *voyageurs* to the same end. In Canada the letters of the Illinois missionaries raised an alarm that the Carolinians planned to establish a post on the Ohio and draw to them the Indian trade as far as the Great Lakes. From Ramesay and Begon as well as from Cadillac, Ponchartrain learned that a new crisis had arrived in the West. When Hughes in June, 1714, returned again to Charles Town with a party of Chickasaw chiefs who came down to ratify their alliance and accept presents, it was evident that the grand design was already well in train. 'En un mot,' wrote Cadillac in desperation, 'les anglois n'epargnent rien pour mettre tous nos sauvages dans leur parti, ce qui sera bien difficile d'empescher.'[105]

The winter of 1714-1715 witnessed the climax of the enter-

[104] JIC, November 31, 1713.

[105] JCHA, December 16, 1714. Cadillac to the governor of South Carolina, March 20, June 3, July 14, 1714, in Arch. Nat., col. C[13] A 3, ff. 489-92. Cadillac to the minister, September 18, 1714, ibid., pp. 518-22. La Harpe, Journal historique, 1713, April, 1714. Pénicaut, in Margry (ed.), *Découvertes,* V. 507, 519; Richebourg, Mémoire, in B. F. French (ed.), *Hist. Coll. of La.,* III. 241; F. Le Maire, Mémoire (1717), in *Comptes-rendus de l'Athénée Louisianais,* September-November, 1889, p. 5; *Wis. Hist. Soc. Coll.,* XVI. 303, 318 f., 325 f., 331-3.

prise, and the *débâcle*. The Carolinians, Bienville reported, had magazines among the Alabama and the Choctaw well-stocked with the essential presents; at the Alabamas, he had learned, they were planning to erect a post and place a garrison of fifty men. After visiting all the old centres of trade Price Hughes made his way to the Mississippi. From his base at the Natchez this enterprising 'mylord anglois' planned to visit the tribes of the Red River, and then descend to the mouth of the Mississippi, hoping to win, by presents and trade, the potent instruments of English expansion, the friendship of the Houma, the Bayagoula, the Chawasha and the Acolapissa. His commission from Governor Craven set forth the sweeping claims of the Carolinian expansionists to the Mississippi, and to the country westward as far as the Spanish settlements.

Meanwhile, Cadillac's efforts to oust the English from their hold upon the Choctaw met with dismal failure: the Charles Town traders laughed at the pompous governor of Louisiana and his handful of *coquins*. It was fortunate, perhaps, for Louisiana that this was the moment chosen by Cadillac for his journey to Illinois to discover the mine. In February, 1715, he set out, leaving to the experienced and adroit Bienville the task of saving the colony in its hour of greatest danger. Sealed orders bade him use every effort, and all the presents sent over from France, to drive out the Carolinians. Bienville knew, none better, that the affair required despatch. He saw, wrote La Harpe, that 'without a prompt remedy the colony would fall into the power of the English.' To allay discontent among the chiefs, and perhaps to vent his own spleen, he assured the Indian council that La Mothe was gone, never to return. At his bidding the Choctaw arrested an English trader, and pillaged the magazine of presents destined for the Mississippi tribes. The tide was turning. But it was not until later in the summer, after Hughes had been arrested, and when the whole southern Indian country was aflame against the English traders, that the Choctaw gave final proof of their reconversion, received in peace the two loyalist villages, and sent down to Mobile the head of Oulactichiton, brother of the great chief and prime agent in the reception of the English.[106]

[106] La Harpe, Journal historique, 1715; Arch. Nat., col., C¹³ A 3, ff. 782-5, 827-32; A 4, ff. 237-43, 518-20; Marine, B¹, IX. 271f.; Bibl. Nat., MSS Fr., nouv. acquis., vol. 9301, p. 300.

As Cadillac made his way up the Mississippi, signs had multiplied of the scope, and the success, of Price Hughes's intrigue. To Crozat's *comis* at Natchez, Sieur de la Loir des Ursins, the governor sent an order for the Englishman's arrest. But this required no little caution, in view of the attitude of the Indians toward him. 'We dared not arrest this mylord in the village of the Natchez,' confessed Pénicaut, who delayed his return to Natchitoches to assist in the capture of 'master You.' Drifting down the Mississippi in April, Hughes was shadowed by the *voyageurs* from Natchez to the Tonicas and to Manchac. There he was taken into custody in the name of the French king, protesting vigorously against this indignity in time of peace, and was delivered with his interpreter to Bienville at Mobile. For three days, Pénicaut wrote, Hughes was Bienville's prisoner, treated with every consideration, and then released to find his way back to Carolina.[107]

When Bienville put Hughes upon his examination, a dramatic moment had arrived in the Anglo-French duel for the heart of America. Their talents in wilderness intrigue so nearly matched, the two men as they talked together in the stockade of Fort St. Louis in the spring of 1715 stood for rival forces of empire in irreconcilable conflict. Not since the issues of Anglo-French rivalry had broadened to include control of the West and its trade had two such agents of French and English policy debated face to face. Why, asked Bienville, have you gone about among all our Indians with your presents, inciting them to revolt? Hughes replied, so Bienville reported to Paris, 'that all this country belonged to them, and that they had a better claim to it than ours; if we chose to dispute it with them, they would know what to do.' He added, said Bienville, that next autumn five hundred English families would be settled by the Crown on the Mississippi. At the moment, with their chief agent in custody, and their Indian alliances already crumbling, the high claims of the Carolinians were subject to heavy discount. But Bienville was sufficiently impressed to retain Hughes's sweeping commission from Craven to send home as evidence of English ambition. To avoid future disputes, it was

[107] Pénicaut in Margry, *Découvertes,* V. 507-9. His chronology is confused; the episode appears under 1713.

highly important, he urged, that the boundaries should be run between Louisiana and Carolina.[108]

From Mobile Hughes passed to Pensacola, to enjoy the hospitality of Señor Guzman. And then, alone, he set out to penetrate the wilderness to the Alabamas. Not far from the mouth of the Alabama River he was waylaid and killed by a party of Tohome Indians, a tribe that had often felt the scourge of the Charles Town slave-dealers.[109] Already the wilderness, from Port Royal to the Mississippi, was ringing with the angry whoop of Indians leagued against the Carolina traders. The great Yamasee-Creek insurrection had begun.

'Dieu rompit ce coup,' a French missionary wrote of the Carolinian trading enterprise of 1713-1715, 'et par la mort du ministre Yousse, le chef de leur ambassade aux Indiens du Mississipi et par la révolte des sauvages des environs de la Caroline.'[110]

[108] Archival materials cited in note 106.

[109] Ibid. See also MS map in C.O. Maps, N.A.C. General, 7, for the route of Hughes and the scene of his assassination.

[110] F. Le Maire, Mémoire, 1717, p. 13, *loc. cit.,* note 105.

CHAPTER V

The Charles Town Indian Trade

Charles Town in the eighteenth century was the one port-town of the South: the residence of prosperous merchants and rice-planters, and the seat of a genteel if not yet a sophisticated society. But every spring the tidewater capital took on, for a few weeks, the aspect of the remote frontier. For Charles Town was also the metropolis of the whole southern Indian country, and it was there that traders from the mountains and the Gulf plains paid their annual visits to civilization.

Down the streets that led to the Bay, bells jingling, plodded caravans of twenty or thirty horses, three or four servants in charge. Or silent files of Indian burdeners sought out the warehouses of the Charles Town merchants. At the wharves where London packets would load with rice and deerskins now lay periagoes and larger trading-boats, paddled by negroes or Indians through river and inland passage from Savannah Town or Augusta. In their offices Mr. Benjamin Godin, Mr. John Bee, Mr. Samuel Eveleigh, and other promoters of the trade reckoned their profits from last year's ventures to the Cherokee or the Talapoosa, or, perchance, counted their losses in some ill-starred Choctaw enterprise. Their shops were freshly stocked with English woolens in bright colors, strouds, duffels, and all the baubles which would fill the packs of the traders on their return journeys. Taverns and punch-houses, Charlton's, the Bowling Green House, and other haunts of the backwoodsmen, were thronged with a roystering crowd. 'Those sparkes,' wrote one who knew them well, 'make little of drinking 15 or 16 £ at one Bout in Towne.'[1] Two or three hundred Carolinians were engaged in the trade, and except for the dealers with the distant Choctaw and Chickasaw, each principal trader must by law renew his license once a year. At this season the Indian commissioners held frequent sessions. There were licenses to approve or reject, charges lodged by the agents to be heard against cheating or abusive traders, projects for the reform of the trade to be considered. If the assembly were sitting traders

[1] S.P.G. MSS A, II, no. 156 (letter of T. Nairne, 1705).

might be summoned also to the province-house to give advice of the situation on the French or Spanish borders. Not infrequently a delegation of Indian chiefs come down to treat for peace or commerce lent another touch of color to the annual pageant of the southern wilderness. Elsewhere in the English colonies only Albany could show such scenes.

Except that each played a great part in the contest for the continent, however, there was little in common between the fur trade of New York and of South Carolina. Indeed, the southern trade was not properly a fur trade at all, but a trade in skins or leather. Beaver and other furs made small part of the returns, and were in quality inferior to the thick pelts of the northern forests. But Charles Town sent off to London each year great quantities of heavy deerskins; skins of lighter weight were consumed at home or shipped to the other colonies. A less respectable branch of the business was the Indian slave-trade. Though the early Indian wars had led to the enslaving of Indians in other English colonies, only in South Carolina did the traffic reach commercial proportions. It was especially among the more distant tribes, upon the frontiers of Florida and Louisiana, that the Carolinians pushed their trade in Indian captives. For the Charles Town traders from an early day penetrated far into the wilderness, and operated among tribes close to the rival colonies of France and Spain. 'Charles Town,' boasted Archdale in 1707, 'Trades near 1000 miles into the Continent.'[2] Thus the Carolinians became notable explorers, whose feats had no parallel among the English in the North. It was only rarely, as in the well-known episodes of 1685-1687, and 1692-1694, that traders from Albany pierced the Iroquois blockade and ventured in person among the western tribes. For the Five Nations, with shrewd commercial instinct, jealously guarded the position of middlemen to which they owed so much of their importance; the trade ran, normally, through Indian channels down to Albany.[3] In the South neither Cherokee nor Creeks could emulate the Long House. The *coureurs de bois* of Canada have been celebrated as a class without parallel among the plodding English farmer-folk of the Atlantic coast.

[2] Carroll (ed.), *Collections,* II. 97.
[3] See Wraxall, *Abridgement,* ed. C. H. McIlwain, Introduction.

But hundreds of English traders each year ranged the forests from the Savannah River to the Tennessee and the Yazoo. Certainly in the first generation of the southern trade there were pioneers, like Thomas Welch, whose feats of daring and endurance challenged comparison with those of Tonti's men, or Dulhut's.

The Indian trade was a life of adventure, no doubt, but primarily it was a business, and the first business to develop in the lower South. The Indian traders, wrote John Lawson (1709), had 'soonest rais'd themselves of any People I have known in Carolina.'[4] Before rice became a great staple the products of the Indian trade were almost the only exports from the struggling colony. In 1687, when the inland trade was just opening, but was still mainly a slave-trade, the Proprietors reported that their people had 'not as yet produced any Comodityes fit for the market of Europe but a few Skins they purchased from the native Indians and a little Cedar with which they helpe to fill the ship that brings the skins for London, both which togeather doe not amount to the value of Two Thousand pounds yearely, and for which London is the best Mercat.'[5] Nairne, in 1705, recalled 'that this Province owed for a long time its Subsistance to the Indian Trade, which,' he added, ' is now the main Branch of its Traffick.'[6] Even as late as the mid-century shipments of deerskins exceeded in value the combined returns from indigo, cattle, beef and pork, lumber and naval stores.[7] The prosperity of South Carolina, wrote

[4] Lawson, *History*, 1718, p. 87, 'The Present State of Carolina.'

[5] C.O. 5:288, p. 120 (probably a report to the Lords of Trade). They added the following picture of early Carolina industry and commerce: 'The Cheif subsistance of the first Settlers being by Hoggs, & Cattle they sell to the New-Comers, and with which they purchase Cloathes, and Tooles from them, and the Ships that carry Passengers from England thither goe from thence to Virginea, Maryland, or the Sugar Islands for a Freight for England, and the Harbours of that part of Carolina that hath been longer settled, and borders on Virginea, are soe barred by sand that shifts often, and thereby soe dangerous to shipping that few or none dare venture thither and that little Trade the few Inhabitants that are there have is by Shallops from Virginea and New England.'

[6] S.P.G. MSS A, II, no. 156.

[7] James Glen, *Description*, 1761, pp. 50-55, reprinted in Carroll (ed.), *Collections*, II. 234-8 (account of exports, 1747-1748). Rice produced about three times the returns from the Indian trade. Cf. account of exports 1748-1749 in C.O. 5:372, I 60. Total value of exports was £1,027,440 6s. 15d. currency, or £144,777 3s. 9d. sterling; of deerskins £187,250 curr.; of rice £615,510. Sterling exchange was about 700 to 100.

a colonial economist of the mid-century, had been achieved from 'its Soil and Climate, producing a good Staple, the best of Rice; and from a neighboring vast Indian Country affording large Quantities of Deer-Skins.'[8]

In contrast to the disappointing dearth of beaver,[9] early writers described vast numbers of deer in Carolina and the hinterland. 'There is such infinite Herds,' declared Thomas Ashe in 1682, 'that the whole Country seems but one continued Park.'[10] The skins sent to England were chiefly heavy buck-skins, weighing on the average close to two pounds when 'half-dressed,' or cured by the Indian method of smoking. Lighter skins, unfit for the English domestic market, or for re-export to Germany, were used in the province or sold in the northern colonies.[11] Of this intercolonial trade there are no adequate ac-counts.[12] But for the trade to England fairly reliable statistics may be reconstructed for practically the whole period from 1699 to 1765,[13] when the new British provinces of East and West Florida became rival centres of the southern trade. From 1699 to 1715 the average annual importation into England from Carolina was nearly 54,000 deerskins. Exports from year to year fluctuated widely, with the fortunes of the Indian hunters, the vicissitudes of intertribal and international warfare, the number of traders, and other influences. The greatest number purchased by the English merchants in one year of this period

[8] [William Douglas], *Postcript to a Discourse concerning the Curren-cies,* reprinted in *Currency Reprints* (Prince Society *Collections*), IV. 52.
[9] In 1699 Great Britain imported from Carolina 1436 beaver skins; in 1702, probably because of an isolated attempt by several *coureurs de bois* of Canada, in the preceding year, to find a market in Carolina for the products of their illicit trade, this increased to 2724; but in 1711, during the Tuscarora War, which interfered with the northern trade, whence came most of the beaver, it declined to a negligible total of 36 skins. In the years immediately preceding the Yamasee War, with the expansion of the Cherokee trade, there was a gradual, and temporary increase. Table of 'Skins and Furs annually imported from Carolina, between Christ: 1698 to Christmas 1715,' in C.O. 5:1265, Q 75. V. W. Crane, in *MVHR,* III. p. 16 and note. By 1747-1748, when the exports of deerskins were valued, in Carolina currency, at £252,000 —approximately £36,000 sterling—the return from beaver was a bare £300 provincial currency. The export of other, inferior furs was also negligible. Carroll (ed.), *Collections,* II. 237.
[10] Ibid., p. 72.
[11] Glen to Board of Trade, September 29, 1746, in C.O. 5:371, H 88. On skin dressing see *Handbook of American Indians,* II. 591-4.
[12] [T. Nairne?], *Letter from South Carolina,* 1710, pp. 16 f., 17; [F. Hall], *Importance of the British Plantations,* 1731, p. 80.
[13] Based on tables received by the Board of Trade from the Inspector General's office, etc.

was 121,355 skins from Christmas, 1706, to Christmas, 1707. In 1716 the ruin of the trade as a result of the Yamasee War was revealed by the importation of only 4,702 skins. Under the public trading régime, in the period of reconstruction, about a third of the old traffic was recovered. From 1721 to 1724 the resumption of the Creek trade and the energy infused into frontier management by Governor Nicholson restored the traffic, temporarily, to pre-war proportions. But in the next five years the troubled relations with the Creek confederacy and, around 1728-1730, with the Cherokee, caused another slump. The two decades after 1730, however, were a golden era for the Charles Town merchants, drawing as they did most of the skins from Georgia as well as from South Carolina. In 1748 the province shipped off over seven hundred hogsheads, containing approximately 160,000 deerskins. Governor Glen reported to the Board of Trade in 1746 that 'the annual Export of Deer Skins from this Port [Charles Town] only, is betwixt six and seven hundred Hogsheads; each Hogshead being worth Fifty Guineas in Charles Town; and to this must be added the Duty, Freight, Insurance, and Merchants' Gains which make altogether a considerable Sum.'[14] There was a falling off in the early 1750's, but another peak was reached in 1763. These exports, of course, represented a tremendous slaughter of deer, comparable to the great wastage, by a later generation, of the buffalo of the Great Plains. Long before 1763 the 'infinite herds' of the late seventeenth century must have been seriously diminished.

Of that other, singular branch of the business, the traffic in Indian slaves, statistical records were meagre. In 1702 Iberville asserted that within the last decade the Chickasaw had taken five hundred Choctaw prisoners at English instigation, and had killed more than three times that many.[15] The Frenchman was addressing an Indian council, when rhetoric was in order, but the proportion of captives to casualties in these wasting contests was probably typical. By such attrition the slave-trade, of small economic significance, wore down the barriers to the English advance. In 1708, when the total popu-

[14] C.O. 5:371, H 88.
[15] Margry (ed.), *Découvertes*, IV. 517.

lation of South Carolina was 9,580, including 2,900 negroes, there were 1,400 Indian slaves held in the province.[16] Probably the number of Indians employed by the Carolina planters did not greatly increase thereafter. The parish of St. Thomas consisted in 1722 of one hundred families who owned nine hundred to a thousand negroes and only ninety Indian slaves.[17] From an early time the exportation of captured Indians was favored both on grounds of public policy and self-interest. Indian slaves were constantly escaping to the woods, and in the settlements their presence in any numbers raised the danger of conspiracies with enemy Indians. One of the earliest alarms of a slave insurrection in the South seems to have been that of 1700, when some Indian slaves were suspected of a plot in Carolina.[18] The Indians, moreover, were at best poor workers in the fields, though some became skilled artisans.[19] Prices in the Charles Town slave market reflected these facts. 'An Indian Man or Woman may cost 18 or 20 Pound,' wrote a well-informed pamphleteer in 1712, 'but a good Negro is worth more than twice that Sum.'[20] On all accounts it was better to ship off the Indians to New England or the West Indies, and to import blacks. When the trade was young, permits were issued during

---

[16] C.O. 5:1264, P 82: 500 men, 600 women, 300 children.

[17] S.P.G. MSS, B, IV, part 1, p. 103. In 1726 there were 60 Indian slaves in this parish (ibid., p. 208).

[18] *Commissions and Instructions, 1685-1715*, 1916, p. 144.

[19] The Indians, Lawson declared, 'are as apt to learn any Handicraft, as any People that the World affords'; he referred to their native crafts and also to 'the Indian Slaves in South Carolina.' *History* (1718), p. 235. Advertisements of runaway Indians in the *South Carolina Gazette* frequently mentioned their trades, viz.: Peter, 'both a Carpenter and Cooper' (September 11, 1736); Jack, 'by trade a Tanner' (May 18, 1738); James, 'a Cooper by Trade' (December 14, 1747); Jack, 'seems to understand something of the shoemaker's trade' (June 4, 1753); Sarah, 'brought up to Household Work' (June 17, 1732); Deborah, 'handy at Women's Work' (November 4, 1732); 'a young Indian House Wench' (December 15, 1746).

[20] [John Norris], *Profitable Advice*, p. 57. In his estimate of the cost of setting up a plantation with £1500 capital this writer included these items:

Imprimis: Fifteen good Negro Men at 45 1. each   £675
Item, Fifteen Indian Women to work in the Field,
    at 18 1. each, comes to   270
Item, Three Indian Women as Cooks for the Slaves,
    and other Household-Business   55

For a small plantation of 100 to 200 acres he advised the purchase of 'Two Slaves: a good Negro Man and a good Indian Woman' at £45 and £18 respectively. The housewife would have the assistance of the Indian woman, they 'diligently Employing themselves in the careful Management of the Dairy, Hogs,' etc. (ibid., pp. 88 f., 93).

one month (October, 1681) for the transportation of forty slaves.[21] Following the Tuscarora War, in 1712-1713 export duties were paid on seventy-five Indians, but there were complaints that this duty was evaded.[22] In 1716, when the punishment of the revolted Indians was going forward briskly, duties were levied on 308 Indian slaves.[23]

The chief markets were in the islands and in New England. In the early eighteenth century the *Boston News Letter* printed frequent advertisements of runaway Carolina Indians. Thus in the issue of September 17, 1711, five southern Indians were described as fugitives, including 'a Carolina Indian Man nam'd Toby,' escaped from the Reverend Mr. Samuel Myles, 'a Carolina Indian woman nam'd Jenny' sought by Colonel Thomas Savage, and three other runaways, two described as 'Spanish Indians,' advertised by less eminent masters. In 1715 Rhode Island passed a law prohibiting importation of Indian slaves, on the ground of frequent conspiracies and the discouragement of white servants from Great Britain.[24] Two Newport merchants advertised in 1717 for runaway Carolina Indians; one, the property of William Bourden, was branded with W on one cheek and B on the other.[25] Thus Yankee merchants and masters, before they became great purveyors of blacks from Guinea to the plantation colonies, had made acquaintance with the slave-trade in their trafficking from Carolina to Boston and Newport. The southerners who supplied them with Indian slaves were ready to justify this commerce by arguments worthy of the 'saints of New England.' 'Some men think,' wrote a Carolinian, 'that it both serves to Lessen their numbers before the French can arm them, and it is a more Effectuall way of Civilising and Instructing [them] than all the Efforts used by the French Missionaries.'[26]

[21] Court of Ordinary Records, 1672-1692 (MS).
[22] C.O. 5:1265, Q 76 (enclosure). From contemporary references the impression is created that these scattering statistics inadequately measure the actual volume of the traffic.
[23] JCHA, December 15, 1716.
[24] *R. I. Colonial Records,* IV. 193.
[25] *Boston News Letter,* July 22, 1717. Ibid., September 29, 1712, printed an offer to sell 'a Carolina Indian woman that can do all sorts of Household work well, and spin Linen.' See other advertisements under dates of April 22, 1706, August 27, December 17, 1711; March 9, June 16, 1712; September 24, 1716; March 18, 1717.
[26] C.O. 5:382 (11): Nairne's memorial of July 10, 1708.

In exchange for skins, furs, and Indian slaves, the colonists provided the Indians within the circuit of their trade with the usual variety of Indian trading goods. These were mainly coarse woolen cloths and hardware imported from Great Britain, which made the business, as Nicholson and Glen and other governors frequently emphasized,[27] of substantial importance to the mother country, or at least to the group of English merchants who traded to the southern colonies. By 1715 the annual outlay for the trading goods was said, on excellent authority, to exceed £10,000 sterling.[28] The trade also brought some small revenue to the Crown, as the colonists often urged in their appeals for royal protection.[29]

From the historical standpoint, however, the imperial significance of the Indian trade of South Carolina outweighed its mercantilistic advantages. Nor did this escape contemporaries. 'The Indian trade,' declared the *South Carolina Gazette* in 1736, 'is of the greatest Importance to the Wellfare of this Province, not only as it affords us near one 5th part of the Returns we make to Great Britain . . . but principally as it is the Means by which we keep and maintain the several Nations of the Indians surrounding this Province in Amity and Friendship with us, and thereby prevent their falling into the Interest of France or Spain.'[30] Only the excellence of the British trade counterbalanced the superior position and diplomacy of the Spanish and the French. 'It's no doubt very favourable for the Inhabitants of South Carolina,' wrote one of their agents, a merchant with interests in the Indian trade, 'that Deer Skins the only Indian Produce are of more value in England than in France or Spain and in Consequence the Traders give a better price for them . . . and indeed that accidental Advantage has proved of more Service than any presents given by the British Nation or Colonies which are in no respect equal to what is given by the French and Spaniards.'[31]

---

[27] See C.O. 5:359, B 16; C.O. 5:371, H 88.
[28] Johnson to Board of Trade, January 12, 1720, in C.O. 5:1265, Q 201
[29] The old duty of 6d. per pound was raised in the Book of Rates of 1725 to 1s. 3d. per lb. (House of Commons Journal, March 16, 1724/5). Cf. Nairne in C.O. 5:382 (11).
[30] *South Carolina Gazette,* July 3, 1736.
[31] James Crokatt, memorial to Board of Trade, November 10, 1752, in C.O. 5:374, K 48.

The progress of the Charles Town traders in their contacts, first with the coast tribes, and then with the Indians of the interior, marked the rise of a picturesque American business and constituted an important chapter in the Anglo-American conquest of the continent. It also produced among the Indians an economic and social revolution. The trade bred new habits and ways of living, and these bred dependence upon the white man. An accurate measure of the economic, and also the political subjection of the southern tribes was furnished by the lists of goods which the traders purveyed. At first peak or wampum, and a few substitutes for the cruder articles manufactured by the Indians, made up the traders' cargoes. The 'Indian trade' sent out by the Proprietors in 1669 included glass beads, hatchets, hoes, hollowing adzes, knives, 'sizzard,' and 'ten striped shirts,' the last as presents for the chiefs.[32] John Lawson, who wrote in 1709 of the piedmont tribes, said that in general only the great men among the Indians, who had plenty of deerskins, bought the English coats, and even they refused to buy breeches. But nearer the settlements were Indians who dressed in hats, shoes, stockings, breeches, and linen shirts of English manufacture.[33] These tastes spread rapidly, however, as the traders pushed westward. At the end of the first period of the Carolina Indian trade, in 1715,[34] a trader bound up for the Indian country carried in his pack-horse train, or on the backs of his Indian burdeners, the coarse cloth which was the staple of the trade: bright red or blue 'duffield' blankets, 'strouds,' and 'plains' or 'half-thicks'; also axes, and broad hoes with which the Indians cleared their fields and cultivated their maize and pulse, salt, brass kettles, hatchets, fusees or trading-guns, knives, flints, powder and bullets for war and the hunt, tobacco, pipes, rum, red-lead and vermilion, petticoats, scissors, thread, needles, 'tensy' lace, flowered calico, red girdles, scarlet caddice for gartering, linen shirts, laced coats and hats for chiefs and beloved men, and even small looking glasses which Indian dandies affected to wear suspended by a cord from the neck. Once a demand for merchandise not manu-

---

[32] *CSCHS,* V. 149.
[33] *History,* 1718, pp. 191f.
[34] The list is compiled from a variety of sources, chiefly the Indian commissioners' journals.

factured by the Indians was created, or the native industries had fallen into disuse, a threat to cut off the trade was often sufficient to bring a recalcitrant tribe to terms. This was especially true when the Indians had been supplied with arms and ammunition. The early efforts to prevent the trade in those articles had been futile. Motives of policy combined with motives of greed to promote it. By 1715 munitions had become with cloth—and rum—the chief commodities of the forest trade.

In 1725 Tobias Fitch was sent as agent to the Creeks to counteract the influence which the Spanish and French had won since the Yamasee War. 'I must tell your Young Men,' he shrewdly declaimed in the upper towns, 'that had it not been for us they would not have known how to Warr nor yet have anything to Warr with; for before we came among you, there was no other weapons than Bows and Arrows to hunt with, you could Hunt a whole day and bring nothing Home at Night, you had no other Hoes or Axes than Stones, you wore nothing but Skins; but now we have learnt you the use of fire Arms, as well to kill Deer, and other Provisions, as to Warr against your Enemies.' 'This you that are Old Men know to be true,' Fitch concluded, 'and I would have you make your Young Men Sensible of it.'[35] It was an Indian, the head warrior of Tennessee, who, according to Colonel Chicken, agent at the same period among the Cherokee, 'got up and made the following Speech to me and the People of the Town. "That they must now mind and Consider that all their Old men were gone, and that they have been brought up after another Manner than their forefathers and that they must Consider that they could not live without the English." '[36] Not often did the oratory of the round house strike so close to the realities of Indian politics. Here was revealed, of course, the whole basis of English influence among the southern Indians.

The Charles Town Indian trade passed through several fairly distinct stages of organization. Roughly these corresponded to periods in border history and in the evolution of colonial commerce.

[35] JC, August 24, 1725, and more briefly in Mereness (ed.), *Travels*, p. 181.
[36] Ibid., pp. 112 f.

During the first decade the Lords Proprietors attempted to turn the traffic with the Indians into a source of dividends upon their investment. The early trade, both proprietary and private, was a plantation trade. 'All the considerable Planters,' wrote an early pamphleteer, 'have an Indian hunter which they hire for less than twenty shillings a year.'[37] It was his duty to supply the plantation with game and peltries, but other Indians also resorted to the plantations for trade. Thomas Ashe wrote in 1682 that he had 'often heard Captain Matthews, an ingenious Gentleman, and Agent to Sir Peter Colleton for his Affairs in Carolina [declare] that one hunting Indian has yearly kill'd and brought to his Plantation more than an 100, sometimes 200 head of Deer.'[38] Disappointed in the meagre returns from Ashley River, Shaftesbury in 1674 projected his abortive Edisto Island settlement, and declared to the Charles Town government his unwillingness 'to be controulled by you in my dealing or trade with any of the Indians.'[39] The same year Woodward opened the Westo trade, which was carried on from Shaftesbury's plantation of St. Giles' Kusso, and from Sir Peter Colleton's Fairlawn plantation, so well located for the interior trade on the western branch of the Cooper River. In 1677 the Proprietors issued their order establishing a monopoly for seven years with 'the Westoes, Cussatoes, Spaniards, or other Indians that live beyond Porte Royall, or at the same distance from our present settlement.' To carry it on, Albemarle, Craven, Clarendon, Sir Peter Colleton, and Shaftesbury, then in the Tower, formed a joint-stock with subscriptions of £100; Shaftesbury's contract of 1674 with Woodward was taken over.[40] The trade along the coast as far as Port Royal and inland for one hundred miles was left open to the planters, and the nearby Indians resorted to the plantation houses with their peltry. But friction developed; the private traders controlled the assembly, and through the Westo War they broke down the proprietary monopoly. It was not until 1691, however, that instructions

---

[37] [Samuel Wilson], *Account of the Province of Carolina*, 1682, p. 12; reprinted in Carroll (ed.), *Collections*, II. 28.

[38] T. A[she], *Carolina*, 1682, p. 21; reprinted in Carroll (ed.), *Collections*, II. 72.

[39] *CSCHS*, V. 439-46, 468.

[40] C.O. 5:286, pp. 120 f. (in Rivers, *Sketch* pp 388-90).

were sent to the governor that he should 'suffer all persons that will, freely to trade with the Indians.'[41]

Meanwhile, the trade had fallen largely into the hands of a few enterprising planters, who sent factors into the Indian country, men who, in Lawson's phrase, 'travel and abide amongst the Indians for a long space of time.'[42] Such was already the organization of the Virginia Indian trade. William Byrd of Westover, son of one of the great Virginia trader-planters of the seventeenth century, said that 'the Common Method of carrying on this Indian Commerce is as follows: Gentlemen send for Goods proper for such a Trade from England, and then either Venture them out at their own Risk to the Indian Towns, or credit some Traders with them of Substance and Reputation, to be paid in Skins at a certain Price agreed betwixt them.'[43]

Among the Carolinians who emulated Abraham Wood, the elder Byrd, and Cadwallader Jones, were several early notables. As surveyor-general Maurice Mathews carried through the extinction of Indian titles south to the Savannah and west to the mountains; as agent for Colleton he early became an extensive trader. He was named by the Proprietors with Percival to reopen the peltry trade interrupted by the Westo War.[44] But with James Moore he soon incurred the displeasure of the Proprietors for slave-dealing; both were removed from all their offices. Mathews had powerful friends in England, but Moore, an indigent Barbadian gentleman with numerous dependents, apparently owed his rise to his own restless energy. As manager of the plantations of Captain William Walley and of Lady Margaret Yeamans, whom he prudently married, Moore launched into cattleraising and Indian trading on a large scale. In 1690 he made his journey to the Cherokee, seeking mines as well as trade.[45] Both Mathews and Moore shrewdly combined politics with business. In 1685 the Proprietors complained that the slave-dealers by the 'packing of parliaments and the grand

[41] C.O. 5:288, p. 195.
[42] Lawson, *History*, 1718, p. 184.
[43] Byrd, *Writings*, Bassett (ed.), p. 235.
[44] R. F., *Present State*, 1682, p. 11; C.O. 5:286, p. 164; *CSCHS*, V. 332 note.
[45] R. F., *Present State*, 1682, p. 10; C.O. 5:288, p. 288; JCHA, April 2, 1702; *CSCHS*, V. 463 note.

Councell . . . have made warrs and peace with the Indians as it best suited their private advantage in trade.'[46] The close alliance of politics and Indian trading was also seen in the attempts of successive governors to monopolize the trade.

The hey-day of the planter interest was the quarter-century following the Westo War. At an early date Colonel Stephen Bull traded northward as far as Cape Fear.[47] In the decade preceding the Yamasee War, Landgrave Thomas Smith was frequently in collision with the council and the Indian board over the licensing of his traders to the northern tribes.[48] Another leading employer at the beginning of the new century was Colonel Thomas Broughton. The son-in-law of Sir Nathaniel Johnson, he enjoyed, for a time, a privileged position in the trade.[49] Like Broughton's Mulberry plantation, Peter St. Julien's place near Dorchester was convenient both to the Cherokee path by way of Congaree and to the Savannah Town route.[50] An important rival of Moore in the southern trade was James Stanyarne, a wealthy planter of Colleton county. Though largely engaged in dealing with the Yamasee, Stanyarne also sent traders inland as far as the Talapoosas.[51]

Early in the new century the privileged position of the governors and the great planters of the council in the Indian trade was being undermined. In 1707 Governor Johnson complained of 'the Multitude of Indian traders that now more and more pester the Trade with their Numbers for their own advantage.'[52] That year the Commons House wrested the regulation of the trade from the upper house. At Charles Town, moreover, there was developing a class of merchants unique in the South; inevitably they succeeded to the dominance of the southern Indian trade. From a profitable side-line of the planter and cattle-rancher, it became a mercantile interest second only to the exportation of rice. Most of the Charles Town merchants

[46] C.O. 5:288, p. 52.

[47] Archdale, *Description,* 1707, p. 21, reprinted in Carroll (ed.), *Collections,* II. 108.

[48] JCHA, December 16, 1708; JIC, October 6, 1713; March 25, May 6, 1714.

[49] See pp. 146-7.

[50] JIC, August 19, 1713, May 5, 20, 1714.

[51] JCHA, January 15, September 2, 1703; November 4, 1709. John Ash, *Present State of Affairs.*

[52] JCHA, March 6, 1707.

in the eighteenth century were in some degree concerned in it. The following were conspicuous in the first quarter-century for their frontier interests: Andrew Allen and his partner, William Gibbon; Benjamin Godin, the Goose Creek planter and Charles Town merchant, whose family connection included several London merchants trading to Carolina; his partner, Benjamin de la Conseilliere; Isaac Mazÿck; Charles Hill and Company; Walter Lougher; Samuel Wragg, nephew of a London merchant; John Bee; and notably Samuel Eveleigh, 'of South Carolina and Bristol, merchant.'[53] For the later years the list was a roster of the little business world of Broad and Tradd streets. Among the conspicuous names were Greene, Godin, Hill, Catell, Pringle, Savage, Croft, Bedon, Beale, Atkins, Crokatt, Grimké, Osmond, Motte, Yeomans, Broughton, Horry, Smallwood, and Roché.[54] Most of these men were importers of Indian trading goods and exporters of furs and deerskins. Some were also actual undertakers in the trade. Jordan Roché was perhaps the only merchant who had lived as a factor among the Indians; in his youth he had traded to the Chickasaw.[55] John Bee maintained a trading factory on the upper Ocmulgee for some years after the desertion of the Lower Creeks, and in 1725 took out licenses for 'a parcel of traders' to the Choctaw.[56]

Probably no merchant in South Carolina was so long or so extensively engaged in the business as Samuel Eveleigh.

[53] The list is compiled chiefly from the Indian commissioners' journals, 1710, 1716-1718. The family and trading connections of several of these merchants with London firms probably led the author of The Importance of the British Plantations in America, 1731, to assert (p. 66) that 'the Indian Trade there being of such exceeding Advantage, and frequently carried on by the Servants of those who live here, all the Profits thereof are sent here by those who design to return to this Kingdom.' This statement led Channing in his excellent brief description of the southern trade (History, II. 551) to overemphasize the direct British interest. I have not been able to discover that it was in anywise differentiated from the Carolina trade as a whole. On the Wraggs see SCHGM, XIX. 121.

[54] Compiled from assembly journals, advertisements in South Carolina Gazette, and from the following documents in particular: memorial of Charles Town merchants regarding Georgia's interference in the trade, July 4, 1735, C.O. 5:365, F 14; schedule of debts due by Georgia traders, JCHA, December 15, 1737; petition to governor and council, JC, September 5, 1749.

[55] JCHA, March 1, 1734; JC, December 14, 1747; Glover's journal, 1728, in C.O. 5:387.

[56] Fitch to Middleton, Kasihta, October 1, 1725, in JC, November 2, 1725.

Instead of employing factors at wages, like Bee, Eveleigh engaged on a large scale in supplying traders to the Creeks and the Cherokee with trading goods on credit. Consequently, he was more than a little interested in the machinery of Indian regulation, one of the chief functions of which was to secure the merchants against defalcation of the traders or thefts by the Indians. From 1712 to the Yamasee War Eveleigh was a member of the Indian board.[57] By later acts the Indian commissioners were forbidden to engage in trade during their incumbency; but through membership in the council,[58] or pressure on the assembly and the commissioners, the merchants were still powerful in Indian management. In January, 1731, Eveleigh presented to the council a memorial complaining that the Creeks had robbed one Thomas Duvall, a Cherokee trader, of 800 lbs. of leather. When the council resolved to order restitution, it was Eveleigh who named the traders proper to carry it out. A few months later he opposed the selection of Tobias Fitch as agent to the Creek nation, asserting that he had great concerns in trade which would suffer by Fitch's appointment and charging him with mismanagement when formerly in office. The Indian act was delayed nearly a month while a committee of the Commons took depositions of traders and heard Fitch's reply. He admitted a project for a trading partnership with Charlesworth Glover at the end of his agency, but denied 'that he had ever formed a scheme of trade with the Choctaw Indians or to engross or monopolize the whole of the Southern Trade in conjunction with Col. Glover.' After once striking out Fitch's name from the bill, the assembly restored it a few days later. But Fitch, possibly in view of the opposition, refused the office.[59]

To a merchant with Eveleigh's stake in the trade, friendly

[57] He first attended on June 27, 1712. Next day the board delivered to the Indian agent 'Accots. of Several Debts due from Mr. Richd. Gower to Samuel Eveleigh, Esqr., Mr. Andrew Allen, and Mr. Porter to be recovered by the Agent' (JIC).

[58] Smith, *S. C. as a Royal Province, 1719-1776*, pp. 234, 330 (control of council by merchants).

[59] JC, January 1, 1730/1; JCHA, June 26, July 9, 14, 22, 24, 1731. See also Mereness (ed.), *Travels*, pp. 119, 141; and record of Eveleigh's will (1766) in *SCHGM*, XII. 216. Eveleigh was later a commercial agent for the Georgia Trustees at Charles Town, and named one of his vessels, a schooner in the West Indian trade, the *Oglethorpe* (C.O. 5:509).

relations with the Indians were quite as important as to the provincial government. In June, 1732, a delegation of Creek chiefs was visiting Charles Town. 'Yesterday,' the *Gazette* chronicled, 'the Head Men of the Indians now in Town were plentifully entertained at Dinner, by Mr. Eveleigh, at his House, who carried them, in the Afternoon, on board the '*Fox*' Man-of-War with the sight of which they seemed mighty well pleased. The civilities showed to these Indians by Mr. Eveleigh,' the writer continued, 'are not, we believe, (as some would suggest) from any private Views of Interest to himself, but a general design of promoting a good understanding, and consequently our Trade with them. It being the known Artifice of the French and Spaniards, who have dealings with the same Persons, to trick us out of our Trade, by Excelling in smooth-faced Strategems of this Kind.'[60]

The profits of the trade accrued mainly to the Charles Town merchants and their London correspondents. Among other classes, especially the planters, there developed a certain resentment that the heavy expense of Indian management, the largest single charge against the public, was incurred for the profit of a small privileged group. In 1736 the Georgians were attempting to divert the inland Indian trade to Savannah, and to regulate from that province all intercourse with the Cherokee and Creek Indians. Oglethorpe appealed to the non-commercial, or anti-commercial, sentiment in South Carolina in his letter to Lieutenant-Governor Broughton of June 5, 1736: 'Notwithstanding the Artifices of a few designing Men you will Joyn with me in judging, that our Taking the Indian Trade with the Expense of treating with the Indians, is taking off a Burthen from the Province of Carolina: the Public there having been at all the Expense and a few private Merchants only receiving the Benefit.'[61] But the merchants prevailed in the assembly, and the measures outlined in the memorial of thirty-one Charles Town merchants,[62] 'all more or less Concerned in the said Trade, either Trading thither directly or in furnishing Goods for the said Trade,' were embodied in an ordinance for its defense.

[60] *South Carolina Gazette,* June 10, 1732.
[61] JCHA, X. 272-4.
[62] C.O. 5:365, F 14.

Thus began the bitter and protracted conflict between Georgia and South Carolina for the control of the western trade. Though the controversy was carried home to the Privy Council, it was actually determined less by the arguments of lawyers and agents in Whitehall than by the commercial preponderance of Charles Town in the South. Though some of the Carolina traders now transferred their headquarters to Augusta, and took out licenses at Savannah, the old lines of trade were little disturbed. The trading-boats which brought the skins down the Savannah River from the new entrepôt at Augusta usually passed right by the empty wharves of Savannah, or only called there on their way to Charles Town, which remained until after 1763 the mart of the whole southern Indian trade.[63]

In their memorial of 1735 the Charles Town merchants had sought to prove 'that the said Trade is of a particular advantage to this Province in regard to the poorer sort of People there being no less than three Hundred who find constant employment therein.' These were the traders with the Indians, a picturesque element in the population of the southern border. Even two decades before, by official estimate there had been 'one way or Other near 200 English Indian traders Imployed as Factors by the Merchants of Carolina.'[64] A few clearly belonged to a class above 'the poorer sort of People.'[65] There was Jordan Roché, who became a merchant; John Musgrove, a member of the Commons House; Theophilus Hastings, a militia officer and frontier fighter; and, at a later period, the extraordinary figure of the historiographer of the southern Indians, James Adair. But most, even of the principal traders, were poor and illiterate, chronic debtors, true types of the first American frontier. Notoriously they were 'not (generally) Men of the best Morals.'[66] The journals of the assembly and of the Indian board were filled with severest strictures on their 'Barbarous, . . . Imorall and unjust way of Liveing and Deale-

[63] See William Stephens, *Journal,* 1752, II. 90, 156, 258, 282, 377.
[64] C.O. 5 :1265, Q 201.
[65] *Warrants for Lands, 1692-1711,* pp. 218, 241, show that Thomas Welch owned a plantation near Round O Savannah in 1709; and that in 1711 he received warrants for 300 and 400 acres in Colleton county. John Jones received warrants, in 1692-1696, for 1100 acres (ibid., pp. 22, 53, 54, 109, 111).
[66] Yonge, *Narrative,* 1726, reprinted in Carroll (ed.), *Collections,* II. 145.

ing,' with allegations that 'the Lewdness and wickedness of them have been a Scandall to the Religion wee Profess.'[67] Though many of the old traders, for their sins, lost their lives in the *débâcle* of 1715, their successors were no more exemplary. One of their worst traits, from the merchants' standpoint, was financial irresponsibility. Unfortunate wretches there were whose great debts to the Charles Town merchants made them exiles for many years in the Indian country; when some crisis required their presence in Charles Town it was necessary for the assembly to publish a moratorium.[68] The names of most of these obscure pioneers of empire in the South have perished, but in the period before 1715 about one hundred traders were named in the records by reason of their public services, or, more commonly, their misdemeanors. About as many are known for the years from 1715 to 1732. In the early century most were of English origin, with a sprinkling of Scotch and Irish, and a conspicuous absence of the thrifty and stable Huguenots. Evidently the restless and indigent members of the English-Barbadian community, and servants whose terms of indenture had expired, drifted back into the wilderness. In the later period, and markedly as the century advanced, the licenses issued at Charles Town bore such names as Campbell, Dougherty, Gillespie, McGillivray, McKinney, McIntosh, MacDonald, McCormick, Millikin, McBain, and the like.

A trader's life, though one of danger and especially of hardships, rewarded usually with poverty, was not without its lure. James Adair, for forty years a trader among the Cherokee and Chickasaw Indians, typified the fascination of the southern wilderness for those who had once followed its paths in the legend of Major Herbert's spring. There were even rude comforts to be had in the Indian towns, which abounded, Adair wrote, 'with hogs, poultry, and every thing sufficient for the support of a reasonable life.' Most traders took Indian wives, who dressed their victuals and taught them the Indian tongue. 'Such a man,' said Lawson, 'gets a great Trade with the Savages.' Among the Indians the traders enjoyed an influence which

[67] As in JCHA, April 2, November 16, 1700. See article xvi of the Indian act of 1719, in Cooper (ed.), *Statutes,* III. 91.

[68] See JCHA, November 21, 1706, and Indian Book (MS) II. 135 (petition of a trader in 1751).

tempted some to play the petty tyrant, with disastrous results. But so long as 'they kept them busily employed, and did not make themselves too cheap, the Indians,' by Adair's account, 'bore them good-will and respect.'[69]

Each principal trader, except such 'poor, loose and vaga-bond persons' as were only able to get 'credit for rum and small quantitys of goods,'[70] employed at least one packhorse-man as his assistant to look after six or seven horses and their burdens. Sometimes this work was performed by indented servants, sometimes, though the government disapproved, by negro or Indian slaves, but usually a trader's man was hired at wages.[71] The average outfit in the Creek trade in the early thirties consisted of three or four men and twenty to thirty horses, and this was probably characteristic. When William Byrd wrote of caravans of a hundred horses setting out across the piedmont from the falls of the James under the conduct of fifteen or sixteen persons[72] he probably described the outfits of several traders, who sought protection in company. To be sure, there were Charles Town trading-firms which sent out quite as imposing trains as any that came from north of the Roanoke. Archibald McGillivray and Company employed one hundred and three horses between New Windsor and the Creeks, in charge of fifteen pack-horsemen besides the principal traders. In 1747, when the Choctaw 'Revolution' opened a prospect of winning that tribe from the French, a company formed by Charles McNaire and several other traders, with the backing of the Rochés, sent up a caravan of two hundred horses, in a venture at once political and commercial, to the farthest trading frontier of the English in America.[73]

---

[69] James Adair, *History of the American Indians*, 1775, pp. 230 f.

[70] Cooper (ed.), *Statutes*, III. 231.

[71] [Nairne?], *A Letter from South Carolina*, 1710, pp. 54 f., describing 'the usual Wages and Prices of Labour,' listed overseers at £15 to £40 currency per annum, and 'such as are employ'd to trade with the Indians from 20 to 100 l.' In 1718, during the public trade, packhorsemen were paid £10 currency per month, with an allowance of 7s. 6d. for board while in Charles Town. JIC, April 12, May 3, 29, 1718. The act of 1719, in Cooper (ed.), *Statutes*, III. 89, proposed to hire thirty free men at not more than 100 lb. weight of skins per year, and to engage thirty servants. In 1725 the council complained that the Indian traders were enticing men away from the garrisons by offering them higher wages (JCHA, March 18, 1724/5).

[72] Byrd, *Writings* (Bassett, ed.), p. 235.

[73] C.O. 5:373, K 34 (examination of John Vann).

Trading companies were in fact very common, and some were of a more or less permanent character. On the eve of the Yamasee War, Richard Gower and William Britt, and John Chester and Weaver were leading dealers among the Creeks. Card, Skeel and Wiggins, Trumbull and Richardson, Holford, Peirce and Griffin, John Graves and Joseph Cundry were other companies of that period. Henry Gustin and Laughlin McBain traded to the Cherokee in the second quarter-century, John McGillivray and Company to the Creeks. The most considerable partnership in the Carolina trade toward the mid-century was the firm of Archibald McGillivray and Company. Besides Mc-Gillivray, 'sole manager and director,' the company included the well-known traders Isaac Motte of New Windsor, William Sludders, Jeremiah Knott, and George Cussings. In 1747 another leading Creek firm, that of Alexander Wood and Patrick Brown, was taken into the combine. Besides effecting economies, such companies were able to parcel out the Indian towns, creating a partial or complete monopoly which was sometimes confirmed by the provincial government. In this way cut-throat competition was abated in the Indian country.[74]

The equipment of the trade was simple. The pack-horses were Indian-bred, or raised by the traders in the Indian country. Cherokee horses were in common use; these were excellent animals, said Adair, 'of a good size, well-made, hard-hoofed, handsome, strong and fit for the saddle or draught.'[75] On the down journey each horse was laden with three packs. An estimate for a cargo of presents to the Choctaw in 1751 throws light upon the cost of transportation to the more distant Indians. 'I compute,' said the contractor, 'that carriage of the said goods will take up 35 horses, and that a horse will be burdened with 150 wt. so then the wt. of the whole will be 5250 wt. and that the Carriage hiring horses for the above goods will amount to 1225 pounds.'[76] Sometimes Indian bur-

[74] Compiled from journals of Indian boards and assembly, etc. See also *South Carolina Gazette*, September 8, 1739; September 12, October 3, 1747.

[75] Adair, *History of the American Indians*, p. 230. Adair explained (ibid., p. 300) that bells were used on the pack-horses partly on account of the 'big flies that infest the country.' JIC, November 20, 1719, notes the purchase of two horse bells, with collars, for pack-horses in the Catawba trade, at £3.

[76] JC, August 1, 1751. See also James Crokatt (1752) in C.O. 5:374, K 48: 'its customary to give from £3: to £5: Sterling for a Horse Load.'

deners were employed instead of horses. This seems to have been the earliest method of conveyance, and the tribes of the Savannah River region, Yamasee, Savannah, Apalache, etc., were of particular service in this capacity.[77] Again, after the Indian war, Cherokee burdeners were used because the unsettled state of Indian affairs made it too risky to send horses. Each burdener shouldered a pack of about thirty skins. The following from the journal of the Indian board in 1717 was a characteristic entry: 'Ordered, that the Cherokee Burdeners this day arrived, be paid out of the Store, two yards of blew duffields to each man, for their labour and travel to Charles Town and home again.'[78]

Some part of the heavy expense of land carriage was saved by the use of the water-route between Charles Town and the falls of the Savannah. Various small craft were employed: canoes and periagoes paddled by Indians or negroes, which were also part of the regular equipment of the traders with the coast tribes, and special trading-boats. About 1710 a large periago cost sixteen pounds in Carolina currency, a small canoe two pounds. A periago paddled by seven or eight slaves could load 500 to 700 skins.[79] In the middle eighteenth century the Charles Town merchants and the up-country storekeepers made use of considerably larger boats. Such was one described in the *South Carolina Gazette* of February 1, 1748:

Stolen, or gone a-drift from Mr. Elliott's Wharf, last Tuesday Night, an Indian-trading Boat, 42 Feet long and upwards of 7 feet wide, with a cabin in her Stern, and Staples in her Side, and a King bolt in her Head. Whoever takes up said Boat, and delivers her to Macartan & Campbell in Charles Town shall have 20 1. Currency reward.[80]

Trading-boats such as this drew three or four feet of water, and were equipped with oars, but not usually with sails.[81] Wil-

[77] Rivers, *Sketch,* p. 424. C.O. 5:1264, P 82: a report of governor and council in 1708 said 'Indians seated upwards of Seven Hundred Miles off are Supplied with Goods by our White Men that Transport them from this River [i.e. the Savannah] upon Indians' backs.'

[78] JIC, November 27, 1717. See ibid., 1716-1718, *passim.*

[79] Ibid.; John Norris, *Profitable Advice,* 1712, pp. 88, 93.

[80] See *South Carolina Gazette,* January 12, 1738, for an advertisement of the sale of 'an Indian trading Boat, with her Oars and Grapling' by Archibald McGillivray and Jacob Motte.

[81] JBT, June 9, 1737 (C.O. 391:46, ff. 125-126).

liam Stephens in his journal often mentioned the trading-boats of Eveleigh and others which plied past Savannah. Five, he said, were owned by the storekeepers at Augusta; they could carry 'about nine or ten thousand weight of Deer-Skins each, making four or five Voyages at least in a Year to Charles Town, . . . and the value of each cargo is computed to be from 12 to 1500 £ Sterling.'[82]

From Charles Town to the up-country the traders followed the water-route or well-beaten roads. The great inland trading paths really began at the fall-line of the rivers. Congaree, at the head of the Santee swamp, distant one hundred and forty-five miles by road from Charles Town, was a focus for paths to the Catawba and the Cherokee. Thence, the Catawba path ran northwestward to the Wateree town on Wateree River, and along that stream to the Waxhaws and the Catawba, where it met the famous Occaneechi path from Virginia.[83]

The Congaree route to the Cherokee country became important after the Indian war, when the more southern trail was exposed to Creek and Yamasee attack, and especially after the building of Fort Congaree in 1718. Its course was clearly indicated on George Hunter's map of 1730,[84] and in the journals of George Chicken[85] and Sir Alexander Cuming. To the nearest Cherokee town was a distance of one hundred and fifty-eight miles. The path followed the southern margin of the Congaree watershed, through Saluda Old Town and Ninety-Six, so-called because ninety-six miles from Keowee, and then crossed over to the headwaters of the Savannah River. From Dividing Paths near Apple Tree Creek one path ran westward to the heart of the Lower Towns on the Tugaloo River, the other to Keowee. At Tugaloo, 'the most Antient Town in these parts,'[86] the English maintained one of their principal facto-

[82] *Ga. Hist. Coll.*, II. 72. See above note 64.
[83] C.O. 5 Maps, N.A.C. General, 7 (manuscript map, official, *circa* 1721-1727). For a description of the Virginia trail to the Catawba, see Bassett's introduction to Byrd, *Writings*, p. xviii.
[84] Library of Congress.
[85] Mereness (ed.), *Travels*, pp. 97-172. See also *Year Book of the City of Charleston*, 1894, pp. 342-52. I have also used maps in the Colonial Office Library, Whitehall: especially C.O. Maps, N.A.C. General, 7, and the Haig-Hunter map of the Cherokee, 1751, ibid., Carolina, 17.
[86] Chicken, in Mereness (ed.), *Travels*, p. 145. Tugaloo and the towns nearby were in Oconee County, S. C., and Habersham County, Ga.

ries. Estatoee nearby, with more than six hundred people, was the 'mother town' of this lower division; Itseyi, Noyowee (Nuyuhi), Chagee, and Toxaway were neighboring settlements. Westward from Tugaloo, at the head of the Chattahoochee, fifteen to thirty miles distant, were the frontier towns towards the Creeks: Soquee or Sukeki, Naguchee, and Echota. From Echota a difficult mountain path led by way of Unacoi Gap over the lofty Blue Ridge, then through the Valley Towns to the head of the Hiwasee, a branch of the Tennessee, and ultimately across the high Unakas, by the Northwest Passage of the traders, to the Overhill Cherokee.

But from Congaree the usual approach to the Cherokee country was by way of famous Keowee, where, in 1753, Fort Prince George was built.[87] A mile above Keowee, Cunasagee (Sugar Town) marked the head of the lovely Vale of Keowee. The botanist Bartram, who saw it in 1776, wrote that 'this fertile vale within the remembrance of some old traders with whom I conversed, was one continued settlement; the swelling sides of the adjoining hills were then covered with habitations, and the rich level grounds beneath lying on the river, was cultivated and planted.'[88] Around 1715 the Lower Cherokee on or near the headwaters of the Savannah River numbered eleven towns and 2,100 people. Westward from Keowee the trading path ran by way of Old Keowee, Tomasee and Oconoee, to Chatooga, Tacoreche, and Stecoe, where again the Blue Ridge raises its barrier three to four thousand feet high. But the Chattooga River and its tributary creeks have etched their valleys deeply into the hills, and by way of Rabun Gap was an easy approach for Indian or trader to the sources of the Little Tennessee, another of the western waters. Beyond the pass this river pursues its first rapid course northward, through the 'extensive and fruitful vale of Cowe'; it is soon 'incredibly increased in size, by the continual accession of brooks flowing in from the hills on each side.' These hills, Bartram observed, had been 'the common situations of the towns of the

[87] Oconee County, S. C. See D. D. Wallace, *Henry Laurens,* p. 98 and appendix IV (pp. 503-10).
[88] Bartram, *Travels,* 1792, p. 330.

ancients.'[89] Here, in the early eighteenth century, Old Estatoee, Tessento, Noofka, and Arachi still looked down from their heights upon this fountain of the Mississippi. Northward the widening valley of the river and the nearby hills were the sites of numerous settlements: Echoy, Nequasse or Nucasse, Watauga and Cowee, and the hill-towns of Catatoga, Cunisca, Ellijay the little, and Jore. From Watauga, where the Little Tennessee curves westward, a path led off to the northeast, through Watauga Gap in the Cowee range, to a second group of the Middle Towns on the parallel course of the Tuckasegee. In all these middle settlements the English noted some thirty towns, with a population of nearly six thousand Indians. Politically the Middle Towns were joined to the Lower Cherokee. From Jore the traders' route to the Overhill settlements struck westward to Little Tellico, and thence by way of Great Tellico, 'an English Factory,' to the Tennessee. The other chief towns of the trans-montane division, the bulwark of the Cherokee, and of Carolina, against the French Indians of the Northwest, were Euphase, Tallasee, Tennessee, Chotte, and Settico. In the Overhill towns was spoken a peculiar dialect, the Atali.

In 1721 the Society for the Propagation of the Gospel received a 'true and exact account of the number and names of all the Towns belonging to the Cherikee Nation and of the Number of Men, Women, and Children inhabiting the same,'[90] which was apparently based on carefully compiled returns from traders and agents. Fifty-three towns of a total of sixty were named, with a population of 10,379, of whom 3,510 were men. This was probably slightly under the actual number.[91]

[89] Ibid., p. 343, Macon County, N. C. Nucasse was near Franklin, N. C.; the path from Keowee traversed Rabun County, Georgia. The Tuckaseegee River towns were in Jackson County, N. C. The Overhill towns were mostly in Monroe County, Tenn. Tellico Plains is the approximate site of Great Tellico.

[90] S.P.G. MSS, B, IV, part 2, 173.

[91] Governor Johnson in 1708 said the Cherokees were settled in sixty towns and had at least 500 men (C.O. 5:1264, P 82). 'An Exact Account of the number and Strength of all the Indian Nations that were subject to the Government of South Carolina, and Solely Traded with them in the beginning of the year 1715,' drawn from the journals of Nairne, John Wright, Price Hughes, and John Barnwell (C.O. 5:1265, Q 201), gave a total for the Cherokees of 11,530 (it should be 11,210), as follows: Upper Settlement, 19 towns, 900 men, 980 women, 400 boys, 480 girls; Middle Settlement, 30 towns, 2500 men, 2000 women, 950 boys, 900 girls; Lower

But relations with the Indians of the Creek confederation were much more important commercially than with either Catawba or Cherokee. The chief inland bases of the trade, therefore, were found at the fall-line of the Savannah River. In the late seventeenth century, Savannah Town, with its Indian villages and its traders' stockades on both banks of the river,[92] foreshadowed the later settlements of New Windsor[93] and Augusta. New Windsor township was laid out in the shelter of Fort Moore. Augusta, which was built in 1735 seven miles upstream on the Georgia side, partially supplanted the Carolina village as the outfitting station for the trade. William Stephens estimated in 1740, perhaps too boastfully, that six hundred traders and two thousand horses resorted to Augusta in the spring.[94] From Charles Town to Savannah Town was a distance by road, *via* Edisto Bluff, of one hundred and forty miles. But the longer water-route was preferred, except when hostile Indians lurked along the river. From Port Royal to Savannah Town was reckoned twenty days' rowing against the current, but the laden periagoes and trading-boats dropped down-stream in four or five days. Five days up from Port Royal, on the right bank, was Palachacola Old Town,[95] abandoned by the Indians in 1715, where provisions were laid in for the river journey. Opposite the town a garrison was maintained from 1723 to 1735.

Long before the founding of Georgia, the Carolina traders followed a path to the Cherokee from Old Fort, opposite Savannah Town, along the right bank of the Savannah River.[96] Later, this became the main highway between Georgia and the mountain towns. But the usual Carolina route from Savannah Town ran northeast of the river. Both trails entered the Chero-

---

Settlement, 11 towns, 600 men, 620 women, 400 boys, 480 girls. The manuscript map, C.O. Maps, N.A.C. General, 7, was probably based on the same data, and the figures are substantially the same.

[92] Gascoyne, Plat, B.M. Add. MSS 5414, roll 24. See instructions to Ludwell, Nov. 8, 1691, to encourage settlement at Savannah Town (C.O. 5:288, p. 195).

[93] See Adair, *History of the American Indians,* p. 340; and Haig-Hunter map, 1751, C.O. Maps, Carolina, 17.

[94] *A State of the Province of Georgia,* pp. 6 f., reprinted in *Ga. Hist. Soc. Coll.,* II. 72. Cf. Martyn, *An Account shewing the Progress of Georgia,* p. 22, reprinted in ibid., p. 294; and *An Impartial Enquiry,* pp. 48 f.

[95] C.O. 5:358, A 9.

[96] See reference, note 92.

kee country at Tugaloo, where also ended the Indian path, sometimes used by traders, from Coweta Town on the Chattahoochee.

From Savannah Town and the neighboring settlements the great southern and western trade routes led away to the populous Creek towns in the Altamaha, Chattahoochee, and Alabama valleys, and beyond to the settlements of the Choctaw and the Chickasaw, and as far as the Natchez and Yazoo villages on the Mississippi.[97] After 1690 and prior to the Yamasee War the first objective of the southern traders was Ochese Creek, the head of Ocmulgee River above the confluence with Tobesofkee Creek. There the Ochese Creek Indians, by abbreviation the *Creeks,* were seated in ten or eleven towns. An official report in 1715 placed their numbers at 731 men, in all, 2,406 souls.[98] In 1708 Governor Johnson had described them as great hunters and warriors, who consumed large quantities of English goods, in contrast to the lazy Cherokee.[99] For fifty miles from Savannah Town a Creek trader guided his caravan a little south of west to the ford of the Ogeechee River. Beyond, the road divided into two paths. If he traded with the Okmulgee and the neighboring towns he turned his horses southwest to follow the Lower Path by way of Oconee Town. Approaching the Ocmulgee River he passed through 'the famous Oakmulgee fields,' where, wrote William Bartram after many years, 'are yet conspicuous very wonderful remains of the power and grandeur of the ancients in this part of America.'[100] 'Good Land' was the brief rubric on an early map at this place;[101] the southern tribes, after their primitive fashion, were notable farmers. It was by the Lower Path to Okmulgee that Moore and the other early invaders marched to the frontiers of Apalache. After the Yamasee War and the retreat westward of the Lower Creeks, it became, with its extension

[97] The description below is based on many cartographical sources, including C.O. Maps, N.A.C. General, 7; Spotswood's copy of Price Hughes' map, ibid., Virginia, 2; William Bonar, 'A Draught of the Creek Nation,' May, 1757, ibid., Carolina, 21; ibid., Carolina, 3; ibid., Florida, 2.

[98] Rivers, *Sketch,* p. 94. The Nairne inset in the Crisp map (1711) showed 'Okesee,' 700 men. The towns were near Macon, Ga.

[99] C.O. 5:1264, P 82.

[100] *Loc. cit.,* pp. 53, 379.

[101] C.O. Maps, N.A.C. General, 7.

the 'Old Sandhill Path,' the direct road to their new towns on the Chattahoochee.

The Lower Creek country, after 1716, extended from a short distance above the falls of the Chattahoochee some forty or fifty miles downstream. Coweta Town was located on the right bank, a few miles from the falls; Kasihta opposite, several miles below. These were the northernmost towns of any importance, though about fifty miles above, where the Upper Path crossed the river, was Chattahoochee town, settled some years before for convenience in carrying on the trade to the Upper Creeks. Below Coweta most of the villages were planted on the western bank. They included the Yuchi town; Osochi, Chiaha, and Okmulgee, the so-called Point towns, and Hichiti, in the sharp eastward bend of the river, opposite the mouth of Hichitee Creek; Apalachicola, Oconee, and Sawokli. Kolomi, Atasi, and Tuskegee were at first neighbors of Coweta, but later moved down below the Point. Eufala town was some distance below, near Clewalla Creek; Chisca Talofa was an outlying southern settlement towards Weopka, or the Forks village, which was located in the middle-century on the west bank, opposite the confluence with the Flint. In the forks proper, Cherokeeleechee in 1716 built his fort, where, for a time, the pro-Spanish faction of the Apalachicola maintained a center of anti-English intrigue.[102]

By the Upper Path the traders before the Yamasee War made their way westward from Ogeechee one hundred and ten miles to Coweta and Kasihta Old Towns near the head of the Ocmulgee. After the rising and the Lower Creek migration, the Upper Path still remained the direct route to the Upper Creek towns. Arrived at Okfuskee on the Tallapoosa, after a toilsome journey from the settlements of at least three weeks, a trader found himself on the margin of the Upper Creek country. But if his license read for the Chickasaw or the Choctaw, he was still only a little more than half-way to his destination.

The Upper Creeks were known to the Carolinians for many years by the names of their three geographical divisions: Tala-

---

[102] C.O. Maps, N.A.C. General, 7; Carolina, 21; Swanton, *Early History*, plates 1, 2, and index under towns. Coweta and Kasihta were near present Columbus, Ga., and most of the other towns were in Russell County, Ala.

poosa, Coosa or Abikha, and Alabama. By one account of about 1715, 'the Tallibooses consist of 11 Towns and 563 men;'[103] a nearly contemporaneous estimate was 13 towns, 636 men, 2,343 souls.[104] After the Ochese this was the largest Indian 'nation' in the Carolina trading system. The Talapoosa villages were strung along the valley of the Okfuskee or Talla-poosa River from their chief village, and the foremost western Carolina factory, at Great Okfuskee, well down to the forks of the Alabama. From Okfuskee to Tukabahchee the river flows almost due south, and then turns sharply westward to its con-fluence with the Coosa. Tukabahchee was another early Caro-lina factory, where the Lower Path from Coweta reached the river, to follow it thence to the towns in the point overlooked by Fort Toulouse. Near the French fort and along the Ala-bama River below lived the Alabama Indians, '4 Towns and 226 Men,' the English reckoned, in 1715.[105] From Charles Town to the Alabamas, said Oglethorpe, was a journey of twenty-seven days for the packhorse trains.[106] The Upper Path continued northwestward from Okfuskee twenty miles to Wa-kokai, then west an equal distance to Abihkutci and nearby Coosa, on the Coosa River, the head towns of the third great division of the Upper Creeks. In 1715 they were said to num-ber '14 Towns and 1773 Souls whereof 500 [are] fighting Men.'[107]

The 'old Chikkasah, or American-Flanders path,' as Adair named it,[108] was a continuation of the Upper Path extending northwestward for about two hundred miles beyond the Abihka country. It ran through 'Rich Oak and Hickery Land mixt with Pleasant Savanas'[109] near the head of the Tuscaloosa; it skirted the southern foothills of the Appalachians where they

[103] C.O. Maps, N.A.C. General, 7. In the present Tallapoosa and Elmore Counties, Ala.
[104] C.O. 5:1265, Q 201. D'Artaguiette in 1721 listed twelve towns of 'Talapouches,' with 715 men, and eight of 'Alibamons,' with 560 men, but his classification was not exactly the same as the English, and made no separate list of the Coosa towns. See Baron Marc de Villiers, in Journ. de la societé des Americanistes de Paris, n.s., XIV. 127-40.
[105] C.O. Maps, N.A.C. General, 7. Near Montgomery, Ala.
[106] Oglethorpe to [Newcastle?] circa July, 1736, in C.O. 5:383.
[107] C.O. Maps, N.A.C. General, 7.
[108] Adair, History of the American Indians, p. 239.
[109] C.O. Maps, N.A.C. General, 7.

merge into the Alabama plains. On the upper branches of the Tombigbee was the small but warlike tribe of Chickasaw, six villages, 700 men, by English account in 1715, but in the next few decades they were wasted by their wars with the French and the Choctaw.[110] Always they were greatly inferior in numbers to the Choctaw, whose country lay southwest of their towns, about the sources of the Pascagoula and Pearl Rivers. With some 15,000 inhabitants in the eighteenth century, the Choctaw was the largest compact 'nation' in the South, only outnumbered, perhaps, by the loosely federated Creeks. On those occasions when the path was open to them, the Carolinians could reach the Choctaw either from the Chickasaw villages, or by the extension of the Lower Path from the Alabama.[111]

From the Ogeechee, then, to the borders of Florida and Louisiana, ran those two main arteries of the southwestern trade, gradually diverging, the Upper and the Lower Paths of the Charles Town traders. Long before the railroad, long before the emigrant trails, they led Anglo-American pioneers to their first conquest, by trade, of a great section of the trans-Appalachian West. With the paths of the Carolina piedmont and the trails to the Cherokee they linked the Carolina border with the most numerous tribes of Indians east of the Mississippi. No such network penetrated the wilderness from any other English colony in the seventeenth or early eighteenth century. No such direct commercial and political hegemony was won by the English traders elsewhere, over so great an area, even by the Albanians. Thomas Nairne might boast in 1705—and Governor Glen echo his words in 1748—'Everybody knows well wee have the greatest quantity of Indians Subject to this Government of any in all America, and almost as many as all other English Governments put together.'[112]

---

[110] C.O. 5:1265, Q 201. Swanton, *Early History,* pp. 437, 448-50.

[111] See the De Crenay map, 1733, ibid., plate 5.

[112] S.P.G. MSS, A, II, no. 156. Cf. Glen to Board of Trade, April 14, 1748, in C.O. 5:372, I 14.

CHAPTER VI

Trade Regulation and Intercolonial Problems
1670-1715

Until the middle of the eighteenth century the regulation and management of Indian affairs in the British American empire were left almost wholly to the control of the separate colonies, with results which approached chaos. The gradual centralization and imperialization of Indian relations during and after the last French war was a major tendency of later British policy, and a factor in the complex causes of the American Revolution.[1] Probably in no other colony was Indian administration so often the subject of provincial legislation, or so much involved in provincial politics, as in South Carolina. Nowhere were the evil possibilities of intercolonial conflicts for the control of the Indian trade more clearly demonstrated than on the southern frontier. Southern experience, moreover, as embodied in the Carolina Indian code, contributed substantially to later imperial attempts to deal with the Indian aspect of the western problem.[2]

For the first two decades, while the Proprietors were monopolizing traffic with the inland tribes, they attempted to exercise from England a rigid supervision over Indian relations. From the beginning they insisted upon orderly purchase of Indian lands, and warned against encroachments by settlers.[3] The Carolina record in these matters was fairly good, judged by frontier standards. Between 1670 and 1686 the land from Charles Town to the Savannah River and westward to the mountains was acquired by formal treaty with the 'cassiques' of Stono, Edisto, Ashepoo, St. Helena, Combahee, Kusso, etc.[4]

[1] See C. W. Alvord, *Mississippi Valley in British Politics.*
[2] The suggestions of the southern superintendent, John Stuart, based upon southern practice, were more influential in the framing of the Board of Trade plan of 1764 than has yet been pointed out.
[3] See instructions to governor and council, July 27, 1669 (C.O. 5:286, pp. 43-6; Rivers, *Sketch,* p. 348) ; 'Agrarian Laws,' 1672 (ibid., p. 358, from C.O. 5:286, pp. 83-6) ; Proprietors to governor and council, April 10, 1677 (C.O. 5:286, p. 125) ; same to same, May 19, 1679 (ibid., p. 141) ; instructions to governor, June 5, 1682 (ibid., p. 195).
[4] C.O. 5:288, p. 100. *Report of the Committee, Appointed to examine into the Proceedings of the People of Georgia* (1737), Appendix, pp. 50-3. *CSCHS,* V. 456 f. note.

But perhaps it was not so much proprietary influence as the slow growth of the colony and the weakness of the Cusabo or settlement Indians, that saved South Carolina from the kind of Indian crisis through which Virginia and New England were passing in those years. The Westo War of 1680 and the Yamasee War of 1715 were clearly of a different order.

Justice to the Indians, peaceful intercourse, and in particular the suppression of the traffic in Indian slaves, these were injunctions to successive governors and councils. Under the Fundamental Constitutions the Grand Council had been authorized 'to make peace or war, leagues, treaties, &c. with any of the neighboring Indians,'[5] but early instructions limited its powers to defense against invasion or injury, and enjoyned 'a fair Correspondence with all the people round about who doe you no harm.'[6] To insure peace, in 1680 the Proprietors set up a separate judicature to deal with disputes 'between Christians and Indians.'[7] The governor and six other commissioners—'the soberest and most disinterested Inhabitants,' they were described by the Proprietors' secretary[8]—were to meet every two months, or on summons, to hear and determine all conflicts. They had competence over trade disputes, but were in fact strictly forbidden to meddle with the proprietary monopoly of the inland trade. The strongest instruction to the commission was to prevent the enslaving or transportation without special proprietary license of any friendly Indians within two hundred miles of Charles Town. This early machinery for Indian regulation failed completely to serve the Proprietors' purposes. Governor West and at least two other members, Maurice Mathews and John Boone, were slave-dealers, whose profits from that business were dependent upon Indian wars. In 1682, following the Westo War, the commission was abrogated. The Proprietors then complained that it had been secured from them 'rather . . . for the opression than protection of the Indians.' At that time they extended their protection to all

[5] William MacDonald (ed.), *Select Charters*, p. 158 (Article 50).
[6] Instructions of May 1, 1671, C.O. 5:286, p. 64, printed in Rivers, *Sketch*, Appendix, p. 368.
[7] C.O. 5:286, pp. 148-52.
[8] [Samuel Wilson], *An Account of the Province of Carolina*, 1682, p. 15, reprinted in Carroll (ed.), *Collections*, II. 31.

Indians within four hundred miles of Charles Town and un-
qualifiedly forbade their enslavement.[9]

The conflict between the Proprietors and the planters over
Indian slavery was embittered by a clash of trading interests.
With their stake in the inland peltry trade, the Proprietors opposed wars and the slave-traffic for selfish as well as humani-
tarian reasons. The colonists, indeed, gave them little credit for
benevolence, and this cynicism found some support in the fact
that proprietary opposition to Indian slavery waxed and waned
with the rise and decline of their trading régime. Moreover,
they never developed similar scruples with regard to the Guinea
trade. In 1671-1672 the 'Temporary Laws' and the 'Agrarian
Laws' forbade Indian slavery or the transportation of any
Indian 'without his owne consent.' The 'consent' of captives
brought in by the Sewee was actually recorded in the Grand
Council journal in 1675.[10] The Westo War undermined the
proprietary Indian traffic and inaugurated an orgy of slave-
dealing which drew down the wrath of the proprietary board.
In September, 1683, the Proprietors sent to the governor and
council a long letter exposing and denouncing the odious business.[11] The colonists' excuse that public safety demanded the
transportation of captives they swept aside, and ridiculed the
argument that 'the Sevanas haveing United all their tribes are
become [so] powerfull that it is Dangerous to disoblige them.'
The exclusive contract with the Savannah for slaves in return
for arms and ammunition was a certain means, they declared,
to attract to them all the other scattered tribes 'and so make
them formidable indeed.' The plea that the Savannahs assisted
the colonists against their enemies met with the reply that 'the
sending away of Indians made the Westoh and Waniah Warrs
and Continue[s] them,' and will 'make other Warrs if the Indians are Suffered still to be sent away and warr is very Inconvenient for Planters.' Humanity, the planters had explained,
induced them to buy slaves of their Indian allies 'to keep them
from being put to Cruell deaths.' But thus, retorted the Proprietors, you induce the Savannahs 'through Covetousness of

---

[9] Instructions to Morton, May 10, 1682, C.O. 5 :286, p. 186.
[10] Rivers, *Sketch*, p. 132; Appendix, pp. 353, 358. *JGC*, December 10, 1675.
[11] C.O. 5 :288, p. 16 *et seq.*

your gunns Powder and Shott and other European Comodities
. . . to ravish the wife from the Husband, Kill the father to
get the Child and to burne and Destroy the habitations of these
poore people into whose Country wee were Ch[e]arefully received by them, cherished and supplyed when wee are weake,
or at least never have done us hurt; and after wee have set
them on worke to doe all these horrid wicked things to get
slaves to sell the dealers in Indians call it humanity to buy them
and thereby keep them from being murdered.' The scandal of
these actions in England, they declared, had prevented 'many
sober, substantiall Men from coming to you.' It was a business,
they charged, which enriched only a few ambitious men with
'a share in the Government.' Against these trader-politicians
the Proprietors proceeded with rigor. The Indian commission
was abolished, West removed as governor, Maurice Mathews
and James Moore discharged as deputies, the former also as
surveyor.[12] To be sure, in 1683, they modified the complete
prohibition, conceding that slaves might be taken by soldiers in
legitimate Indian wars to encourage enlistments. But for their
exportation they required the consent of the parliament, signi-
fied in each case by special act.[13] With the decline of the Proprietors' interest in the Indian trade, and the slackening of their
efficiency in government their opposition to the slave-trade became more and more perfunctory. In any case the traffic survived as an important instrument in Carolinian expansion. The
dispute, meanwhile, had helped to stir up anti-proprietary feel-
ings which never disappeared until the proprietorship ceased.
The address to Seth Sothell in 1691[14] voiced the mingled
grievances of a growing party 'concerninge Fundamentall Constitutions, Indentures for land and in matters of orderinge
the Indian trade.'

The proprietary monopoly of 1677-1684 lapsed, but individual Proprietors were tempted by Shaftesbury's vision of
wealth in the Carolinian wilderness, as were also ambitious
governors and councillors. Landgrave Colleton, brother of the
Proprietor, was accused by the anti-proprietary party of at-

[12] C.O. 5:288, pp. 16, 17, 18, 20, 50, 64, 67.
[13] C.O. 5:288, pp. 18 f.
[14] Rivers, *Sketch*, Appendix, pp. 426 f.

tempting to secure a trade monopoly, and it was insinuated that there were 'rational grounds' for believing that he had a partner in England. 'Wee have never wanted courage to regulate, by Lawes, the Indian Trade,' declared these memorialists, 'so as that the Colony should not be in any danger from thence; yett wee have been always interrupted and obstructed by such doings as these.' Apparently the earliest act 'for Regulating-of the Indian Trade'[15] was passed in Sothell's time. It is not extant, and was soon superseded by the extraordinary measure of September 26, 1691.[16] The preamble recited that previous invasions of the colony had found the government without funds to rout the enemy, and without the services of the persons employed in the Indian trade, 'by reason of the distance the most convenient place for that tradeing lyes from the settled part of this Collony.' Duties were therefore levied upon the export of skins and furs, and at the same time all trading was forbidden south of the Savannah River, north of the Winyah River, or beyond Savannah Town and the Congarees. Provision was made for the withdrawal of traders from the Lower Creeks and Cherokee and other distant tribes within a specified period. Probably the law was intended to create another monopoly to be enjoyed by Sothell and his friends. In any case the governor would profit largely from it: for two years he was granted a third of the duties and a third of the penalties for illegal trading. Although Sothell's acts were annulled by the Proprietors, this one seems to have been enforced against James Moore in 1692, but it did not long restrain the inland advance of the traders.[17]

With Joseph Blake (deputy-governor, 1694, 1696-1700) began the great westward push of the Carolina traders to the Mississippi, and also ten years' struggle over trade regulation. Everyone agreed that some sort of reform was imperative, in view of the character and the conduct of the traders. Both Blake and Moore, magnates of the trade, repeatedly called for

[15] Cooper (ed.), *Statutes,* II. 55.
[16] Ibid., p. 64.
[17] *JGC,* April 14, May 28, 1692. In 1693 and 1696 acts were passed 'for destroying beasts of prey and for appointing magistrates for the hearing and determining of all causes and controversies between white man and Indian, and Indian and Indian.' *JCHA,* September 12, 14, 16, 18, 21, 1693; Cooper (ed.), *Statutes,* II. 108.

legislation, though both were accused by their enemies of obstructing reform for monopolistic reasons. Edward Randolph, a chronic scandal-monger, accused Blake of a partnership with Amy, a Proprietor, and Thornburgh, their secretary. 'This triumvirate,' he said, 'carry on the Government and the Indian Trade together, for one must support the other else both are ruined.'[18] Certainly the conflicting interests of governors and councillors who were also traders, of merchants, planters, and Proprietors, long prevented agreement upon any measure of regulation. In December, 1697, the Proprietors urged Blake to get the trade regulated so 'that it might be a Strengthening to the Country.'[19] Already, in February, 1697, the assembly had debated the problem, and resolved 'that the said Trade be Regulated' but had postponed the issue to another session. A great smallpox epidemic which raged among the Indians for four or five hundred miles inland seemed for the moment to make legislation less urgent.[20] But soon rumors of the French project to settle on the Mississippi supplied a new motive for reform. In September, 1698, the Commons House unanimously resolved that the Indian trade as then conducted was 'a grievance to the Settlement and Prejudiciall to the Safety thereof.'[21]

The issues of this early American debate over state regulation of business had curiously modern implications. In the Commons House there was considerable sentiment for a public trade. In October, 1698, the committee of the whole agreed that 'the Indian trade should be managed by a Publick Stock for the Use of the Publick'; but probably in deference to the merchants the public commissioners were to be forbidden to trade directly with England.[22] When a public stock was again proposed in 1703 this restriction was waived.[23] Meanwhile, under Moore's government, various other schemes of reorganization had been brought forward, including a bill in 1701 for an open trade under strict public regulation, the method

---

[18] Randolph to Blathwayt, Bermuda, April 8, 1699, in *Prince Society Publications,* XXXI (Randolph Papers, VII), 554.

[19] C.O. 5:289, p. 38.

[20] *JCHA,* February 24, March 2, 1696/7; Blake and council to Proprietors, April 23 [1698], *Commissions and Instructions, 1685-1715* (1916), p. 105.

[21] *JCHA,* September 28, 1698.

[22] Ibid., October 4, 1698.

[23] Ibid., January 21, 1702/3.

ultimately adopted.[24] In 1702 the assembly rejected both a public trade and a 'farmed trade' such as Colonel Thomas Broughton, a member of the assembly and a considerable trader, had proposed. For a monopoly northward to the Saxapahaw and 'as farr Southward and westward as the Same may be done with Safety,' Broughton offered to pay £800 a year into the treasury, and to maintain twenty armed and mounted rangers to guard the frontier.[25] A few months later the former Carolinian, Robert Quary, was urging the colonial authorities to take over the proprieties and appoint royal governors, especially in Carolina, where a law to regulate the Indian trade in the public interest might, he said, be made to defray all the expenses of the government. Quary elaborated his ideas in another memorial. He proposed that the Crown create companies to control the Indian trade in America, which would provide frontier defense in return for monopoly rights.[26] Nicholson supported the plan before the Board of Trade. This was substantially the scheme which Spotswood, a decade later, set up in Virginia.

In the Colleton county representation, June 26, 1703, Moore's enemies charged that 'by his Artifices' he had been 'the chief (if not the only) occasion of obstructing' regulation, 'designing nothing less than the ingrossing the same for himself and accomplices.' And his successor, Johnson, alluded to the fact as of common knowledge that the upper house under previous governors had consistently refused proposals of regulation.[27] But the assembly records throw some doubt upon

[24] Ibid., February 6, 1700/1. See ibid., January 29, 1701/2 for similar proposal. See John Ash, *Present State of Affairs in Carolina* (1706?), Number 4 of [collection of papers relating to the church controversy], p. 30: 'Finding himself too poor, even with the Countenance of his Office, to make any considerable Profit of the Indian Trade, he lays a Design of getting it wholly into his Power. This he attempted by getting a Bill brought into the Assembly at the latter end of the Year 1700, Intituled, *A Bill for Regulating the Indian Trade,* but so contriv'd as to have made him wholly Master of it. But Mr. Robert Stephens, Mr. Trott (then no Courtier) and some others so plainly shew'd its ill Aim, that it was thrown out of the Assembly, as it was again in the beginning of the Year 1701.'
[25] Ibid., January 22, 27, 29, 1701/2.
[26] C.O. 323:3, E 31, 32; Memorials read by Board of Trade, March 31 and April 7, 1702. Quary also urged the settlement of the Port Royal border. In the Archdale papers (MSS, Library of Congress) is an undated project for an Indian company to consist of 'the joynt stock of all Inhabitants, who puting in to the saide stock according to their capacities, shall receive their proportion of all Devidents made of proffets.'
[27] Rivers, *Sketch,* pp. 455 f.

these accusations. In April, 1702, Moore made an unusual, but apparently an ingenuous appeal for trade reform to prevent an Indian war. 'I have the most Numerous Family of Relations and children in the Collony,' he declared, adding that he had laid out most of his fortune 'in Settling Plantations for them, and those in the most Inland Parts of the Collony.' Therefore in case of war he had 'Reason to Expect to be the first and greatest Sufferer.' He believed it was better for himself and his family 'to prefer the Saveing of what we have already to the Prospect of gitting more by that Trade,' which, unless regulated, would certainly bring on disaster. Accordingly he promised his assent to any regulatory law 'even to the Ceasing to trade with the Indjans or to be Concerned any way Relateing to it Whilst I am Governor,' provided that the assembly's bill aimed 'at nothing but the Publick Safety.' At the same time the governor freely denounced the abuses of the traders.[28] He often warned that care must be taken to prevent the Yamasee and Creeks from deserting to the Spanish and French. And it was his initiative that led to official investigations which uncovered many acts of petty tyranny by the traders.[29] In January, 1702, the assembly awarded judgment against seven Yamasee traders for failing to pay for skins, for burning Indian houses, killing hogs, stealing guns, etc. The method used to enforce satisfaction marked the beginnings of a regulative system. The governor was requested to empower Thomas Nairne, who had already performed some of the duties of an Indian agent, to carry out the assembly's orders.[30] Another law was also passed in that year, at Moore's request, to prevent traders selling goods on credit and to appoint 'a judicious man' to regulate trade and political relations among the Upper Creeks.[31] Apparently Moore was not entirely responsible for the failure to adopt an adequate Indian code.[32]

[28] JCHA, April 2, 1702. See *Warrants for Lands, 1680-1692,* pp. 33, 66, 103, 166; ibid., *1692-1711,* pp. 12, 17, 21, 32, 126, for warrants for over 4000 acres to James Moore.
[29] JCHA, November 16, 1700; January 14, 15, 20, 21, 1702.
[30] Ibid., January 24, 1702.
[31] Not printed, but referred to in journals; ibid., April 2, August 14, 15, 20, 22, 25, 27, 29, 1702. Colonel Stephen Bull was sent as agent to the Talapoosas, his salary to begin at his departure from Savannah Town.
[32] From an allusion during the discussions of 1707 it appears that in 1703 Moore was an advocate of public trade.

As a matter of fact, Indian regulation was now hopelessly entangled in the bitter factionalism of Carolina politics. The failure of the St. Augustine campaign and the debts then incurred had stirred up vociferous opposition to Moore and his friends. The malcontents were especially numerous in Colleton county, the stronghold of the dissenters. Under Sir Nathaniel Johnson, who was supported by Trott and others of Moore's party, provincial politics for several years revolved around the famous church controversy. Johnson, wrote Archdale, in hostile vein, 'by a Chimical Wit, Zeal and Art, transmuted or turn'd this Civil Difference into a Religious Controversy.'[33] But other issues were also involved in the protracted dispute: the claims of the Commons House of Assembly to control administration, and, not least, the complex problem of regulating the Indian trade.

One of Johnson's stoutest opponents, along with John Ash, was Thomas Nairne of St. Helena. According to his own account, Nairne drew up and introduced into the assembly the addresses of thanks to the Queen and the House of Lords for the repeal of the obnoxious Conformity and Church Acts, and so laid himself open 'to the hatred of the Governor.'[34] Nairne had already aligned himself with Dr. Edward Marston, whom Johnson denounced as 'the pest of the country,' in an attack, in 1705, upon a clerical protegé of the governor, the Reverend Samuel Thomas. This clergyman had been sent out to Carolina in 1702 by the Society for the Propagation of the Gospel in response to the appeal of Nairne and Robert Stevens for a missionary to the Yamasee. Thomas reported on his arrival that those Indians, at war with Florida, were 'not at leasure to attend to instruction, nor is it safe,' he added, 'to venture among them.' His prudence was rewarded by the governor, who appointed him to the pleasant cure of Goose Creek, where he convinced himself that efforts to convert the negro slaves were as laudable as hazardous missionary labors in the 'Indian Land.' But Nairne and Stevens excoriated him for abandoning his charge. For over a century, Nairne recalled, the Spanish

---

[33] Archdale, *Description*, 1707, p. 23, reprinted in Carroll (ed.), *Collections*, II. 110. See Rivers, *Sketch*, chs. viii-x, and McCrady, *S. C. under the Prop. Gov.*, chs. xviii-xx.
[34] C.O. 5:306, no. 4.

Indians now in Carolina had had Christian churches among them. 'Now if we take not care equal of their Salvation as the Spaniards always have done, what a good fight have wee been fighting to bring so many people from something of Christianity to downright Barbarity and heathenism.' But Nairne's interest in Indian missions was not altogether the product of piety. He also saw the usefulness of having among the Indians persons not interested in trade to protect them from injustice and to send the government intelligence of Indian affairs. In 1705 he proposed a fund for the purpose: the Queen to settle £100 annually out of her dues in Carolina, the Proprietors to allow £80, and the rest to be raised by a tax of £4 a year on the traders.[35]

By 1706 the ecclesiastical dispute was abated. But much of the heat of the quarrel was carried over into the debates on Indian affairs. On this new ground the opposition to the ruling clique of Johnson, Rhett, and Trott was reinforced by many supporters of Johnson's church policy. By 1707 they were securely in control of the assembly. As before, the organization of the trade was involved. But the crux of the debate was now whether the governor and council, or the Commons House should control the Indian administration? And who should enjoy the Indian presents, the governor or the public? This clash of interest was intimately connected with the parallel struggle for the appointment by the assembly of the public-receiver. It was characteristic of this frontier province that the first notable contest between the executive and the popular branch of the legislature for administrative power—a struggle which developed in most of the provinces and produced profound changes in their constitutions in the eighteenth century—should have had as one of its issues the administration of Indian affairs.

In the spring of 1706, urging regulation, the governor assured the assembly that neither 'relations or any particular Interest' would bias him.[36] The reference was probably to his

[35] S.P.G. MSS, A, II, no. 156; *SCHGM,* IV. 221-30, 278-85; V. 21-55; [Collection of printed documents relating to church controversy, etc. London, *circa* 1706]: letter of Marston, May 3, 1705; Humphreys, *Historical Account,* 1730, pp. 81-3; E. B. Greene, 'The Anglican Outlook,' in *AHR,* XX. 72.

[36] JCHA, March 7, 1705/6.

son-in-law, Colonel Thomas Broughton, a great trader. But one 'particular interest' proved to be a great stumbling-block. This was the valuable perquisite which Johnson and earlier governors had enjoyed of retaining all presents made by the Indians to the province. In December, 1706, Johnson refused as 'penurious' £200 a year in lieu of these presents, an amount equal to his salary.[37] The opposition scented scandal in the practice, and later brought up the case of James Child in confirmation. The slave-dealers, Nairne asserted, had a trick of setting Indians in the English alliance to surprise each other's towns in order to make a quicker sale of their goods for slaves; and to escape punishment they had 'the address to be industrious in procuring presents for the Governor and tradeing in partnership with his Son-in-Law.' James Child, he said, had set the Cherokees upon some friendly Indians in 1706, pretending that he acted on the governor's orders. They took about 160 captives, thirty of whom Child exposed for sale in the Charles Town slave-market, declaring that half were for the governor. The assembly set the captives free, but the governor paid no heed to their petitions to prosecute Child.[38] It was this affair, apparently, that led to the temporary act of April, 1706, to restrain traders charged with offenses from going into the Indian country, for the Commons promptly requested Johnson to apply the ban to Child. Similar charges against John Musgrove, John Pight, and Anthony Probat, traders, were ventilated in the assembly in 1706. The state of the trade had become notorious, and there were 'private whispers that the governor privately Encouraged these Kinds of Actions.'[39]

Late in 1706 the Commons sent up a bill to prohibit presents to the governor and to place the regulation of the traders in the hands of their own commissioners. The issues were clearly drawn. To be sure, the Commons insisted that they were divesting the governor of neither power nor profit, but merely endowing their commissioners with authority not already possessed by the governor. In case of refusal they threatened to carry the affair not only to the Proprietors but to the Crown.

[37] Ibid., December 20, 1706.
[38] C.O. 5:306, no. 4; and petition to Proprietors in Huntington Library.
[39] C.O. 5:306, no. 4; JCHA, April 2, 9, November 23, December 20, 1706; Cooper (ed.), *Statutes,* II. 274 (act of April 9, 1706, enacted for six months).

Johnson was resolute. 'I offer you,' he replied, 'a regulation of the Indian trade, but so that it may be safe to the country, honourable and profitable to myself, and no ways chargeable to the public.'[40]

The first session of 1707 was stormy. The opposition was in a mood for conquest, and pressed the attack on all fronts. Nairne was again directing the fight. It was Nairne with George Smith who drafted the bill declaring the right of the assembly to name the public receiver.[41] It was Nairne who drew up an address to the Crown on the grievances of the country.[42] It was Nairne who led the battle to place control of Indian affairs in the hands of the Commons House. Most of the members, the House later declared, had received specific instructions from their constituents to pass the Indian act, 'Demanded by so many Assemblys and the Universall cry of the People.'[43] In the spring the province had been further aroused by the affair of the Savannah Indians. Resenting encroachments and other injuries, part of the Savannah had begun to desert their towns at the fall-line and move northward, a migration which led them eventually to Maryland and Pennsylvania. Richard Berresford of the Commons House was posted off to check the desertion, without any commission at first from governor and council, who claimed sole authority over Indian negotiations. June 20, Berresford received the thanks of the Commons for reducing the Savannahs and investigating abuses. The same day Johnson complained that the lower house had taken exclusive possession of Berresford's journals.[44] But it was the control of the Indian trade, rather than of Indian diplomacy, that was the real objective of the popular party. This control was won through Nairne's Indian act of July 19, 1707.

Early in July, 1707, Johnson, without a conference, rejected a bill for a public stock in the Indian trade as 'a grand

[40] JCHA, December 20, 1706, January 29, 1706/7.
[41] Ibid., July 2, 1707.
[42] Ibid., June 27, 1707.
[43] Ibid., July 5, 1707.
[44] Ibid., April, June, 1707, *passim*. Further difficulties with the Savannah in 1708 led to the despatch of Captain James Moore (son of the old governor) to reduce them; cf. ibid., February, October, November, 1708, *passim*; Swanton, *Early History*, pp. 317 f.; *Handbook of American Indians*, II. 533.

monopoly and against the Express words of the Charter.'[45]
He invited legislation 'agreeable to the Charter and their
Lordships' instructions'; but when next day the Commons sent
up a new bill under a similar title the upper house returned it
on the technical ground that a bill once rejected could not be
reintroduced in the same session. The Commons then threatened
to hold up the governor's cherished project for fortifying
Charles Town. 'We are not solicitous to provide a defence for
our breasts,' they declared, 'when we may at the same time receive a mortall Stabb thro our Backs.'[46] This threat, or perhaps
the menace of an appeal to the Crown, proved effective.[47] But
Johnson's stubbornness had won the concession of £100 a year
payable to the governor and his successors in lieu of Indian
presents; and also a lump sum not mentioned in the act but
entered in the schedule of debts:

[To] the Rt. Honble. the Governor Sr. Nath. Johnson for Con-
centing to the Indians Trading Act . . . £400.[48]

The Commons sought to make this payment contingent upon
Johnson's securing the approval of the Proprietors for the act,
but he only agreed to press it upon them.[49] 'That a free province
should be forced to purchase their deliverance from abuses'
was denounced in a memorial to the Proprietors as 'a corrup-
tion almost beyond example.'[50]

The anxiety of the assembly to secure a guarantee of rati-
fication was no doubt due to the fact that their act 'for Regulating the Indian Trade and making it Safe to the Public'[51]
involved a considerable encroachment by the popular branch of
the legislature upon administration. The whole Indian trade
outside of the settlements[52] was subjected to a system of licensing and regulation under the control, not of the governor
and council, nor of the assembly as a whole, but solely of the

---

[45] JCHA, July 4, 1707. See also ibid., March 6, April 23, 1707.
[46] Ibid., July 5, 1707.
[47] Ibid., July 5, 7, 11, 14, 15, 17, 18, 1707, for legislative history.
[48] Ibid., July 19, 1707.
[49] Ibid., July 14, 15, 1707. Nairne wrote of this deal: 'This they [the
Commons] did with much reluctancy, only fear of danger prevailed with
them.' C.O. 5:306, no. 4.
[50] JCHA, October 20, 1709.
[51] Cooper (ed.), *Statutes*, II. 309 *et seq.*
[52] On the Cusabo and the other 'settlement Indians,' see Swanton, *Early
History*, pp. 31-72, especially 71.

Commons. The machinery consisted of a board of Indian commissioners, a secretary, and an agent, all appointed for indefinite terms by the act, and removable by vote of the Commons House.

There were nine Indian commissioners, who were usually members of the assembly. As a rule they had had experience in Indian affairs, though like the agent they were under oath not to engage in trade, directly or indirectly, during their tenure. Ralph Izard was the first president; Richard Berresford, another commissioner, had acted in the Savannah affair; Samuel Eveleigh and Captain Musgrove were, respectively, merchant and Indian trader. An act of 1712 added the governor, the popular Charles Craven, to the board, but he served only a few months.[53] The board was required to meet twice a year, in February and August, in three-day sessions. Other meetings, however, were frequent: from 1710 to 1715 they averaged two or three each month from March to December. In their corporate capacity the commissioners were vested with considerable powers. They granted, or, at their discretion, withheld, the licenses, good for one year, which all traders except those in the settlements must procure. They issued instructions to the agent and to the traders; the latter must obey or forfeit their licenses. As a court they heard appeals from the agent's decisions.[54]

But it was the Indian agent who stood at the centre of the new regulative machinery. For a salary of £250 he was obliged to live for ten months in each year among the tribes subject to South Carolina, to visit all their principal towns, redress grievances and supervise the trade. He was a justice of the peace, with authority to decide all cases among traders, or between Indians and traders, involving sums of under £30

[53] Cooper (ed.), *Statutes,* II. 381. Not extant, but the journals of the assembly and the board indicate its character. In 1713 and 1714 there was much discussion of further legislation; JCHA, 1713, 1714, *passim.* See Rawlinson MSS C, 943, for a report of the commissary, the Rev. Gideon Johnston, *circa* 1713, which reveals his unsuccessful effort to secure appointment to the board in order to promote missionary efforts among the Indians.

[54] Act of 1707, articles i, v, xiii, xxiv-xxvi, xxix-xxx. The pay during sessions was 10s. per day. The journals and other records were kept by a secretary who was paid 10s. a day for his attendance, and a 20s. fee for each license.

currency. He could examine witnesses under oath, send down offenders for trial at Charles Town, and direct orders and warrants to all whites in the ·Indian country. On complaint of a merchant against a trader for debt, a common occurrence, the agent was required to demand securities or commit the debtor to prison.[55] To these duties defined by law the board added others in their instructions: supervising the traders' morals, upholding their influence over the Indians, preserving peace between tribes in the Carolina alliance, and converting 'as many Nations of Indians as possibly you can to embrace our Amity and Friendship.' He was also to act as a political adviser to the tribes within the English sphere of influence, 'Giving the King and head men advice in Relation to the managing their people the Better to keep them in Subjection, and with Example and arguments drawn from a parralell with our Government; and always as much as in you lyes keep in favour with the Chief Men, advising and assisting them to Maintain the Authority given them by this Government.'[56] The Indian agent, moreover, was the chief adviser of the Charles Town government in all Indian affairs.

The agent's office took him frequently upon a great circuit of the southern wilderness. In July, 1712, John Wright was ordered by the board to set out for the Indian country upon a day prescribed, and his route and duties were laid down in his instructions. First, he should go to Pocotaligo Town, to settle all differences between the traders and the Upper Yamasee, thence to Altamaha, in the lower towns, then upstream to hold another court at Palachacola. To the Alabamas he was instructed to travel by way of Savannah Town, and on his way to send an express to the trader, Captain Thomas Welch, to get the Chickasaw chiefs down to the Alabamas. But if they failed him, he must push on to the Chickasaw country. His special mission was to prevent the threatened defection of the Alabama to the French, by redressing their grievances, by arguments and presents, and, if necessary, by taking hostages and inciting the loyal tribes to oppose the renegades. This accomplished, he had still to settle ordinary affairs among the Tala-

[55] Articles vii, xi-xviii, xx, xxii-xxiii.
[56] JIC, July 9, December 18, 1712.

poosa and the rest of the Upper and Lower Creeks. From
Coweta he was directed to follow the path to the Cherokee, to
act once more as a magistrate before returning to Savannah
Town.[57] His itinerary thus involved a journey by trading path
of more than fifteen hundred miles.

Obviously an extraordinary task was placed upon the
agent's shoulders, calling for physical courage and endurance,
discretion, and skill in the arts of forest diplomacy. The early
agents, especially Nairne, were perhaps as successful as could
have been expected. But Nairne's real accomplishments were
as a diplomat and a partizan leader rather than as an 'itinerary
justice among the Indians.' The weakness of the Carolina Indian system lay in the character of the average trader, and that
the laws of 1707 and 1712 conspicuously failed to reform.
In New France, where the *coureurs de bois* had a comparable
reputation for evil living, there were missionaries at hand to
check some of the worst abuses. But the efforts of Nairne and
others to secure English missionaries even among the nearest
tribes were unsuccessful. In 1712 the Reverend Francis Le Jau
reported to the Bishop of London that the Yamasee wanted
missionaries, but that 'the Indian traders have always discouraged me by raising a world of Difficultyes when I proposed anything to them relating to the Conversion of the
Indians. It appears they do not care to have Clergymen so near
them who doubtless would never approve those perpetual warrs
they promote amongst the Indians for the onely reason of
making slaves to pay for their trading goods; and what slaves!
poor women and children; for the men taken prisoners are
burnt most barbarously.'[58]

In 1707 certain notorious abuses were outlawed: the ex-
tortion of presents for governors, the enslaving of free Indians,
the sale of rum and the supplying of hostile Indians with ammunition.[59] Other practices were banned by instructions from
the board, especially the accumulation of the great Indian

[57] Ibid., July 9, 1712.
[58] Fulham Palace MSS, South Carolina, no. 10. Le Jau said he intended
to consult Mr. Barnwell regarding this project when he returned from
North Carolina 'as his plantation and settlement borders upon the Yamon-
seas.'
[59] Act of July 19, 1707, articles iii, iv, viii, ix. Traders were required to
file bonds of £100 to obey the law and the agent's instructions (article ii).

debts.[60] One witness examined by the Commons described the vicious circle of rum, chicane and debt, which was in a fair way to ruin the trade.[61] 'It was a general thing among the traders there,' he said, referring to the Yamasee, 'to meet the Indians at a great distance off their Towns when they come from Warr, and . . . by giving rum and making them Drunk get their Slaves or Skinns for little or nothing, to the great dissatisfaction of the Indians when they are Sober, and that by their Selling such great quantities of rum, hath occasioned them to be very much in Debt, which if not timely prevented will Occasion Murther to be Committed amongst them.' Complaints of ill conduct filled the agents' letters, the minutes of the board, and the debates on frontier affairs in the Commons House.[62] For the Commons often intervened directly in Indian management. In June, 1711, Benjamin Quelch, a recent appointee to the board, laid before the House an abstract of the agents' letters dealing with the state of the trade, and the Commons entered in their journal 'Remarks on the Agent's Letters' which were closely followed by the Indian commissioners in their next instructions to the traders.[63] Both the board and the assembly seem to have striven earnestly to put the trade on a footing of justice to the Indians, profit to the merchants, and safety to the province. But the system of licenses upon which the whole regulative machinery was based broke down. Many traders neglected or refused to pay the £8 currency for a license and to give the bond in £100 to obey the instructions of agents and commissioners. In 1713 the board confessed that it was powerless as the law stood to prosecute for arrears of license fees. In August, 1714, the secretary reported that practically all of the traders were without licenses.[64] A general prosecution was planned, but the Indians within a few months undertook a reformation of the trade in their own drastic and terrible fashion.

The Indian frontier in the South was a zone of intercolo-

[60] JIC, August 3, 1711.
[61] JCHA, October 12, 1710.
[62] See below, pp. 165-7, for the causes of the Yamasee War. Efforts to amend or replace the act of 1707 were made in November, 1707, and in 1710, 1711, 1712, 1713, 1714. JCHA, passim.
[63] Ibid., June 13, 1711.
[64] JIC, July 7, 1713; May 20, August 31, 1714.

nial as well as international contacts and rivalries. Except when Indian wars in 1711 and 1715 prompted some mutual aid, the usual relations of the Carolinians with Virginia, and later with Georgia, were those of jealous rivalry for the Indian trade. This led to discriminatory legislation and to bitter controversies which were carried home for settlement.

The area of conflict with Virginia comprised the Catawba and Cherokee nations. Curiously, the Charles Town government was aroused to the French danger on the Mississippi quite as early as to Virginian rivalry in the piedmont and the southern Appalachians. Carolinian expansion in the seventeenth century had been mainly southward and westward. Meanwhile, the elder William Byrd and the other successors of Abraham Wood in the 'foreign' trade had been sending their caravans to the Catawba towns by the famous Occaneechi path, described by the younger Byrd in his 'History of the Dividing Line,' and by a circuitous route through the North Carolina foothills, to the Cherokee beyond. In 1686 Byrd reported that two of his traders had been killed more than four hundred miles from the falls of the James. But even at the height of this trade Virginia exported only a fraction of the deerskins despatched from Charles Town to England, though considerably more beaver. From 1699-1715 the average was about one-quarter of the Carolina exports of deerskins.[65]

By 1698 Jean Couture and James Moore were arousing interest at Charles Town in the Cherokee country and the land beyond. In October the assembly made the first of a series of efforts to eliminate Virginian competition within the charter limits, when the Commons resolved 'that the Virginians be Prohibited from Tradeing in this Province.' This resolution, and one of 1701 proposing confiscation of goods, died with the abortive Indian bills of those years.[66] In 1701, however, there was passed a curiously worded act 'to prevent Horses being brought by Land from the Northern Settlements into this Province,' which was probably intended to stop the pack-horse

[65] William Byrd, *Writings* (Bassett, ed.), preface, p. xviii; also pp. 184 f., 235-9; Spotswood, *Letters,* I. 167; *Va. Mag. of Hist. and Biog.,* XXV. 51f. In 1716 the agent of the Virginia Indian company told the Board of Trade 'that formerly there were 10,000 Skins Yearly Imported from Virginia' (JBT, July 10, 1716).
[66] JCHA, October 4, 1698; February 20, 1700/1

trains of the Virginia traders.[67] If so, it apparently remained a dead letter. Though the Indian act of 1707 made no mention of the Virginia traders, the problem of barring them from the province was now more than ever under discussion at Charles Town. 'As to the Seizure of the goods belonging to the Virginia Indian Traders, now dealing within this Government it does not appear to us,' the Commons reluctantly admitted, 'that they are seizable by any law of this province, but if it may be done by the Laws of England we pray your Honor to put them in Execution in those Cases.' Governor and council, however, found a Carolina statute to their purpose: the act of 1703 laying duties upon exports and imports, which included a three-pence export duty upon deerskins.[68] The Virginians refused to pay the Carolina customs, an addition, of course, to the Virginia levies, and their skins were confiscated. When a trader, Robert Hue, presented a petition for redress to the Commons House it was not entertained.[69]

But in Virginia and in England these complaints found a more sympathetic hearing. Jenings, the lieutenant-governor of Virginia, denounced this 'new practice never offered at before,' though Virginia had long traded with those Indians. Carolina's aim was clearly to engross the trade. He urged strongly the adverse effect upon exports to Virginia of English manufacturers. Most of the Indians in question, the Virginia council declared, lived some hundreds of miles beyond the Carolina habitations. The College of William and Mary, supported by the Virginia duty on skins and furs, also joined in the remonstrance.[70]

For nearly a year the Board of Trade delayed its report for the reply of the Proprietors. They then asserted their fixed

[67] Cooper (ed.), *Statutes*, II. 164. The original motion of Stephen Bull and Robert Fenwick, both traders, pretty clearly indicates the purpose of the measure: 'that Care be taken to prevent horses being brought into this Government from Virginia & that such Care be taken to bring the Essawees [Catawba] Indians more dependent on this Government by discourageing the Virginians trading among them' (JCHA, February 13, 1700/1; and see ibid., February 19, 20, 24, 1700/1).

[68] Cooper (ed.), *Statutes*, II. 200; JCHA, June 13, 1707.

[69] Ibid., October 25, 1707.

[70] Minutes of the Virginia council, October 19, 1708, in *Col. Rec. N. C.*, I. 691; *Calendar of Virginia State Papers*, I. 124; Maggs Brothers, *Bibl. Am.* (Catalogue 429), no. 465.

doctrine in all such disputes. The trade must be 'left Free and Open to Virginia.' The western Indians were not under the government of South Carolina. On general principles, 'the laying of Duties on European Goods Carryed through one plantation to another, has ever been and ought Still to be Discouraged.' From Great Britain Virginia bought quantities of manufactured goods to sell to the Indians, while the Carolinians carried on a contraband trade in European commodities from Curacao and St. Thomas. With inferior shipping facilities her traders must charge higher prices to the Indians. If they engrossed the trade, and raised prices as they saw fit, there was danger that the Indians would be supplied by the French, who would use them to annoy the English colonies. Apparently the Board did not understand that the Carolinians had actually a monopoly against any other English traders in that quarter and were the only real champions of English against French trade. The Privy Council concurred, and forbade the levy of the duties.[71]

But the Privy Council could not save the declining Virginia trade. The Carolinians of that generation understood nullification in practice if not yet in theory. Despite the passes which the traders brought from Williamsburg,[72] they met with frequent obstructions. The new governor, Alexander Spotswood, made himself their champion, and at the same time sought to penetrate by a new route through the mountains to the western tribes and so outflank the Carolinian blockade.[73]

In 1711 the South Carolina assembly prepared for a new attack by an address to the Proprietors complaining of the 'great mischief and danger to this province by the intrusions and approachments of the Virginia Traders.' This time the Proprietors should be better informed of 'the bounds of this Government and the Indians,' and therefore better prepared than in 1708 to assert 'their just rights therein.' The new act of June 28, 1711, was nominally one of regulation. But the

---

[71] *Acts of the Privy Council, Colonial, 1680-1720,* pp. 610-4; JBT, November 8, 10, 1707; February 1, May 3, August 9, 19, September 5, 1709; C.O. 5:1264, P 48, P 56, P 72, P 76; C.O. 5:292, pp. 6, 8, 22, 29. C.O. 5:289, p. 153.
[72] *Calendar of Virginia State Papers,* I. 135.
[73] See below, pp. 220-1.

memorial made clear that exclusion was intended.[74] Again the Virginians were made subject to the duties, were obliged, indeed, to make returns of their skins to the agent or at Savannah Town, remote from their usual route. Moreover, they were now brought within the scope of the provincial system of regulation, and required to take out licenses, in person or by agent, at Charles Town. The preamble argued, plausibly, that freedom from restraint gave them an unfair advantage in trade rivalry, and that it was essential that South Carolina have the power to enforce embargoes against disobedient tribes. But all this proved chiefly the need of intercolonial coöperation or imperial control. The law was enforced with some rigor. Several Virginians had taken licenses at Charles Town even before its enactment. In 1712 there were seizures of goods and slaves.[75] Spotswood protested at home, the Board of Trade drew up another representation, and the Privy Council directed the Proprietors to repeal the statute.[76]

But already South Carolina had abandoned its efforts, twice pronounced illegal, to check the Virginia western trade by restrictions and confiscation. Probably the chief reason was that they had succeeded. No doubt there were other factors in the decline, especially geographical ones, but certainly by 1715 the Indian trade from the James had sunk to a low ebb. In 1716, Cary, the London agent, declared that three-fourths of the old commerce was lost. Spotswood gave similar testimony, and defended his monopolistic Indian company as a means of recovery. Even the Yamasee War did not permanently affect Carolina's primacy. Eventually Spotswood had to admit that the South Carolina government had 'engrossed all the Indian Trade on the Southern Continent of America.'[77]

The North Carolinians had no part in these contests, intercolonial and international, for the frontier trade. In an agricultural sense, to be sure, North Carolina was completely a

[74] Cooper (ed.), *Statutes,* II. 357-9; JCHA, February 3, 13, June 20, November 3, 1711.
[75] See additional instructions to John Wright, JIC, August 3, 1711; and ibid., March 22, 1710/11, July 9, 1712. See also JCHA, August 12, 1712, regarding seizures and fear that the Virginians might take a different route.
[76] C.O. 5:1335, no. 78; JBT, December 19, 1712; *Col. Rec. N. C.,* I. 863; *Acts of P.C., Colonial, 1680-1720,* p. 614.
[77] JBT, July 10, 1716; Spotswood, *Letters,* II. 235.

frontier colony. But trade with the Indians on more than a local scale required the capital accumulations of prosperous planters and merchants, and direct mercantile connection with England. One frontier problem, however, was shared by all three southern colonies: the problem of defense against the Indians in the crises of 1711 and 1715.[78] In spite of some mutual aid, these episodes increased rather than diminished the prejudices and suspicions which were the normal atmosphere of intercolonial relations in the South.

Virginia, certainly, played less than a generous part in the Tuscarora rising of 1711-1712.[79] In the end the royal province furnished only a loan of clothing for three hundred non-existent North Carolina troops. Spotswood, to be sure, was able to make out a case in England to acquit himself of standing 'an idle Spectator of the Miserys' of his fellow-subjects. He was hampered by factionalism in North Carolina and by political opposition at Williamsburg. The Virginia Burgesses declared for the extirpation of the Tuscarora, but quarrelled hopelessly over raising requisite funds. They also opposed the governor's prudent efforts to isolate the conflict by making a treaty with eight towns of Tuscarora neutrals. Barnwell's sneer that Virginia 'begged a most ignominious neutrality of those cowardly miscreants, which they were gracious to grant'[80] was unfair, but nothing in Spotswood's own conduct justified his eagerness to publish at home 'this Mr. Barnwell's Treachery' or to pose as the warden of the southern and western border. His patronising allusions to hopes of reducing the enemy 'by the Assistance of the forces sent from South Carolina' were made ridiculous by the brilliant campaign of the South Carolina 'army' in 1712.[81] It was not in human nature, perhaps, for the Carolinians to refrain from asserting their sense of moral

[78] JBT, August 16, 1720: testimony of John Barnwell that North and South Carolina were independent in all respects, with different courts, laws, etc., 'and but little Communication with each other, except that when the People of North Carolina have been in Danger from the Indians, they have been supported from South Carolina.'

[79] Col. Rec. N. C., I. 810-992, especially pp. 888 f., 890 f., 895; Journals of the House of Burgesses, 1712-1726, passim (see index under Tuscarora, South Carolina, Barnwell, etc.); H. L. Osgood, Am. Cols. in the Eighteenth Century, II. 227-33, and references below.

[80] Va. Mag. of Hist. and Biog., V. 400.

[81] Col. Rec. N. C., I. 862.

superiority. 'We are sorry and amazed,' the Commons House declared, 'that they to whom God has given greater power and opportunities, should be so deficient in giving that assistance, which was ever due to human nature, and that any who have British blood in their veins should regard the destruction of their neighbors as a Tragedy on a Theatre.'[82]

From worse calamities North Carolina was saved by aid from the south. On the first news of the massacres the assembly at Charles Town appropriated £4000 and sent off an army of thirty whites and several hundred Indians, commanded by Colonel John Barnwell.[83] But the Indians, mainly recruited from the smaller tribes, were constantly deserting, and proved thoroughly insubordinate. Only Barnwell's own Yamasee company could be measurably trusted. At the end of a march by way of the Congaree, Waxhaw, and Saraw towns, Barnwell found himself in January, 1712, in the midst of the Tuscarora forts on the upper Neuse and Pamlico, without guides or supplies, for the news of his approach had miscarried. The Torhunta (or Narhontes) fort he carried by assault, whereupon most of his Indians made off with their spoils. But with his 'brave Yamasee' he plundered and destroyed several towns in a march which, he boasted, 'to the immortall Glory of South Carolina has struck the Dominion of Virginia with Amazement and Wonder.' To the wretched settlers at Bath he brought relief, and built Fort Barnwell at the junction of Cotechney Creek and the Neuse to protect the German Palatine settlements. But he was soon hopelessly at odds with his North Carolinian allies. Hancock's Town was the remaining Tuscarora stronghold. Barnwell raised his first siege of the place to save a number of prisoners from execution. But the Tuscarora broke their promise to release the prisoners and early in April Barnwell again invested the fort. Many of his white troops were nursing wounds, and his Indians showed themselves unsteady in assault. One attack convinced Barnwell that this method of ending the war was too costly. Supplies were running low; the attitude

[82] JCHA.

[83] JCHA, October 26, 27, November 2, 3, 6, 8, 9, 1711. See *Va. Mag. of Hist. and Biog.*, VI. 42-55, for journal of Barnwell expedition; also *Col. Rec. N. C.*, I. 839, 874 f. Barnwell's route is shown on C.O. Maps, Carolina, 4, reproduced in *Crown Collection*, III. 17, 18. See also maps in *SCHGM*, X, opposite pp. 33, 37.

of the northern Tuscaroras was uncertain; the Virginia troops had not yet been raised. He therefore decided to accept a surrender upon terms which left 'above 100 murderers unpunished.'

This was the clapped-up peace which Governor Hyde denounced and against which Spotswood railed. Another charge against Barnwell was that after the truce some of his Indians attacked the Tuscarora and provoked new massacres. But no white commander could ever be held fully responsible for the insubordination of his Indians. Barnwell lacked neither courage nor good faith, but certainly he failed in tact. He was openly contemptuous of the North Carolinians, and had apparently won the special enmity of the Pollock faction by his association with Moseley—hence the worst charges against him, to which Spotswood gave currency without scruple. Rather naturally the distressed and incompetent North Carolina government in their later appeals for aid at Charles Town described him as *persona non grata*.[84]

On his return, wounded, Barnwell was thanked by the South Carolina assembly, and helped to plan the new campaign.[85] For Craven had appealed to the assembly to overlook the bad conduct of the neighboring government and to send another expedition. The Indians, Barnwell advised, would never attempt a fort unless led by a considerable number of whites, nor could the Tuscarora be destroyed within a reasonable period, but a lasting peace, which was more to the interest of North Carolina, might be imposed. When Robert Daniel, of St. Augustine fame, demanded an 'extravagant reward,' James Moore, son of the old governor, was given command. His officers—Mackay, Cantey, Hastings, and the rest—were a notable group of Indian fighters, as their services in this war and the next were to show. This time the auxiliaries were recruited from the larger warlike tribes: Cherokee, Creek, and Catawba. Spotswood's report of 850 Indians was probably exaggerated.

[84] See Craven's complaint against Barnwell in *Col. Rec. N. C.*, I. 903.
[85] On the second campaign see Joseph Barnwell, 'The Second Tuscarora Expedition,' in *SCHGM*, X. 33 *et seq.* (with map). See also JCHA, April 2, 4, 9, May 14, December 2, 1712; August 6, 7, 8, November 17, 19, 27, December 5, 18, 1713; May 13, June 8, 1714; *Col. Rec. N. C.*, II. 881f., 892-4; *Boston News Letter*, March 9, 1713. Heinrich, in *La Louisiane*, p. lxviii, assumes without warrant that the Tuscarora War arrested the English trading offensive for two years.

Fewer Indians were raised than Craven had hoped, and charges were laid against several Creek and Cherokee traders of hindering the Indians from marching against the Tuscarora —'profligate wretches,' said Craven, 'that for sordid gain would betray their country.' But in any case the army proved, as the governor predicted, 'a sufficient Body to put a good end to the War.' Moore marched northward by the traders' path. In North Carolina his auxiliaries had to forage for their own supplies, and made themselves almost as dreaded as the Tuscarora. However, on March 20, 1713, Moore stormed and burned the Indian fort of Nooherooka. It was a hard-fought action. The Carolinians lost 22 whites killed, and 24 wounded, besides 35 Indians killed and 58 wounded. The army took 392 prisoners, and 192 scalps. Many of the Tuscarora were burned in the fort. Moore thought the total loss of the enemy, killed and captured, was nearly 1,000. Their power, certainly, was broken. But before Moore had completed their reduction, all his Indians except 180 decamped to South Carolina to sell their slaves to the traders. Peace was soon made. Most of the Tuscarora who survived their terrible punishment retired in the next years to New York to join the Iroquois league as the sixth nation.

Moore's success, and his gallantry, helped to restore the goodwill of the harassed North Carolinians, ruffled by Barnwell's bluntness. Two years later they were able to repay the aid of South Carolina. In 1715 Maurice, a younger brother of James Moore, headed the North Carolina militia who came to the assistance of South Carolina in its most dangerous hour. And these men joined in the march to the Cherokee country, an exploit which for forty years gave measurable security to the whole southern border

CHAPTER VII

The Yamasee War, 1715-1716

The Yamasee War, so-called, differed notably from King Philip's War in New England, and from the Virginia troubles of 1675-1676. Episodes, these were, in the advance of the farming frontier. But the events of 1715-1716 on the southern border constituted, rather, a far-reaching revolt against the Carolinian trading régime, involving the Creeks, the Choctaw, and to a less extent the Cherokee, as well as the tribes of the piedmont and of the Savannah River and Port Royal districts. To be sure, the Yamasee, and perhaps also the piedmont Indians, were to some degree apprehensive of encroachment upon their lands. But they shared with the Creeks, probable authors of the conspiracy, and with the other interior tribes a greater resentment of the tyrannies of the Charles Town traders. In its causes, then, the Yamasee War was *sui generis*.[1] In its results, leading as it did to the awakening of the English colonial authorities to the danger of French encirclement, to a constitutional revolution in South Carolina, to far-reaching migrations of the southern tribes, and to a re-orientation of wilderness diplomacy in the South which altered seriously the prospects of English, French, and Spanish rivalry, it takes rank with the more famous Indian conspiracies of colonial times.

After the destruction of the Scotch colony in 1686 the Port Royal region was left vacant for some years by the Carolinians. The Yamasee, meanwhile, moved from St. Helena and Hilton's Head Island, where they had been settled by Cardross, to the adjacent mainland, between the Combahee and Savannah Rivers. As late as 1703, the removal of the Yamasee even nearer the settlements was discussed, and room was found for the Yoa, the last migrants from Guale, north of the other Yamasee towns.[2] By the end of the seventeenth century, however, the English frontier was again advancing towards Port Royal.

[1] This is not, certainly, the usual view. For a too sweeping generalization regarding the colonial Indian wars see Edward Channing, *History of the United States,* I. 454. See also H. L. Osgood, *Am. Col. in the Seventeenth Century,* II. 432. The significance of this war in Indian history is clearly recognized by Swanton in his *Early History,* pp. 100 f.

[2] JCHA, January 15, 16, 19, February 3, 18, 1702/3.

After 1694 Colleton county was becoming a region of great cattle-ranches. Southward, in Port Royal (later Granville) county, the coastal islands were rapidly occupied between 1698 and 1707. Thus in 1698 the surveyor was directed to lay out a thousand acres on St. Helena Island for John Stewart, on 'a neck of land formerly inhabited by the Pocatalagoes lying Northwest of the lands settled by Mr. Thomas Niern.'[3] Nairne was a leading planter of the Colleton-Granville border, and a partizan leader of the Yamasee in the Florida raids of Queen Anne's War. For some years before he became a regularly appointed provincial Indian agent, he had been employed to keep the Yamasee traders in order. Between 1703 and 1711 he received six additional grants in Granville County, totalling 2,130 acres.[4] John Barnwell was a later settler on this frontier who also became a notable Indian fighter and negotiator, sharing Nairne's expansive views of western policy. An Irishman of good family who came out to Carolina about 1701, Barnwell lost his offices through opposition to Johnson and Trott, and retired to Port Royal to rebuild his fortunes.[5] His plantation and settlement lay at the northern end of Port Royal Island, directly across from the Yamasee lands. Under 'Tuscarora Jack' Barnwell the Yamasee served effectively in the North Carolina Indian war.

The intrusion of the cattle-raisers which reached its peak in 1707, led that year to the passage of an important act 'to Limit the Bounds of the Yamasee Settlement, to prevent Persons from Disturbing them with their Stocks, and to Remove such as are settled' within the bounds described.[6] The reservation embraced the island of Coosawhatchie, and the mainland between the Combahee, Port Royal, and Savannah Rivers and

[3] *Warrants for Lands, 1692-1711,* pp. 152, 174. *Present State of Europe.* XI. 295 f. (August, 1700), referred to recent letters from Carolina reporting 'that the River of *Port Royal* becomes every Day better known, and more inhabited.'
[4] JCHA, January 20, 21, 24, 1701/2; C.O. 5:398, 'South Carolina, An Abstract of the Records of all Grants of Lands.'
[5] Letters in *SCHGM,* II. 47-50 and notes. From C.O. 5:398 it appears that Barnwell received grants of 2,038 acres, 1705-1708.
[6] Cooper (ed.), *Statutes,* II. 317; 9,376 acres were granted in Granville county in 1707 (C.O. 5:398). For other years the figures were: 1702, 6,272 acres; 1703, 1,470 acres; 1704, 2,230 acres; 1705, 8,428 acres; 1706, 7,394 acres; 1708, 800 acres; 1709, 3,780 acres; 1710, 4,835 acres; 1711, 8,094 acres; 1712, 1713, none; 1714, 1,796 acres; 1715 (to the war), 2,984 acres.

an inland boundary drawn vaguely from the head of the Combahee River to the head of the Savannah. All of Granville county with the exception of the sea-islands was thus set apart for the ten towns of the Yamasee. The Broad River was apparently the line between the two divisions of the tribe. The Upper Towns were Pocotaligo, Huspaw, Yoa, Sadkeche and Tomatly; the Lower Towns comprised Altamaha, Pocasabo, Chasee, Oketee, and probably Tulafina.[7] For generations after its desertion by the Yamasee this region north of Port Royal retained the name of the 'Indian Land.'

By 1711, certainly, Indian resentment had been aroused by the continued infiltering of the whites. In July the Yamasee chiefs complained to the Indian commissioners that certain persons had taken up land within their reservation. A prosecution was ordered against nine interlopers and the deputy-surveyor who had illegally run out their lands; apparently the offenders were vigorously dealt with.[8] In 1711 a highway was

[7] Compare with the list in Swanton, *Early History,* p. 97, where Sadkeche, Tomatly, Oketee, and Tulafina are omitted. Swanton also includes Ilcombe, Dawfuskee (with some question), and possibly Peterba, but on questionable evidence. JIC, July 9, 1712, named Pocotaligo and Altamaha as head-towns of the two divisions. Pocataligo River, a small tributary of the Broad, bounds present Beaufort and Jasper counties. Huspah Neck is between the Combahee and the Whale Branch. The Yoa occupied adjoining lands. Sadkeche (see JCHA, February 5, 1703) survives in Salkehatchie, the name of a hamlet at the Atlantic Coast Line crossing of the Combahee. Farther north, probably in Colleton county, was fought in 1715 the Sadkeche or 'Saltketchers' fight. Probably this town was the Spanish Salchiches, according to Swanton 'an unidentified tribe living inland' from Guale, apparently Muskhogeans with 'numerous relatives in . . . Guale' (pp. 60, 83). Tomatly town of the Yamasee was mentioned in JCHA, February 5, 1703, and in JIC, July 28, 1711; it probably gave the name to Landgrave Bellinger's great barony (*SCHGM,* XV. 9), and hence to the village in Beaufort county. The name appears also among Creeks and Cherokees; in this connection it is of interest that Cherokee tradition in 1727 held that the Yamasee (possibly this town?) were formerly Cherokee, driven out by the Tomahitans (C.O. 5:387, p. 132). Pocasabo is another surviving place-name. The 'Okata' cassique was named in JCHA, January 24, 1702; Sir John Colleton's barony, laid out in 1718 north of Hilton's Head Island, was called 'Oketee' (*SCHGM,* XIII. 119-25), and the name is a common one in Jasper county. Ocute and Altamaha were neighboring towns in central Georgia in the 16th and 17th centuries (Swanton, *Early History,* p. 95). Swanton, to be sure, identifies Ocute and Hitchiti (p. 174), but 'Aëquité' in the De Crenay map was more likely Achitia. There is no contemporary Carolinian record of Tulafina, but an estuary of the Coosawhatchie, in Jasper county, is named Tulifinny, which is strikingly like the name of the interior town in Guale associated with Salchiches (Swanton, *Early History,* pp. 60, 82, 83).

[8] JIC, July 27, August 15, September 13, 1711.

ordered extended from South Edisto River to the islands of Port Royal and St. Helena.[9] In 1711, also, after two years' discussion, the Lords Proprietors issued a patent for the erection of a seaport on Port Royal, to be called Beaufort Town.[10] Efforts were made in England to attract new settlers to the region, especially west-countrymen and Swiss, and its convenience in carrying on the Indian trade was one of the advantages extolled in the advertisements.[11] In 1712 the parish of St. Helena was created, embracing all of Granville county, and William Guy, a minister supported by the S.P.G., was appointed to the charge.[12] Possibly rumors of these plans to make Port Royal at last a real settlement produced the uneasiness among the Yamasee that their lands were to be taken away, which the Indian commissioners in 1712 were at some pains to allay.[13]

But in none of the contemporary analyses of the causes of the war was the pressure of settlement accounted a real factor. It was generally agreed that the real mischief had been done among the Yamasee as well as among their confederates by lawless and oppressive Indian traders, 'notoriously infamous for their wicked and evil actions.'[14]

The sessions of the Indian commissioners supplied detailed evidence of the callous brutality of some of the traders, of petty thieving, of illegal enslavement of free Indians, of the abuse of rum to facilitate sharp dealing, of the use of cheating weights, and like knaveries.[15] At many points they confirmed the prejudiced but telling indictment of the Carolina traders sent by a Virginia trader in 1715 to the Virginia agent in London.[16] David Crawley accused them of killing the Indians' hogs and fowls, gathering corn and peas and watermelons without leave, and paying not half the value, or balancing the account with blows. For a paltry wage Indian burdeners, he charged, were

[9] McCord (ed.), *Statutes*, IX. 14; and see also ibid., p. 32.
[10] C.O. 5:292, pp. 14, 15, 36, 38, 39. See H. A. M. Smith, 'Beaufort—the Original Plan and the Earliest Settlers,' in *SCHGM*, IX. 141-60.
[11] See the promotion tracts, *A Letter from South Carolina*, London, 1710, of which Nairne was probably the author, and [John Norris], *Profitable Advice for Rich and Poor*, London, 1712.
[12] Cooper (ed.), *Statutes*, II. 372.
[13] JIC, June 20, 1712.
[14] Cooper (ed.), *Statutes*, III. 91 (Article xvi of trade act of 1719).
[15] Above, pp. 152-5.
[16] C.O. 5:1265, Q 51.

forced to carry packs seventy to one hundred pounds in weight for three hundred to five hundred miles. 'And when they had sent the men away about their business, or they were Gon a hunting, [I] have heard them brag to each other of Debauching their wives.' The agent, John Wright, he denounced for maintaining a great state among the Indians, requiring many of them 'to wait on [him] and carry his Lugage and packs of skins from one town to another purely out of Ostentation, saying in my hearing hee would make them Honour him as their Governour.' Traders were frequently arrested and brought before the Indian board for especially scandalous behavior, but the agents' jurisdiction was too large to be effective. Even so, a frontier clergyman was probably justified in asserting that 'the Indians of late years have had as little grounds of Complaint as ever they had since the settlement of the Province.'[17] Certainly special care had been taken by the assembly and the board to keep order among the Yamasee, whose alliance was an essential defense of the southern border. But the grievances of the Indians were real, and regulation had failed to remove them. The essence of the Carolina system was a licensed trade. In practice many traders neglected to take out licenses and disregarded the instructions of commissioners and agent. Nor were the greed and lust of the traders at all restrained by the presence of missionaries, as among the French. The attempt of the Society for the Propagation of the Gospel in 1702 to Christanize the Yamasee had come to nought.[18] On the eve of the war, to be sure, a young Yamasee chieftain was sent over to England 'to be instructed in Literature and Religion and dispos'd to a Love of the English Nation,' and there received baptism from Bishop Compton. But Prince George returned to find his kinsfolk in revolt, fleeing to Florida.[19]

'Another occasion and that a very great one of the Warr,' declared the Rev. Mr. Bull, grew out of 'the vast Debts' of the Indians to the traders.[20] Repeated efforts had been made by the

[17] S.P.G. MSS, B, IV, part 1, 23 (Letter from William Tredwell Bull, August 10, 1715).

[18] Ibid., A, II, no. 156; *SCHGM*, IV. 221-30, 278-85; V. 21-55, 95-99.

[19] S.P.G. MSS, B, IV, no. 34; 'Abstract of the Proceedings of the S.P.G., 1712-1713,' in *A Sermon*, 1714, p. 46; Pascoe, *Two Hundred Years of the S.P.G.*, pp. 16 f.; C.O. 5 :292.

[20] *Doc. cit., supra*, note 17; JBT, July 16, 1715.

board to prevent this practice. Rum debts had been declared void, and traders forbidden to hold the Indians of a town collectively responsible for a private debt. No debt was valid, the board finally ruled, unless formally consented to by the debtor's kin or the headmen of the tribe.[21] But great debts nevertheless accumulated. In 1711 it was asserted that they amounted to 100,000 skins, or more than a year's produce of the whole Carolina trade.[22] 'This war,' Bull remarked, 'at once blotts out all their Debts.'[23]

Much was made at the time of alleged Spanish and French complicity. Naturally the colonists saw a connection between the collapse of their western enterprise and the calamity which spread massacre and destruction from the plantations on the Stono and the Santee to the trading factories among the distant Chickasaw. Before the Board of Trade in July, 1715, the charge was squarely made by the Carolina agent and several planters that 'the Spaniards at St. Augustin, and the French at Mobile, have instigated and incouraged the Indians to fall upon us.'[24] And the next year affidavits were sent home in which Carolinians who had visited Florida after the outbreak of the insurrection deposed that the Spaniards bought slaves and plunder from the Yamasee, and that the latter 'had a constant Supply of Ammunition from the Spanish Government.'[25] These and similar charges against the French contained no proof, however, that the revolt was actually instigated by Carolina's southern and western rivals.

The war came with terrible suddenness to the dispersed frontier settlers of St. Helena's and St. Bartholomew's parishes, and to the widely-scattered Indian traders. At Charles Town there was a brief warning. On April 12, 1715, two traders hurried into town with grave news for the Indian board and the gov-

[21] JIC, June 13, August 3, 1711; July 9, 1712. See also JCHA, October 12, 1710.
[22] Ibid., June 13, 1711.
[23] *Doc. cit., supra,* note 17. Bull added that another reason for the war commonly asserted was that the Indians were 'especially addicted to war and bloodshed.' But South Carolina had brought the intertribal wars to an end; united, the Indians thought themselves 'a sufficient Match for us.' Had this design of peace among the Indians been promoted by the province for God's glory, rather than for 'trade and commerce,' he thought it would have prospered better.
[24] JBT, July 16, 1715.
[25] C.O. 5:1265, Q 97.

ernor. They had ridden night and day, William Bray from the Yamasees, Samuel Warner from Palachacola. Both asserted that the plot was hatched by the Creeks. While Bray was hunting for runaway slaves near St. Augustine, 'a Yamasee Indian came to his Wife and told her he had a great matter to tell her which was that the Creek Indians had a design to Cut off the Traders first and then to fall on the settlements and that it was very neare.' Warner, too, had heard from the Palachacola that the Creeks were dissatisfied with their traders, especially John Jones, against whom they had made several complaints without redress, and 'that upon the first afront from any of the Traders they would down with them and so go on with itt.' The final entry in the old 'Indian Book' of the board was a direction to Warner to proceed immediately to the Yamasee and Palachacola towns, to summon the Indians to conference at Savannah Town where Craven promised to hear and redress their grievances.[26]

But the hour of which Cuffy, the Yoa Indian, had brought friendly warning was too near. Craven, hastening to the parley, was met with sickening news of massacre near Port Royal. 'This calamity of Warr was first fomented by some of the lower Creeke people,' declared a well-informed Carolinian, 'but the first stroke was given by the Yamasees.'[27] On Good Friday, April 15, the blow fell at Pocotaligo Town. There Bray and Warner had joined Captain Thomas Nairne, the Indian agent, and several traders. The Yamasee headmen had seemed pleased with their assurances of redress, and on the night of April 14 the Carolinians had retired without thought of imminent danger. But at break of day they were awakened by the war-whoop, to meet the attack of Indians horrible as 'demons risen from Hell' in their red and black war-paint. Some were slain outright. For others—among these Thomas Nairne, veteran of the warpath and the council house, the ablest frontiersman of his day in the South—fiendish torments were prepared. Nairne, it was

[26] JIC, April 12, 1715. The friendly Yamasee who gave warning was identified as Cuffy, a Yoa, in JCHA, August 10, 1715. Compare the tradition of Sanute and the Frasers in Hewat, *History*, I. 215-6, reprinted in Carroll (ed.), *Collections*, I. 192-4. See also Craven to Townshend, May 23, 1715, in *Col. Rec. N. C.*, II. 177.

[27] *Year Book of the City of Charleston*, 1894, p. 337 ('Journal of the March of the Carolinians').

reported, was burned at the stake 'à petit feu,' a refinement of torture which was protracted several days.[28]

From this scene of terror at Pocotaligo only two or three whites escaped. One of these was a seaman who, though wounded, succeeded in swimming the river, to carry the alarm to Barnwell's plantation. A ship, seized for smuggling, lay in the harbor, and was soon crowded with three hundred or more terror-stricken Port Royal planters and their families. Hardly had they found this asylum when the Indians appeared. Their shots fell short of the ship, but ashore they destroyed horses and cattle, sacked the deserted plantations, and murdered those few unfortunates who fell into their hands.

Northward the savages took heavier toll, as a second party swept through the widely scattered plantations in St. Bartholomew's parish, between the Combahee and the Edisto. Here about one hundred settlers fell into the hands of the Indians, and many others, including the Rev. Mr. Osborn, had narrow escapes. Here, too, 'most of the Houses and Heavy Goods in the Parish were burned or spoil'd.' As the news spread to St. Paul's, now the frontier, and to Goose Creek, plantations were deserted for a few improvised garrisons, and women and children, with cart-loads of goods, scurried into Charles Town for shelter.

At a stroke the Yamasee had massacred the traders and destroyed the border settlements. Meanwhile, among the towns of their southern allies, Cowetas, Talapoosas, Abihkas, Alabamas, and Choctaws, the traders everywhere were 'knocked on the head' or forced to flee when their trading-houses were broken open and despoiled. A few were rescued by the French and Spanish, others were protected by friendly Indians until the storm had passed. In this revolt against the traders the Lower Creeks gave the lead: the old Emperor Brims, of Coweta, was charged by the French as well as the English with directing the plot. Creeks from Coweta Town even stole into the Chickasaw country and murdered several of the western traders.

[28] George Rodd, 'Relation' (in French), in C.O. 5:387, no. 1; W. T. Bull to S.P.G., August 10, 1715, and William Guy to same, September 20, 1715, in S.P.G. MSS, B, IV, part 1, 23, 25; *Boston News Letter,* June 13, 1715; Humphreys, *Historical Account,* 1730, pp. 92-8. These references apply also to the two following paragraphs.

The Chickasaw, however, guarded the survivors, and in 1716 sent down word that 'they knew nothing of the Warr tell it was all done; and that their desire is still to continue in friendship with the English.' But the Choctaw killed their new friends, the Charles Town traders, and were soon smoking the calumet again at Mobile. Rumors of these events in the distant Indian country added to the general alarm in the province. It appeared at first that all the southern Indians as far as the Mississippi were leagued together to drive the English into the sea. Most disquieting was the report, based on a few murders of traders and the flight of others to Charles Town, that the Cherokee had joined the conspiracy. It was certain, moreover, that the Yuchi, Apalache, and the remnant of the Shawnee at the Savannah fall-line had taken the war-path. Northward the Catawba and the lesser tribes of the coastal plain and the piedmont—Saraws, Waccamaws, Santee, and Cape Fears—were also hostile. Early in May news that the northern Indians had slain the traders threw the French Protestants of St. James Santee into panic. They took refuge in garrisons, one of which was the house of their pastor, Richebourg. Around Charles Town was drawn a menacing circle of fire and destruction.[29]

That South Carolina escaped complete ruin was due to the energy of a gallant governor, to the skill of the seasoned Indian fighters who commanded her militia, to assistance in arms and men from neighboring provinces, and to the conversion of the Cherokee at a critical moment to peace and friendly assistance.

Met by news of the massacres, Craven, without returning to Charles Town, summoned the militia of Colleton county. Alarm cannons were fired, martial law proclaimed. An attack on the camp was defeated and an advance hastily improvised. Colonel Barnwell and Captain Mackay were despatched by water to attack Pocotaligo with the southern scouts. The week after Easter, Craven marched with two hundred and fifty militiamen and settlement Indians directly towards the 'Indian Land.' Near the head of Combahee River he discovered the

[29] *Doc. cit., supra,* note 27, pp. 332-6; Spotswood, *Letters,* II. 122; S.P.G. MSS, B, IV, part 1, 23, 48; Pénicaut in Margry (ed.), *Découvertes,* V. 509 f.; anonymous French account, MS, Ayer collection, Newberry Library, quoted in Swanton, *Early History,* pp. 225 f.

Yamasee in front of him in a wood. They attacked in a crescent line and nearly surrounded his camp, but he rallied his deserters and drove them into swamps, where pursuit was hopeless. Sadkeche Fight checked the Yamasee incursions for the moment, but Craven had not made the expected junction with the scouts. Mackay, however, captured Pocotaligo Town 'with vast quantities of provisions that they had stored up, and what plunder they had taken from the English.' At another town, 'a young Stripling, Palmer,' first distinguished himself by driving the Indians from their fort while Mackay cut down the fugitives. Mackay and his swamp-hunters now pressed the campaign so vigorously in the 'Indian Land' that the Charles Town merchants were soon shipping captive Yamasee to the markets of Jamaica and New England, as the Ten Towns withdrew to Guale and Florida.[30]

When the assembly convened in May, refugees were pouring into Charles Town from all sides. In the streets were heard 'the cries and lamentations of women and children.' Men talked of a continental conspiracy of the Indians, abetted by the Spanish and French, to kill all the English in America or drive them into the sea. The timid were already fleeing the province when Craven sternly prohibited emigration. 'Expedition,' the governor warned the assembly, 'is the life of action.' Craven, too sanguine, pledged the Proprietors' aid as well as his own. May 7 the Commons House resolved 'that a Treaty with the Cherokee Indians be set on foot immediately.' This, the first decision of the Commons, had to be postponed, but it revealed a clear perception of the fundamental strategy of the war. Agents were despatched to New England to purchase arms and to Virginia and North Carolina to appeal for troops. Three defense acts were passed. The emergency measures of the governor were confirmed, and the governor and council impowered to impress vessels and stores. Negroes were drafted into the army. A ring of plantation garrisons was established along the fighting frontier, nowhere more than thirty miles from Charles Town. These included stockades upon the Edisto River at Edisto Bluff and Jackson's Bridge (Pon Pon), to

---

[30] George Rodd, 'Relation,' *loc. cit., supra*, note 28; *Boston News Letter*, June 13, 1715. Humphreys, *Historical Account*, p. 99.

command the two principal land approaches from the south. A garrison was also established at New London, and at St. Helena a dozen men were placed in a little fortification 'to watch the motions of the Indians by water.' In Berkeley county, nearer Charles Town, other garrisons were posted at the Percival plantation called the Ponds near the head of Ashley River, at Walter Izard's Wassamaw plantation, and at Wantoot, the Ravenel place in St. John's parish, near the head of Cooper· River. Schenkingh's Cowpen on the Santee was the northernmost outpost. With the passage of these acts, and the despatch of urgent addresses for assistance to the King, Proprietors, and the Admiralty, the assembly stood prorogued until August.[31]

Early in June the Santee frontier was attacked by the northern conspirators. Mr. John Herne, a planter, was murdered, and a party of ninety mounted men, marching northward to compel the allegiance of the Congarees, fell into an ambuscade in the woods. Captain Barker, 'a Brave young gentleman,' and nearly a third of his men were lost. The Santee settlements were now abandoned; rich Goose Creek was exposed. A new stream of refugees from the north poured into Charles Town. The danger in this quarter was increased by the disaster at Schenkingh's Cowpen, when the commander, one Redwood, foolishly admitted a party of Indians proposing peace, who then put the defenders to the tomahawk. A gang of Cherokee, it was reported, had a part in this affair. Captain George Chicken, a 'brave and bold' officer, marched northwards from the Ponds with one hundred and twenty of the Goose Creek militia. In a pitched battle, June 13, he roundly punished the raiders, released several prisoners and recaptured some of the arms seized at Schenkingh's.[32] By this prompt stroke the prestige of the militia was restored after a series of humilia-

[31] George Rodd, 'Relation,' in C.O. 5:387, no. 1; JCHA, May 6-12, 1715; *Journals of the House of Burgesses,* August 8, 1715; Spotswood, *Letters,* II. 121. Several garrisons may be located on C.O. Maps, N.A.C. General, 7.

[32] *Doc. cit., supra,* note 17; Samuel Eveleigh to Boone and Berresford, July 19, August 24, 1715; Commons House commissioners to same, August 25, 1715 (C.O. 5:1265, Q 66); *Boston News Letter,* July 11, 1715; Humphreys, *Historical Account,* pp. 99 f.; Rivers, *Sketch,* p. 265; C.O. Maps, N.A.C. General, 7.

tions. But it was not yet certain that the northern Indians were finally repulsed. And meanwhile, what of the Cherokee?

Southward all had been quiet since early June. In mid-July Craven felt secure enough to undertake a northern expedition, to join the North Carolina forces under Maurice Moore and Theophilus Hastings in the subjugation of the Saraws and the other piedmont hostiles. He had crossed the Santee with about a hundred whites drawn from the garrison, and another hundred negroes and Indians, when expresses from the south brought news of a fresh incursion threatening Charles Town. From five hundred to seven hundred Apalaches and their allies had swiftly penetrated the line of forts and crossed the Pon Pon bridge over Edisto River undiscovered. Their attack on New London beaten off by the garrison, the raiders spread out eastward and northward along Stono River to within a dozen miles of Charles Town. About twenty plantations were destroyed in St. Paul's parish, including Lady Blake's and Joseph Boone's, where a ship was burned on the stocks. Of the houses in their path only Landgrave Morton's escaped destruction. But they were checked in their effort to cross over to Stono Island, and fled, burning Pon Pon bridge in their retreat. At Port Royal Captain Stone cut off several canoes, but most of the raiders escaped to the woods. The great damage done in this foray was due to the fact that the garrisons were undermanned, and only by deserting them could the plantations be protected. It was believed at Charles Town that the marauders had withdrawn to Savannah Town to watch for another chance to renew their incursions.[33]

Before the assembly reconvened, August 2, in one respect the situation had improved. The aid anxiously awaited from the north had begun to arrive. At the outbreak of the attacks Craven had immediately appealed to Spotswood for arms, and the assembly, a little later, had sent Benjamin de la Conseilliere to Boston with deerskins, to purchase 'buccaneer' guns. By the middle of July H. M. S. *Valour,* guard ship on the Virginia station, had brought 160 muskets and powder and shot sorely

[33] Letters cited in note *32*; *Boston News Letter,* August 15, 1715. Bull and the commissioners said that the raiders were stopped by South Carolina forces; see Spotswood's claim that Virginia troops saved Charles Town (*Letters,* II. 240).

needed for the garrisons, and a force of Virginia volunteers had arrived. The New England supplies were not received until more than a month later; the agent reported scant encouragement from Governor Dudley.[34] But at first the attitude of Virginia gave great satisfaction.[35] Spotswood, with his frontier interests, saw the seriousness of the situation—and also, no doubt, an opportunity to assert Virginian leadership. Fearing that the Iroquois and other tribes might be drawn into the great conjuration, he sent expresses to Maryland, Pennsylvania and New York, warning their governors to keep a watchful eye on the Indians and suggesting aid to Carolina. To the Board of Trade and the Treasury he urged a store of arms in Virginia, and asked leave to use the quit-rent fund to raise and equip troops to defend the royal colony and her neighbors. The French, he warned Stanhope, might easily seize Port Royal or Charles Town. 'But grant,' he added, 'that the French or Spaniard is not any ways concern'd with these Heathen, yet would it be of the most dreadful Consequence that these inhuman Enemies should prove their own Strength and Valour to be sufficient to conquer and extirpate an English Province.' 'A Triumph over that very Province, which has been the most famous for keeping the Indians under Subjection' would destroy the legend of English invincibility, their chief security against the Indians, and invite a union of all the Indians in America to over-run the English colonies. By such arguments he justified his aid to South Carolina. It is significant that he felt that intercolonial coöperation in defence required justification.[36]

Spotswood and his council had quickly come to terms with Arthur Middleton, the South Carolina commissioner. Virginia agreed to despatch a force of three hundred whites, to serve at 22s 6d, Virginia money, and under their own officers, but on the somewhat extraordinary condition that an able-bodied negro slave woman be sent from South Carolina to Virginia to take the place of each soldier for the duration of the war.[37] Middleton

[34] Letter of August 25, 1715, cited in note 32.
[35] C.O. 5:1265, Q 66 (1).
[36] Spotswood, *Letters*, II. 122f.
[37] Ibid., pp. 135 f., 206, 228. Spotswood described the South Carolina offer as generous, *Journals of the House of Burgesses*, August 4, 1715. See *Col. Rec. N. C.*, II. 253.

returned at once with one hundred and eighteen volunteers. Later, thirty more volunteers and a band of tributary Indians went south with Colonel Evans, commander of the Virginia troops. After some delay, caused by opposition in the North Carolina assembly, Colonel Theophilus Hastings and Colonel Maurice Moore, old Indian fighters of South Carolina, with two companies of fifty men each, marched down the coast to the Pedee, and thence to a rendezvous at St. Julien's plantation on the upper Cooper. With them were sixty North Carolina Indians, Tuscaroras and Corees.[38]

From the first the planters in the South Carolina assembly stoutly opposed the terms of Middleton's agreement as impracticable and extortionate. In vain Craven urged observance; how else, he asked, could the further aid promised by Spotswood be expected? The new army bill of August, 1715, proposed to retain in service 100 Virginians at the same wages as the Carolina troops (viz., £4 per month), providing the treaty were modified. If new terms were refused, the slaves should be sent north sometime before April 1, 1716.[39] Negotiations failing with the Virginia officers, two commissioners were sent to Williamsburg to propose an equivalent of 50s Carolina currency in lieu of each slave. But the Virginians refused the concession, and in February, 1716, Craven renewed his appeal to the public faith of South Carolina, twice pledged, by treaty and by act of assembly. With mutual recriminations the controversy was prolonged for several years. The Carolinians denounced the Virginian troops as 'the most ignorant creeping naked people that ever was seen,' while Spotswood repeatedly complained to the Board of Trade, to Secretary Stanhope and to his fellow governors of their ill-usage. Virginia's assistance he described as unique in American annals. Her disappointment must discourage intercolonial aid in the future. But Virginia was eventually forced to accept such wages for her soldiers as the Carolina troops had received.[40]

[38] Letters cited in note 32. *Boston News Letter*, September 5, 1715. C.O. Maps, Carolina, 4, in *Crown Collection*, III. 17, 18, shows route.
[39] JCHA, August 4, 6, 9, 10, 20, 1715.
[40] Ibid., August 23, 1715. Cooper (ed.), *Statutes*, II. 626 (title only); Spotswood, *Letters*, II. 114, 117, 119, 121, 126-9, 131, 136, 141, 144, 164, 207, 238, 242; *Col. Rec. N. C.*, II. 202, 203, 225, 227, 234, 252-4; JBT, June 28, 1716; *Journals of the House of Burgesses*, May 8, 1718; H. L. Osgood, *Am. Col. in the Eighteenth Century*, II. 348 f.

Probably the Virginian terms were too harsh. Certainly Spotswood's hauteur as a royal governor dealing with a proprietary province created ill-feeling, which was raised to bitterness by his Indian policy. Charges made during the Tuscarora War that Virginia traded with the hostiles were revived. Again were demonstrated the evils of decentralized control of the Indian trade and Indian diplomacy.

It is clear that Spotswood at the beginning of the Indian war saw a chance to restore the waning prestige of Virginia among the southern tribes. To the Burgesses he declared, August 4, that 'never had Virginia so fair an Opportunity as now, to acquire Glory, and appear to the Heathen the most formidable Dominion in America.'[41] His first vision of a triumphant intervention of Virginian arms was frustrated by quarrels with the Carolinians and with his own assembly. Meanwhile he had embarked upon a policy of negotiation with the piedmont tribes. After Chicken had successfully punished the northern raiders in July, 1715, Spotswood transmitted to Charles Town with his endorsement the overtures of the Saraws for peace. The Carolinians, resenting his interference, were quick to discover ulterior motives. They insisted that the Indians in question must submit to South Carolina and make reparation, and protested against any treaty by Virginia which would recognize their neutrality. Through the neutrals, it was predicted, arms and ammunition would find their way to the enemy Indians. And then, as one indignant Carolinian asserted, 'the Sweat and Blood of our People will centre in the coffers of the Indian trading company of Virginia.'[42] The King was petitioned to order assistance of men and arms from all the royal colonies, especially Virginia, to forbid sale of warlike supplies to the Indians, and to require instead an immediate declaration of war against Carolina's enemies.[43] Spotswood, however, clung to his policy of neutrality, and pressed his negotiations with the piedmont tribes, Saraws and Catawbas. But he strenuously denied that one pound of powder or shot was sold to them on the three occasions when they visited Vir-

---

[41] *Journals of the House of Burgesses,* August 4, 1715.
[42] Ibid. Letter of August 25, 1715, cited in note 32; extract from a letter from South Carolina, dated August 30, 1715, in C.O. 5:1265, Q 96.
[43] C.O. 5:382, f. 16.

ginia.[44] On the other hand the Carolina agents transmitted to the Board of Trade letters from America, asserting, to be sure on Indian evidence, that the Saraws had a constant supply of munitions from Virginia, which were distributed through inter-tribal trade to others of the enemy.[45] In 1716 Spotswood re-fused to join in attacks upon the Saraws, though solicited from North Carolina as well as Virginia.[46] In an angry me-morial to the Board in December, 1716,[47] Boone and Berres-ford roundly charged the Virginians with encouraging the war on South Carolina. Else why were the Virginians buying In-dian trading-guns, which they never before had required? The custom house books, they declared, showed large quantities of deerskins recently imported from Virginia 'which must be bought of Indians that are at Warr with Carolina, their trade with their Neighbour Indians never having produced such Quantities, and can be no other than the Stores the Indians plundered from the Carolina traders and sold to them.' The special object of their attack was Spotswood's Indian trading company of 1716. Through this enterprise the ambitious royal governor was suspected of seeking to wrest from Carolina, in her extremity, the remnants of her great southern Indian trade. Moreover, Spotswood's exploring efforts in 1716 to open a route through the Blue Ridge were thought to be aimed specific-ally at the acquisition of the Cherokee trade.[48] Against this background the failure of coöperation by the two provinces was inevitable. The Board of Trade had it in mind when in 1720 the first royal governor of South Carolina was directed to consult with the governor of Virginia and agree upon a com-mon Indian policy.[49] The experience of trade rivalry in the midst of the Yamasee War thus dictated the first effort to place Indian affairs in the South upon something like an imperial footing. Already the war had produced an interesting effort to correlate Indian policy on the northern and southern frontiers. Long since Virginia had made peace with the Five Nations, and had joined in the councils with the Iroquois at Albany.

[44] Spotswood, *Letters,* II. 127, 131, 147, 209.
[45] C.O. 5 :1265, Q 95, 96.
[46] *Col. Rec. N. C.,* II. 242, 243, 246, 247.
[47] C.O. 5 :1265, Q 94.
[48] C.O. 5 :1265, Q 125.
[49] See below, pp. 231, 233.

Now Governor Hunter, at the request of South Carolina, sought to engage the warlike Senecas against the revolting southern tribes. The chief result, apparently, was to support Carolinian morale at a period of intense discouragement.[50]

In August, 1715, the South Carolina assembly admitted that 'our former measures for managing the war have not answered the end,' and undertook to put the defenses of the province upon a better footing. The new army act provided for twelve hundred men to serve under pay: six hundred Carolina whites, one hundred Virginians, the rest slaves and free Indians. But no offensive was planned until the crops were harvested. Instead, the troops were posted in three regiments to defend the country northward, westward, and southward. The former garrisons had been too widely spaced; ten posts were now fixed within supporting distances. James Moore, the younger, commanded as lieutenant-general.[51]

So effective were these measures that during the later summer the war degenerated into a species of bush fighting. The Indians, a Bristol sea-captain wrote, 'endeavour to Cut us off piece meal and won't come to a generall Engagement being very Sensible the Warr enricheth themselves and impoverisheth us. They are all Freebooters and carry all their Estates about with them, and are never from home or out of their way; a little parcht Corn and puddle water is good Victuals for them and fattens them like hogs.'[52] These tactics were demoralizing to planters, but bumper crops were gathered and meanwhile a couple of skirmishes southward augured success for the fall and winter offensives that were planned to end the war.[53]

From a captive taken in one of these small affrays, 'the Dawfusky fight,' it was learned that part of the Yamasee had returned to Guale, which they had deserted thirty years before for the 'Indian Land.' In the fall the lieutenant-governor, Robert Daniel, led a considerable expedition against Huspaw town,

[50] *Boston News Letter,* September 19, 1715; JCHA, May 7, 1715, February 29, 1715/16; cf. S.P.G. MSS, B, IV. 25.

[51] JCHA, August, 1715, *passim.* The act is lost but can be partly reconstructed from the journals. See commissioners to agents, August 25, 1715, C.O. 5:1265, Q 66.

[52] John Tate to Sir John Duddleston, September 16, 1715, in C.O. 5:1265, Q 60.

[53] Ibid., Q 66 (Eveleigh to Boone, October 7, 1715); S.P.G. MSS, B, IV. 29; *Boston News Letter,* September 26, 1715.

on the mainland near the northern mouth of the Altamaha. But the Indians had warning and deserted the settlement. Their flight to Apalache and St. Augustine marked the final abandonment of Guale by its ancient inhabitants. Close to their summer's refuge John Barnwell in 1721 built Fort King George, the historic link between the old Guale and future Georgia.[54]

Meanwhile, what of those great inland tribes, the Creeks and the Cherokee? How long would the Creeks, authors of the conspiracy, rest content with the assassination of the traders? Which way would the mountaineers throw their weight in the war? If against Carolina, then the ruin of the colony still seemed inescapable.

Gradually hopes of Cherokee neutrality, then of aid against the Muskogee, were aroused. In August the province accepted proposals from two escaped Indian traders, Eleazer Wigan and Robert Gilcrest, to undertake a dangerous journey to the Cherokee towns. They were outfitted at public charge, and promised £500 apiece if they persuaded the Cherokee to give aid. Late in October the province was immensely cheered by their return with a great Cherokee delegation: eight head-men, including Caesar of Echota, a frontier town against the Creeks on the Chattahoochee, a dozen head-warriors, and a hundred attendants. With all the ceremonies of the peacepipe and the solemn exchange of garments they made peace for their nation with the governor and council, and promised to send their best warriors to Savannah Town to march with the English against the Creeks. Heartened by this event, the planters returned in greater numbers to the devastated parishes. 'Had it not been for this singular Providence,' wrote one of their clergy, 'we could

[54] References as in note 53, and also Gideon Johnston to secretary of the S.P.G., December 19, 1715, in S.P.G. MSS, IV, part I, 37. The clergyman deplored the militaristic spirit of the province. 'It is certain,' he declared, 'Many of the Yammonses and Creek Indians were against the war all along; But our Military Men are so bent upon Revenge, and so desirous to enrich themselves, by making all the Indians Slaves that fall into their hands, but such as they kill, (without making the least distinction between the guilty and the innocent, and without considering the Barbarous usage these poor Savages met with from our vilainous Traders) that it is in vain to represent to them the Cruelty and injustice of Such a procedure. And therefore all that we can doe is, to lament in Secret those Sins, which have brought this Judgement upon us; for what we Say out of the pulpit, are words of course, and are little minded, notwithstanding the general calamity.'

not have taken the Resolution of returning to our Settlements with so good a heart as we have done.'[55]

At the end of November the army was assembled at the Ponds for the Creek campaign, which was designed to end the war by destroying the source of the conspiracy.[56] While the Cherokee and a few whites should attack the Upper Creeks, the main force would operate against the Lower Creeks and their Savannah and Apalache allies. From the Ponds, they marched to Savannah Town, where it had been decided to settle a strong garrison, later Fort Moore, to overlook both the northern and the southern border at the focus of the trading paths. But the Cherokee had not kept the rendezvous. Once more disturbing doubts were raised of their real intentions.

To resolve these doubts and secure their aid against the Creeks were the objects of the most spectacular enterprise of the war: the march of Colonel Maurice Moore with three hundred men into the heart of the Cherokee country.[57] This exploit, it seems clear, turned the scale of Cherokee policy at a most critical juncture, when Creek emissaries were at work to persuade the mountaineers to break once more with the English. So vivid a tradition of the crucial character of the affair was cherished in South Carolina that forty years later Governor Glen, in praising the character of one of the heroes of the march, Captain William Bull, later lieutenant-governor, declared that 'it is probably owing to that March, that we have this opportunity, so long after, of commemorating that Era; for had the Cherokee and Creeks joined at that time, which nothing prevented but the resolute Behaviour of our Militia; it might have proved fatal, it must have been, at least very dangerous to the Province.'[58]

Under Moore served a number of practised Indian fighters,

[55] JCHA, August 6, 1715; Eveleigh to agents, August 24, 1715 (C.O. 5:1265, Q 66); assembly to agents, March 15, 1715/16 (ibid., Q 72); S.P.G. MSS, B, IV, part I, 31, 32. G. Johnston wrote, December 19, 1715, that he had prevailed upon 'the Emperour of the Cheriquois to let me have his Eldest Son' to be brought up a Christian like the Yamasee Prince.

[56] The account here given of the Cherokee expedition is based chiefly upon the anonymous [Journal of the March] kept by one of the officers, printed in the *Year Book of the City of Charleston*, 1894, pp. 342-52, and attributed by the editor, Langdon Cheves, to George Chicken.

[57] C.O. 5:1265, Q 72.

[58] *South Carolina Gazette*, April 3, 1755.

including Major John Herbert and Captain George Chicken, both Indian commissioners after the war, Captain Nathaniel Broughton, Captain Thomas Smith, Captain John Cantey, and Captain John Pight with his negro company. But their mission called for skill in Indian diplomacy, rather than fighting, though their show of force in the Lower Towns no doubt made an impression. From Savannah Town they followed the old traders' path on the left bank to Toccoa and Tugaloo. Their march was undisturbed, but later they learned that they had been shadowed all the way by the scouts of Brims of Coweta. In the council at the round house of Tugaloo on December 30, they discovered that there were two parties among the Cherokee. The Conjurer and Lower Towns were for peace, declaring they would never fight the English, but they were loath to attack any of their enemies except the Savannah, Yuchi, and Apalache. The Yamasee, the Conjurer asserted, were 'his ancient people.' As for the piedmont tribes, he recalled their parleys with Spotswood and sought to clear the Catawba of blame. The Creeks themselves, he declared, had accepted a flag of truce and promised to come up to negotiate with the English when they should appear. The Carolinians therefore agreed that the Creek headmen be summoned up within a fortnight to treat for peace, and to bring with them their white prisoners. The problem was now to hold in check the war party, Caesar of Echota and the Overhill Towns. Moore and Herbert, with twenty men as a guard, met the headmen of the Chattahoochee frontier towns and of most of the Overhill settlements at Echota. They heard Caesar harangue the warriors to take the war-path as he had promised the English governor they would do. But the old men restrained the ardor of their youths, and the council agreed to wait two days beyond the appointed time for the coming of the Creeks before they should send the 'redstick' through the nation. At Echota the English received letters from James Alford—their first assurance that the Chickasaw had resisted French intrigue and still held to the Carolina alliance. John Chester, trader, was sent West to conduct a party of their chiefs to Charles Town to renew the treaty. With the paths to the Cherokee and the Chickasaw once more open, and the promise of a peace with the Creeks, the speedy rebuilding of the shattered South Carolina Indian system was now in prospect.

So far as these hopes were built upon peace with the Creeks they were doomed to disappointment. Two weeks, three weeks passed, no Creeks appeared. Had they gone instead to Savannah Town to meet the governor? This might well be; therefore Major Herbert with another officer was sent to Hiwasee to persuade the bellicose Overhill towns to turn their arms against the northern enemies of Carolina. Angrily the Indians charged the governor with having 'two talks.' They recalled that they had ceased their old wars with the Creeks only at English intercession, and complained that without these wars 'they should have no way in geting of Slaves to buy amunition and Clothing and that they were resolved to get ready for war.' With difficulty they were persuaded to await further word from the English before they should attack.

For the *dénouement* the English were quite unprepared. Late in January it was known that a dozen Creek headmen had arrived. Then, at Tugaloo, headquarters of the peace party, suddenly the war-whoop was raised and the Creek emissaries were put to the knife. Later the English learned the secret of this extraordinary affair.[59] The Creek 'talk,' it appeared, had been not of peace with South Carolina, but of a joint massacre by Creeks and Cherokee of the Carolinian army scattered among the Lower Towns for convenience in victualling. In the woods nearby had lurked a large force of Creeks, variously estimated at two hundred to five hundred warriors, ready at a word from their messengers to join in the surprise. The arguments of the Creeks, so the Carolinians had reason to believe, had almost won Cherokee consent when suddenly, 'as Providence order'd it they Chang'd their minds and fell upon the Creeks and Yamusees who were in their Towns and kill'd every man of them.'[60] Hoping to cut off the Creek army in the woods before they had news of this overwhelming defeat of their diplomacy, English and Cherokee pursued them several days, but by the end of January it was clear that they had escaped.

---

[59] Compare [Journal of the March], pp. 345-6, with assembly to agents, March 15, 1715/16, *loc. cit.*, and Le Jau to S.P.G., March 19, 1715/16, S.P.G. MSS, B, IV, part 1, 58.

[60] Assembly to agents, March 15, 1715/16, *loc. cit.*

The consequences of this wilderness drama were far reaching. Apparently the extermination of the Carolina force, which must have rekindled the fires of war on a larger front, had been narrowly averted. Among the Cherokee divisions and hesitations were ended. On the other hand the mirage of peace with the Creeks, the center of the old trading system, retreated into the distance. The Lower Creeks themselves shortly made their great migration westward from the Ochese country to their old village sites of the years before 1690 on the Chattahoochee. It was the massacre at Tugaloo, the South Carolina assembly reported, that induced 'the Whole nation' to move themselves 'nearer to the French at Moville.'[61] With the flight of the Yamasee to Florida the Creek hegira brought to a full period that cycle in southern Indian history which began three decades before with the intrusions of the English traders into Guale and Apalachicola.

Soon after the Tugaloo episode the expedition was reduced to fifty brisk men under Colonel Theophilus Hastings; at the Conjurer's request Captain Pight's negroes also remained. The rest of the army returned by the Keowee trail to Savannah Town and was dispersed among the garrisons. Caesar, however, was angered that so small a force had been left, and later it was agreed to maintain one hundred men in the mountains under Lieutenant-General Moore.[62] Moore went up to the Cherokees as an agent to reopen the trade as well as to direct the war against 'their and our Enemies,' the Creeks. In March 1716, the Assembly reduced the size of the army in the settlements, and the number of the garrisons.[63] The forces from Virginia and North Carolina, too, were returned to their homes.

The Reverend Mr. Le Jau of Goose Creek probably reflected the general view in the province when he hailed the surprising turn of events in the Cherokee country as this 'wonderfull Deliverance for us, and for me in particular who had my only Son in our Army in the Cherikee towns. It seems,' he added, 'we have nothing more to do but send some of our men

[61] C.O. 5:1265, Q 78.
[62] Assembly to agents, March 15, 1715/16, *loc. cit.* JCHA, February 29, March 1, 2, 5, 8, 1715/16.
[63] Cooper (ed.), *Statutes,* II. 634.

to head the Cherikees against the Crick if they think fit to stand against us.'[64] Craven also asserted confidently that 'the war is in a fair way to be extinguished.'[65] The assembly, to be sure, continued to send gloomy reports home to the colony agents. But there existed, certainly, a political motive for this pessimism: to complete the discrediting of the proprietary régime. Sporadic forays continued during 1716 and, indeed, for many years after; in a real sense, however, Maurice Moore's march to the Cherokees, following Daniel's expulsion of the Yamasee from Guale,[66] ended the great Indian conspiracy. Peace was soon concluded with the Catawbas and the smaller northern tribes who took their cue from the Cherokee. It was not, to be sure, until 1717 that a peace, and then an uncertain one, was effected with the Creeks. But in 1716 preliminary negotiations were opened, and these caused the abandonment of the joint campaign against the Muskogee from the Cherokee country. By the spring of 1716 South Carolina had begun to count the costs and to plan reconstruction.

'We are just now the poorest Colony in all America,' declared a Carolinian in 1718, 'and have both before us at Sea and behind us at Land very distracting appearances of ruine.'[67] Actual loss of life had fortunately been small, but the border areas, especially Granville county, had been depopulated. Only slowly did settlers return to a region which for many years lay open to Yamasee forays. The province had received an ill name for safety at a time when foreign Protestant emigration was rapidly rising. With the white population static, and a continual importation of slaves, the increasing disproportion of blacks to whites caused alarm for colonial defense. The destruction of crops was soon repaired, but the blow to cattle-raising in the southern parishes and hence to the provision trade with the West Indies seems to have been serious. 'The Trade for Beef and Pork,' wrote Francis Yonge in 1722, 'which was to Barbadoes, and the several Leward Caribbee Islands, the Bahamas,

[64] S.P.G. MSS, B, IV, part 1, 58.
[65] JCHA, February 29, 1715/16.
[66] Assembly to agents, March 15, 1715/16, *loc. cit.*, and Johnston's letter of January 27, 1715/16 (S.P.G. MSS, B, IV, 21) refer to capture of Yoa King, father of the Yamasee Prince.
[67] Fulham Palace MSS, South Carolina, no. 117 (transcript, Library of Congress).

Jamaica, &c., has been very much interrupted by the late Indian War, which not only destroyed the Stocks of Cattle, but drove most of the Inhabitants to the Southward, where the greatest Stocks of Cattle were, from their Plantations. . . . Thus, (for some Years at least) those unfortunate People have lost that Branch of their Trade.'[68] More serious was the total loss, for the time being, of the Indian trade, in 1715 still the main branch of South Carolina commerce.[69] To the recapture of this trade, however, the best energies of the province were devoted. Measured by exports of deerskins, the recovery was complete by 1722. But in terms of empire, the influence of South Carolina arising from Indian alliances had notably declined since the climax of her western expansion under Nairne and Hughes.

For the Spanish and French had not failed to take advantage of South Carolina's extremity. When, after many anxious months, the attacks on the settlements had been suppressed, the wavering Cherokee secured in their allegiance, communication reopened with the loyal Chickasaw, and an uncertain peace concluded with the Creeks, the situation on the southern frontier had been seriously altered, in a sense unfavorable to English ambitions. With the desertion of the Yamasees to Florida and the removal of the Lower Creeks to the Chattahoochee, the Spaniards, from negligible rivals, had become formidable contenders for the alliance of the Creek Indians. Under Brims and his successors the Creeks were able to play for many generations the rôle of the custodians of the wilderness balance of power in the South. The French, moreover, had recovered their control of the Mississippi River tribes. By planting Fort Toulouse at the forks of the Alabama, a few months only before the English peace with the Creeks, they secured the most valuable strategic position in the southern Indian country.

In one important respect, however, the situation of South Carolina as the southern frontier of the English colonies was markedly improved as a result of the Indian war. The colonial authorities at home were soon forced to recognize the existence of an imperial problem in that quarter of America with which

[68] Francis Yonge, *View of the Trade of South-Carolina,* 1722, p. 6.
[69] Ibid. Cf. *Boston News Letter,* November 5, 1716; Commons House answers to queries, C.O. 5:1265, Q 205.

the Proprietors had been unable to cope. A direct result of the war, and of the Proprietors' opposition to provincial measures of reconstruction, was the overthrow of their discredited government. By slow degrees, as control of the province passed to the Crown, there was impressed upon the Board of Trade and the Privy Council the point of view developed by Blake and Moore and Nairne, and now set forth by the South Carolina assembly and its agents: that South Carolina was 'a Barrier and might be made a Bulwark to all his Majesties Collonys on the South West Part of the Continent.'[70] The culmination of a series of efforts to strengthen the southern frontier against the French as well as the Spanish was the establishment of the march colony of Georgia.

[70] C.O. 5:1265, Q 76.

CHAPTER VIII

Defense and Reconstruction, 1715-1732

The larger strategy of the southern frontier, as Carolinians constantly urged in England, was an imperial concern; but defense of the immediate border and reconstruction of the shattered Indian system were obviously provincial problems. To them much energy was devoted in the years which followed the Indian rising.

On the whole the militia had served the province well, and it was continued after the Indian war substantially as organized by the acts of 1703 and 1707. In 1721 dragoons were added, and the patrols were absorbed into the militia.[1] The chief result of the *débâcle* of 1715 was the creation of a new system of defenses for the southwestern border, deserted by the friendly Indians who had constituted its screen, exposed, indeed, to attack by those same Indians, now renegades. Frontier posts and rangers accordingly took the place of the sentry-towns of Palachacolas, Savannahs, Apalache, Yuchi, and Congaree.

Some sort of traders' blockhouse had from early days overlooked the focus of the western trails at Savannah Town, and very early, indeed, there was an 'Oldfort' on the right bank near where Augusta later rose.[2] It was apparently some such traders' strong-house that was garrisoned by the Cherokee-Creek expedition in the winter of 1715-1716. Soon, however, a new fort was constructed, appropriately named Fort Moore. This served both as garrison and trading-post for the supply of the inland tribes, and in 1717 was placed under the inspection of the Indian commissioners. In August, 1716, they instructed their factor to build the main storehouse within the

---

[1] McCord (ed.), *Statutes,* IX, appendix, pp. 617, 625, 631. Smith, *South Carolina as a Royal Province,* chapter v. In 1708 Johnson and the council reported that the militia comprised some 950 whites in two foot-regiments, each of eight companies of about fifty men; an independent company of Huguenots, forty-five men; the governor's guard troop, forty men; and ten patrols, each of ten men, to hold the slaves in check, and in invasions to protect the women and children. There were also negro auxiliaries, for each militia captain was required by law 'to enlist, traine up and bring into the field for each white, one able Slave armed with a gun or lance.' Besides, there were the Indian allies (C.O. 5:1264, P 82).

[2] Above, p. 44.

body of the fort, and to provide a small trading-room for Indians in the outworks. 'I look upon Savano Garison,' the
deputy-governor wrote at this time, 'as the key of our Settlement. It is the Storehouse where we lay our Arms, Ammunition
and Necessaries for the Supply of the Cherikees, and other our
Friendly Indians.'[3] From 1716 to 1725 Fort Moore was commanded by Captain Gerard Monger; he was succeeded by Major
David Durham. Men for this and other garrisons on the frontier were drawn from the militia. So long as the public trade
continued the province servants also made up part of its com-
plement. The garrison was somewhat reduced in 1721, in the
expectation that part of the King's independent company would
be stationed there until they could proceed to the Altamaha.
In 1724 and 1731 it was composed of a commander, a lieutenant, a sergeant, and twenty-four privates.[4] As in the case of
Fort King George efforts were made to strengthen the post by
permanent settlement.[5]

A second logical location for a fort and factory in the upper
country was at Congaree, near the site of Columbia, where
the Catawba path branched off from the trail to the Cherokee
via Ninety-Six. A post was projected in 1716, in keeping with
Moore's promise to the Conjurer, but was not actually built
until two years later. In December, 1717, the province authorized the payment of a captain and twelve privates 'for a garrison to be built at Congarees,' and Charles Russell was given
command. In 1720 the garrison numbered twenty men. But its
maintenance proved burdensome at a time when the cost of
frontier defense was agitating the assembly, and in 1722 the
council ordered its reduction. With the abandonment of Congaree Fort the inland defenses were confined to the line of the
Savannah River.[6]

In the new system of Indian defense another position of
considerable strategic value was the place long known as 'Pal-

[3] Cooper (ed.), *Statutes*, II. 634, 696; III. 23-30. JIC, August 11, 1716.
JCHA, December 28, 1716. The first use I have found of the name Fort
Moore is in ibid., November 22, 1716.
[4] Cooper (ed.), *Statutes*, III. 84, 238, 308. JCHA, August 5, 11, 12, 15,
1721; June 11, 1724; March 12, 28, 1724/5. Smith, *op. cit.*, p. 208.
[5] See below, pp. 282-3.
[6] Cooper (ed.), *Statutes*, III. 23; JCHA, May 19, June 15, 30, November
17, 1716; August 5, 11, 12, 15, 1721; JC, June 5, 1722; JIC, July 10, 11, 1716.

achacolas,' at the extreme western corner of Granville county, on the left bank of the Savannah, opposite the deserted Palachacola Old Town. Thirty miles by land from Port Royal, a five days' row upstream, this had long been an important stage on the traders' route to the interior. Moreover, it commanded the usual route of invasion of Yamasee and other raiders. A company of rangers had been established there for a number of years when, in 1723, the assembly appropriated £400 for the building of a small palisaded fort, equipped with light cannon. William Bellinger was appointed to command, with a lieutenant, a sergeant, and nineteen privates, later reduced to fourteen, and then to ten. Once a fortnight this garrison was required to range down to the old 'Indian Land' about the Coosawhatchie and Tulafina Rivers, and northward also towards the traders' path from Charles Town to Fort Moore. Their special duty was to maintain the bounds of the Indian hunt at the Savannah River. Inducements similar to those at Savannah Town were made in the hope of attracting settlers.[7]

The third key to the southern border was Port Royal, commanding as it did the inland passage to Florida and the river-route to the interior. A garrison of twenty-eight men was placed there by act of March, 1716; reinforced by the Tuscarora Indians, they prosecuted the punitive campaigns against the Yamasee in Guale. Nearby, Beaufort Town was settled in the years immediately following the war; Beaufort Fort became the base for the two scout-boats which comprised the provincial 'navy.' The garrison was divided into two crews, one to remain constantly at the fort, except in emergencies, the other to patrol the inland passage between Port Royal and the Altamaha. But the fort fell into decay; in 1723 the assembly had to appropriate £400 for repairs to make it serviceable against Indian attack. For several years it was quite unoccupied. Then in 1727, after the burning of Fort King George, the invalid company retired to Port Royal. In 1734 the old Indian fort and scout-base was replaced by Fort Frederick, an oyster-shell construction, maintained thereafter until 1743.[8]

[7] Cooper (ed.), *Statutes,* III. 179, 238, 257, 308; JC, February 23, 1723; C.O. 5:358, A 9; 359, B 23. Smith, *op. cit.,* p. 209, incorrectly located the fort on the Georgia side of the river; but see C.O. Maps, N.A.C., General, 7.
[8] Cooper (ed.), *Statutes,* II. 634; III. 7, 23, 186; JC, August 3, 1727; March 14, 1727/8; August 13, 1731; February 16, 1731/2; *SCHGM,* IX. 145; Smith, *op. cit.,* p. 210.

None of the frontier forts was formidable except against the Indians; moreover, they were too widely spaced to prevent marauders from penetrating into the settlements. Consequently they were supplemented in December, 1716, by a scheme of rangers, based on the experience of the Yamasee War, and also, probably, on the example of Virginia. Like the garrisons, the rangers were paid wages and recruited from the militia. Three ranges were described by the act of 1717. The first, 'the old Palachacola range' between the 'Indian Land' and the Savannah path, was patrolled by a captain, lieutenant, and twenty-eight men. A second band of five privates and a captain, 'commonly called the western rangers,' had their headquarters at Rawlings' plantation at Edisto Bluff. Nine men and a captain composed the northern rangers. Although for several years the ranges were apparently discontinued, in 1727 and in 1731 small bodies of rangers again appeared on the province rolls. Similar guard against Indian and other enemies was kept by the Port Royal scout-boats, which also helped to apprehend runaway slaves. The scouts were in service as early as 1713, when one boat was directed to cruise from Port Royal to St Augustine, the other from Stono to Port Royal. In 1717 they were reëstablished with Colonel Barnwell as a commissioner in charge. These were the rough-and-ready frontiersmen whom he employed in 1721 to erect the Altamaha fort.[9]

At various times the provincial government made not very successful attempts to rebuild the old Indian bulwark on the southern border. In 1721 the agent Hastings undertook to draw part of the Creeks back to the Altamaha River, and an act was passed appropriating not more than £1000 for the expenses of removal. The next year the province encouraged the Chickasaws, hard pressed by the French and their allies, to retreat to the Carolina borders. The Commons proposed to place them on the Oconee or Ogeechee, but the small band which migrated eastward preferred to settle on the left bank of the Savannah near Fort Moore. Several years later it was suggested that they remove to a place opposite Palachacola Fort.

[9] Cooper (ed.), *Statutes,* II. 607, 691; III. 9, 23, 180; JCHA, November 13, 1716; June 12, August 23, 1717; December 19, 1722; JC, January 19, 1723; September 22, 1727; Smith, *op. cit.,* pp. 182, 187f.

The Commons, however, opposed another scheme to transfer the Cape Fear Indians to the southern border.[10]

Thus on the immediate border of South Carolina, the Port Royal-Savannah River line was reëstablished. In the Indian country, beyond, other frontier forts were from time to time proposed to support the Carolina traders and to offset the 'encroachments' of the Spanish and French. In 1720 John Barnwell persuaded the Board of Trade to endorse an ambitious scheme for distant royal posts throughout the southern Indian country, and in 1721, as the first step in this policy, Fort King George was built for the Crown at the mouth of the Altamaha.[11] But the province was too poor, and the colonial authorities at home too indifferent, to complete the program. Nevertheless these suggestions in the period immediately preceding 1730 were significant of a provincial interest in southwestward expansion which had a more than casual relation to the colonization of Georgia.

In the spring of 1725, just before Nicholson's return to England, the royal governor, with the support of the council, urged the building by province funds of a fort at the forks of the Altamaha, in the heart of the former Lower Creek country. But the Commons, begrudging the expense, and already locked in the long struggle with the council over paper-money issues, would only admit that private persons, that is, such merchant-traders as John Bee, might undertake the task. Twice the bill was rejected and the project lapsed.[12] In the next years relations with both the Creeks and the Cherokee grew increasingly complex. During the crisis of 1727 the council and the conference committee on Indian affairs agreed that a fort should be built at Okfuskee in the Upper Creek country as an asylum for the traders; and the following year, when the Creek expedition was abandoned, proposed to erect another fort in the Lower Towns in lieu of sending out an army.[13] The committee on Indian affairs in 1729 favored two garrisons, of twenty-five

[10] JCHA, August 28, 1721; June 21, 1722; JC, June 21, August 4, 1722; May 21, 1726; August 3, September 21, 1727; February 29, 1727/8; C.O. 5:359, B 28 (10); Cooper (ed.), *Statutes*, III. 158.
[11] See below, pp. 229-34.
[12] JCHA, March 6, April 9, 13, 14, 15, 1725; JC, May 29, 31, 1725; Tobias Fitch, journal, in Mereness (ed.), *Travels*, p. 203.
[13] JC, September 22, 1727; April 10, 1728.

men each, in the Cherokee and Creek nations 'to prevent the encroachments of the French and Spaniards and any disturbances that may otherways happen among the Indians,' the cost to be defrayed by a 10% levy on the Indian trade. Again in 1731 a Cherokee fort was proposed, but until Governor Glen's time it was not effected.[14] In 1733 Georgia took over the task of supporting the southwestern border against the Creeks and the French and Spanish Indians.

After the Yamasee War the expenses of defense and of Indian management constituted the principal items in the budget of South Carolina, and furnished the chief excuse for the issue of bills of credit. A paper received by the Board of Trade in 1730, entitled 'Answers of Merchants to Queries,' stated that there were then outstanding bills to the amount of £106,-355 currency, or £15,193 11s sterling. The fund for paying them consisted of duties upon negroes and liquors, but this had been broken in upon to pay the expenses of expeditions against pirates and Spanish privateers, and 'to maintain Guards, Garrisons and Scout Boats upon the Frontiers.'[15]

The appropriation bill of 1725,[16] to cover the expenses of the year from September 29, 1725, to September 29, 1726, may be taken as typical. It provided for the raising of £20,260 18s 10½d (£2,894 8s 5d sterling). The following items are of particular interest:

Commander of Fort Moore, one year	£250 curr.
Lieutenant of Fort Moore	144
Serjeant of Fort Moore	96
24 men at Fort Moore, £6 per month	1,728
Provisions at Fort Moore, twelve months	810
Medicines, etc.	50
Commander of Pallachucola garrison, one yr.	250
Lieutenant	144
Serjeant	96

[14] JCHA, January 31, 1728/9; February 25, 1730/1.

[15] C.O. 5:361, C 68.

[16] Cooper (ed.), *Statutes,* III. 257. Miscellaneous expenses of Indian management, aside from salaries of commissioner, secretary, etc., included: 'to Colonel Hastings as a linguist, upon occasion, for one year, one hundred pounds, to be paid quarterly; to John Chester, for going with an express to the Cherokees, forty pounds; to charges of expresses, etc., one hundred pounds; . . . to Colonel Hastings, for salary, three hundred and fifty pounds; . . . to Colonel Herbert, for mapps, twelve pounds.' An increasing item was the entertainment of Indian delegations, which became a great burden.

14 men	1,008
Provisions	510
Necessaries	25
Commanders of two scout boats	360
12 men, £8 per month	1,152
Provisions for 14 men	364
Necessaries	20

As the best means to insure lasting peace with the Indians, Governor Craven, in February, 1716, exhorted the assembly to consider 'in the most disinterested manner . . . in what method the trade with the Indians ought now to be carried on and regulated, fatal experience having taught us, that the measures hitherto taken are neither safe nor beneficial to the public.'[17] The result was the act of June 30, 1716,[18] altering the whole system of Indian trade regulation. For the first time there was set up the régime so often advocated by the planters of the Commons House, and so strenuously resisted by the merchants of the council: a public monopoly. Probably only the existing emergency could have broken down mercantile resistance to this plan. The chief objection raised by the council was on the score of their claim to a share in the control of the trade. But when Daniel insisted that one of the commissioners should be a councillor, the Commons in reply cited the act of 1707 declaring their right to name and remove all public salaried officers.[19]

Thus in the period of reconstruction the South Carolina Indian trade constituted a monopoly, closely controlled by the popular branch of the assembly. It was conducted by a public corporation of five commissioners, subject to the instructions of the Commons House. The first commissioners were named in the act; and though the board was made self-perpetuating, in several instances it appears that the Commons dictated changes in personnel. These occurred rather frequently, for the duties were onerous. The commissioners were uniformly men of standing and experience in Indian affairs, great planters, for the most part, who had served in the Indian wars. They included Colonel George Logan, Ralph Izard, and Major John

[17] JCHA, February 29, 1715/16.
[18] Cooper (ed.), *Statutes,* II. 677ff. Articles i and ii, not extant, may be inferred from the JIC.
[19] JCHA, March 7, June 15, 16, 20, 21, 27, 29, 30, 1716.

Fenwick, of the old Indian board, Colonel Barnwell, after Nairne the ablest frontiersman in the province, George Chicken, Jonathan Drake, and Francis Yonge.[20] The board held frequent meetings: in the first year there were over one hundred sessions. The salary of a commissioner was £150 a year.

Another striking but unsuccessful innovation in 1716 was the restriction of trade to factories on the frontiers. It was the 'resolution and Sense of the whole Country,' the commissioners informed Hastings, 'not to have any more a settled store among the Indians, but by degrees cause the Indians to come to our Forts and purchase what they want.'[21] At Charles Town the public trade employed a cashier (a member of the board), and a storekeeper. The latter received and sold the skins and furs and slaves sent down from the factories, and traded with the settlement Indians and with visiting delegations of Indian chiefs.[22] At first three factories only were provided: Winyah, Congaree, and Savannah Town. On the Black River, William Watis, Sr., and later Meredith Hughes, traded with the coast tribes of the North Carolina border.[23] The Catawba trade was in charge of Eleazer Wigan, succeeded in 1718 by Captain James How.[24] Virginian competition among the Catawba compelled the abandonment of the use of burdeners, and in 1717 James Coleman was made manager of the pack-horses in that trade, and next year of the pack-horses sent to the Cherokee.[25] The duties of Major Blakeney and his assistant, later his successor, Charlesworth Glover, were more onerous than those of the other public employees. For Savannah Town was both a factory where the Cherokee, and later the Creeks, were encouraged to trade by the offer of lower prices and the sale of rum, elsewhere pro-

[20] Logan, Izard, Barnwell, Charles Hill, and James Moore (who refused to act) were the original members.

[21] JIC, July 24, 1716.

[22] Thomas Barton, the first storekeeper, was succeeded by John Barnwell (ibid., July 4, 1716; March 30, 1717). Sales were usually by public vendue. There were frequent sales of slaves, viz., February 9, 1717, four women and their two children for £76 3s.; February 20, seven Indians for £110; February 25, five Indians for £200 15s.; March 2, five Indians for £122 5s.; April 11, one woman for £30; June 18, nine Indians for £468 10s.; May 10, 1718, one boy, £44 10s.

[23] Ibid., July 10, 1716; February 14, 1717. For a time a trade was carried on at Santee with the Winyah (ibid., September 18, 1716; March 7, 1718).

[24] Ibid., May 23, 1718.

[25] Ibid., November 9, 1717; June 12, 1712.

hibited, and also a depot for a restricted traffic in the Indian country.[26]

Among the Cherokee, Colonel Theophilus Hastings served as chief factor until his talents were requisitioned for the difficult business of negotiating peace and trade with the Creeks. Originally it was intended to keep Hastings in the Cherokee towns on a pretense of trade, but actually in the capacity of intelligence officer and diplomat.[27] In 1716 James Moore had reached an agreement with the Conjurer that Cherokee burdeners should go down to Savannah Town to carry up all goods to the mountains.[28] The board then instructed Blakeney to send Hastings cargoes not to exceed £600 in prime cost, provided returns were received before more goods were despatched.[29] Invoices of these Cherokee consignments revealed the character of the trade. On July 23, 1716, when a campaign was being planned against the Creeks, the following goods were sent up by twenty Indians: 400 lbs. of fine gun powder, 250 lbs. of bullets, 1000 flints, seven brass kettles, and '20 yards of half thicks, the powder is packed in 7 pieces strouds.' On other occasions invoices amounting to £1437 14s and £1849 8s 8d were despatched by 91 and 159 burdeners respectively. In October, 1717, two burdeners were sent off with liquor for Hatton and the assistant factors, with the explanation that 'it is not, nor ever was, the intention of the Board, to hinder or deprive any of their Factors from a glass of liquor (at their own charge).' A periago from Savannah Town brought down to Charles Town in October, 1716, 2087 dressed skins, 89 raw skins, 36 beaver from the Cherokee factory, and 29 dressed skins from the Savannah factory. In June, 1717, Hastings accompanied thirty-one burdeners bearing nearly a thousand skins, and turned over twenty-one Indian slaves which he had purchased. For the carriage of skins from Tugaloo, Hastings in 1716 wrote that each man should receive a quarter of a yard of strouds and the same of half-thicks, or a pair of cotton stockings.[30]

[26] Ibid., July 10, August 11, September 25, 1716.
[27] Ibid., July 24, 1716.
[28] Ibid., July 10, 1716.
[29] Ibid., August 11, 1716.
[30] Ibid., July 12, 23, October 10, 1716; January 30, June 11, October 4, December 2, 1717.

From the first, Hastings had warned Charles Town that the 'Cherokees utterly dislike coming down to the Garrisons, to deal, and will not agree to that proposal, on any account (except for Rum).'[31] In January, 1717, Daniel called the assembly into special session. The dissatisfaction over the method of trade he thought alarming. 'Caesar assures me,' he said, 'that if they cannot be supplied with what Goods they want, up at their Towns, having now a great Number of Skins, They will be forced to go to those that will seek their Friendship.' But on a motion 'whether if the said Cherikee Indians, being satisfied or not, this House will stand by the Indian trading law?' the Commons resolved in the affirmative. At Hastings' insistence, however, five sub-factors were assigned to him, and the restriction on the amount of the Cherokee consignments was removed. Several factories were now established in the Cherokee country: at Keowee and Cowee, and later at Tugaloo, in the lower towns; at Quanasse in the middle settlements; and at Tellico among the Overhill towns. In 1718 pack-horses were again despatched to the mountains.[32, 33]

Other difficulties arose with the Indians over the price of goods as established by treaty or by the instructions of the Indian board.   In November, 1716, Hastings supported a Cherokee plea for abatements.[34] The prices, he said, were higher than those agreed upon by Moore. The next year Glover reported Indian complaints that prices at Savannah Town were only a little lower than those in the Cherokee towns, and that too much water was mixed with the rum. The commissioners made several reductions and ordered 'in the mixture with Rum, a convenient proportion.'[35]

More effective than the complaints of the Indians in lowering prices among the Catawba and the Cherokee was the renewed competition of the Virginia traders. An additional act had given the commissioners considerable authority to deal with interlopers in the trade,[36] but in spite of the fact that they

[31] Ibid., November 7, 1716.
[32] JCHA, January 17, 18, 24, 1716/7.
[33] JIC, November 1, 21, 1716; January 25, 29, 31, March 22, June 17, 1717.

[34] JIC, November 1, 1716.
[35] Ibid., September 10, 1717.
[36] Cooper (ed.), *Statutes,* II. 691.

commonly described the Virginians by that term, their powers were actually limited to excluding Carolinians. In the fall of 1717 Wigan warned of Virginian pack-horse trains among the Catawba, and of the seduction of their lower prices. Governor and council in conference with the Indian board agreed that the northern trade must be continued, even at a loss to the public.[37] By 1718 similar competition had developed among the Cherokee. The board then ordered a reduction of rates to the level of the recent Creek schedule.[38]

In spite of these and other difficulties the monopoly was maintained until 1719, and on a smaller scale the public trade continued until 1721. Unquestionably it abated most of the old abuses, and so helped to restore peace with the exasperated inland tribes. The commercial results were more dubious. Some years later, Thomas Lamboll, clerk of the board, gave a plausible account to an assembly committee of the reasons for the failure of the experiment.[39] The original stock of £5000 currency was appropriated in bills of credit and soon proved inadequate, but the board also received loans from the treasury, the use of public property, and the services of a number of public employees. On the other hand serious losses were incurred by Indian attacks and accidents. Moreover, Lamboll declared, the commissioners set out 'under great disadvantages by buying Goods on Credit at about 20% advanced price.' This reflected the widespread suspicion among the Charles Town merchants of the soundness of the corporation, and also, perhaps, their hostility to a public monopoly. One of them wrote to a London correspondent, after two years of the public trade, that 'we have not yet nor dare yet Venture to sell any Indian Trading Goods to our Company who have no foundation nor Stock for any person to depend on, and it's but too likely that should they come to any Loss our Assembly would not be so Just as to make it good, but would tell their Creditors that they did not Compell them to Trust the Commissioners.'[40]

Mercantile opposition crippled the public monopoly. Eventu-

[37] JIC, April 27, September 11, 20, October 24, 1717; April 11, May 8, June 14, 1718.
[38] Ibid., October 4, November 2, 23, 1717; July 5, 19, 1718.
[39] JCHA, May 21, 1734.
[40] C.O. 5:1265, Q 158 (letter of June 13, 1718).

ally the merchants brought about the repeal of the act by the
Lords Proprietors. When the act was renewed for five years,
in 1717,[41] this action was denounced in letters to the London
merchant, Stephen Godin, as likely to lose 'all our Indians who
will goe over to the French Interest and become greater enemies
than ever.'[42] Much was made of the commerce in Indian trading
goods which had sprung up from Charles Town to Mobile and
Pensacola. The issue was clearly drawn between the planters,
whose interest in the trade was mainly one of defense, and the
merchants, who though a small minority in the province had
powerful friends in London. 'The country has engrossed the
Trade through a Mercenary and Ignorant Temper which reigns
in most of our people,' one Charles Town merchant complained. "Tis highly reasonable this should be Remedied by
Disallowing the Act at home as they have done that of the
Virginia Company.' The Virginia Company, to be sure, was a
private and not a public corporation, but the distinction was
not regarded by the London merchants, who attacked both
acts. Stephen Godin, Joseph Boone, Samuel Barons, and other
merchants trading to Carolina petitioned the Proprietors, and
in July, 1718, the latter notified the governor and council of
the repeal.[43] This action, with the simultaneous repeal of the
land-grant acts by which the province had attempted to repeople
the southern border, was one of the grievances which underlay
the anti-proprietary revolution in 1719. There was a certain
irony in a resolution of the Commons in 1720 directing that
the merchant Boone be informed, as colony agent in London,
that the recent Indian ravages might have been prevented 'had
the Indian trading Act continued in force.'[44]

The merchants had destroyed the public monopoly, but it
is evident that the planters dictated the substitute act of 1719,
which inaugurated a mixed régime of public and private
trade.[45] The stock of the public corporation was restored by

[41] Cooper (ed.), *Statutes,* III. 21.
[42] C.O. 5:1265, Q 158 (letter of December 17, 1717).
[43] C.O. 5:290, p. 117; 292, p. 99.
[44] JCHA, May 6, 1720.
[45] Cooper (ed.), *Statutes,* III. 86-96. In October, 1720, sixteen London
merchants with Carolina connections memorialised the Board of Trade on
'what may be done to retrieve the desolation of Carolina'; they urged especially regulation of the Indian trade to prevent abuses and recover the
cld alliances, without providing a monopoly 'exclusive to other private
adventurers' (JBT, October 27, 1720; C.O. 5:358, A 14 + 15).

another appropriation of £5000, its debts were guaranteed to reëstablish its credit, and the commissioners were authorized to purchase goods in England to the value of £3000 each year. But their stock was limited to the value of 30,000 lbs. of dressed deerskins, and except in emergencies, the public trade was restricted to the garrisons at Fort Moore, Congaree, and Palachacola. The employees were reduced to sixty men under three factors, with the rank of captains, and three sub-factors, with the rank of lieutenants of the forts. Within twenty miles of each factory private trading was prohibited. Elsewhere, so soon as traders were settled in any Indian nation with sufficient stocks, the public effects were ordered withdrawn. Defense was still the keynote of regulation. The proceeds of the public trade were appropriated to the pay of the garrisons and of the commissioners and their servants; any surplus was to be used to build three stone or brick forts at the trading-garrisons. All skins brought by private dealers from the Cherokee, Catawba, or from beyond the Savannah, paid a tax of 10% for defense. But the system was transitional, and by 1721 the change to private trade was completed. Meanwhile, as Lamboll pointed out, 'the Public Trade maintained [for] about three years, two Garrisons, one at Savanna, the other at Congarees.'[46]

One of the first results of the establishment of royal government in South Carolina was the loss by the Commons House of its exclusive control over Indian regulation. Naturally a royal governor, backed by the colonial authorities, was a more formidable opponent of the Commons than an appointee of the Proprietors. Nicholson, moreover, was experienced, vigorous in his assertion of prerogative, and able to capitalize the prestige of a régime ushered in by popular revolution. But the board system of regulation survived for several years. In 1719 and again in 1721,[47] when the inspection of the garrisons was added to the board's duties, the three commissioners were designated by the assembly. In February, 1723, however, the powers of the commissioners were vested in the governor and any three members of the council.[48] For a year Nicholson, who

---

[46] See note 39.
[47] Cooper (ed.), *Statutes,* III. 141.
[48] Ibid., p. 184.

gave great attention to frontier affairs, was busily engaged in efforts to bring order among the traders, in issuing instructions, receiving delegations of Cherokee, Creek and Chickasaw chiefs, and in all the manifold details of Indian management.[49] By October, 1723, however, he was ready to acknowledge that 'the Various Interests of the Persons concerned in the . . . Trade makes it very Difficult to Manage it,' and to call on the assembly once more for reform.[50] The difficulties that the irascible governor had encountered with 'refractory and insolent traders' were reflected in his suggestion that it be made 'a felony without Benefit of Clergy for any that shall disobey the orders given them.'

In the act of 1724[51] the single commissioner system of regulation was adopted, and the Commons House recovered part of its former authority over Indian management. Thereafter it was the assembly, by agreement of both houses, that determined policies, appointed commissioners and agents, and advised the governor in his negotiations with Indian tribes; and in most cases the Commons House dictated both appointments and procedure. It was the speaker of the House, James Moore, who became the first sole commissioner, with all the regulative powers of the acts of 1721 and 1724. At his death, soon after, George Chicken was chosen.[52] In 1727 Colonel Herbert became commissioner,[53] and Tobias Fitch in 1733.[54] With only a brief interruption this method of the single commissioner was continued in force until the establishment of Crown control over Indian affairs in 1756.[55]

Each spring the Indian commissioner sat at Charles Town to issue licenses and instructions to the traders. But at other seasons he was usually on his travels far into the interior. At least once a year he was required to inspect the frontier garri-

[49] C.O. 5:359, B 28 (10), (11), (12).
[50] JCHA, October 2, 1723; January 22, February 13, 1724; Nicholson to Board of Trade, December 4, 1723, C.O. 5:359, B 43.
[51] Cooper (ed.), *Statutes,* III. 229.
[52] C.O. 5:412 (act of March 28, 1724, not in Cooper or Trott).
[53] Ibid. (act of September 30, 1727).
[54] Cooper (ed.), *Statutes,* III. 371.
[55] See Smith, *op. cit.,* p. 218, for later commissioners. In 1728 and 1731 an 'open company' was considered but not pressed because of the settled policy of the colonial authorities (JCHA, March 6, April 13, 1728; February 25, 1731).

sons. Longer journeys to regulate the trade and uphold the Carolinian interest against French and Spanish were also part of his office. The act of 1727 required that Colonel Herbert visit the various Creek and Cherokee towns once a year, and his salary was therefore increased from £600 to £1000 currency. In 1731 it was fixed at £100 sterling. In all respects the commissioner was subject to the directions of the governor and assembly, though in great emergencies he was expected to use a larger discretion.[56]

Thus Chicken and his successors served as Indian agents as well as Indian commissioners. But one man could hardly be expected to cover the whole circuit of the Carolina alliances. Several special agents were therefore employed primarily as Indian diplomats, until in 1725 something like a regular Indian agency again came into existence. In view of his great services in 1717 in reopening relations with the Creeks, Colonel Hastings was retained as factor in the Creek nation until the abandonment of the public trade. Thereafter from 1721 to 1725 he resided almost continuously among the Creeks in the double character of a private trader and an Indian agent. William Hatton, his successor as Cherokee factor, also became an agent of this type among the mountaineers.[57] But the critical state of Indian affairs in 1725 demanded the undivided attention of entirely disinterested officials. Tobias Fitch was therefore appointed Creek agent, and the commissioner, Chicken, received an addition to his salary to undertake a mission to the Cherokee. Again in 1726 Fitch and Chicken were appointed.[58] During the winter of 1727-1728 Charlesworth Glover, as agent to the Creeks, negotiated so successfully that it was possible to shelve the Creek punitive expedition. Governor Johnson in 1731 recommended a reward to Glover for his 'constant readiness and good services' for several years past.[59] Until 1731 the agents were appointed by special action

[56] Cooper (ed.), *Statutes*, III. 230, 231, 328; C.O. 5:412.

[57] See below, pp. 259, 265, 267; also, JCHA, February 11, 1723; May 11, 1725; JC, November 26, 1725.

[58] JC, March 17, 1724. JCHA, 1725, 1726, *passim*. The journals of Fitch and Chicken in 1725 are printed in Mereness (ed.), *Travels*, pp. 97-212. A report in JCHA, March 25, 1736, indicates that in 1727 Fitch received an allowance of £1112 for his journey to the Creeks, and Chicken £780 for his special mission.

[59] See below, pp. 271-2. Glover's journal is in C.O. 5:387.

of the assembly in each case, the Commons House usually dictating the person. The Indian act of that year for the first time authorized the appointment of a permanent Creek agent at £80 a month, to exercise all of the powers of a commissioner except the granting of licenses.[60]

Indian diplomacy centred in the Indian trade, and the chief problem of the trade was the conduct of the individual Indian trader. With the return to individual enterprise the old problem of regulation had reappeared, underscored by the terrible experiences of 1715. In the decade before the establishment of Georgia seven statutes were passed in South Carolina, most of them creating new restrictions. The culmination of this tendency was the act of 1731, which really established an Indian trading code for the whole southern frontier, since the Georgia act of 1735 was closely patterned upon it.[61]

The essence of the system, as in 1707, was the requirement of licenses and the subjection of the traders to the instructions of the Indian administration. Licenses were usually renewable once a year, but in the case of the Chickasaw traders at intervals of eighteen months. They were issued by the secretary under the authority of the commissioner, and the personal appearance of the principal trader in Charles Town was required. The fees advanced from £23 in 1721 to £30 in 1724 and 1731. Bonds for good conduct were also required.[62] Many evils arose from the cut-throat competition between wandering traders; in 1724 each trader was required to declare to which nation he intended to go, and was so restricted in his license.[63] In 1731 there was a further restriction to specified towns in each tribe, except among the Chickasaw. The commissioner was empowered to allot the towns according to their size; only in the larger towns was more than one licensed trader permitted to reside.[64] In a further effort 'to encourage persons of interest and reputation to trade amongst the Indians and to make quick sales and returns,' each principal trader was allowed to insert in his license the names of two white assistants. For additional

[60] Cooper (ed.), *Statutes*, III. 334.
[61] *Colonial Records of Georgia*, I. 31-42.
[62] Cooper (ed.), *Statutes*, III. 90 f., 143 f., 230, 330; C.O. 5 :412.
[63] Cooper, *Statutes*, III. 230.
[64] Ibid., pp. 331f.

servants separate licenses were required.[65] The trader must give
bond for the conduct of his servants, and he was forbidden to
discharge them in the Indian country. The employment of
slaves or of free negroes was strictly forbidden. Penalties were
imposed for such offenses as the refusal to obey instructions
or warrants, trading without license, trusting Indians, trading
with enemy tribes or the subjects of Spain or France. These
might be fines, forfeiture of license, or both. To enforce these
rules the commissioner was given judicial powers, and could
issue warrants against offenders; the commanders of the frontier posts might also be called upon to send detachments to
arrest recalcitrants.[66] By such provisions of the code the trade
was kept fairly free from danger, though never free from
scandal.

By 1732 the South Carolina regulatory system was probably as well planned and as efficiently enforced as any such system could have been under colonial conditions, and in view of
the vast extent of the Carolina Indian country. No great advance could be made until provincial control of Indian affairs
gave way to imperial control, a reform which was not actually
begun for more than a score of years. But as early as 1720 the
necessity of an imperial policy in these matters had begun to
appear. To this end Sir William Keith's famous 'Report on
the Progress of the French Nation,' submitted to the Board
of Trade in 1719, proposed 'a compleat body of Instructions'
to 'all the Governours on this Continent,' to establish complete
freedom of trade from one colony to another. Once the Indian
trade was regarded as an imperial interest, 'we should not have
the traders of New York jealous and uneasie at the profits
gained by the Traders of Virginia, nor those again of the Im-
provements which may possibly be made in Carolina, but every
Colony would find a solid and certain Advantage by an Union
among them according to their situation Power and Ability to
advance their trading Settlements Westward.'[67] In 1720, at the
suggestion of John Barnwell and Francis Nicholson, the Board
of Trade advised the new royal governor to confer with the
governor of Virginia 'for promoting, settling, and inlarging

---

[65] Ibid., pp. 230, 331.
[66] Ibid., pp. 90-2, 141-3, 230 f., 329-32.
[67] C.O. 5:1265, Q 179.

the Indian Trade, . . . and to settle matters on such a foot, that neither of these Colonies should have reason to complain of the other.'[68] The consultations thus authorized were continued, by correspondence, as late as 1722, and drew in also the governor of North Carolina. They marked the first halting steps towards the development of an imperial policy in the regulation of the southern Indian trade.[69]

Little, however, was actually accomplished at the time. One of Barnwell's suggestions had been that the assemblies of Virginia and South Carolina pass equitable and complementary laws regulating trade. Yet so strong were the old jealousies that Spotswood found matter for complaint in the South Carolina Indian act of 1721. To be sure, the Virginians were not mentioned therein, but the Virginia agent argued that the requirement of licenses to be taken out at Charles Town was principally aimed at them. Richard West, counsel of the Board, saw no essential difference from the act of 1711, previously disallowed, and declared that the new act was 'not proper to be passed into law.' He went out of his way to reveal his ignorance of the American frontier when he observed that the hardships imposed on the Carolina traders themselves were 'very grievous, and the powers granted to the commissioners . . . very arbitrary.' In rebuttal the Carolina agent asserted that the whole scope of the law was to keep the Carolina traders 'in a due Oeconomy,' and denied that there was any intent to exclude the Virginia traders. To seize their goods or otherwise submit them to the law would be in effect, he said, a declaration of war between the provinces—an interesting commentary on the relations which had actually existed from 1707 to 1712.[70] This time the Board paid no heed to the Virginian complaints. As a matter of fact it was no longer necessary for the Carolinians to stretch the legitimate function of regulation for the illegitimate purpose of excluding the Virginians. Despite Spotswood's activities, the competition from the Chesapeake colony had become practically negligible. In 1725 George Chicken wrote from the Cherokees that 'the Virginia traders . . . I am

[68] C.O. 5:358, A 11; 400, p. 132.

[69] JCHA, January 26, February 1, 1721/2. See also C.O. 5:401, p. 45.

[70] George Chalmers (comp.), Opinions of Eminent Lawyers, II. 300-6. JC, December 4, 1722. C.O. 5:371, H 56.

certain can do no prejudice to ours in the Way of Trade there
not being above two or three of them and their goods no ways
Suitable or Comparable to ours.'[71] The Virginians continued
to enjoy a small share of the Catawba and Cherokee trade, but
the real rivals of the Carolinians, in the next generation, were
the colonists of Georgia. Between South Carolina and Georgia
quite as bitter a conflict was to be waged, with resort, again, to
the Board of Trade and Privy Council. But now the tables
were turned, and the Carolinians found themselves in the
former situation of the Virginia traders, compelled to defend
the trade which they had long enjoyed against the monopolistic
designs of their new neighbors.

[71] JC, November 2, 1725 (Chicken's journal for August 30).

CHAPTER IX

BEGINNINGS OF BRITISH WESTERN POLICY, 1715-1721

The Yamasee War began a new era in British frontier policy as well as in the border history of the South. The threatened ruin of South Carolina for the first time definitely focussed the attention of the colonial authorities upon the southern frontier. The Indian war and its aftermath served also to arouse the English as never before to the encroachments of the French west of the Appalachians. Persistently exploited by the Carolinians in their appeals at home, these apprehensions led in the next five or six years to the establishment of royal government in Carolina and to the assertion by the Board of Trade of the first clearly formulated British program for challenging the progress of the French in the West.

In the spring and summer of 1715 something like panic spread along the Atlantic seaboard, and even to England. The Board of Trade was warned by William Byrd that if the Cherokee joined the conspiracy, the destruction of Carolina could not be prevented.[1] From New York Colonel Heathcote communicated to Lord Townshend his dread of a general Indian rising, with French support, against all of the English colonies.[2] Carolina, wrote Cotton Mather, in characteristic vein, 'is newly destroy'd by the dreadful Judgments of God, for which an uncommon measure of Iniquities had ripened it.' It was much to be feared, he added, 'that the Combination of the Indians is more general, than meerly for the Destruction of Carolina; and under a French and Spanish Instigation. And that some other Colonies, which, alas, are too obnoxious, may shortly suffer grievous Depredations from them.'[3] Craven and Spotswood pictured the French occupying Carolina on the heels of the barbarians.[4] Soon there arrived in England from South Carolina a series of addresses and petitions appealing for aid of arms and men and also for the establishment of direct royal control.

[1] JBT, July 15, 1715.
[2] *Docs. rel. Col. Hist. N. Y.*, V. 433.
[3] *Mass. Hist. Soc. Coll.*, seventh series, VIII. pp. 328 f.
[4] Spotswood, *Letters*, II. 122; *Col. Rec. N. C.*, II. 179.

At the first report of the crisis, the Board of Trade was directed by Secretary Stanhope, on July 7, to report on the question of assistance.[5] There followed consultation with the Secretaries, and the Cabinet, eager scanning of the letters from America, questioning of planters and merchants, and pointed interrogation of the Lords Proprietors.[6] Though the latter had themselves appealed to the Board for aid, they pleaded the minority of two of their number as a reason for not pledging their charter as security.[7] The Board now proposed an outright surrender, but failed to arrive at terms. On July 19 they reported to Stanhope that the Proprietors were unable 'or at least not inclin'd, at their own Charges, either to send the necessary Succours upon this Exigency, or to support that province under the like for the future.' The results of proprietary neglect in the Bahamas were recalled, and the value of South Carolina set forth, as a producer of rice, naval stores, and skins, and also as a frontier. 'The situation of Carolina,' they declared, 'makes it a Frontier, as well against the French and Spaniards, as against numerous Nations of Indians, which last, at the Instigation of the former, seem to have enter'd into a General Confederacy against all our other Plantations on the Continent.' Therefore they raised the question whether it was not proper for his Majesty 'to take the preservation of so valuable a province upon him at this Juncture.'[8]

The attack upon the Lords Proprietors was pressed both by the Board and by the Carolina agent. It soon shifted to the House of Commons, and broadened out into a general assault upon the colonial charters. August 2, 1715, a petition of the Carolina agent and several merchants trading to that province was presented. They recited the plight of the colony, complained of French encroachments, and prayed for immediate relief. August 10, the committee, which included members of the Board of Trade and merchants, reported substantially in the

[5] Ibid., p. 193.
[6] JBT, July 8, 13, 14, 15, 1715 (printed in *Col. Rec. N. C.*, II. 193-6). See also McCrady, *South Carolina under the Prop. Gov.*, pp. 538 ff., and L. M. Kellogg, 'The American Colonial Charter,' in *Am. Hist. Assoc. Rep.* (1903), I. 309.
[7] JBT, July 13, 1715; *Col. Rec. N. C.*, II. 188.
[8] C.O. 5:383, no. 1; Rivers, *Sketch* (1856), pp. 271-4. See also memorial of Kettleby and the merchants, July 18, 1715, in *Col. Rec. N. C.*, II. 196-9.

terms of the Board's earlier letter to the Secretary of State, whereupon the House ordered an address to the Crown for the relief of Carolina. At the same time leave was given to bring in a bill 'for the better Regulation of the Charter and Proprietary Governments in America.' Though this bill advanced to a second reading, it soon met formidable opposition. Petitions were offered by Baltimore and Penn, by the agents of Massachusetts, Connecticut, and Rhode Island, and by the guardians of Lord Craven and the Duke of Beaufort. These special interests, marshalled by Lord Carteret, were reinforced by the Whig antipathy to encroachments upon vested rights. Confronted by so formidable an opposition the legislative attack upon the charters in 1715 broke down.[9]

Henceforth the strategy of the dominant anti-proprietary party in the province was to exploit to the utmost the perils of their frontier situation and the inefficiency of the Proprietary régime. No doubt they colored their reports of the Indian revolt and of the French peril; on the other hand the Proprietors and their servants constantly minimized these dangers.[10]

In London the campaign was vigorously pressed by the assembly's new agents, Joseph Boone and Richard Berresford. They bombarded the Board and the Secretary of State with formal addresses from the assembly, with extracts from American letters, and with their own memorials. Thus in June, 1716, they submitted a sheaf of papers,[11] including a list of exports and imports for a year before the rising, to emphasize the mercantilist interest in preserving the colony. Again and again they stressed the Proprietors' neglect in face of the new French program of encirclement from Canada to Louisiana. South Carolina, they asserted, was 'a Barrier and might be made a Bulwark to all his Majesties Collonys on the South West Part

[9] *Journals of the House of Commons,* August 2, 10, 13, 15, 16, 17, 19, 1715; C.O. 5:1265, Q 50, 52; *Political State of Great Britain,* X. 170 f. (August, 1715) ; Kellogg, in *Am. Hist. Assoc. Rep.* (1903), I. 310 f.; H. L. Osgood, *Am. Col. in the Eighteenth Century,* II. 294.

[10] Thus in July, 1716, the Proprietors told the Board of Trade that the Yamasee and Creek Indians were almost entirely destroyed (C.O. 5:1265, Q 118), but a few months later the Commons House in an address asserted that only a miracle or royal intervention could stave off ruin (C.O. 5:387, f. 8 i). See also JCHA, April 18, 1716; JBT, June 28, 1716; C.O. 5:290, p. 92

[11] C.O. 5:1265, Q 74, 75, 76, 77; *Col. Rec. N. C.,* II. 229-33.

of the Continent against the French, Spaniards and Indians.' Forts in the Bahamas and at Port Royal were proposed to control the shipping route from the Gulf, and others 'towards Mobile on the borders of our Frontiers.' In December, 1717, the Board of Trade received from Berresford a memorial relating to 'the Designs of the French to Extend their Settlements from Canada to Mississippi behind the British Plantations.' This paper made a strong impression, and led to inquiries of colonial governors which produced in the next two years the confirmatory warnings of Spotswood and Keith. Berresford denounced the Crozat grant as 'a direct Encroachment on the patent from our Crown to the Proprietors of Carolina.' He described the new Western Company as an even greater menace. The French had already imperilled the Iroquois alliance, and now threatened to fall with their Indians upon the Cherokee. If they should succeed, he predicted, 'We shall not only lose all our Commerce with the Natives, which will Sink our Trade but be evidently expos'd to be drove out of the Continent by the French and their Numerous Allies; and what a Loss as well as Disgrace this will be to England 'tis not easy to be conceiv'd and far less to be express'd.'[12]

These clamors of the French peril were accompanied by repeated overtures for royal government in Carolina. While the House of Commons bill of 1715 was expiring in committee, in South Carolina the Commons House of Assembly was preparing another address to the King, praying 'that this once Flourishing Province may be absolutely under your Majesties care and Government.' In March, 1716, and again in November, the plea was renewed.[13] Finally, in 1717, the agents, who meantime had thanked the Board of Trade for its previous efforts, again carried to Parliament the case of South Carolina, 'the only Southern Frontier of all British America, both to the French and the Spaniards.' But this time the friends of the chartered governments prevented even a reference of the subject to committee.[14]

---

[12] C.O. 323:7, K 116.
[13] C.O. 5:382, ff. 14, 19; 1265, Q 71, 72, 73; 387, f. 12, enclosure; JCHA, April 17, 1716.
[14] C.O. 5:1265, Q 117, broadside, 'The case of the colony of South-Carolina in America: humbly offered to the consideration of both houses of Parliament.' *Journals of the House of Commons*, May 22, 1717.

While the Proprietors were under attack, their failure as wardens of the southern marches the chief count against them, there was developed a plan—the best remembered of the pre-Georgia schemes—for solving the problem of southern border defense quite in the feudal spirit of their régime. The Margravate of Azilia was designed to occupy precisely the region which fifteen years later became Georgia. Otherwise it has seemed chiefly remarkable as involving a degree of sub-infeudation unique among English colonial projects,[15] and for its singular plan of settlement.

The projector was a Scotch baronet, Sir Robert Montgomery of Skelmorly (1680-1731). His was a family interest in colonization. He claimed a Knight of Nova Scotia among his ancestors; his father, moreover, had been a backer of Lord Cardross, and the charming descriptions of Carolina which he had heard in his youth inspired him, he wrote, with a particular affection for that part of America.[16] Among his associates were Abel Kettleby, discharged as agent by the South Carolina assembly in November, 1716;[17] and the poet-projector, Aaron Hill.[18] Hill's pen, perhaps, produced the flamboyant descriptions of 'our future Eden,' which set a new record for exaggeration in colonial promotion literature. The very name of the colony was eloquent of the confused utopianism and decadent feudalism which inspired the scheme.

In June, 1717, Montgomery and Kettleby presented their proposals, to which the Proprietors readily agreed, anticipating quit-rents and an easy solution of the vexing problem of defense. Details were negotiated by Kettleby and the Proprietary secretary, Shelton, and on July 11, 1717, the deeds of lease and release were executed.[19] For a penny quit-rent for each acre occupied, the Proprietors conveyed to Montgomery and his heirs and assigns 'all that Tract of Land which lies between the Rivers Altamaha and Savanna.' Farther southward, too, Mont-

[15] Professor C. M. Andrews has characterized this project as an attempt to establish 'the most remarkable feudal estate within the colonial area' (Introduction to B. W. Bond, *Quit Rent System*, p. 20).
[16] *Dictionary of National Biography*, XXXVIII, 321f.; Montgomery, *Discourse* (1717); Insh, *Scottish Colonial Schemes*, p. 203.
[17] C.O. 5:387, f. 8. Kettleby had served as agent since 1712.
[18] Dorothy Brewster, *Aaron Hill: Poet, Dramatist, Projector*, 1913, pp. 50-9; Aaron Hill, *Works*, 1753, II. 187-96.
[19] C.O. 5:1265, Q 144, 145(1); 292, pp. 93, 94.

gomery might make settlements, but beyond the Altamaha the
Proprietors reserved the right to grant unoccupied lands. Profit-
ing by the Cardross episode, or, more probably, by recent quarrels between Virginia and South Carolina, they withheld from
Montgomery the right to tax or in any way obstruct the navigation of the Azilian rivers by inhabitants of North or South
Carolina, or to interfere with 'their free Commerce and Trade
with the Indian Nations, either within, or to the Southward of
the Margravate.' Moreover, if Montgomery should fail to effect
a settlement within three years the Proprietors might repossess
themselves of the grant.

Within a few weeks Montgomery published his well-known
*Discourse concerning the design'd Establishment of a New
Colony to the South of Carolina, in the most delightful Country of the Universe.*[20] 'Paradise with all her Virgin beau-
ties,' declared the exuberant pamphleteer, 'may be modestly
suppos'd at most but equal to its Native Excellencies.' He unfolded a highly artificial plan for planting compact fortified
township settlements in Azilia, with servants to till the proprietors' lands and a class of gentlemen-tenants. An illustrative
chart showed a great tract, four-square and surrounded by
fortifications. Within were concentric zones parcelled among
the proprietors and the resident gentry, or set aside for the uses
of a park and a town. At the precise centre stood the palace of
the Margrave. Hopefully Montgomery listed the many valuable
exotic commodities, olives, wine, raisins, almonds, etc., which
Azilia, like all colonies projected in the South, was expected to
produce. Less was said, naturally, of the buffer character of the
proposed colony in an advertisement intended to attract investors. But Montgomery was aware of Cardross's disaster, and
of recent events in Carolina. Azilia, he hoped, might not only
'resist a Storm Herself, but . . . also spread her Wings to a
Capacity of shadowing others : a British Colony, shou'd, like the
Roman, carry with it always something of the Mother's Glory.'

[20] A note in the first issue announced that subscriptions would be taken
at the Carolina Coffee House, Birchin Lane, after August 1. In a later issue
(copy in John Carter Brown Library), a revised plan was announced :
purchasers would pay the first half of their subscriptions not to Montgomery but to Messrs. Turner, Caswell, and Co., at the Sword Blade office,
to be held until completed or until trustees were chosen by the subscribers.
These trustees would make all expenditures and hold all supplies prior to
embarkation. Books would be opened September 2.

So far as it was in their power the Proprietors had agreed that Azilia should be a province distinct from Carolina. But royal approval was necessary if Montgomery was to become, as he hoped, governor for life. In July, 1717, the Proprietors commended the scheme to the Privy Council.[21] The appeals to the colonial authorities placed great emphasis upon Azilia's strategic value, in Anglo-French even more than in Anglo-Spanish rivalry. It was pointed out by Montgomery, or by his associate, the poet-projector Hill, in terms which strikingly recall the Nairne memorial of 1707, that under cover of this grant, 'a settlement may unexpectedly, and without noise, be made somewhere on the river of Apalachia.' Seated upon the Gulf, the English would then be in a position to watch the designs of the French, 'and be a Check to their Ambition.'[22]

Montgomery in 1718 insisted that he had in prospect sufficient subscriptions to carry over the first colony of five or six hundred settlers. Already aroused to the French danger in the West by the Carolinians and by Spotswood of Virginia, whose well-known warnings were largely an echo of the clamors from South Carolina, the Board was favorably disposed towards a new barrier colony, which was also endorsed to them in general terms by Colonel Blakiston and the colonial merchant, Micajah Perry. But in line with their fixed policy, and with the sceptical opinion of Attorney-General Northey, the Lords of Trade first proposed that the Carolina Proprietors surrender their powers of government in the new province.[23]

With this qualified approval by the Board the matter rested until 1720. Meanwhile, declared Hill, Montgomery's advertisements meeting with less success than expected, 'I bought his grant of him with a firm resolution, to pursue the design by myself.'

> No gain-polluted aim inspires my view,
> I seek not office, nor reward pursue.
> More nobly fir'd my thoughts high schemes design,
> To stretch dominion, and make empire shine.

[21] C.O. 5:1265, Q 142; JBT, February 20, 1718.
[22] C.O. 5:1265, Q 143. Compare Aaron Hill's 'Letter to Lord ——,' n.d., in *Works*, 1753, II. 187-96.
[23] C.O. 5:1265, Q 146; 383, nos. 2, 2 i, 3; JBT, February 20, 25, 27, March 4, 5, 1717/18.

Thus Hill appealed to a noble lord for patronage. At the moment he was seeking to set up a lottery in Scotland to make good the dearth of subscriptions,[24] for Azilia had many competitors for public support in that period of the South Sea excitement. The collapse of the South Sea stock turned opinion strongly against all projectors. Transformed into a 'bubble,' so John Barnwell of South Carolina charged,[25] the project disappeared with the ebbing of the tide of speculation.

It left only a name on contemporary maps,[26] and several interesting promotion pamphlets. Two of these, of 1720, advertised the modified scheme for colonizing St. Catherine's and the other so-called 'Golden Islands' of the Azilian coast.[27] Investors were enticed with the promise not merely of quit-rents from military-industrial colonies like those proposed in 1717, but also of profits from a monopoly of trade with Azilia. Preparations were described for a first settlement at St. Catherine's with a stock of £25,000 already in hand. From the Carolina agents, however, the revised scheme met with opposition. To be sure, on his first arrival in England John Barnwell had written to Montgomery commending his 'worthy Design of planting Azilia.' This letter, with its stress on the commercial and strategic value of the colony, and its prediction that the Indian trade would centre there, was conspicuously displayed in both the Golden Islands tracts. But by September, 1720, the situation was greatly altered, and with it the agent's attitude. The results of the revolution of 1719 in the colony had now been accepted by the Crown. A provisional royal governor was to be sent out; and, at Barnwell's urging, a garrison was to be established at the mouth of the Altamaha, on the southern margin of Azilia. Boone and Barnwell accordingly complained to the Board of Trade that Montgomery's advertisements raised fears of a conflict between the royal garrison and the Golden

[24] Aaron Hill, *Works,* 1753, II. 187-96; and Brewster, *Aaron Hill,* p. 58. But note that Montgomery petitioned for a lottery in 1718 and made affidavit that he had a *bona fide* intention to make a settlement (C.O. 5:383, ff. 3, 4). In 1720 Montgomery was again connected with the Golden Islands scheme.

[25] Historical MSS Commission, *Eleventh Report,* part IV, p. 256.

[26] See Herman Moll, *A New Map of the North Parts of America claimed by France,* 1720; and *C.O. Maps,* N.A.C. General, 7.

[27] *An Account . . . of a Design* (1720) and *A Description of the Golden Islands* (1720).

Islands colonists. Declaring that no powers of government claimed from the Proprietors could interfere with his Majesty's authority, the Board referred the complainants to the Lords Justices.[28] But the Azilia 'bubble' had already burst.[29]

In the affair of Azilia the Proprietors had shown some appreciation of the existence of a frontier problem in their vast estate, not undivorced from hopes of revenue in quit-rents. Meanwhile they evaded the inquiries of the Board of Trade regarding more tangible aid of arms and money.[30] But it was their land policy, and especially the affair of the Yamasee tract, that most strikingly revealed their indifference to the strategic needs of the colony.

By an act of 1707, approved by the Proprietors, a reservation had been created between the Combahee and Savannah Rivers for the Yamasee Indians. Their revolt and expulsion from the province now raised the question of the disposition of these lands, the immediate frontier, towards Florida, of the existing settlements. The war had shown the disadvantages from the defense standpoint of large grants only partially occupied by scattered plantations sparsely settled by whites, disadvantages which were particularly obvious in this border land. Apparently the assembly urged a new policy. In February, 1716, the proprietary board, rebuking the assembly's agent, Joseph Boone, for his 'very insolent manner,' nevertheless declared its intention to parcel out the Yamasee lands in holdings of not over two hundred acres, free of quit-rents for five years, for the encouragement of actual settlers. This pledge was recorded in the minutes, and shortly repeated in a letter to the colony.[31]

Thereupon the assembly somewhat rashly passed an act to

[28] JBT, September 15, 1720.

[29] The ghost of Azilia occasionally walked. See C.O. 5:358, A 48, p. 131; 362, D 57; 290, f. 260; also Percival, *Diary*, I. 398.

[30] On the controversy over proprietary aid, see C.O. 5:1265, Q 78, Q 118, Q 121; 1293, pp. 97, 98; JCHA, April 18, 25, 1716; also, McCrady, *S. C. under the Prop. Gov.*, pp. 571-2, and Osgood, *Am. Col. in the Eighteenth Century*, II. 354. Probably the donation of quit-rents was all that the Proprietors could offer in their situation. In November, 1718, they received an address of the governor and assembly to procure from the Crown a stationship to cruise for pirates, and '500 men to protect them against the Encroachment of the French Indians.' The appeal for the ship was apparently pressed, but it does not appear that the Proprietors interested themselves in the plea for a garrison (C.O. 5:292, Proprietors' minutes under November 28, 1718, and February 27, 1718/19).

[31] C.O. 5:292, pp. 84, 86; 290, p. 92.

appropriate the 'Indian Land' for the 'publick benefit of this Province.'[32] To encourage newcomers from Great Britain, Ireland, or from other colonies, grants were offered of three hundred to four hundred acres on condition of actual settlement and occupation for ten months in the year. While retaining the usual quit-rent of twelve shillings per hundred acres, the assembly imprudently undertook to suspend for four years the payment of the purchase price of £3. A special plea was made to the Proprietors to permit this concession to the poverty of the new settlers. Other acts in the same session offered bounties for bringing in white Protestant servants, and placed a check upon the importation of blacks from Africa. Together these measures represented an attempt to convert the southern border into a region with a predominant white population, ready to defend the province in an emergency.

The publication of the settlement laws in England, it was said, soon attracted some five hundred Protestant Irish to South Carolina. Other settlers, old Carolinians, began to enter the portion of the tract, Huspaw Neck, reserved for them.[33] But this hopeful movement to repeople the ravaged border was abruptly halted by the Proprietors, who, in July, 1718, repealed these acts as an encroachment upon their property.[34] At that time, indeed, the Proprietors made a wholesale attack upon provincial legislation assertive of the powers of the assembly. The discriminatory customs act, the Indian-trading act, the law establishing elections in the parishes, and the act of 1707 for the election of the public receiver by the assembly, all went by the board. These vetoes clearly proclaimed the intention of the Proprietors to recover a dominant voice in the government of the province. The assembly was ordered dissolved, and new elections held under the old law. News of the vetoes came to the colonists in the midst of their bitter quarrel with Chief Justice Trott, the unpopular representative of proprietary prerogative. Trott vigorously defended the Proprietors when the assembly presumed to question their right of veto. Though Francis Yonge of the council was sent to England to persuade the

[32] Cooper (ed.), *Statutes,* II. 641-6.
[33] C.O. 5 :382, f. 20.
[34] C.O. 5 :292, p. 98 ; Cooper (ed.), *Statutes,* III. 30 f.

Proprietors to give way, they were inflexible. Reluctantly, Governor Johnson bowed to their will.[35]

Meanwhile, whatever the justification of the vetoes, the Proprietors' proceedings in the matter of the Yamasee tract gave culminating evidence of bad faith. In February, 1718, they had ordered that a copy of their resolution 'and agreement' relating to the Yamasee lands should be sent to the colony.[36] In July, 1718, following the vetoes, and in answer to a 'manifesto' of the governor and council, the order of March 3, 1716, was again transmitted, with the strictest injunctions for its enforcement.[37] The tracts taken up by newcomers were, it appears, reduced to the size required by the order,[38] for the Proprietors were committed even more emphatically than the assembly to a policy of small holdings along the frontier. Already, however, the Board had empowered Mr. Bertie to act upon a petition from one Hodgson that his land-grant of five thousand acres be run out in the old Yamasee settlement. In September further sales of land by agents were forbidden without the previous consent of the Proprietors. And in November, 1718, the proprietary pledge was definitely dishonored. It was then resolved that in a new distribution of baronies among the Proprietors, half of each grant might be taken up, at the individual Proprietor's option, in the Yamasee Land. In February, 1719, sixteen baronies of 12,000 acres each were ordered surveyed for the eight Proprietors, and another barony for their secretary.[39]

At the time, apparently, the Proprietors did not trouble to justify their action. In 1728, however, they insisted that the method was adopted for the 'better Peopling [of] the Province by engaging the Proprietors separately to cultivate and improve their own Lands.'[40] But the history of baronies and of other large grants surely belied this assertion. In 1720, when the colonists were justifying their revolution, they emphasized this breach of faith as a principal article in their case. The order, they declared, was received with indignation in the province;

[35] See Rivers, *Sketch,* chapter x, and Osgood, *Am. Col. in the Eighteenth Century,* II. 351-8 for narratives of the crisis.
[36] C.O. 5:292, p. 95.
[37] C.O. 5:290, p. 118; 292, p. 99.
[38] C.O. 5:382, f. 20.
[39] C.O. 5:292, pp. 88, 103, 104, 108, 110, 114, 115, 119; 290, p. 140.
[40] C.O. 5:290, p. 261.

the Proprietors had appropriated for themselves more land than the Yamasee settlement had ever been accounted to contain. Even *bona fide* settlers who had paid their purchase money to the receiver general, it was charged, were refused confirmation of their titles. The old settlers who had returned to the exposed plantations expecting reinforcements, again deserted.[41] In September, 1719, the reactionary land policy of the lords of the soil was capped by the closing of the land office, on the ground of excessive grants, provincial encroachments, and disorders in the collection of quit-rents.[42] This action was taken before and not, as the Proprietors later asserted, after the revolution.[43]

By the Proprietors the revolt against their rule in 1719 was set down as an affair of the quit-rents, the work of 'some needy Tumultous persons.'[44] Actually the revolution was engineered by the richest and most influential inhabitants, and represented the culmination of a conflict almost as old as the colony. This conflict had taken many forms. Since 1715 the crux of the controversy had been the failure of the Proprietors to provide adequate defense. Hatred of the proprietary machine, Trott and Rhett at Charles Town and Secretary Shelton at home, added fuel to the fires; the proprietary vetoes and the dissolution of the assembly precipitated the crisis. The immediate occasion was furnished by rumors of an impending attack by Spain, now at war with France and England to upset the peace of Utrecht.[45]

Early in July, 1719, the Proprietors had received intelligence from the governor and council that six hundred Indians, headed by Spaniards, were ready to fall on the southern settlements. This emergency they decided to take into consideration at 'the first opportunity,' but only four meetings of the board were held thereafter in 1719, or, indeed, until 1725, and the plight of the colony was apparently ignored.[46] More ominous

[41] C.O. 5:382, f. 20.
[42] C.O. 5:290, pp. 155-7.
[43] Ibid., p. 264.
[44] Ibid., p. 165.
[45] Francis Yonge, *A Narrative of the Proceedings of the People of South Carolina,* London, 1726, reprinted in Carroll (ed.), *Collections,* II. 141-92, was the only detailed contemporary narrative, and the chief source used by Rivers, McCrady, and others. A fair statement of the causes of the revolt was made by Johnson to the Board of Trade in his letter of December 27, 1719 (C.O. 5:1265, Q 200).
[46] C.O. 5:292, p. 128.

were preparations known to be going forward at Havana for an attack by sea, from which Charles Town was saved by an unforeseen turn in the Franco-Spanish conflict in the Gulf. Meanwhile, according to Yonge's narrative, Governor Johnson summoned a conference of councillors and members of the new assembly to secure a subscription for fortifications. But the conference broke up in a quarrel over the validity of the vetoed acts. When Johnson then proceeded to call out the militia, the occasion was seized by the anti-proprietary leaders to create an association in November, 1719, to set up his Majesty's government. This movement soon spread through the province. In December the assembly met and was promptly converted into a convention. After a bloodless conflict with Johnson, who recognized the futility of resistance, James Moore was designated governor in the name of the King. Moore was a son of the old frontier magnate and conqueror of Apalache, and himself a hero of the Yamasee War. To justify these extraordinary proceedings a long paper was drawn up, later printed in England as *A True State of the Case between the Inhabitants of South Carolina, and the Lords Proprietors* [1720].[47] Therein were set forth in great detail all of the accumulated grievances of the planters. But special stress was laid upon the strategic importance of the neglected province, on the necessity of ousting the Spaniards from St. Augustine, and on the failure of the Proprietors, in face of frequent warnings, to represent the encroachments of the French in the West in such light as to forestall their advance. Since the building of Fort Toulouse and the recent capture of Pensacola, it was declared, the French 'surround this settlement from the mountains to the Sea.' Between Carolina and their borders lay 'an open level Champion Country' with abundant game to support an invading army in its march against the English frontier. Without royal protection in the next war 'this hopefull Province will be lost to the British Empire to the endangering Virginia and other your Majesties Dominions and the Irreparable Loss of the beneficial Trade of the Same.' To support these somewhat melodramatic

[47] C.O. 5:1265, Q 203. Cf. ibid., Q 199; and C.O. 5:382, f. 20. In B.M. Add. MSS 35909 (Hardwicke papers, DLXI), ff. 9-18, is a manuscript copy, evidently intended for use as a brief in the proceedings against the charter. 'Collo. Barnwell proves this' or similar comments appear frequently in the margin.

warnings the frontier planter and Indian fighter, John Barnwell, was sent over to London on a special mission.

The revolutionary régime had no real difficulty in sustaining itself, despite the attitude assumed by the commander of H. M. S. *Flamborough* stationed at Charles Town.[48] In England the news of the revolt led to futile efforts by the Proprietors to cash in on their property at the height of the speculative excitement of that mad 'bubble' era. Two attempts to sell Carolina were made. An agreement seems actually to have been reached in 1720 to sell the charter to three Quakers for £230,-000. 'Their design,' declared Barnwell, 'was to make a Buble of it.' Yonge asserted that they intended 'to divide the Country into shares, which were to be Stock-Jobb'd in Exchange Alley,' but were prevented by the act for suppressing bubbles. News of these proceedings naturally heightened provincial resentment and protest was lodged with Secretary Craggs against this attempt to 'elude that Justice we might Reasonably hope.'[49] The second negotiation, in 1720-1721, was for the sale of Carolina to the reorganized South Sea Company. In 1726 a pamphleteer bitterly denounced the Proprietors for adopting in these affairs 'the Practice of the Coast of Africa' in bartering 'for the Sale of free, and natural Subjects' to 'a Set of Jews and Brokers.'[50]

John Barnwell's first task in England, the reconciling of the home government to the *fait accompli,* was easily accomplished. His mission had been prepared by persistent anti-proprietary propaganda in recent years, which was now intensified by a new flood of letters and memorials from South Carolina.[51] The Board of Trade saw the triumph of a long-established policy in

[48] Carroll (ed.), *Collections,* II. 183-7; *Boston News Letter,* June 5, 1721; Rivers, *Chapter,* pp. 52-9; Cooper (ed.), *Statutes,* I. 58 f. On the attitude of North Carolina, see *Col. Rec. N. C.,* II. 374 f., 384.

[49] Historical MSS Commission, *Eleventh Report,* part IV, pp. 255, 256. C.O. 5:358, A 18; Yonge, in Carroll (ed.), *Collections,* II. 190 f.

[50] This forgotten episode was revealed to Nicholson by Kettleby as a great secret in a letter of January 17, 1720/21, in S.P.G. MSS, B, IV, part 1, p. 97. Confirmation appears in Bertie's letter to Lord Carlton, August 14, 1724: 'I must observe to your Lordship that at that time the South Sea directors had set up a treaty for the purchase of the whole Province from the Proprietors; and hastened the Prosecution against their Charters in order to lessen their Demands and at the same time a Scire facias was directed to be brought against our Charter, but none was ever issued out, or any further proceedings had, and by his Majesties Act of Grace in 1721 all proceedings of that kind were determined' (C.O. 5:290, pp. 165-6). See also *Liberty and Property,* 1726, p. 27.

[51] See especially C.O. 5:358, A 3, and documents cited in note 47.

sight. Nor was the Privy Council slow to act. By an order of August 11, 1720, which pointed to the great importance of South Carolina as a frontier as well as its commercial value, the government was taken provisionally into the hands of the Crown. The Board was directed to prepare a commission and instructions for Francis Nicholson, and to propose such further measures as were necessary for the safety of the province.[52] Another Order in Council of September directed that a *scire facias* be procured to vacate the charter.[53] But the Proprietors bowed to the inevitable, and this attack was not pressed. Until 1729 the Proprietors retained their title to the soil of Carolina.

The second purpose of Barnwell's mission was to convert the colonial authorities to a vigorous program of frontier defense in the South. Since the death of Captain Nairne no Carolinian, perhaps no American, was better qualified than this Beaufort planter and veteran of numerous Indian campaigns to assist the Board of Trade in laying the groundwork of an imperial western policy. Though Barnwell based his program upon the Indian system of South Carolina, it was conceived on a truly continental scale; its object was to offset the rapid expansion of French influence all along the back of the English sea-board colonies. The notable reports of the Board of Trade upon South Carolina in 1720 almost literally reproduced Barnwell's suggestions. His ideas were again incorporated, with those of James Logan, in the great representation upon the state of the colonies of September 8, 1721. With these documents, issuing from Whitehall in 1720-1721, British western policy may be said to begin.

Much, to be sure, had been done before 1720 to stir the home government to a realization of the western problem in its international bearings, by Alexander Spotswood and William Keith as well as by the Carolinians. The energetic royal governor of Virginia, in particular, had already appropriated to himself the rôle of guardian of British interests in trans-Appalachia.[54] As early as 1710, when he first came out to

---

[52] C.O. 5:358, A 1. Nicholson's instructions are in Rivers, *Chapter,* pp. 68-91.

[53] C.O. 5:358, A 24; *Liberty and Property,* 1726, p. 28.

[54] Historians have been inclined to accept Spotswood's leadership in western enterprise too nearly at his own valuation. See the sweeping assertion of so cautious a scholar as Osgood in his *American Colonies in the Eighteenth Century,* II. 238.

America, he had proposed to the Board of Trade a scheme for preventing the French from linking their settlements in Canada and Louisiana.[55] But the plan was a singularly immature one: to restrict settlement to one side only of the James River, so that it would soon be colonized all the way to the lake beyond the mountains where it was reputed to take its rise. Spotswood aroused no more interest at home than had Nairne with his extraordinary memorial of 1708. Comparison of the two schemes leaves no doubt that the Carolinian was master of a subject where Spotswood was yet a tyro. The difference was essentially a matter of knowledge and of experience of the West. Spotswood's imagination had been stirred by a two-hundred miles' reconnaissance of his horsemen to the crest of the first Virginia mountains, but Nairne had matched wits with the French on the Mississippi. Indeed, the Virginia expedition in the fall of 1710 fell far short of earlier exploits of Virginia traders, lost to memory in the Old Dominion. This affair of 1710 was a precursor of the more famous summer junket of Spotswood and the Knights of the Golden Horseshoe in 1716. Two years later the governor asserted that 'the Chief Aim of my Expedition over the great Mountains in 1716, was to satisfy my Self whether it was practicable to come at the Lakes.' Contemporary comment emphasized other motives: the discovery of mines, the extension of the trade of Spotswood's Indian Company, hampered by the discriminatory policy of South Carolina, and the rehabilitation of his political fortunes by western adventures.[56] In any case the affair has been grossly exaggerated as an episode in the westward advance of the English empire. It was not even the first *official* exploration into the Shenandoah. A letter from North Carolina in July, 1716, revealed that Spotswood's rangers that spring had penetrated forty miles beyond the newly discovered pass.[57]

It was not until the summer of 1718, apparently, that Spots-

[55] Spotswood, *Letters,* I. 40.

[56] Ibid., II. 295. See the very interesting abstract of a letter from Chowan, N. C., unsigned, of July 4, 1716, in C.O. 5:1265, Q 125, for Carolinian speculation on Spotswood's efforts to reach the western tribes, and for evidence regarding the rangers' exploit of that spring.

[57] Ibid. See 'Journal of the Lieut. Governor's Travels and Expeditions Undertaken for the Public Service of Virginia,' in *William and Mary College Quarterly,* second series, III. 40-5.

wood returned in his voluminous correspondence to the subject of checkmating the French, and then in reply to queries from the Board prompted by Berresford's noteworthy memorial of 1717.[58] He had learned a good deal in eight years, partly from his own travels and investigations among the Indians, though he was too easily persuaded that only a five days' march separated his pass from the Great Lakes. But most of his information seems to have come from Charles Town, the southern capital of the Indian trade. To give point to his theme of French encirclement he sent home a table of distances from Montreal to Mobile, given him by three Frenchmen who had accompanied the ill-fated Ramesay-D'Adoucourt expedition against the Fox Indians when it was attacked by the Cherokee.[59] The French, he warned, were now able to engross the whole skin trade of the West. If they completed their connections from Canada to the Gulf, 'they might even possess themselves of any of these Plantations they pleased.' To forestall them he proposed that he be permitted to finance a Virginia expedition to the Great Lakes out of the provincial surplus. An English post on Lake Erie would serve to cut the line of French communications.

This project was Spotswood's only real contribution to that discussion of anti-French strategy which the Carolinians had set in train, and even in this matter he had been anticipated by Nicholson. It was based, of course, upon a serious miscalculation of trans-Appalachian distances. Again in 1720 Spotswood added his voice to the chorus of demands from America for an aggressive English western policy.[60] In 1719 the Board of Trade was convinced that the opportunity of the war with Spain should be used for an attack upon St. Augustine. In a set of queries to Virginia and Carolina they invited comment on the projected campaign. Spotswood endorsed it heartily, and applied for the command. His old army associates should no longer assert that he had buried himself in America. The conquest of Florida, he said, would give England control over French and Spanish communications with their Gulf colonies. Moreover, it would enable the English to frustrate the French

[58] Spotswood, *Letters,* II. 295-8; and see ibid., p. 300.
[59] L. P. Kellogg, *French Régime in Wisconsin,* 1925, pp. 283 f.
[60] Spotswood, *Letters,* II. 329-33, 336 f.

design to advance eastward from the Mississippi at the expense of Carolina. For Spotswood accepted completely the Carolinian theory of the eastward push from Louisiana. 'The greatest danger of Encroachm'ts,' he declared, 'is on the side of South Carolina.' He referred to the recent French capture of Pensacola, to French activities among the Creeks, and, in a second letter of 1720, to the establishment of Fort Toulouse, of which he had just heard, as evidence in point. He proposed to occupy not only St. Augustine but also Apalache, and from thence to check the French, divide the Indian trade, and in time of war annoy Louisiana. But this, essentially, had been the Carolinian dream for over twenty years. Spotswood derived most of his information of French encroachments from Charles Town sources. The map which was enclosed to illustrate his report was a crude chart of 'the Country adjacent to the River Misisipi' which he had copied from the original draught by the adventurous Carolina planter, Price Hughes.[61]

No doubt endorsement of the main features of the Carolinian propaganda by the royal governor of Virginia added greatly to its effect in London. And from other authoritative sources came the same cry that the French were rapidly drawing a circle around the English colonies. In July, 1719, the Board of Trade received from the deputy-governor of Pennsylvania, William Keith, his notable report upon the progress of the French in America, also prompted by Berresford's memorial.[62] Keith insisted that only one method was hopeful to break through the bounds which the French were seeking to establish beyond the mountains, or, indeed, to preserve intact the existing line of seaboard colonies. The English must gain the friendship of the Indians, and this could be acquired by trade only. Complete intercolonial freedom of trade was requisite, and the suppression of such jealousies as existed between New York and Virginia, Virginia and South Carolina. 'A National Interest' must take the place of selfish localism. In drafting his report Keith had made use of a striking 'Account of the French Trade' prepared at his request by James

---

[61] C.O. Maps, N.A.C. Virginia, 2.
[62] C.O. 5:1265, Q 179. Save for the Iroquois, Keith said, the English Indians north of Carolina were fewer than 1500.

Logan.[63] Logan endorsed Spotswood's project for western settlements and a Lake Erie fort, and urged that special encouragement should be given to the Indian traders of South Carolina, 'who have very good Opportunities of making Alliances with all the Indians to the Southward of the Lakes, and to the East of the Mississippi.'

Thus South Carolina, Virginia, Pennsylvania spoke almost with one voice. From New York, meanwhile, came reports of a new western offensive of the Albany traders, but also of the resistance of the French: of Joncaire's intrigues among the western Iroquois, and of the French project for a post at Niagara.[64] These tactics naturally seemed part of the same policy as recent menaces against the Cherokee in the South. In the light of such evidence, North and South, of French aggression, the current advices from Paris of the efforts of the Western Company to colonize Louisiana, and in 1720 of the great scheme of the Compagnie des Indes, took on an ominous significance.[65] In 1718 the royal cartographer of France, Guillaume Delisle, had issued his famous map of Louisiana and the course of the Mississippi. Englishmen could not but view with astonishment and alarm the restricted western boundaries which he gave to the middle and southern English colonies, at no point west of the Appalachians, and at the two ends of the frontier, where the English trading advance had been most successful, far to the east. The alarmist warnings of the little group of Anglo-American imperialists were confirmed by every despatch from the French capital.

In the summer of 1719 the Board of Trade had a special reason for seeking all possible information of English western claims and French encroachments. By the peace of Utrecht the boundaries of the English and French colonies in North America had been left for later negotiation. Parleys were now about to begin in Paris.[66] Martin Bladen and Daniel Pulteney were

---

[63] C.O. 5:1268, S 33.

[64] Wraxall, *Abridgement,* edited by C. H. McIlwain, pp. 112, 117, 118, 124; Buffinton, 'The Policy of Albany and English Westward Expansion,' in *MVHR,* VIII. 357; Osgood, *Am. Col. in the Eighteenth Century,* III. 363-6.

[65] Heinrich, *La Louisiane,* liv. I, chapters i, ii; Jean Buvat, *Journal de la régence, 1715-1723,* II. 14.

[66] See Henri Le Clercq, *Histoire de la régence,* 1921, III. 352, for the origin of these negotiations, in French resentment of English encroachments. The Regent's proposal concerned Acadia and Hudson Bay.

named commissioners, and the Lords of Trade were ordered to draft Bladen's instructions.[67] Thus was raised at Whitehall the whole complex problem of colonial grants and claims, westward of the Appalachians as well as in Nova Scotia and in the Hudson Bay region, to the great perplexity of the Board, but also, certainly, to their education. From every available source they now sought data to substantiate the English title to the West: from representatives of the Hudson's Bay Company, from agents of New York, Pennsylvania, Maryland, and Virginia, and from the Proprietors of Carolina.[68] The latter were called upon for the ·best available map of the province as well as information of its boundaries. The Board seems to have developed a special interest in the alleged intrusions of the French into the territories granted by the Carolina charter. Among other witnesses called in at the Cockpit was that indefatigable promoter, Dr. Daniel Coxe, claimant of Carolana under the old Heath patent. This opportunity he eagerly seized to reassert his sweeping claims to the western part of Carolina, which had lain dormant since the collapse of the Mississippi project in 1699. With a gesture of conciliation he now offered to abandon over half of Carolana 'totally and finally to the French,' and to draw the boundary at the Mississippi. To establish his own case and the fact of English priority in this region he produced his deeds of grant, his memorial of 1699, and several new memorials and some maps. Though he was able to cite the undoubted achievements in western exploration of the Virginians and Carolinians, Needham, Woodward, and Blake's traders, he had, as usual, mislaid the requisite proofs. At the hearing on Coxe's claims, however, Danson, one of the Proprietors, produced a witness with first-hand knowledge of the extent of the Carolina Indian trade, one Byth, formerly a trader among the Upper Creeks. He declared that

[67] C.O. 391:117, JBT, July 21, 1719 to April 13, 1720; *Calendar of Treasury Papers, 1720-1728*, p. 47; O. M. Dickerson, *American Colonial Government*, p. 63 note.

[68] See especially JBT, July 24, 28, August 4, 6, 7, 13, 14, 18, 19, 1719. Danson, a Proprietor, 'being ask'd how far Westward the people of Carolina understood their Boundaries to extend he said, they extended Westward as far as the Ocean, and that they traded wth. all the Indians that way, but that they had no Forts that Way at all' (August 19). Previously Joshua Gee had referred to the mountains as 'the natural Bounds of that Province' (July 24). See also C.O. 323:7, K 159, 160.

the English had traded with these Indians 'above 30 years; that the Indians were not then subject to the French.' Coxe made no great headway in his own interest. In 1720, however, Barnwell wrote: 'I am informed he is reviving his pretensions in order to make a bubble of it.'[69] Two years later the younger Daniel Coxe made literary salvage of his father's memorials in *A Description of the English Province of Carolana.*

The investigation had elicited many assertions of English western interests, and a whole new crop of warnings against the French. But little enough had been disclosed in the way of adequate proof of English continental claims. The Board decided, therefore, to hold them in abeyance. The instructions[70] to the Paris negotiators excluded all mention of boundaries save those of Nova Scotia and Hudson Bay. The explanatory report to the Privy Council,[71] however, marked a stage in the evolution of British western policy. With refreshing realism the Lords of Trade disposed of the charter grants: though many of these were very extensive, 'the French would not perhaps be determin'd by these Authoritys alone.' Unable to secure as yet dependable maps of the plantations, or such further data as might be required to support the British title 'to places which the French possess or pretend to either on the back or Westward of the British Plantations from New England down to the Gulf of Mexico,' they advised perforce a limited negotiation. But lest this should be construed at Paris as a tacit admission of French rights, Bladen was charged to assert that Great Britain had reason to believe the French had made several encroachments 'upon the British settlements,' which might be discussed when fuller accounts had been received from the colonial governors. Meanwhile, at Paris, he should gather information of the situation, strength, laws and government of the French colonies in general, and especially of the Mississippi Company. Without passing judgment upon Coxe's rights, the report referred particularly to the Heath patent which over-

---

[69] Historical MSS Commission, *Eleventh Report*, part IV, p. 256.
[70] C.O. 323:7, K 163; and draft in C.O. 391:117, pp. 133-50, especially p. 147.
[71] Ibid., pp. 122-6; and commissions, pp. 127-32. See C.O. 323:7, K 165, for a copy of the French instructions; and ibid., K 166, for Pulteney's letter from Paris, December 5, 1719, with information from French sources on Louisiana.

lapped both Florida and Louisiana. In this connection they expressed a lively hope 'that in imitation of our Industrious Neighbors of France, some means could be found to extend our Settlements likewise towards the Bay of Mexico more especially while we are at War with Spain, and might possibly preserve by a future Treaty whatever might be now acquir'd.' The conquest of St. Augustine they specified as 'a great Security to our plantations on that side.' Thus far had these matter-of-fact mercantilists of Whitehall gone along the path of aggressive 'imperialism' pointed out by Coxe and the Americans.

With the entrance of Spain into the Quadruple Alliance the conquest of St. Augustine naturally dropped out of the discussion. But the Anglo-French *entente* was not proof against continued suspicions and alarms. By July, 1720, the Board of Trade had before it two detailed replies from South Carolina to queries of the preceding year.[72] Col. Johnson and the assembly differed in their emphasis upon the culpability of the Proprietors, but they were in essential agreement as to the population of the colony, the effect of the Indian war, the number of the Indian allies, and especially the grave frontier situation. French preparations to colonize the Mississippi, declared the deposed governor, 'cannot but very much alarm all the Continent of America, and especially Carolina.' If war should recur with France, 'this Province would fall an easy Prey to them and very probably Virginia, New York, and the other Plantations to which this Colony is a Frontier, would feel the effects of the French growing so powerfull in America.' The assembly described the building of Fort Toulouse, so disastrous to the Indian trade, the founding of New Orleans, the wholesale importations of settlers, the capture of Pensacola, and recent French activities at the mouth of the Chattahoochee—probably the Fort Crèvecoeur episode—and added an alarmist rumor that French 'Emissarys have been viewing the coast between this settlement and St. Augustine,' which 'putts us into a terrible Consternation.'

The excitement in America had already awakened echoes in

[72] C.O. 5 :1265, 201 (from Johnson), and Q 205 (from the assembly). These are in Rivers, *Chapter,* appendix, pp. 91-109.

England. Popular interest in John Law's Mississippi Bubble was widespread. In February, 1720, a contemporary French diarist reported news from London of great agitation in Parliamentary circles over the activities of the Compagnie des Indes.[73] Sceptics might scoff at the speculative character of the French enterprise, but in the spring there appeared in London an anonymous pamphlet written to prove that behind the financial legerdemain of John Law lurked a real menace to Great Britain in the expansion of French power in the West. The author of *Some Considerations on the Consequences of the French Settling Colonies on the Mississippi* was probably not the Carolina agent, Richard Berresford, as has been thought, but James Smith, late advocate-general in New England, who a little later secured appointment as admiralty judge in South Carolina.[74] The English in North America, he declared, believed that the French Mississippi scheme was no chimera, 'as some not far from Whitehall can testify, from the many Letters, Memorials, Representations and Remonstrances, which have been written on that Subject from time to time, and transmitted to England.' This 'very remarkable pamphlet,' as one London journal[75] described it, was well calculated to stir public and especially official interest at the moment when John Barnwell was placing before the Board of Trade the anti-French program of the Carolinians.

As a veteran of Queen Anne's War, of the Tuscarora War, and of the Indian rising of 1715, John Barnwell had first-hand knowledge of the Indian and Spanish frontiers from Virginia to the neck of Florida; moreover, as the greatest planter of the Port Royal district, he had a direct interest in safeguarding the harassed southern border. His career in provincial office gave him standing as a colonial expert which the average agent, chosen from the merchant group in London, seldom possessed. In England his advice was sought by the Azilia

[73] Jean Buvat, *Journal de la régence,* II. 14.
[74] Ascribed to Richard Berresford by Heinrich, *La Louisiane,* p. 151 note, following Justin Winsor, *Narrative and Critical History,* V. 76. But see Winsor, *Mississippi Basin,* p. 141, for ascription to James Smith, for which there is strong internal evidence. The author showed no first-hand acquaintance with the southern frontier, much with the New England border, and he recounted the troubles of an advocate-general in New England.
[75] *Political State of Great Britain,* XIX. 359-82, with abstract of the tract.

promoters, by the Board of Trade, and Lord Townshend, and he largely wrote the instructions to the governor of South Carolina in 1720. With Boone he frequented the lodgings of the veteran colonial official, General Francis Nicholson, soon to go out to Carolina as provisional royal governor.[76] In that company did Nicholson perhaps recall that a quarter-century earlier his had been one of the first voices raised to warn Englishmen of the danger of French encirclement?

Before the Board of Trade in August, 1720, Barnwell and Boone presented the essence of their program, proposing to check French aggression by imitating the most striking feature of their policy. 'The Method of the French,' they recalled, 'is to build Forts on their Frontiers which it wou'd be our Interest to do likewise, not only to preserve Our Trade with the Indians and their Dependance upon Us, but to preserve our Boundaries.' They also confirmed the most alarming item in the recent report of the assembly, 'that the French particularly pretend a Right to the River May [Altamaha].' 'Therefore,' they urged, 'it wou'd be more immediately necessary for Us to possess ourselves of the Mouth of that River.'[77]

These proposals, with supporting arguments, were elaborated in a series of documents which the Carolina agents now filed with the Board of Trade and Secretary Townshend. They, too, prepared a set of answers to the Board's queries of 1719.[78]

[76] Many years later the Rev. James McSparran of Rhode Island wrote that in 1720 he was in London 'and often saw the Provincial Agents at the lodgings of my great friend and patron, General Francis Nicholson' (W. Updyke, *History of the Episcopal Church in Narragansett*, Appendix, p. 488). Compare Nicholson's eulogy of Barnwell, recently deceased, in JC, June 9, 1724. He deplored the 'great loss that his Majesty's Province in generall, and more particularly that part to the Southward, hath sustained .., I having been an eye and ear witness of the great service he did for this country in Great Britain.'

[77] JBT, August 16, 1720.

[78] C.O. 5:358, A 7, 8; presented August 23 (see JBT), along with 'An Account of the proper places fit for Garrisons in Carolina and the absolute necessity of doing the same speedily' (ibid., A 8); a table of distances between the proposed forts (A 9); and Thomas Smith's 'A Description of Pansecola, Mobile and the Mississippi River,' dated February 22, 1719/20 (A 10), also in C.O. 5:12, no. 1. The latter, based on reports of Captain Byrchall and Mr. Owen, who had recently arrived overland from the West at Smith's plantation, gave considerable detail of the French possessions on the Gulf and Mississippi. See also Historical MSS Commission, *Eleventh Report*, Appendix, part IV, pp. 254-6, for other copies in the Townshend MSS.

In these they set forth, more clearly than elsewhere appears, the basis of the western claims of Carolina, first, the charters, secondly, and particularly, the Indian alliances. For further definition, they referred to Nairne's map. The Carolinians, it appears, still claimed the whole Indian country from the Cherokee nation westward along the Tennessee to the Mississippi, the Gulf coast from Apalache Bay nearly to Pensacola, and the lands of the Creeks and the Chickasaw. To recover these rightful boundaries and to check further encroachments upon his Majesty's domains, as well as to hold the Indian trade, they specified six or seven strategic locations in the South which should now be fortified. Port Royal should be made a port of entry and the magazine of supply for the whole southern frontier. At Savannah Town should be built a stone or brick fort to guard 'the ordinary thorowfare to the Westward Indians.' A similar fort was needed at Palachacola Town. But the most urgent requirement of anti-French defence was the fortification of the mouth of the Altamaha. Westward, a post on the Chattahoochee at the crossing of the trading-path would support English influence among the Lower Creeks. If possible the French should be compelled to surrender Fort Toulouse as a usurpation; otherwise, it would be well to build another post upon the Tennessee River, 'by means whereof we may interrupt the communication between the French of Mississippi, and those of Canada, and prevent them from gaining the Cherokees.' This, obviously, was a reversion to the Nairne project of 1707-1708. With emphasis they insisted that the Indian trade was not the only interest that would be served. The province, they declared, carried on the trade with the French Indians at a loss, 'yet they are under a necessity of supporting it, for their own preservation.' Once more the 'next war' with its anticipated horrors was predicted. 'As Carolina is the South west Frontier to the rest of the Collonys and by its Situation has a more easy Communication with the Indians, it must be there that care must be taken; a penny now laid out may save pounds hereafter and enable us in time of War, even to dispossess the French.'

The Carolinian scheme for frontier posts was elaborated only for the Southwest, but it was applicable to the whole continental frontier. Other memoranda indicate that Barnwell expected the Altamaha Fort and the others projected to become centres of settlement as well as defense, and that the project was considered adaptable to Nova Scotia, to Virginia, and to that maritime frontier, the Bahamas, as well as to Carolina. To prevent the engrossing of the soil by 'the several Proprietors pretending to them by Charters,' Barnwell suggested that lands immediately adjacent to the forts should be reserved for the support of officers and troops, or granted under tenure of castle-guard, without quit-rents, to attract traders and planters who would assist in defense.[79] In another memorial he strongly urged a conference of governors to adjust the long-standing trade rivalry between Virginia and South Carolina. This might well prove fatal to both in face of French aggression. Virginia, he added, was now in a better situation than ever before to aid, out of her own treasury, a plan for securing her frontiers along with those of Carolina.[80]

How strong an impression Barnwell and his colleagues had made was soon evident. Within exactly a week from the presentation of the scheme for frontier forts it was endorsed almost verbatim by the Board of Trade to the Lords Justices;[81] this action approached a record for celerity in Whitehall. But the Board of Trade was now thoroughly aroused. There was truth as well as flattery in the agents' reply to the stereotyped query, 'What Effect have the French settlements on the Continent of America upon his Majesties Plantations?' 'The effects,' they wrote, 'are better known to your Lordships than to any body of Men whatsoever.'[82] That Barnwell's scheme was avowedly an imitation of the grand French design was probably not its least merit in the view of Whitehall. Along with fear that their rivals might realize the imputed ambition to achieve 'an Universal Empire in America,' went a very wholesome respect for supposed French efficiency, in frontier management as well as in centralized colonial control.

[79] C.O. 5:358, A 11 (enclosure).
[80] Ibid.
[81] See Delafaye to Board of Trade, August 18, 1720, directing the Board to hasten the report 'of what is further necessary to be done for the safety' of Carolina (C.O. 5:358, A 7).
[82] C.O. 5:358, A 7, 8.

At the moment the Board was engaged in framing the elaborate representation upon the state of the plantations which was completed in September, 1721.[83] Into that document when it was issued they incorporated their new western policy, combining the proposals of the Carolinians, of Spotswood, and of Governor Burnet, who suggested the occupation of Niagara. But in 1720 they recognized the special urgency of the affairs of 'Carolina and Nova Scotia, the two Frontiers of the British Empire in America to the North and to the South.' The chief care of the French, they believed, was to make themselves strong 'at the two Heads of their Colonies, North and South.' In the next war the conquest of Nova Scotia from Quebec and Cape Breton might be expected. Even greater was the danger of Carolina, 'where our Bounds have never yet been Ascertained any other way, but by the Charters to the Lords Proprietors,' and where, recently, the negro slaves had conspired to massacre their masters.[84] Accordingly, on August 30, 1720, the Board submitted to the Privy Council, along with Nicholson's instructions, an emergency report upon the two border colonies.[85] Four battalions of foot should be sent to each, and in the South the Barnwell plan of frontier forts should be put into immediate execution. The Board, indeed, recognized the utility of the scheme for the whole continental frontier. The French had realized that 'a continued Possession in an uninhabited Country was a better Title than a Charter without Possession; and for the same reason no doubt it would behove us to extend ourselves as far as may be by building Forts in convenient Places to mark our Possessions likewise on the frontiers of our several Colonies on the Continent of America.' The location of most of the Carolina posts might be left to Nicholson's discretion, but there was a special urgency in securing the river Altamaha. The failure of the French to retain possession of Pensacola in the Treaty of Madrid, and the difficulties which they had encountered in the navigation of the mouth of the Mississippi made it more than ever probable that they would

---

[83] *Docs. rel. Col. Hist. N. Y.*, V. 591-630; extract in *Col. Rec. N. C.*, II. 418-25.
[84] C.O. 5:358, A 2.
[85] C.O. 5:400, p. 31-40. All quotations in this paragraph are from that document.

seek to intrude into the region between St. Augustine and the Carolina border, whereby 'the British Interest in America wou'd receive a more fatal Blow . . . than from any other Possession the French have hitherto acquired on the continent of America.'

In this first item only of the new western policy was the Board able to carry the Privy Council with it. To the program as a whole, as propounded from Whitehall in 1720 and again in 1721, there were formidable objections. The expense would be considerable; and in any case such a conception of territorial 'imperialism' on a continental scale was alien to the temper of Whig colonial administration. Even so, the discussions of 1720-1721 mark a significant stage in the development of British 'imperialism' and especially of British western policy in face of French encirclement. The provincial origins of that policy were indubitable.

At the direction of the Lords Justices the Board of Trade on September 23, 1720, reported again upon measures immediately necessary to safeguard the southern frontier.[86] Barnwell's proposals for the Altamaha garrison, for the allotment of lands for 'the new projected Town' at Altamaha River, and for the Indian trade conference, were heartily approved. It was urged, moreover, that the command of the garrison should devolve on the Carolina special agent 'whose knowledge of the Country and Experience in matters of this Nature will highly conduce to the promoting a Settlement on this Frontier.' The Board also adopted a memorandum of instructions for the commander drawn up by Barnwell, which included a direction 'not to suffer any other Nation to take possession of any Part of the said River, or of the Sea Coasts from Port Royal to St. Augustine.'[87]

The building of Altamaha Fort was readily approved by the Privy Council, and Governor Nicholson received the necessary instructions.[88] In 1721, therefore, began the actual English occupation of the old Spanish province of Guale, the future English colony of Georgia. It is significant that in the whole preceding discussion there had been no mention of Spanish

[86] C.O. 5:400, p. 126.
[87] C.O. 5:358, A 11.
[88] C.O. 5:358, A 19, A 21, A 23.

rights. Nor was the dubious military value of the post in shielding the border from the Spanish and the marauding Yamasee an important reason for its location. In fact it was intended, as was Georgia later, in large measure, as a strategic move in the Anglo-French conflict for the West. Not Oswego in 1727, but Altamaha, in 1721, saw the inception of the British eighteenth-century scheme of frontier posts to counteract French expansion.

Both in Barnwell's memorials and in the Board's reports, moreover, it was intended that this fort and the others in contemplation should become centres of frontier settlement. Thus as early as 1720, under pressure from the Carolina expansionists, the occupation of the region which became Georgia had been definitely approved by the Board of Trade as part of a plan to defeat the supposed encircling policy of France. For a decade various obstacles prevented the fruition of this purpose. Nevertheless Fort King George, rather than Azilia, pointed the way to the establishment of the march colony of Georgia.

CHAPTER X

The Carolina-Florida Border, 1721-1730

On May 22, 1721, H.M.S. *Enterprise,* with Governor Francis Nicholson, John Barnwell, and the royal troops aboard, dropped anchor at Charles Town bar. Her arrival, anxiously expected by the supporters of the temporary government, put an end to the attempts of Johnson and Captain Hildesley to defeat the popular revolution.[1]

Amid rejoicing at the beginning of a new order in the colony government, and in defense of the southern frontier, there were reasons for dissatisfaction on the part of Barnwell and the old soldier who had supported him so vigorously in his dealings with Whitehall. Official lethargy in England had come near to defeating in advance the one item in the expansionist program of the Carolinians and the Board of Trade to which the government had given assent. Instead of a battalion of foot, a single company of soldiers had come over on the *Enterprise*; and not the young artificers for whom Nicholson had pleaded, but a hundred invalids, half of them now ill of scurvy. Tools for building the fort had indeed been furnished by the Board of Ordnance, but the engineer had failed to sail with Nicholson as he had agreed. Barnwell had expected the lieutenancy of the independent company and a command on the same footing as at Annapolis and Placentia, but had been disappointed. 'Without an Engineer, without Carpenters, Smiths, Brick-layers and other Trades-men, and even without men Capable of doing any work, it was hopeless,' he declared, to employ the independent company in making the projected settlement on the Altamaha. But delay might be fatal. He therefore proposed that some of the province scouts should be sent at once to 'secure possession of that place by a small Palissado Fort and a few Huts,' until the regular royal fort could be built.[2] Nicholson and his council concurred, and entrusted the task to Barnwell himself as the

---

[1] C.O. 5:387, ff. 23, 24. McCrady, *S. C. under the Royal Government,* p. 34.
[2] C.O. 5:358, A 34: 'Letters and Papers relating to Landing His Majesty's Independent Company now in South-Carolina &ca. and likewise concerning Coll. Barnwell's going to Altamaha River in order to Build a Small Fort there' (16 folios), especially Barnwell's memorial, June 3, 1721.

commander of the southern scouts. He was ordered to take possession of the Altamaha in the King's name 'for use of the Crown of Great Britain,' and if interrupted by Indians or Europeans 'to repel force by force.'[3]

At Port Royal Barnwell met with further discouragement. The scoutmen, during his absence in England, had lost all semblance of discipline: 'a wild idle people,' he described them, 'and continually Sotting if they can get any Rum for Trust or Money.'[4] Yet, he added, 'they are greatly usefull for such Expeditions as these if well and Tenderly managed.' Early in July he was ready to sail southward with twenty-six of these 'hopeful fellows,' 'all drunk as beasts,' and a white sawyer with his Indian slaves. At the 'passage fort' Captain Palmeter and several other scouts were added. Barnwell, with two small boats, followed the inland passage, and on July 13 made rendezvous with the supply sloop from Beaufort in the *embouchure* of the Altamaha. Meanwhile, in that vast expanse of marshland and cypress swamps, he had selected a site for the post. Several branches of the estuary were explored before he found a suitable bluff on the north bank of the northern branch, five miles below its exit from the principal stream, and near the town occupied by the Huspaw people in 1715.[5] There he made ready to erect the temporary fort, save for the warehouses of the traders the first English establishment in the land which became Georgia.

It was well that Barnwell had brought such seasoned frontiersmen as the Port Royal scouts. No timber could be found within three miles of Garrison Point, so he decided to build with cypress plank, four inches thick and musket-proof, instead of logs. 'This cypress,' he wrote in his journal, 'can't be gott out of the Swamp without wading naked up to the waist or sometimes to the neck, which is a Terrible Slavery, especially now in the dog days, when the Musquetos are in their Vigour.' By such herculean labors was built the Altamaha Fort, a 'planked house,' or gabled blockhouse, twenty-six feet square.

[3] Ibid.
[4] S.P.G. MSS, B, V, no. 257: Barnwell to Nicholson, dated 'Garrison at Altamaha point, July 21, 1721.' This vivid journal of a neglected episode in the Anglo-American frontier advance has recently been printed in *SCHGM,* XXVII. 189-203.
[5] C.O. Maps, Georgia 2.

There were three floors: a magazine floor, a gun-floor at six feet from the ground, with walls pierced for cannon and musketry, and above a 'jetting floor to clear the sides,' with more loopholes for small arms. High in the gable a lookout window commanded a wide view of river and marsh and old Indian fields, and of St. Simon's Island to the east and southeast. On the land side the blockhouse was defended by an earthen parapet, five to six feet high, with a bastion, and surrounding palisades and a moat. Another parapet of fascines fronted the river, and the palisades were continued along the marsh on the northeast. Within this irregular triangle, in a space measuring two hundred by three hundred feet, stood several palmetto-roofed huts and barracks.[6] Such was Altamaha Fort, or Fort King George as it was grandly named, a frontier improvisation which the King's officers mocked and reviled.[7] Barnwell himself thought it serviceable only as a temporary shelter, until a strong fort could be constructed on St. Simon's Island to command all the mouths of the Altamaha and the sea-approach.[8]

While 'Tuscarora Jack' and his rangers were toiling in the swamps of Altamaha, at Charles Town Nicholson was persuading the assembly to advance the charges of the enterprise. As a matter of course the assembly grumbled. 'This Infant Colony,' they asserted, 'is so farr from being able to bear the Charges of making new Acquisitions to the Crown that it is scarce in a Condition to support the Garrisons already settled without his Majesty's Aid and Assistance.'[9] But in the end they complied. In fact, within a year the province laid out nearly a thousand pounds sterling upon the Altamaha project.[10] Until the independent company was fit for border service provincial troops from the colony posts were quartered at Fort King

---

[6] Barnwell's journal, *loc. cit.*; C.O. Maps, Georgia 1, 2, 4, 5, 7, 8. Several of these maps and plans are reproduced in *Crown Collection,* series III, 132, 133 f., 135 f., 137. See also P.R.O., M.P., G 13 (plan, 1726). Winsor, in *Mississippi Basin,* p. 135, incorrectly described the post as located at the forks of the Altamaha, and has been followed by others, as Heinrich, *La Louisiane,* p. 158.

[7] C.O. 5:360, C 2 (enclosure).

[8] Barnwell's journal, *loc. cit.*; endorsed by assembly in instructions to Yonge and Lloyd, in C.O. 5:358, A 48. See C.O. Maps, Georgia 3, for Barnwell's chart of St. Simon's harbor, September 2, 1721.

[9] JCHA, July 21, August 5, 11, 12, 15, 1721; February 1, 1721/2.

[10] JC, June 15, November 24, 1722.

George.[11] There was genuine anxiety at Charles Town to hold the line of the Altamaha. In August, 1722, a conference committee expressed a lively fear that if the place were deserted before royal troops arrived 'the Spanish or the French would take immediate possession.' Barnwell was chairman of this committee, which proposed an address to the Crown to reimburse the province for the outlay on the fort. At the same time, in keeping with Barnwell's program as endorsed by the Board of Trade, they advocated land-grants for towns on the Altamaha and Savannah Rivers.[12] But the land policy of the Lords Proprietors and the dubious constitutional status of the colony prevented for a number of years this logical development in a defense policy of which Fort King George itself represented only the first step.

Though fears of French intrusion into the region south of the Savannah had been the chief consideration dictating the southward advance, Fort King George represented, of course, a flagrant intrusion into ancient Spanish territory. A generation had passed since mission bells had sounded over the Bocas de Talaje, but Spain had never yielded title to Guale. Barnwell, hunting for Spanish figs and garlic among the ruins of Zápala and Asao, had grounds for fearing Spanish opposition to his adventure; indeed, he fixed upon the more sheltered mainland rather than St. Simon's for just that reason.[13] News of the invasion came to Benavides too late to prevent it, but protests were not long delayed. Challenging France, Barnwell and his backers had provoked another contest with Spain for Guale, a contest in diplomacy and war which continued until 1763.

The dispute over boundaries was embittered by other familiar issues. Since the end of the War of the Quadruple Alliance, Indian raids had continued along the Carolina-Florida border. Already the Marquis Pozobueno, Spanish ambassador at London, had complained that the Floridians 'could not stir out of

[11] JCHA, August 12, 15, 1721. It was also proposed to enlist prisoners lately arrived from Havana to serve at the Altamaha River at £6 per month. See also JC, August 3, 1722.

[12] JC, August 2, 1722; JCHA, June 19, 1722. See ibid., June 15, 1722, for message to the Commons suggesting that Barnwell be designated 'governor' or 'lieutenant-governor' of Fort King George, 'which will be a means to encourage his settling there.'

[13] Barnwell's journal, loc. cit.

their Houses to Cultivate their Lands, nor turn out their Cattle without apparent danger from the said Indians.' Carteret thereupon sent orders to Nicholson, September 6, 1721, that violence against the Spaniards and their Indians should cease, and that all treaties and conventions should be observed.[14] In March, 1722, there appeared at Charles Town a diplomatic mission headed by Don Francisco Menéndez Marqués, auditor of St. Augustine, proposing to settle by treaty all matters at issue. In particular, Menéndez was instructed to secure regulation of partizan warfare, and to demand the return of certain negro and Spanish prisoners. Retaliation was hinted if the Indian raids should continue. Nicholson replied that he had no powers for negotiating a treaty, and warmly resented the charges of ill-usage of Spanish prisoners. In turn he set up counter-claims for the restoration of runaway slaves and of prize vessels taken since the peace. Shrewdly he demanded that the Spaniard define those tribes claimed as subjects of Florida. And he expressed great surprise at another demand in Menéndez's memorial on which his instructions had been silent. 'My Governour,' the Spaniard had declared, 'is informed by the Indians under his Command of a New Settlement that is made by this Government in the time of the Suspension of Arms upon the Land of the King my Master near the Island of St. Catherine, upon the Mainland. It seems very Strange, and [he] desires to know the Reason of doing it.' The fort, Nicholson retorted, was built under royal orders 'for the better Securing of those his Majesty's dominions,' and would be maintained so long as the King saw fit.[15]

The boundary question, unsettled since 1670, was at last squarely raised. On Menéndez's return Benavides lost no time in reporting to the Council of the Indies the recent English usurpation and the uncompromising attitude of South Carolina. Nicholson he accused of aiming at the capture of St. Augustine, in order to command the Bahama Channel. At London Pozo-

---

[14] C.O. 5:387, f. 64; also 359, B 62, and 324:34, p. 208. On a second protest from Pozobueno that the grievances complained of were not redressed, Carteret sent a duplicate of this letter, November 28, 1722 (C.O. 5:387, f. 64). For one specific Spanish complaint see C.O. 5:358, A 96.

[15] C.O. 5:358, A 103, A 104. See Benavides to Nicholson, February 11, 1721, and enclosing letter to the Crown, April 21, 1722, in Brooks (comp.), *Unwritten History*, pp. 168-71.

bueno protested vigorously, stipulating that the fort at Talaje should be demolished and none built in its place in the future. Confronted by this peremptory demand, and with the vaguest notions, apparently, of the merits of the dispute, Lord Carteret referred the matter to the Board of Trade for examination and report.[16] Nor were the members of the Board in a much better position to argue the merits of the case, despite their whole-hearted support of English pretensions and their own responsibility as authors of the 1720 reports. In a brief representation of December 20, 1722, the commissioners recalled the genesis of the recently adopted policy for the southern frontier. Categorically they asserted the English title to the land where the fort was built, as part of the province of South Carolina. If further discussion were thought necessary they promised confidently 'to produce sufficient proofs to verify the same.'[17] But a covering letter to Carteret revealed their actual ignorance, explaining that the short and general terms of the report were designed for Spanish consumption, 'whereby we have reserv'd to Ourselves an Opportunity of applying such particular Proofs arising from charters and otherwise as we are already masters of, as well as those we may further discover.' Except for the dubious plea from the charters, the Board obviously had no plausible legal case. But of one weighty sanction they were complacently aware. 'We were the rather induc'd to take this Method,' they added, 'because His Majesty being in Possession it will certainly be incumbent on the Spaniards to produce Proofs of their Title before His Majesty can be under any Necessity of justifying his own Right.'[18]

Meanwhile Carteret had notified Nicholson of Pozobueno's protest and called for information. In response, a committee of both houses of the assembly in May, 1723, drew up a set of 'Observations,'[19] which constituted the chief English brief in the whole long drawn out dispute, as Arredondo recognized when, in 1742, he assailed its arguments in his 'Demonstración

---

[16] Ibid.; and C.O. 5:358, A 62 (December 8, 1722). On the Spanish discovery of the intrusion and the subsequent proceedings in Spain and Florida, see Bolton (ed.), *Arredondo's Historical Proof* (1925), pp. 172 ff.

[17] C.O. 5:382, f. 35 (1).

[18] C.O. 5:382, f. 35.

[19] JCHA, May 10, 1723. C.O. 5:387, f. 65.

Historiographica.'[20] The charter, it was asserted, granted not only the Altamaha River, but a large territory to the south,[21] and never since had the Spanish possessed or settled any lands on the Altamaha. Here the assembly revealed an amazing, but convenient, ignorance of the extent of the Spanish missions in Guale so late as 1684. Since the settlement of South Carolina, the English had always regarded the Altamaha as under their government. For forty years they had traded with the Indians of that river without interruption, 'and Several of the Inhabitants of this Province, had houses and plantations' there. Ignoring the treaty of 1670, they remarked that the Spanish had quite as good a claim to Port Royal or to Charles Town as to Altamaha. Weak in law and in history, the assembly found firmer ground in its assertions of policy, reviving the arguments with which Barnwell had impressed the Board of Trade in 1720. The fort, they recalled, had been built by order of the King 'to Secure his Dominions in those parts against the Incroachments of the French.' A rival power in control of a river which led so far into the continent could cut off the whole western trade of South Carolina, and in war render the province 'scarce tenable.'

Carolinian anxiety was increased by the persistency with which the authorities of Florida pressed their grievances, by repeated missions to South Carolina. Suspicion that these embassies covered designs against the fort became a settled conviction. In August, 1722, Benavides had sent a captain and a friar with a body guard by the inland passage to Charles Town to demand restitution of ships and merchandize under the convention of the Hague, and also the return of Spanish Indians held as slaves. With the advice of the assembly Nicholson only consented to exchange Indian slaves for runaway negroes, and demanded the return of English vessels and prisoners taken since the peace. This reply the Board of Trade later approved. The assembly demurred at the cost of entertaining such unbidden guests; and Nicholson insisted that future agents must come directly to Charles Town by sea and enter no other har-

[20] Edition cited in note 16.
[21] In the committee's report it was asserted 'that St. Augustine is within the Proprietors' charter,' but this was later struck ouᵗ (JCHA, May 10, 1723).

bors.[22] Despite this warning, in February, 1724, an officer of the presidio visited Fort King George, but was promptly sent down to Charles Town with his guard. 'We are apprehensive,' Nicholson informed Carteret, 'that the Governor of St. Augustine sent them there as Spyes to see what condition Fort King George was in and what other things they could inform themselves in.'

These and other alarms revived in South Carolina the old jealousy of Florida. In December, 1722, the assembly received a report from the Creek agent that the Spanish were inciting the Yamasee to attack Fort King George.[23] Just at this time it was rumored in America that the surrender of Gibraltar and Port Mahon to Spain was impending. Declaring that Spanish possession of St. Augustine was of pernicious consequence to South Carolina, the assembly proposed that instead of West Indian colonies the equivalent demanded should be the continent as far as the Mississippi, and also St. Augustine.[24] Nicholson, who shared the provincial suspicion of the Spanish, hoped that in the next war Fort King George would provide a base for the conquest of Florida.[25]

The importance which the Spanish on their side attached to the Altamaha affair appeared in the measures of the Council of the Indies and of Governor Benavides. In 1724 the latter received orders to negotiate at Charles Town, and to permit no discussion of an equivalent for the fort.[26] But diplomacy in America had to wait upon the slow course of diplomacy at London. When, after many months, no reply had been vouchsafed to the demand for the demolition of Fort King George, Pozobueno pressed for an exact determination of the Carolina-Florida boundary under the terms of the treaty of 1670, with its guarantee of existing possessions at that time. He proposed that the governors of the two provinces should be empowered to settle these limits by negotiations on the spot. On July

[22] C.O. 5:358, A 58; 400, p. 170. JC, August 4, 1722. In C.O. 5:382, no. 34, vi, is a copy of Nicholson's safe-conduct for the seventeen Spaniards of the embassy, requiring that they return to St. Augustine by direct route in sixteen days, without entering any harbors except in emergency.
[23] JCHA, December 8, 1722.
[24] Ibid.
[25] C.O. 5:387, f. 60.
[26] *Arredondo's Historical Proof*, p. 173; JC, September 8, 1725.

3, Newcastle announced the King's assent to a conference of governors. But he parried the reiterated claim for the immediate destruction of Fort King George, agreeing only that it should be razed if it were found to stand on Spanish soil, which he was careful not to concede.[27] And it was nearly a year before the authorization for a conference received his signature. Meanwhile, in December, 1724, he transmitted to the Spanish ambassador the assembly's 'Observations,' and explained the delay in the matter of the fort by the expectation that Nicholson would soon arrive in London, and the desire of the King to suspend judgment until the governor could be questioned.[28] The Spanish were led to believe that instructions had been sent to the provincial council to investigate the facts in consultation with Florida, but this order was not actually signed until June 2, 1725. It authorized, of course, not a real negotiation, but a joint inquiry respecting boundaries, the final decision being reserved for the King and Privy Council. Moreover, this letter was either further delayed in transmission, or, not improbably, pocketed by President Middleton. At all events it was not entered in the council's journal until November, 1725, after another Spanish embassy had vainly sought a conference at Charles Town. Evasion and delay in diplomacy, were not, apparently, a monopoly of the Spanish.[29]

For the abortive negotiation of September, 1725, Benavides had made elaborate preparation. At St. Augustine depositions had been taken from veteran officers of the presidio that the English fort stood upon Spanish territory, and that they had served in the garrisons of Guale, at Santa Catalina, Zápala, Guadalquini, Santa María, and San Juan, long after 1670, the year of the Treaty of Madrid.[30] As commissioners Benavides again named Don Francisco Menéndez Marqués, and also the commander of the presidio, Joseph Primo de Rivera.[31] Their instructions[32] repeated the injunction of the Council of the Indies

[27] Ibid.; Serrano y Sanz (ed.), *Documentos,* pp. 248 f. Compare *Arredondo's Historical Proof,* p. 174.

[28] Ibid., pp. 179-80, citing archives of St. Augustine and Havana.

[29] C.O. 324:35, p. 141. JC, November 2, 1725. See Middleton to Newcastle, December 20, 1725, in C.O. 5:387, f. 81.

[30] *Arredondo's Historical Proof,* pp. 175 f.

[31] Serrano y Sanz (ed.), *Documentos,* pp. 243-5.

[32] Ibid., pp. 249-52.

that no equivalent for Fort King George should be admitted. The post, moreover, must be demolished in their presence, and no English settlers or Indians allowed to remain. In settling the boundary they were charged to assert the Spanish claim to ancient Santa Elena on the north, and on the west to the province of Apalachicola, to the lands, that is, of the Lower Creeks. But should opposition be raised on these points, they were to show their instructions and demand a written receipt to be transmitted to Spain. Another instruction related to the prohibition of trade between Florida and Carolina. To forestall the expected dispute over runaway slaves, by which the English had clouded former negotiations, they were to declare that only seven were held at the presidio. In keeping with former royal orders they were instructed to refuse the return of slaves, but to offer compensation to their owners.

When the Spanish delegation, thirty in number, arrived at Charles Town in September,[33] they met with a cautious reception. With inveterate suspicion of Spanish faith where negro slaves were concerned, the council ordered special care by the watch to prevent cabals. If any of the visitors, except the two plenipotentiaries, were found abroad after beat of tattoo at seven in the evening, the marshal was directed to lodge them in custody. The failure of the mission was immediately apparent when the Spaniards' credentials were presented. The necessary powers, they were assured, had not been received from England, and pending further negotiations, the fort would be maintained. The council, too, refused the Spaniards' petition to be permitted to buy a sloop to carry them home, fearing that this covered a sinister design against the Altamaha garrison. Eagerly assuming the diplomatic offensive, the Carolinians protested against the harboring of their slaves at St. Augustine. Both in the parleys and in Middleton's letter to Benavides much was made of this old grievance, the stock in trade of the Carolinians in all their border disputes with Florida. When the Spaniards talked with righteous indignation of the flouting of the treaty of 1670, the Carolinians retorted that their planters were unjustly robbed of their property by the connivance of Spain.

[33] Bolton and Ross, *The Debatable Land,* p. 70, date given incorrectly as March, 1725. Negotiations in JC, September 6-13, 1725. See C.O. 5:387, f. 80; also Serrano y Sanz (ed.), *Documentos,* pp. 255-8; and Mereness (ed.), *Travels,* p. 159.

Addressing the assembly in November, 1725, President Middleton characterised the boundary dispute as 'an Affair of the utmost Importance that can possibly happen to this province.'[34] Already he had written to Nicholson and Newcastle appealing for support for the provincial policy. To the absent governor he did not need to argue the value of Fort King George. But he described the doubtful posture of affairs among the Lower Creeks, who had recently given insulting replies to the talks of the agent. Abandonment of the fort, he declared, would 'be owning that all the Creek Indians are depending on the Spaniards.' Instead of withdrawing from the Altamaha, Creek policy demanded that the English should build another fort at the forks of the river.[35] To Newcastle Middleton objected that he was directed to settle the bounds under the treaty of 1670, 'at which time the English were in possession of no more land than in and about Charles Towne, so that with Submission I think that the Spaniards may as well claime all the Lands within a few miles adjacent, as those lying on the Allatamahaw River.'[36] On November 4 a conference committee of the assembly decided that negotiations must wait for spring and good weather.[37] With spring, however, the Carolinians took no steps to reopen the unwelcome debate. Nor did Newcastle exhibit further interest in the drawing of the boundary, now that he was apprised of the consequences of acceding to Spanish pressure.

But why did the Spanish neglect to revive the question? In Europe, Spain and England were already headed towards war. Perhaps St. Augustine was lulled into false security by a disaster which occurred a little later at Altamaha. In mid-winter a fire destroyed the barracks and damaged the wooden defenses of the makeshift English fort.[38] Captain Massey's investigation at the direction of the Secretary at War failed to show that the fire was of incendiary origin, but he suspected that the men were not so active as they might have been in extinguishing it, 'in hopes by the destruction of the Fort they should be

[34] JC, November 2, 1725.
[35] C.O. 5 :387, f. 80.
[36] Ibid., f. 79.
[37] JC, November 4, 1725.
[38] C.O. 5 :387, f. 73.

delivered from the Miseries they had so long suffered.'[39] A dismal picture of the hardships of the garrison was drawn by the commander in his report of 1727, advocating removal to Port Royal, in which he complained bitterly of the neglect of the soldiers by the Carolinians. Surrounded by malarial marshes, Fort King George had been little more than a hospital of sick and dying soldiers. Unwholesome food had provoked frequent mutinies; on one occasion twelve soldiers had decamped to St. Augustine. 'It might as usefully have been placed in Japan,' Massey asserted. But Nicholson, who knew something of the inevitable hardships of frontier service, attributed most of the troubles at Altamaha to the unfitness of the garrison, 'old, Infirm, inactive and Morose,' too lazy and mutinous to fetch good water or make gardens to provide wholesome food.[40] Middleton shared Nicholson's disgust with these ill-assorted pioneers. He wrote in 1726 to the governor: 'I have had a continual plague and trouble with those people of the Fort ever since your Departure.'[41]

After much haggling with the assembly, President Middleton secured an ordinance[42] in February, 1726, advancing £2000 currency as a loan to the Crown for rebuilding the post, until a permanent royal establishment could be made. He strongly deplored the possibility of withdrawal from the Altamaha in face of the controversy with Spain: 'As possession gives a right in this case, so the abandoning of what we have held so many years is tacitly giving that right away.'[43] The treasury was empty, the tax bill for the year already passed, so Middleton and the council reluctantly agreed to a re-issue of paper bills.[44] In spite of opposition at home to such practice, the ordinance was not disallowed. Fort King George was rebuilt, and for a few months the King's soldiers continued to hold the line of the Altamaha.

For a few months only, however, for in the fall of 1727 the garrison was withdrawn to Port Royal. This retreat was

[39] C.O. 5:360, C 2 (enclosure).
[40] C.O. 5:360, C 8.
[41] C.O. 5:387, f. 73.
[42] Cooper (ed.), *Statutes*, III. 246f.
[43] JC, February 2, 1725/6.
[44] Ibid.; and see C.O. 5:387, f. 85.

not the result of Spanish protests, though certainly Spanish border policy had much to do with it. The years 1726 and 1727 were marked by Indian raids along the Carolina-Florida border, and by increasing tension among the Creeks. At just this period in Europe, Spain and England, with France and Prussia also opposing Spain, were drifting into the brief and desultory War of the League of Hanover.[45] Spain declared war in February, 1727, and began a languid siege of Gibraltar. But hostilities were ended before the year was out, and two years later Spain came to terms with France and England in the Treaty of Seville. In America, except for the attempt of 1726 at Puerto Bello and Sir Charles Wager's efforts to capture the plate fleet, England undertook nothing offensive. To be sure, an expedition against the Spanish West Indies with colonial assistance was canvassed. Carolina, a memorialist asserted, could render no aid, for the Spaniards would find them business enough at home. Alluding to Spanish intrigues among their slaves, he declared 'that either the People of Carolina must take St. Augustin, or St. Augustin will take them.'[46] This was hyperbole, but there was reason for dread at Charles Town. The Creek problem was never more vexing. Port Royal lay open to the enemy, and partizan warfare again ravaged the southern plantations.

In 1728 President Middleton furnished Newcastle with a circumstantial account of a whole series of border forays of the past two years.[47] These, he protested, 'may be rather termed Robberys, Murders, and Piracys.' The militia were constantly under arms, plantations were going to wreck, the planters again threatened to desert the most valuable part of the province. The Yamasee tribe especially was a thorn in the side of Carolina. Though reduced to three villages close to St. Augustine[48] they had lost none of their skill as marauders. They were frequently joined by recalcitrant Lower Creeks, especially the Indians of Cherokeeleechee's town, and by negroes, the runa-

[45] *Cambridge Modern History*, VI. 59 f. Bolton and Marshall, *Colonization of North America*, pp. 359 f.
[46] C.O. 5 :4, no. 36.
[47] C.O. 5 :387, f. 167.
[48] JC, August 4, 9, 1727. Compare Swanton, *Early History*, p. 104, where four towns are named.

ways whose retention in Florida had been a constant article of complaint against the Spaniards. The Carolinians cited evidence in the reports of English captives in Florida that these raiders were outfitted at St. Augustine, and usually led by two or three soldiers, and that on their return they exchanged scalps for pieces-of-eight. Repeated incursions produced a panic among the southern settlers, especially of Granville county, where the nightmare of 1715 was not easily forgotten. In June, 1727, they petitioned the province for removal of the independent company to a position near Beaufort.[49]

In the midst of these alarms came news of a fresh disaster to a party of traders near Fort King George. Mathew Smallwood had lately established a trading-post at the forks of the Altamaha, and had been engaged by Middleton to win over the Yamasee to the English trade and alliance. With seven other traders he was on his way to his post by periago when, on July 23 or 24, he was attacked by a gang of Yamasees and Creeks. Smallwood and four companions were scalped, and the rest carried prisoners to St. Augustine. The store at the Forks was broken open and despoiled.[50] The Smallwood affair seemed to prove the uselessness of Fort King George; it aroused, moreover, the liveliest fears of a general Indian rising. The scout-boats were ordered to cruise constantly between Port Royal and the Altamaha, and the assembly was hastily convened to deal with the border crisis.[51]

Two tasks confronted the assembly: to protect the border plantations, and to punish the enemy Indians, and so check the spreading disloyalty among the Lower Creeks. The obvious solution of the border question was to transfer the royal troops to Port Royal. Already the council had taken Massey's advice and had agreed that a detachment should be posted there.[52] Massey, however, favored the removal of the whole company, and it was he, according to Middleton, who converted the assembly to this measure. Middleton himself was probably persuaded to agree by a report brought in by traders, late in August, that seven or eight periagoes were fitting out at St.

[49] JC, June 15, 1727.
[50] C.O. 5:387, f. 167. JC, August 1, 2, 3, 1727.
[51] JC, August 2, 3, 24, 1727.
[52] Ibid., June 15, 17, 1727.

Augustine to attack Port Royal and on their return to destroy the fort. But the council sought to throw responsibility for the retreat upon the King's officer. After Massey had objected to the first phrasing of the request, these words were used: 'If you believe it will not be of any Injury to his Majesty's Claim to the River Altamaha.'[53]

More important, it seemed, at the moment, than a show of possession on the coast, was actual domination of the interior tribes. With Port Royal protected by the King's men, the Carolinians, by an aggressive Indian policy, might hope to become once more really supreme upon the Florida and Louisiana borders. In September, accordingly, plans were set on foot for two expeditions to complete the half-conquest of the southern Indians.[54] One was designed to annihilate the remnant of the Yamasee. The other, the principal campaign, as first planned, was meant to overawe the Creek confederation, and to put an end to recurrent Creek intrigues with the Spanish and French. Only the first expedition was actually carried through. In February, 1728, Colonel John Palmer, a member of the Commons House and a veteran of the great Indian war, embarked upon the campaign in Florida.[55] Meanwhile, the major expedition was postponed, and Colonel Charlesworth Glover was sent up to the Creeks to make a last effort, by diplomacy, to win them wholly to the English league.[56]

A picturesque version of the inception of Palmer's raid appeared in a letter of Alexander Parris, the province treasurer, to the factor of the Royal Asiento Company at Havana. Early in February, 1728, he said, some returned prisoners from St. Augustine brought 'a very impudent sawcy letter' from the Spanish governor, with a verbal query whether Middleton was asleep 'that he suffer'd his Frontier plantations to be cut off,

---

[53] Ibid., August 25, 30, 31, September 1, 22, 30, 1727. In the last entry Ralph Izard had it recorded in the minutes 'that he is against Removing the Garrison.'

[54] Ibid., August 3, 25, 26, 31, September 1, 12, 13, 15, 16, 21, 22, 23, 29, 30, 1727; February 1, 1728. The act of September 30 is not in Cooper, but appears in C.O. 5:412 (83).

[55] C.O. 5:387, ff. 167-97, *passim* (Middleton's account to Newcastle, June 13, 1728, with enclosures of letters by Alexander Parris and Wargent Nicholson, the muster roll, etc.). See also *Boston News Letter*, April 25, 1728.

[56] See below, pp. 271-2.

and his people carry'd away prisoners by Indians.' 'I was in company with the Governor when this message was Delivered him,' wrote Parris, 'on which he smiled, and gave orders immediately' for Palmer's despatch. With two companies, each of fifty whites, and about a hundred friendly Indians, Palmer took the inland passage to Florida. Landing at San Juan's, he left a guard for the boats, and advanced upon St. Augustine. He had learned, meanwhile, that the Yamasee had taken refuge in their strong town of Nombre de Dios, within half a mile of the Spanish castle. Before dawn on March 9 he attacked. About thirty Indians were killed, and others wounded, besides fifteen who were taken prisoners. 'Instead of our Governour being asleep,' exulted Parris, 'they found the Governour of St. Augustine so.' But the rest of the Yamasee now took refuge in the Spanish fort. For three days the little army lingered in front of St. Augustine, hoping to complete the destruction of the Yamasee. According to English report, the Spanish continually fired their guns at them, but attempted no sortie, and Palmer in turn refrained from attacking the Spanish town. Before retiring, however, he laid Nombre de Dios waste, burning the chapel as well as the Indian town. Another fortified Yamasee village he had to leave unspoiled because it was commanded by the guns of the fort. But the extent of his victory was greater than the petty Indian casualties and the few prisoners would indicate. Prestige was a great imponderable in the rivalries of the American wilderness. Spanish Indians had been punished under the walls of St. Augustine, and henceforth Yamasee was not so much a name of terror to the English borderers. 'We have now Ballanc'd accounts with them,' Parris declared, 'and it's my opinion that they never will come neare us more.'[57] English prestige was also restored among the interior tribes, for news of Palmer's exploit had come at a critical moment in Glover's negotiations, and had helped to turn the wavering scale of Lower Creek policy once more toward

[57] See JCHA, March 23, 1728, and JC, April 5, for references to Palmer's success. A Spanish version of the affair is in Swanton, *Early History,* p. 341. In April the Commons House proposed that Palmer's force be sent again to Florida to complete the destruction of the Yamasee, but Middleton replied that it was disbanded, and the articles of pacification signed with Spain (JCHA, April 4, 1728; JC, April 15, 16, 1728).

peace and alliance with Great Britain.[58] Never since 1715 had the situation on the Florida border been more favorable than in the years 1728-1732 for another English advance.

Meanwhile, in England, events were preparing an effective impulse for the occupation of Guale. Fort King George had been abandoned, but under circumstances which made probable a reassertion of English control in that part of Carolina within the near future. The Board of Trade, certainly, was thoroughly committed to the retention of the Altamaha border. When the Board first learned of the proposed removal of the independent company, Nicholson was promptly consulted. The aged governor urged that in spite of the emergency a detachment should remain at the Altamaha to keep possession, and that an engineer should go over from England to fix a proper site for a permanent establishment 'to answer His late Majesty's intention of securing the property and Trade of the said River from the French and the Spaniards.'[59] This procedure the Board endorsed in a representation of December 1, 1727,[60] 'the Reasons being at present rather Stronger for Maintaining of this Fort than they were at first for the Erecting of it.' Though nothing was done immediately, in 1730 the reoccupation of the Altamaha was made an item in the instructions to Robert Johnson, and also the colonization of that river and of the Savannah. Soon the Board's plan for southward expansion from Port Royal was transformed into the project for the march colony of Georgia. When, in 1736, Oglethorpe built Frederica on St. Simon's Island, he was carrying to completion the ideas of Barnwell, Nicholson, and the Board of Trade.

In 1728 the negotiations with Spain which led to the Treaty of Seville were about to begin. In May, the Duke of Newcastle called upon the Board for a report upon the English possessions in America which were disputed by Spain, specifying the Bahamas, Campeche, and Fort King George. In preparing its reply the Board took account of a number of papers submitted by persons in England claiming special knowledge of the southern frontier.[61] The Proprietors' secretary, Shelton, asserted

[58] See below, p. 272.
[59] C.O. 5:360, C 8.
[60] C.O. 5:383, no. 30 ii.
[61] C.O. 5:360, C 21, C 22, C 23, C 24, C 25.

that 'tho the Inhabitants usually reckoned the Bounds of Carolina to extend no further than St. Maria River; yet by persual
of Mr. Nairne's Mapp and other more antient Mapps, I find
that the Fort of St. Augustine is included within the Proprietors' Charter.' He cited the occupation of the forks of the
Altamaha as a basis for Carolinian claims, as did also Robert
Johnson, Francis Yonge, and Samuel Wragg in another paper
of information. The merchant Godin thought that 'the Inhabitants always took the Alatamaha River to be a naturall boundary
between us.' There was general agreement that the Spaniards
had not for many years enjoyed any control farther northward,
and that the maintenance of an advanced southern border was
imperative in face of the French as well as the Spaniards.
One Captain John Bowdler gave an eye-witness's description of
Fort King George. On June 20, 1728, the Board transmitted to
Newcastle a representation and a report; a copy of the latter
was furnished to the English plenipotentiaries.[62] In these documents appeared once more the familiar arguments expounded
by Dr. Coxe, and by the assembly in its 'Observations' of 1723.
Ignoring the Spanish missions in Guale, the Board gave a
forced interpretation to the treaty of 1670, which was held to
confirm not merely actual possessions of that date, but also the
charter grants to Heath and the Lords Proprietors. Against
these grants the Spaniards had never protested, and under all
of them settlements had been made. If Spain would not admit
'that planting one part of a Province secures the Title to the
whole, any Nation,' the Board contended, 'is at liberty and may
settle the remaining part of Florida,' outside St. Augustine,
the only place over which the Spaniards had maintained possession. With these papers went also a schedule of losses suffered by English vessels since 1718.

In the Treaty of Seville, however, American boundary questions were left for later settlement. In 1730 three British commissioners were named for the negotiation, Benjamin Keene,
Arthur Stert, and John Goddard. They were instructed to insist that all disputed limits in America should be settled in
accordance with information furnished by the Board of Trade,
which supplied copies of the report and representation of 1728.

[62] C.O. 5:383, no. 32 ii.

To Newcastle the Board in August, 1730, suggested a rewording of the instructions. Instead of the phrase, 'the limits between our province of South Carolina and the King's province of Florida' they would insert: 'the limits of our Province of South Carolina.' 'We are far from acknowledging,' they explained, 'that Florida belongs to the King of Spain.'[63]

Though nothing developed from this proposed negotiation, it had served to draw from the Board of Trade another uncompromising assertion of the English claim to Guale. Already, in fact, the Board had evolved the logical sequel to this repeated claim, a program for the effective occupation of the debatable land between the Savannah and the Altamaha.

[63] Ibid., no. 32 iii.

CHAPTER XI

INTERNATIONAL RIVALRIES IN THE OLD SOUTHWEST
1715-1730

The Yamasee War had set the stage for international rivalries in the old Southwest throughout the colonial era. For the southern Indians it was the most disturbing event since the coming of the whites, followed as it was, immediately, by the wholesale removal of the hostile Indians from the South Carolina border. The war, and this migration, promoted a further amalgamation of tribes, Muskhogean and non-Muskhogean, into that remarkable league, the Creek confederation. Moreover, in the presence of the three-sided rivalries of England, France, and Spain, there occurred a significant reorientation of Creek policy.

For a generation past South Carolina had sought to consolidate a double bulwark of Indian allies in the zone of the Savannah and Altamaha Rivers, a region now completely deserted. Later, a few fugitive Chickasaw were induced to settle upon the Savannah, but all efforts failed to draw back the Yamasee and Creeks. In the new provincial defense system border forts and rangers were substitutes for sentry-towns of friendly Indians. Inevitably, too, the dispeopling of the Savannah-Altamaha country led to schemes for English settlement on that advanced frontier. The Indian retreat, then, furnished the occasion and the setting for the projects of Montgomery, Barnwell, Purry, and ultimately Oglethorpe.

'In 1716 the Ocheese Creek Indians with the Cowetas, Savanas, Hogologees [Yuchi] and Oconees and Apalachees and several remnants of other small tribes moved to this river. They are now at peace with us but suffer the French as well as us to trade with them. They are in all about 1000 men, the most warlike Indians in these parts.' Thus a legend on a contemporary English map[1] described the return of the Creeks with part of their confederates to their old land of Apalachicola, on the Chattahoochee, at the meeting of the trails from Charles Town, Apalache, and Mobile. No other region in the South,

[1] C.O. Maps, N.A.C. General, 7.

henceforth, was so much the theatre of international intrigue. Meanwhile, other allies, more completely committed to Spain, had fled farther southward. They established a new border for Florida from the St. John's River to Apalache Bay, the forks of the Apalachicola, and Santa María de Galve. Most of the Yamasee took shelter near the presidio of St. Augustine. In 1727 they were settled in three neighboring towns: Tolemato, where the Huspaw and Altamaha people lived together, Nombre de Dios, and Pocotaligo.[2] Their skill in border forays, developed under English tutelage, was still in requisition, but now for scalping and negro-stealing raids against the plantations of Port Royal and Pon Pon. For several years their usual partners in these incursions were the Creeks of Cherokee-leechee's town, migrants from the Palachacola Town of the old Carolina border. Contemporary maps showed the fort which the Apalachicola built in 1716 at the confluence of the Flint and Chattahoochee Rivers.[3] The Apalache were at first widely dispersed. Some found shelter with the Creeks, some near Pensacola, others joined their tribesmen who had fled from Moore in 1703 to Mobile.[4]

With these changes in the map of the southern Indian country occurred also a great revolution in wilderness politics. The eclipse of English prestige, for the moment complete, was reflected in the enhanced influence of the Spanish and the French. In the midst of the war Creeks and Yamasee had resorted to St. Augustine and Pensacola. They had been eagerly welcomed and supplied with trading goods and ammunition. In 1717 the Spanish achieved a master-stroke of diplomacy. Seven Apalache and Creek chiefs were sent from Pensacola to Mexico to give their allegiance to the King of Spain in the person of his viceroy.[5] The Choctaw and the Mississippi tribes in the West reverted to the French league. Bienville in 1715 had hastened to extend the existing peace with the Alabama to the other divi-

[2] JC, August 4, 9, 1727 (testimony of the Squirrel King of the Chickasaws regarding a recent raid). Cf. Swanton, *Early History,* p. 104.

[3] C.O. Maps, N.A.C. General, 7; Florida, 2. Compare Popple (1733) and Mitchell (1755).

[4] Serrano y Sanz (ed.), *Documentos,* p. 228; Swanton, *Early History,* pp. 124 f.

[5] Ibid., pp. 101f. (from Brooks transcripts); Serrano y Sanz (ed.), *Documentos,* pp. 238-42; Barcia, *Ensayo cronológico,* p. 330; JBT, July 15, 1716. C.O. 5:1265, Q 152.

sions of the Upper Creeks.[6] Now for the first time the Lower Creeks also came within the effective orbit of French policy. The key to the Creek country and the most valuable strategic position on the Carolina-Louisiana border was within French grasp. It was not, however, until the summer of 1717 that Fort Toulouse *aux Alibamons* was actually built.[7]

The establishment of this post had been approved in 1714, before the Indian revolt, but had been repeatedly postponed for lack of troops and supplies, and because Cadillac frowned upon the schemes of Bienville and Duclos. Had it been started immediately after the rising, Cadillac argued, he would have been accused of instigating the Carolina massacres. He still thought it imprudent in 1716 to risk French lives to the faith of their old Indian enemies. But this year saw the launching of a new aggressive American policy by the Regency, and the appointment of Lespinay and Hubert as governor and commissaire ordonnateur. Thoroughly convinced that the English aimed to oust the French from America, the Conseil de Marine described Louisiana as 'une espèce de garde avancée sur les colonies anglaises.' Colonists were recruited, troops despatched. Eight posts, later reduced to four, were decreed. In Louisiana the new officials hastened the Alabama expedition, for there, they determined, was the most pressing need of frontier defense. Late in July, 1717, twenty French soldiers under the lieutenant La Tour arrived at the forks, and on the point of land at the confluence of the Coosa and Tallapoosa rivers erected the new eastern outpost of Louisiana towards the English colonies. The French had come none too soon. At the end of August, English emissaries appeared among the neighboring Talapoosa to reopen the Charles Town trade. A month later, La Tour believed, he must have failed, and the English have seized control again of the whole country of the Upper Creeks.[8] With the building

[6] Arch. Nat., col., C[13], A 3, ff. 830 f.; La Harpe, Journal historique, July, 1715, *et seq.* Compare Pénicaut, in Margry (ed.), *Découvertes,* V. 511.

[7] Much confusion exists, even in contemporary records, regarding this date. Pénicaut, in Margry, *Découvertes,* V. 511, said 1713; *Present State of Great Britain,* 1755, p. 26, 1714, etc. C.O. Maps, N.A.C. General, 7, shows 'A French fort at the Halbamas usurped by them 1715'; and the South Carolina assembly in March, 1716, reported a French fort there (C.O. 5:1265, Q 72). Possibly the seizure of an English trading factory at the forks led to the confusion.

[8] Arch. Nat., col., C[13], A 3, ff. 780, 791, 797-8; A 4, ff. 54-62, 64, 211-31, 499-507, 515 f., 567-9; A 5, ff. 229-36, 517; Marine, B[1], IX, ff. 274 f.; Heinrich, *La Louisiane,* pp. lxxii-lxxix.

of Fort Toulouse, and the reappearance of the English traders, there began, in 1717, the sharpest sort of triangular contest by soldiers and traders and Indian agents for the Creek trade and alliance. Until the establishment of Georgia, and for many years after, the diplomacy of the southern frontier largely revolved upon this pivot.

The Creeks were the last of Carolina's foes to consent to peace. The first proposals, from an Anglophile faction, were made in the spring of 1717, when John Chester, a trader long since given up as dead, came down to Charles Town with two Coweta headmen. They promised to surrender their prisoners and plunder, and Brims was assured of a safe-conduct to the Ponds garrison. Soon, however, it was rumored that the powerful and wily Emperor knew nothing of these parleys. But Captain Jones, sent up by the governor, found him friendly; June, he reported, would see the chiefs at Charles Town. Meanwhile the Spanish faction had been busy, and Seepeycoffee, son of Brims, and other chiefs had run down to St. Augustine. Danger from the north also threatened the incipient peace. The Senecas, it was learned from New York, were raising an army to attack their old foes the Cherokee and Catawba. Jones, returning from the Chattahoochee, reported the Creeks in alliance with the Iroquois. Spotswood joined in urging coöperation from New York to hold the Senecas in leash. In all this intrigue the hand of France was clearly seen. To add to the anxiety, only one chief, Bocachee, came in from Coweta. Peace could not be made, he explained, until the corn was ripe.[9]

It was this emergency which prompted the despatch of the extraordinary peace mission of 1717, under two veteran frontiersmen, Theophilus Hastings, public factor among the Cherokee, and the trader John Musgrove. With a caravan of pack-horses and eight or ten men they were welcomed at Coweta in July. The leaders of the pro-Spanish faction were still absent. Leaving two traders on guard, the agents pressed on westward, to find the French at Alabama forks. Though challenged by a French trader at Tukabahchee, they won over the Abikha and the important Talapoosa towns. Lespinay had sent soldiers,

[9] C.O. 5:1265, Q 121, 126, 131. JCHA, April 23, May 24, 29, 31, June 7, 14, 15, 27, 1717.

but in spite of Bienville's urging had neglected to furnish the essential Indian presents. Soon English trading-factories appeared upon both rivers above the forks.[10]

Meanwhile, civil war threatened along the Chattahoochee. In July, some sixty Lower Creek and Apalache headmen and warriors had been regaled at St. Augustine, among others Seepeycoffee, the war captain Talichaliche, and Adrian, the Christian Apalache chief. With them returned a dozen soldiers under Lieutenant Diego de Peña. Peña was charged to buy horses and fix the site of the frontier fort which Ayala now proposed to build in Apalachicola, nearly thirty years after Spanish troops had withdrawn from that province. Struggling across flooded lowlands to the down-river towns, Peña in September learned of the recent exploits of the English agents. To the loyalists he purveyed Spanish whiskey, and in council they determined to send the Carolinians bound to St. Augustine. But Kasihta and Sawokli towns had not joined in the Spanish 'talk,' and Coweta was divided, with the Emperor shielding the English. When at last Peña was admitted to Coweta, Brims evaded his reproaches. He proposed to reconcile all his white friends, Spanish and English. After protracted debates and obscure plots and counterplots, Peña withdrew to St. Augustine under escort of the dissident Creeks. The conflict had divided the nation into hostile parties. A new migration of the Apalache and certain of the Lower Creeks nearer Florida occurred. Peña urged that the new fort be built not in Apalachicola but in Apalache, to encourage the repeopling of that frontier. In 1718 Ayala sent Primo de Rivera to establish the presidio of San Marcos. But only two Apalache villages could be induced to re-colonize there. The fort, however, furnished a link with Pensacola, and a base for Spanish influence among the Lower Creeks.[11]

[10] C.O. Maps, N.A.C. General, 7. In 1723 the South Carolina council examined two deserters from Fort Toulouse, who declared that the French there had 'no Trade with the Indians who goes all to the Okfuskees to Trade with the English, they sell Ammunition to the Indians for provisions; a very little is planted by such as are discharged from the fort' (JC, February 11, 1723). See also La Harpe, Journal historique, August, 1721, regarding a mutiny at Fort Toulouse; and Mereness (ed.), Travels, p. 200.

[11] Peña's narrative in Serrano y Sanz (ed.), Documentos, pp. 227-37; Barcia, Ensayo cronológico, pp. 329, 336, 344, 347 f.; reports of Ayala and Vega in Swanton, Early History, pp. 125, 127; Arch. Nat., col., C¹³, A 5, ff. 117 f., 119; JCHA, June 15, 29, December 6, 1717; C.O. 5:1265, Q 152; Bolton and Ross, The Debatable Land, pp. 65 f.

The partial victory of Hastings and Musgrove was followed by a partial and precarious treaty. Early in November, 1717, Musgrove brought down to Charles Town eleven Creek chiefs; Hastings and three or four companions remained as hostages at Coweta. On November 15, the new governor, Robert Johnson, reported to the Commons that the Indians in town were well satisfied with the terms proposed, and thought their headmen would agree, 'and even the Alabamas, when they hear their Talk, tho' they have no power to conclude anything for them.' Early in December, therefore, the assembly directed the Indian commissioners to reopen the trade with the Chickasaw and Creek nations. Theophilus Hastings was named as factor among the Creeks.[12]

The Charles Town treaty of 1717 was but an entering wedge; it must be driven home by a vigorous program of trade and diplomacy. The friendly Creeks had asked for Englishmen 'to show the French and Spaniards that they do not want friends to assist them, notwithstanding all their lies to the contrary.' In January, 1718, Musgrove hurried back with a quantity of goods and some thirty whites.[13] But emissaries from Florida and Louisiana were again on the scene. This year witnessed another dramatic contest in the Creek towns. Again faction was opposed to faction. But the Emperor's policy became clearer—to have peace with all his neighbors, and to preserve, in the Indian interest, a real balance of power in the South.

Indeed, at the moment of Musgrove's return, old Brims was holding a council at Chewale, on the Tallapoosa, with the Creek ambassadors returning from Mexico City, and their Spanish escort from Pensacola. To the delight of the adjutant, Juan Fernández, Tixjana was acknowledged *señor de la Talipuces,* and Seepeycoffee designated successor to Brims. But Fernández could not persuade the Emperor to remove with his people closer to Pensacola. At this juncture a courier brought

[12] C.O. 5:1265, Q 147 (2); JC, August 13, September 11, 1717; JCHA, October 31, November 1, 7, 8, 13, 14, 15, December 4, 6, 1717; JIC, September 11, November 9, 1717. The text of the treaty has not been found. Later tradition held that it established the southern bounds of English settlement at the Savannah River. See Benjamin Martyn, *An Impartial Enquiry,* 1741, pp. 54 f.; and Percival, *Diary,* II. 204.

[13] JCHA, December 6, 11, 1717, and the source cited in the next note.

news of the return of the Carolinians. The scene now shifted to Coweta, where complex cross-currents of intrigue were set in motion. Hastings and Musgrove were at length admitted to the Coweta council, where they broke a knife to confirm the peace, and the Indians shattered a bow and arrow. But another bow they kept, and a bloody knife, explaining that they still had a war with the Cherokee, to whom the English had sent arms and ammunition. For another decade the Cherokee-Creek feud was to complicate the relations of Charles Town with those two great tribes. The arrival of a French agent from Fort Toulouse injected a new element into the situation. He bore a flattering letter from Bienville, Lespinay's successor, inviting the Emperor to Mobile to receive gifts lately sent from France. The Frenchman made a certain impression, but La Tour was convinced that the Emperor was a friend of England, and even more of Spain. Fickle Seepeycoffee hurried down to Mobile; henceforth he was rather a pensioner of Louisiana than of Florida. When Fernández withdrew to Apalachicola, the peace with Carolina still stood upon uncertain footing. But English trading-goods had their usual effect. An agreement was soon reached regarding prices. So when Rivera, responding to Fernández's appeals for support, set out for Coweta, he was met at Sawokli, March 23, with news that turned him back. The Indians, he learned, had decided to live in peace with the Spanish, French, and English, and the great council at Coweta had dissolved.[14]

By 1718 most of the elements of the conflict in the Gulf plains had been revealed. From this epoch dates the extraordinary influence retained by the Creeks throughout the colonial period as the custodians of the wilderness balance of power in the South. Even the division of the confederacy into opposing factions reinforced what seems to have been the deliberate policy of the powerful Coweta chief, the Emperor Brims, 'as great a Politician,' declared one Carolinian, 'as any Governor

---

[14] In the detailed narrative of the mission of Juan Fernández in Barcia, *Ensayo cronológico,* pp. 331-40, the English agents were disguised as Chanmasculo (i.e., John Musgrove), and Chiaflus (i.e., Theophilus [Hastings]). See also C.O. 5 :1265, Q 147 (2), Q 152, Q 157. On French relations with the Creeks see Arch. Nat., col. C¹³, A 5, ff. 117f., 184-7, and Barcia, *Ensayo cronológico,* p. 344. See JIC, July 16, 1718, for appointment of three sub-factors for the Creek trade.

in America.'[15] 'No one has ever been able to make him take sides with one of the three European nations who know him,' wrote an anonymous Frenchman, 'he alleging that he wishes to see everyone, to be neutral, and not to espouse any of the quarrels which the French, English and Spaniards have with one another.'[16] This policy was so strongly impressed upon his people that sixty years later James Adair could write that 'they held it as an invariable maxim, that their security and welfare required a perpetual friendly intercourse with us and the French; as our political state of war with each other, would always secure their liberties.'[17]

On the margins of the Creek country the European competitors for their favors set up frontier forts: French Toulouse, Spanish San Marcos, and, in 1721, the English fort at the mouth of the Altamaha. Other posts were frequently projected. Barnwell's program of 1720 called for English forts on the Chattahoochee and on the Alabama or the Tennessee. At the forks of the Altamaha it was proposed in 1725 to convert a traders' factory into a colony post, and in 1727 and 1729 other posts were mooted in both divisions of the confederacy.[18] The French, too, pressed eastward. Soon after Fort Toulouse was built Bienville attempted to create an advanced base nearer the Lower Creeks. While La Tour was sending agents to the Emperor, Bienville, early in 1718, despatched Chateaugué to build a stockaded post, Fort de Crèvecoeur, on Baie St. Joseph, just west of the mouth of the Apalachicola River. But the Spanish soon discovered this flagrant intrusion into Florida, and protested vehemently to the commandant and to Bienville. Bienville referred to orders from France, but shortly abandoned Fort de Crèvecoeur as untenable. In South Carolina the affair did not escape notice. With the building of Alabama Fort, and a rumored French reconnaissance near Altamaha, it was cited in propaganda at home as further evidence of the dangerous French policy of encirclement.[19]

[15] C.O. 5:1265, Q 121.
[16] Quoted in Swanton, *Early History*, p. 226.
[17] James Adair, *The History of the American Indians*, 1775, p. 260.
[18] See above, pp. 191-2.
[19] A narrative of this forgotten French intrusion is in Barcia, *Ensayo cronológico*, pp. 338 f., 341, 345. See Bienville to conseil de marine, June 12, September 25, 1718, in Arch. Nat., col. C[13], A 5, ff. 154-159, 161; Commons

That the French were in fact looking eastward, the Franco-Spanish conflict in war and diplomacy between 1719 and 1721 afforded ample evidence. In 1719 occurred a brief, and localized, intercolonial war: the American phase of a European contest in which the quadruple alliance of England, France, Holland and Austria opposed the Italian ambitions of Philip V and Elizabeth Farnese. There were Indian raids on the Carolina-Florida border, and at Havana an expedition was prepared to attack Charles Town.[20] But the zone of active hostilities was confined to the Gulf of Mexico. There the exciting Franco-Spanish duel for Pensacola acquired a special significance from the triangular contest in progress in the hinterland.

From the time of Iberville the French had coveted Pensacola as a base for the extension of their sway among the Creeks and to block the westward progress of the Carolinians. With news of the declaration of war, Bienville acted promptly upon orders from the Compagnie d'Occident to seize Pensacola before the English could forestall him. In the south of America the sharpest conflict of interest was actually between these nominal allies. Pensacola, however, proved easier to take than to hold. May 15, 1719, a half-famished garrison surrendered and was sent in two vessels to Cuba. But these transports were captured off Havana by the armada sailing against Charles Town. Augmented by the French vessels, and their crews, the fleet took aboard the Havana garrison, and soon reoccupied Pensacola. Had aid from Mexico materialized, had the Spanish even shown a little more resolution, Louisiana might indeed have been lost. But early in September the fleet from Brest saved the French colony and made possible the retaking of Pensacola, again in a bloodless struggle. Bienville now dismantled the defenses. When the spring of 1720 brought news of a suspension of arms French colors still waved at Santa María de Galve.[21]

But in the diplomatic sequel the one objective of France in America was sacrificed to the Regent's eagerness for the al-

House answers to queries (1720) in C.O. 5:1265, Q 205; Carte nouvelle (1718), MS, in Bibl. Nat. MSS 4040, C 6 (photostat, W. L. Clements Library) ; and D'Anville, *Carte de la Louisiane dressée en Mai, 1732* (1752).
[20] C.O. 5:1265, Q 197. Barcia, *Ensayo cronológico,* pp. 350 f.
[21] Ibid., pp. 346-62. Heinrich, *La Louisiane,* livre I, chapitre iii, 'La guerre Franco-Espagnole (1719-1721).'

liance of Spain. Dubois' original instructions to Moulevrier had insisted upon the retention of Pensacola, to keep out other maritime powers who might interrupt the commerce of Louisiana, and to check Carolinian encroachments. In addition he was instructed to secure inclusive boundaries for Louisiana on the Gulf: on the west, the Rio Grande, or at any rate Baie St. Louis, on the east, Tampa Bay, or at least 'la rivière des Apalache.' But Philip insisted upon the *status quo ante bellum* on the Gulf, and Dubois' program of expansion was perforce abandoned. In 1721 the Spanish returned to Pensacola.[22] Thereafter, in general, Spanish and French worked together to defeat their common rivals in the old Southwest.

In the tortuous diplomacy of the southern wilderness the skein of international intrigue was frequently tangled by tribal politics and intertribal relations. Two problems of this sort especially complicated the task of Carolina governors and Indian authorities in the decade after the peace with the Creeks: the Cherokee-Creek war, and the *rapport* of Yamasee and Creeks.

Prior to the Yamasee War South Carolina for some years had aimed to promote peace among all allied Indians. But this, men believed, had made possible the great conspiracy of 1715. Hence there was no haste to bring the Creeks and the mountaineers to agreement. One Carolinian wrote home cynically of the early overtures of the Creeks: 'This makes the matter of great weight to us, how to hold both as our friends, for some time, and assist them in Cutting one another's throats without offending either. This is the game we intend to play if possible.'[23] It was an embarrassing, even a dangerous game. The Cherokee, not content to be called the 'best friends' of the English, reproached them for supplying their implacable foes with arms. On the other hand the Creeks denounced the Carolinians for warning the Cherokee of impending raids; they even attacked English traders in the Cherokee towns. By 1725 it was evident that a policy which endangered English trade and

[22] Morel-Fatio, A., and Léonardson, H. (ed.), *Recueil des instructions,* XII (Espagne, 1701-1722), pp. 374-6; Heinrich, *La Louisiane,* pp. 70-80; H. Le Clercq, *Histoire de la régence,* III. 132-50; JC, February 11, 1723.
[23] C.O. 5:1265, Q 126.

weakened English prestige was bankrupt and must be abandoned.

Meanwhile, the Yamasee were causing annoyance out of all proportion to their numbers. Their raids,[24] supported by Creek hostiles, checked the repeopling of the southern parishes, and gave occasion for the projects brought forward in England and America between 1717 and 1730 for townships or barrier-provinces along the Savannah and Altamaha. 'It is a very great discouragement to the settlers of our Southern Frontiers,' wrote President Middleton, 'to be always obliged to hold the plough in one hand and the sword in the other.'[25] The Yamasee, moreover, were regarded as the focal centre from which the Spanish infection might spread throughout the Creek nation. There were two alternatives: to draw them back from Florida, or to destroy them. Success in either course required support from the Creeks. For more than a decade the conversion of the Yamasee was vainly attempted by agents who undertook dangerous missions to Florida,[26] or by pressure upon their Lower Creek friends. Meanwhile, a number of punitive expeditions went out against them.[27]

The coming of Francis Nicholson, that old antagonist of the French, as provisional royal governor, infused new energy into Indian affairs, which had suffered during the dispute with the Proprietors. 'An old War Captain, especially among the Senecas and the Northward Indians,' Nicholson described himself on his arrival in 1721 to Ouletta, the son of old Brims and

[24] C.O. 5:358, A 2, A 4; 382, f. 23; 387, f. 167.

[25] Ibid.

[26] In 1716 Major James Cochrane and Mrs. John Charlton were employed in two attempts to bring back the Huspaw King and his people (Cooper ed., *Statutes,* II. 695; JCHA, April 18, May 3, 4, 19, June 28, November 22, 23, 1716). John Barnwell renewed the attempt in 1719 during the Anglo-Spanish war, but his Indian messengers found the Huspaw King in a refractory mood, 'the Spaniards having made him Chief General of 500 and odd Indians to come immediately Against Us, he was carried about the town in triumph with drums and Trumpets' (C.O. 5:1265, Q 185). John Bee in 1723 (C.O. 5:359, B 28, 29), and Mathew Smallwood's trader, John Jones, in 1727 (JC, September 22, 1727), made other unsuccessful attempts.

[27] See JCHA, June 13, 15, 22, 1717, and C.O. 5:1265, Q 202. The latter includes 'An Exact acct. of the late Expedition against the Yamasees and Spaniards of St. Augustine performed by 50 Indians, Melvin a white man and Musgrove and Griffin half breed or Mustees under the leading of Oweeka a Creek Indian their generall, Wettly his Second a Palachacola Indian' (1719). They burned three towns, including the mission at the Yoa town, and carried off the friar's plate and other plunder.

the English candidate for the Creek succession. Nicholson denounced the French scheme of building forts as 'a Design of Theirs, so to keep you under in Time, that none of the English shall bring up any Goods amongst you to trade without Leave of the French.' By the English, he declared, they had been treated as a free people, and constantly supplied with goods, 'which we know the French can't do without buying it of the English.'[28] Again in 1722 Ouletta appeared in place of the Emperor. 'We take this to be a critical juncture of time,' declared the governor and council. To make head against French and Spanish intrigues commissions were sent to Brims 'to act and be headman of the Creek nation,' and under him to Ouletta, to the Tukabahchee chief, and to the Okfuskee war captain; and English colors were also sent to be displayed in their towns. Theophilus Hastings was engaged as a special agent to go from town to town to impress the governor's talk upon the Creeks. He was offered £300 for the journey, or £500 if he induced the Yamasee to submit and return to South Carolina. If persuasion failed, and the governor should authorize a Creek expedition against the Yamasee, the Commons promised him £50 for each Yamasee killed or enslaved and £1000 when the Yamasee were utterly destroyed.[29]

But this scheme to convert the Yamasee broke down, as did another attempt in 1723 through offices of John Bee, who maintained a trading factory at the forks of the Altamaha. Ouletta and Brims, it was charged, 'stifled the talk' among the Lower Creeks. Only at Kasihta, where Cussaba was a notable friend of the English, did Hastings find coöperation. The Anglophile party was stronger in the Upper Towns, though the Alabama, overlooked by Fort Toulouse, were hostile. Oulatchee of Tukabahchee Town, with the Okfuskee Captain, took the 'talk' directly from Nicholson at Charles Town, and raised a war-party against the Yamasee. To force the Lower Creeks into line the governor and council in June, 1723, laid an embargo upon trade with their towns or with the Alabama; the Talapoosa traders were warned to follow the Upper Path.

[28] Report of the Committee, Appointed to examine into the Proceedings of the People of Georgia (1737), Appendix, p. 60.
[29] JC, May 25, 26, June 14, 1722; JCHA, May 26, 31, June 14, 21, 1722; May 17, 1723.

The Talapoosa that year took a few Yamasee scalps in Florida. Creek hands were dipped in their blood, and at the moment it seemed that even in the Lower Towns the scales had been tipped. Returning from Florida by way of Fort Moore and Charles Town, the Talapoosa band reported the notorious nest of marauders, Cherokeeleechee's Town, broken up, and Cowetas and Okmulgees sending out war parties against the Yamasee. But they also reported the French actively opposing the Yamasee campaign. Seepeycoffee had gone to Mobile, where the governor had threatened to send a force to arrest Hastings and Cussaba as authors of the breach. With good reason Hastings doubted the Lower Creek promises. When Ouletta came in again in the fall he was given a very strong 'talk,' denouncing the deviousness of his people. He protested his own good faith, but admitted there were many divisions. Within a year the English lost their chief client: Ouletta was slain by the Yamasee. Seepeycoffee, the old antagonist of Charles Town, was the accepted heir of Brims.[30]

Only the Upper Creeks now showed any diligence in the Yamasee affair. In June, 1724, when several of their chiefs were in town, a thinly-veiled suggestion was made that they would do well to punish the Chattahoochee towns before the latter should join hands with the French against them.[31] This extraordinary incitement to civil war within the confederation was due to recent portents of danger: an empty rumor that the French meant to build a fort at Coweta, and new complications in the Cherokee-Creek feud. On the path to the mountains a trader had been insulted by some Lower Creeks. In November, 1724, came a more ominous incident. A gang of Upper Creeks, under Gogel Eyes, attacked and plundered a trader's storehouse near Tugaloo and wounded the trader, John Sharp. South Carolina must join the Cherokee to subdue the treacherous Creeks, warned Hatton and the Cherokee traders, else again all the Indians would unite against the province.[32]

[30] C.O. 5:359, B 26, B 28 (11), (12), B 49; JCHA, October 4, November 14, 1723. See Benavides to the King, August 18, 1723, in Brooks (comp.), *Unwritten History,* summarizing Peña's report of English activities among the Talapoosa, and his distrust of pretended Spanish friends among the Lower Creeks. The English faction, he thought, greatly outnumbered the Spanish.
[31] JC, June 10, 1724.
[32] C.O. 5:359, B 125, B 126.

Clearly the affairs of the Indians approached another crisis. From 1725 to 1728 the Carolinians put forth a series of extraordinary diplomatic efforts. To checkmate Spanish and French intrigue, to end the war between Creeks and Cherokee, to settle finally with the Yamasee, to come to a clear understanding with the Lower Creeks—these were problems demanding skill and persistence. Accordingly, the Indian agency was reorganized and the trader-agents, Hastings and Hatton, discharged. In the summer of 1725, Colonel Chicken was sent to the Cherokee, Tobias Fitch was made an agent for the more difficult mission to the Creeks.[33]

From July to October, 1725, Chicken travelled through the Cherokee towns on both sides of the mountains, supervising traders, and giving the English 'talk' in councils at Keowee and Tennessee.[34] Everywhere he strove to prevent the Cherokee from making a separate and unauthorized peace with the Creeks, to explain why Carolina still refrained from war with the Creeks, and to warn against the French. The Cherokee reply was given in a great council at Elejoy. 'It is my humble Opinion,' Chicken wrote to Middleton, 'that these people are so well Affected to us that they may be brought into any Measures the Government pleases.' Soon proof was offered them of English solicitude for their safety. Fitch reported to Charles Town that the Upper Creeks and Choctaw were about to attack the mountaineers. This news was forwarded to Chicken, who hastened to obey Middleton's instructions to warn the Cherokee. Thus the Creek-Choctaw raid was foiled, and a new claim upon Cherokee loyalty established. But at Okfuskee Tobias Fitch was hard pressed to explain how the news had been carried to the mountains. The blame he sought to throw on that useful scapegoat, the Indian trader.

Even before this complication arose Fitch had faced a difficult task.[35] To it he brought assiduity and a considerable skill in negotiation. Between July and December, 1725, he visited

---

[33] See above, p. 201.

[34] Chicken's journal (C.O. 5:12, ff. 14-34) is printed in Mereness (ed.), *Travels,* pp. 97-172. As transmitted to Middleton in letters it is in JC, August 24, November 2, 1725.

[35] Fitch's journal (C.O. 5:12, ff. 35-55) is printed in Mereness (ed.), *Travels,* pp. 176-212. Some matter not in Mereness appears in JC, August 24, 25, November 2, 1725.

every town in the confederation, making frequent journeys between the Chattahoochee and Alabama settlements. The Upper Creeks readily promised redress for the Sharp outrage. Later, Fitch persuaded the Abikhas to withdraw from the Cherokee expedition, which was reduced from a formidable army to a small raiding gang. But both the upper and the lower towns rejected the proffered mediation with the mountaineers, which was therefore dropped until a more favorable juncture. For the future Brims promised better compliance with English orders, and a brisk war against the Yamasee. He also interceded with the agent for Seepeycoffee, who was seeking English support for the succession to Ouletta. Seepeycoffee, indeed, now offered the fruits of repentance. He led an army of two hundred Cowetas, Sawokli, Tukabahchee, etc., against the Yamasee, and on his return, at Fitch's recommendation, received the coveted commission in a council at Coweta. To be sure, he had done little damage to the Yamasee, who had been warned of the attack by the towns below the Point, still strongly pro-Spanish. At Coweta, in August, Fitch had been able to stage a bit of melodrama with the assistance of the Kasihtas, and 'stop the talk' of a Spanish emissary. But in November a hostile chief at Apalachicola released a negro taken into custody under Fitch's warrant. Moreover, there were signs that the French were again intermeddling to support Florida and the Yamasee. A few days after Seepeycoffee's army had set out, Fitch learned, it was overtaken by a negro from Fort Toulouse, who turned back some seventy warriors. When Fitch returned to Charles Town in December, he had no illusions as to the loyalty of any of the Lower Creeks except the Kasihta. Fear of the Cherokee, and pressure from the Upper Creeks, not love of the English, held them in line.

With the new year, 1726, there developed a new and more dangerous emergency. Fitch and Chicken were again despatched into the wilderness, the former with an escort of ten men on account of his 'extremely hazardous' errand, and the assembly was summoned into special session.[36]

About the middle of March, 1726, a sizable party of Cherokee and Chickasaw had attacked Kasihta Town on the Chat-

[36] JC, April 21, 1725.

tahoochee. An ordinary incident, this, in intertribal warfare, except that the invaders had carried a flag and drum presented them some time before by the Charles Town government. Here was evidence, then, to support Spanish insinuations: Fitch had been sent to close their eyes while another beloved man, Colonel Chicken, incited the Cherokee against them. Samuel Sleigh, a Creek trader, warned Charles Town that a plot to massacre the English was afoot. Even the Upper Creeks were wavering, though Chekill, Long Warrior of Coweta, was rebuffed when he carried up the Spanish present. As for Brims and Seepey-coffee, Sleigh reported that he had seen them at Apalachicola, with headmen from each of the Lower Towns. They were hastening to St. Augustine, he said, 'to make a firm peace with the Spanish and not to regard the English any more.' Meanwhile King Hott (or Liquor) of Kasihta was rallying the English party.[37]

The assembly was now convinced that the collapse of English prestige could only be stayed by peace between Cherokee and Creeks. Late in May the agents set out to promote the treaty.[38] After six months the Cherokee headmen arrived in the settlements to accept mediation. For weeks they were fed at provincial expense, until Hobihatchee, King of the Abikhas, came in with the Upper Creeks, and later Chekill and twenty-four Lower Creeks appeared. On January 26, 1727, with much ceremony, the formal mediation occurred in the presence of both houses of the assembly. The Cherokee were seated at the right hand of President Middleton, the Creeks at the left. Already in separate conferences Middleton had warned them against the French: 'in time they'l make you all slaves.' All who had been friends of the English before the war, he said, 'should be united in Peace, to be on theire Guard against them.' In the council the Cherokee heaped scorn on Chekill for the small number of his followers, and required a pledge that they would never more harm the English. 'Why do you goe to the French and the Spaniards?' demanded the Long Warrior of Tennessee. 'What do you get by it? how can you goe to so many

[37] JC, April 20, 1726, contains Sleigh's journal, March 23-April 6, 1726.
[38] JC, April 25-30, 1726. Middleton to Nicholson, May 24, 1726, in C.O. 5:383, no. 28 (viii, b).

of the white People? This great Town is able to Supply us with everything wee want, more than all the French and Spaniards.' After royal healths had been drunk 'by the whole Company under the Discharge of all the Cannon at the Fort,' the council adjourned. The Indians then went off to smoke the peace-pipe together.[39]

Despite these solemn ceremonies in the province-house at Charles Town, the following year, 1727, found the Lower Creeks again at odds with the English. To be sure, they refused an overture from Florida for the expulsion of the Carolina traders. But the Creek hostiles were deeply involved in those border forays which, at this time of the breach with Spain, terrorized the southern parishes, and led to the withdrawal of the garrison from the Altamaha. The murder of Mathew Smallwood near Fort King George put the final seal upon Creek guilt. The council was now convinced that a great Indian war impended. The assembly was hurriedly summoned and extraordinary measures adopted to defend the border and put to the touch, once for all, the vexed relations with the Lower Creeks. The traders were withdrawn from their towns and assembled for safety in the Upper Creek country. At the end of September, an act was passed to authorize two expeditions 'against our Indian and other Enemies'—Palmer's expedition against the Yamasee, and another against the Lower Creeks. One hundred whites were designed for the first, three hundred for the latter, with as many Indians, Cherokee, Upper Creek, etc., as could be raised. The council was anxious to attach a body of Catawba to the Creek army, partly to commit them against alliance with the Creeks should the campaign miscarry. For if South Carolina should fail in this, the most ambitious and hazardous attempt yet made to impose English authority among the southern Indians, it was realized that 'it might prove of the worst consequence to the province and a means to encourage all our Indians to insult us.' But the council decided to postpone the major Creek offensive until the success of Palmer's invasion of Florida was assured. Meanwhile, the field officer in charge, Colonel Charlesworth Glover, was sent up to the

[39] C.O. 5:387, ff. 131-141; JCHA, January 4, 11-13, 21, 26, 1727.

Creek nation as a special Indian agent, in a final attempt to substitute diplomacy for war.[40]

Glover's mission in 1727 was one of extraordinary delicacy and importance.[41] The Upper Creeks he found still loyal, and this temper he confirmed, warning them against French encroachment. But the Lower Creeks were badly divided: the 'Cowetas and Pallachacolas had declared for the Spaniards and the rest for us.' 'Now you are going the Broad Path to destruction,' he warned Chekill, 'for fighting against one another, some for the Spaniards, some for us.' So long as they received the Spanish they need expect to see no English traders. To this ultimatum Chekill craftily replied: 'Brims bid me ask you what harm it did to receive the Spaniards, French or any White People; he could see no harm in it.'

In March, Glover hurried down to the Chattahoochee to challenge a French officer just come up the river from Florida. Coöperation was never more complete between Florida and Louisiana. In 1727 Périer had earned Spanish thanks for checking the Talapoosa plan to attack Pensacola. In November, though he had learned of the war in Europe between France and Spain, he wrote that he expected to aid St. Augustine indirectly against the English, because the safety of Louisiana demanded that the Carolinians be held at arms' length.[42] Glover managed to reach Coweta a day before 'the King of France's son' and to 'stop his talk.' He knew well that the whole basis of English influence was the Indian trade. Therefore he painted to the Indians a vivid contrast between the meagre commerce of Florida and Louisiana and the great colonial trade of England. 'There's been several of you down in Charles Town and seen Ships coming in every Day, and did you ever hear the English talk of such Things? We won't get out of our Chairs to go and look at so foolish a thing as one Ship. When a small Spanish Canoe is coming to your Towns the whoop will be

[40] JC, June 14-17, August 1-4, 9-10, 14, 18, 24-26, 29-31, September 1, 12-16, 21-23, 29-30, 1727; February 1, 1728; C.O. 5:412, no. 82, act of September 30, 1727, not in Cooper or Trott.

[41] Glover's journal, October, 1727-April, 1728, is in C.O. 5:387, f. 171 et seq.

[42] Arch. Nat., col. C¹³, A 10, ff. 230-239. See ibid., A 11, f. 14, for Périer's report to the minister, August 15, 1728, of his correspondence with Middleton, who had protested against French aid to Florida.

carried to the Abickaws before she gets to Cowetas, but I can never hear any of you talk of our Pack Horses coming till you hear the bells Gingle.' Though he had won this skirmish, Glover was apprehensive of increasing French influence on the Chatta-hoochee and among the Lower Creeks. It was on this account that he strongly opposed the despatch of soldiers against the Creeks. 'It's my Opinion,' he wrote to Middleton, that 'there will be no occasion of them: it is the Trade Governs these People. If there comes any army they'll fly to the French.' More useful than troops, he advised, would be a permanent Creek agent. 'The lower Creeks will soon make friends with the Spaniards again if there is not somebody to prevent it; and in short every two or three traders ought to have an agent or Commissioner to keep them in order.'[43]

It was news of Palmer's victory over the Yamasee that completed the success of Glover's mission. Trade was reopened with the Lower Creeks, and a special effort was made to win old Brims by liberal presents. After ten years of uncertain peace, after three anxious years of increasing tension, something like stability had been restored in Anglo-Creek relations. Fitch and Glover had helped notably to make possible the later frontier achievements of James Edward Oglethorpe.

By 1728 the attention of South Carolina was again focussed upon rivalry with the French in the West. Franco-Spanish co-operation among the Creeks despite the European war, and now rumors of French overtures to the Overhill Cherokee, who so long had borne the brunt of the attacks of the French Indians of the Northwest, raised profound alarm. On the other hand the Carolinians for some years had been even more aggressive in striving to build an Anglophile party in the great French tribe of Choctaw Indians. French and English Indian diplomats and traders were now playing for the highest stakes in the game of forest intrigue. Equally disastrous to Louisiana or to South Carolina would be the loss of the Choctaw or the Cherokee.

The Yamasee-Creek War had ruined the far-western trade from Charles Town at the moment of its greatest expansion. But by 1720 the French were again talking of the English menace in Louisiana. That year the Chickasaw attacked a French trader and took to the war-path, at English instigation it was believed. Bienville undertook to raise his own allies. The Choctaw responded, though part of the tribe opposed the Chickasaw war. The Alabamas, complaining that the French refused to pay English prices for deerskins, could be won only to neutrality, but they persuaded the Chickasaw not to attack the French water-route to Fort Toulouse. Along the Mississippi the Chickasaw raided the Yazoo and Koroa villages, quite in their old manner. Again the Natchez, as in 1715, caught the contagion from their eastern neighbors, and the so-called second and third Natchez wars added to the difficulties of Louisiana. Bienville, too, was again disturbed by English overtures to the Choctaw. Prices of Indian goods were lowered at Mobile, rewards offered for Chickasaw scalps, and at length the Choctaw were induced to throw all their weight against the Chickasaw. In a great attack in January, 1723, they were said to have killed some four hundred English Indians, and to have laid waste to the largest Chickasaw town. The disruption of the Chickasaw had begun.[44] In August, 1722, they had been invited by South Carolina to remove to the vacant lands south of the Savannah. In 1723 a small band settled near Savannah Town, and gave considerable aid against the Yamasee. Other bands of Chickasaw found asylum among the Cherokee and Creeks, and joined in the intertribal wars.[45] But in 1724 Bienville brought the western towns into peace with Louisiana.[46]

This peace, however, proved more profitable to the English than to the French. Early in 1725 Bienville was recalled, and Indian affairs in Louisiana suffered from his absence. The Carolina Indian act of 1725 made special provision to encourage trade with the Choctaw as well as the Chickasaw. In August, 1725, six Choctaw headmen came to Fitch, at the Upper Creeks, to sue for peace. A great part of the nation, he reported to

[44] Arch. Nat., col. C¹³, A 6, ff. 146f., 172-75, 303-11; La Harpe, Journal historique [January], July, 1720; November 12, 1721; April 18, May 1, July 6, 1722; January, 1723; Charlevoix, Histoire et description générale, 1744, VI. 271; Heinrich, La Louisiane, pp. 157, 163 f.; Swanton, Indian Tribes of the Lower Mississippi, pp. 206-20.
[45] JC, August 4, 9, 1727, report of a raid under the Squirrel King against the Yamasee.
[46] Heinrich, La Louisiane, pp. 206 f.

Charles Town, was disaffected to the French 'and might be brought into our Interest.' The Choctaw were therefore invited to send down their chiefs to Carolina. In the fall the Oakchoy Captain, 'a politick fellow,' went west to offer his escort. He was accompanied by several traders, with goods to reopen the trade. But one of these traders, John Gillespie, was attacked, and his man killed. 'Now its all spoilt,' lamented the Coosaw King of the Choctaw, who for several years had been trying to open the path to the English. Boisbriant and Périer were still fearful, however, that the Choctaw would succumb, and with them, the colony. Hence the extraordinary French diplomatic efforts between 1726 and 1728, in Florida as well as on their own borders. To be sure they still lacked the essential reserves of presents and trade. However, in 1728, they were able to use the Choctaw to good effect to menace English traders among the Chickasaw, and to awe the Creeks. In that year Jordan Roché, for many years the most enterprising of the distant traders, wrote from the Chickasaws to Glover that the French had sent a 'bloody flag' through all their Indian towns, to prepare a punitive attack upon the Upper Creeks 'for intermeddling with the Spanish Indians.' But next year Louisiana was again in a fever of anxiety over the threatened defection of the Choctaw to the English trade and alliance.[47]

Such was the situation on the Louisiana border a dozen years after the French colony had been saved by Bienville's vigor and the outbreak of the Yamasee War. In 1729 there developed the great Natchez conspiracy, involving also the Chickasaw and Choctaw. The massacre at Natchez was apparently part of a scheme to root out all the French on the lower Mississippi. Coveteousness of English goods, but probably not direct English pressure, was the efficient cause. The Choctaw, however, broke faith with their fellow-conspirators and the tragedy of the Natchez followed, the first chapter in the series of Indian wars on the Louisiana border which finally destroyed

[47] JC, June 17, 1724; August 24, December 3, 1725; JCHA, December 3, 1725; April 10, 1728; Fitch journal in Mereness (ed.), *Travels*, pp. 194, 196, 202, 206 f.; Fitch to Middleton, August 4, 1725, in JC, August 24, 1725 (not in Mereness) ; C.O. 5:412, no. 60, act of April 17, 1725; Arch. Nat., col. C¹³, A 10, ff. 138-41, 158-60, 215-19, 223-5, 228 f., 230-39, 251 f., 273 f.; *Canadian Archives Report for 1905*, I. 453-5, 457; Heinrich, *La Louisiane*, pp. 205-28.

the power of the western English clients, 'our old friendly Chikkasah.'[48]

Meanwhile, French fears for the Choctaw were matched by growing English fears for the loyalty of their own best friends, the Cherokee. For a decade after 1717 the mountaineers had been regarded at Charles Town as the most faithful of allies. Their chronic wars with the French Indians of the Illinois country in a measure guaranteed immunity from French influence. The only fear had been that the French might join their own Indians 'to reduce them to the obedience and dependence of that enterprising nation.' In 1717 that danger seemed imminent; the threatened alliance of Creeks and Seneca was thought to be part of a great French plan to subdue the Cherokee. In 1718 the governor was authorized by act to send troops to their aid if the French should join the Indians in the rumored Cherokee expedition. 'The safety of this Province does, under God, depend on the friendship of the Cherokees,' the assembly declared.[49] But this danger passed. 'Very hearty to the English' was the report of Gregory Haines, in 1723,[50] and in 1725 Chicken found them wholly committed to Carolina. At the Elejoy council they promised to arrest any Frenchman who came among them.[51] Commissions were distributed by the Carolina governors to friendly chiefs, and their authority was supported by the Indian agents. Thus in 1723 Outassatah, of Keowee, was confirmed as 'King of the Lower Cherokee' in face of the claims of a rival, Konotiskee.[52]

In the midst of the alarms of 1727, however, when a war with the Lower Creeks had seemed inevitable, news came to Charles Town that the Tennessee Warrior, acknowledged 'King of the Upper Cherokee,' had lately received some French

[48] Ibid., pp. 229-48. Adair, History of the American Indians, pp. 3 (Preface), 353. Swanton, Indian Tribes of the Lower Mississippi, pp. 221-51. South Carolina Gazette, April 27, 1734, reported that the 'King of the Natchees, a nation of Western Indians, faithful Friends of this Province,' had come down and asked leave to settle with all his people at Savannah Town. On the Louisiana Indian frontier at this period see the documents just now published in D. Rowland and A. G. Sanders, eds., Mississippi Provincial Archives, 1729-1740, I (1927).
[49] Cooper (ed.), Statutes, III. 39; JIC, July 19, 1718.
[50] C.O. 5:359, B 26. Cf. Barnwell's testimony, JBT, August 16, 1720.
[51] Mereness (ed.), Travels, pp. 127, 138.
[52] C.O. 5:359, B 48; JCHA, November 8, 1723.

Indians who came to sue for peace, and that a number of Cherokee had returned with them. In the spring, it was said, the Miamis were expected in the Upper Towns. Eleazer Wigan was sent at once on a secret mission to defeat these overtures. The Overhill Cherokee were warned that these French Indians were tools of the whites who lived among them and who sought this peace in order to build a fort in the Cherokee country and to enslave the Indians. The French, they were reminded, lived so far from the Cherokee country that they could neither supply them with goods nor aid them against their enemies. Peace with the French Indians was denounced as 'inconsistent with our Friendship.' In reply to these remonstrances the Tennessee Warrior assured Wigan that 'it is only with red men I talk—as for whites where they live, I have nothing to say to them and they shall never come here.'[53]

The Creek situation was slowly mending, but relations with the Cherokee grew more and more perplexed. Colonel Herbert, as Indian commissioner, made repeated journeys to the mountains to regulate the traders and forestall French intrigue. Serious disturbances were revealed in his journal of 1728: there had even been consultations to destroy the traders. Early in 1729 the committee on Indian affairs proposed a fort in the middle settlements, and another among the Creeks, with garrisons of twenty-five men, 'to prevent the encroachments of the French and Spaniards.' The situation was especially serious among the Overhill towns, the bulwark against the French Indians of the Northwest. The Long Warrior of Tennessee continued to champion peace with the French Indians, but was opposed by the head-warrior of Great Tellico, the famous Moytoy.[54] With the spring of 1730 ominous signs of Cherokee discontent again appeared.

Across this stage, set, perhaps, for tragedy, there strode in 1730 the mock-heroic figure of Sir Alexander Cuming. His self-appointed 'mission' to the Cherokee with its aftermath, the visit of the seven Cherokee Indians to England and the noteworthy treaty with the Board of Trade, was perhaps the most singular incident in southern border history.

[53] JC, August 30-September 1, 1727; C.O. 5:387 (Wigan to Middleton, October 7, 1727).
[54] JC, February 22, 1727/8; January 24, February 7, 1728/9; JCHA, July 16, 1728.

Sir Alexander Cuming of Coulter was a Scottish baronet and advocate; born about 1690, he died, a poor brother of Charterhouse, in 1775. There were many evidences of an erratic mind in the checkered career of the self-vaunted 'King of the Cherokees.' At one period he dabbled in alchemy. For nearly thirty years (1737-1766) he was confined as a debtor to the limits of the Fleet. A chronic projector, his schemes ranged from a plan for banks to support the colonial currencies to an absurd proposal to pay off the British national debt by settling three hundred thousand Jewish families in the Cherokee mountains.[55]

Cuming's visit to South Carolina in 1729-1730 was in no sense an official mission.[56] 'The Great King,' he told the Indians at Nequasse, 'did not know of his coming among them.' At Charles Town he busied himself during the winter with his currency scheme.[57] On the eve of his return to England, however, he decided to make a rapid excursion into the back-country and the mountains. With tourist enterprise he crowded this journey of nearly a thousand miles by rough trading-paths into a single month (March 13 to April 13, 1730). To the Congarees and beyond he was escorted by Colonel Chicken and the surveyor, George Hunter.[58] But their pace was too slow, and the impatient Briton hurried on to Keowee and engaged a trader, Ludovick Grant, as his guide. Sir Alexander was a member of the Royal Society, and he seems to have set out as a scientific explorer rather than a political agent, searching for minerals, especially iron-stone, medicinal herbs, and the 'natural curiosities' of the land. Before he reached the first Cherokee town he had gathered so many specimens that his 'intent in

[55] *Notes and Queries,* first series, V. 257, 278 f.; *Dictionary of National Biography,* XIII, 294 f.

[56] The sources for this extraordinary incident are: Ludovick Grant's deposition, January 12, 1756, in *SCHGM,* X. 54 ff.; and two accounts based on Cuming's journal in London *Daily Journal,* September 30, October 8, 1730. Cf. S. G. Drake, 'Early History of Georgia,' in *New England Historical and Genealogical Register,* 1872, pp. 262 ff.

[57] See his memorial to Newcastle, 'Observations relating to the present ill-state of South Carolina,' in C.O. 5:361, C 99. The list of the original members of St. Andrew's Society, Charleston, 1729-1730, includes 'Sir Alex. Cumming, Bart.' (*Year Book of the City of Charleston,* 1894, Appendix, p. 282.)

[58] On this journey Hunter revised Herbert's map of the Cherokee country, and the route thither. This map, with itinerary, is in the Library of Congress.

going up to the Cherokee Mountains was more than answered by the Discoveries already made.'

But another purpose had taken shape in his mind as he listened to accounts by frontier settlers and traders of the dangerous posture of Indian affairs. In the settlements there had been rumors when he left that the Indians would rise in the spring, and on the way Captain Russell had told him that a French agent had been busy for two years among the Lower Cherokee. At Keowee, too, the traders talked of the sullen temper of the Indians. It was at Keowee that Sir Alexander's enterprise, mad or inspired, was first revealed. On the night of March 23 the Indians were assembled as usual in the town-house. There Sir Alexander dramatically appeared, armed 'with three cases of Pistols, a Gun and a Sword under a Great Coat.' Against this extraordinary breach of decorum the traders expostulated in vain. Cuming had determined, single-handed if need be, to overawe the Cherokee and force them to submit to the British interest. Of what ensued after Sir Alexander's speech in praise of King George two versions were given, the baronet's and Ludovick Grant's. They differed chiefly in interpretation. According to Grant, Cuming invited the traders, and they in turn persuaded the Indians, to join in drinking the health of His Britannic Majesty on bended knee. This strange ceremony Cuming chose to regard as an acknowledgment of 'his Majesty King George's Sovereignty over them,' such a submission, in fact, as 'they never before made either to God or Man.' Intoxicated by success in his vice-regal rôle, he summoned a general council of the three divisions of the Cherokee to meet at Nequasse on April 3.

In the interval Sir Alexander continued his hasty progress through the lower, middle, and upper settlements as far as those remote towns on the western waters, Great Tellico and Great Tennessee. 'He seldom staid above two or three hours,' Grant later deposed, 'never above a night at any place.' Everywhere he collected minerals and herbs, everywhere he repeated his speech and recorded in his notebook the names of headmen and conjurers whom he had made his friends. To him Moytoy revealed his ambition to be made Emperor of all the Cherokee. Several towns had already agreed, but 'now it must be whatever Sir Alexander pleased.' Cuming in turn was anxious to add to his collection one of the Indian 'crowns.' 'It resembles a wig,' said Grant, 'and is made of Possum's hair Dyed Red or Yellow.' So Moytoy and other headmen sent messengers to bring down to Nequasse the famous 'Crown of Tennessee.'

The climax was reached when Cuming returned with a great train of Overhill Cherokee to Nequasse Town. 'This was a Day of Solemnity,' ran the baronet's inflated account,[59] 'the greatest that ever was seen in the Country; there was Singing, Dancing, Feasting, making of Speeches, the Creation of Moytoy Emperor, with the unanimous consent of all the Head Men assembled from the different Towns of the Nation, a Declaration of their resigning their Crown, Eagles Tails, Scalps of their Enemies, as an Emblem of their all owning his Majesty King George's Sovereignty over them, at the desire of Sir Alexander Cuming, in whom an absolute unlimited Power was placed, without which he could not be able to answer to his Majesty for their Conduct.' Even though substantial discount be made for Cuming's exuberance, the eccentric Scot had evidently appealed to the dramatic instincts of the Indians, and had made a notable impression at a crucial moment in their relations with the English. Of course they had no real notion of acknowledging English 'sovereignty,' much less of parting with their lands to Cuming himself or to 'the Great Man on the other side of the Great Water.' Cuming knew that doubters in Charles Town and in England would discredit his claims. He therefore invited the Cherokee to send some of their headmen to bear him company on his return to England. They readily consented; only the dangerous illness of his wife, Moytoy protested, kept him from joining the embassy. Of the six Indians whom Sir Alexander selected, only two were actually chiefs. These were Ouka Ulah, 'Head King that is to be,' head-warrior of Tasetche, and the Skalilosken or second warrior, who was also by right a Ketagustah, 'Prince.' Tathtowe and Kollanah were simply warriors; they were to appear, however, as 'Generals' in the London press. From Tennessee, remotest of the Cherokee towns, came the warriors Clogoitta and Ukwaneequa. The latter, a youth, was probably the famous Little Carpenter, who in his prime was wont to recall his visit to England and 'the great King's Talk.' Near Charles Town a seventh Indian was added, by chance, to the party. Without credentials from the Nequasse council, Onaconoa's name did not appear in the London treaty.[60]

Nursing a grandiose dream of a vice-royalty of the Cherokee, Sir Alexander with his party took passage for England, May 13, 1730, on the *Fox* man-of-war. Little profit did Cuming reap for himself from his bizarre American adventure. But for the southern frontier he had achieved a diplomatic *tour de force*. English prestige was decisively restored in the mountains. In England his protegés furnished the sensation of the London season. Their appearance at court and everywhere in town no doubt dramatised for many Englishmen the existence of a frontier of empire of which few had yet been aware.

Significantly, the year 1730 saw the rise of a new English interest in Carolina. It saw, also, the beginnings of a new advance of English colonization upon the southern frontier.

[60] See below, pp. 295-302, especially pp. 299 f.

CHAPTER XII

THE BOARD OF TRADE AND SOUTHERN COLONIZATION
1721-1730

Georgia was the last successful enterprise of English colonization within the limits of the United States; it was also one of the first notable achievements of modern philanthropy. The dual character of the project was widely advertised by the charter and in the promotion literature of the Trustees: it has become a commonplace of colonial history. But how did these two movements, charitable and strategic, chance to converge in 1730-1732?

Since the beginning of effective English occupation of Carolina, in 1670, the region south of the Savannah had repeatedly attracted colonial projectors as different in station and interests as Lord Cardross and Captain Thomas Nairne. The Margravate of Azilia had exactly coincided with the later Georgia tract; the Golden Islands were, of course, the sea-islands of the Georgia coast. Barnwell's scheme for the fortification of the mouth of the Altamaha had assumed that this fort, and the other frontier garrisons which he advocated, would become centres of English settlement. These projects revealed a continuous interest in a region which geography and the strategy of empire had marked as a zone for English expansion. Reinforcing the propaganda from South Carolina, the projectors asserted the claims of frontier defense in the South at a time when the Board of Trade was just awakening to the peril of French encirclement. By 1720 the Board was fully committed to the settlement as well as the fortification of the land which became Georgia.

But for more than a decade various obstacles prevented the fruition of this purpose. Despite the zeal of the Board, the Privy Council was indifferent. Moreover, until 1729, so long, that is, as the Proprietors held title to the soil, the proprietary land policy checked all efforts at southward expansion, either by planting from South Carolina or by diverting the mounting stream of foreign Protestant emigration to the southern frontier.

'The Misfortune of this Country at Present,' wrote Nicholson in 1724, 'is the Uncertainty . . . whither his Majesty will keep it or the Lords Proprietors be restored, and their Lordships having been Pleased to shutt up their Land Office which hinders people from taking up lands in Order to Settle the Frontiers especially to the Southward which Borders on the Spaniards and French who are now United and we find that they are not only Endeavouring to sett their Indians upon ours but likewise Inveighling them from us.'[1] From 1719 to 1730 the land office remained closed. In self-justification the Proprietors pointed to the arrears of quit-rents, and the obstacles Nicholson had placed in the way of their collection. Land grants would be resumed, declared their secretary, Richard Shelton, 'as soon as the present Governor is removed.'[2] Indifferent, seemingly, to the need of repeopling and extending the ravaged Carolina frontiers, the Proprietors made use of their ownership of the land as a lever to secure restoration of their powers of government. The colonists were naturally confirmed thereby in their anti-proprietary bias.

In the midst of this quarrel the provincial government developed an interesting scheme for border settlements, which had an important place in the evolution of the Georgia enterprise. It served to link the projects of Barnwell with the Board of Trade's noteworthy instructions of 1730 to Governor Robert Johnson for the establishment of townships on the Carolina rivers, including the Savannah and the Altamaha, instructions which determined the precise *locale* and the border character of Oglethorpe's colony.

Nearly a decade before 1730 this policy in all essentials was proposed by the South Carolina assembly. The basis, apparently, was John Barnwell's idea of a settlement at the Altamaha. Indeed, Barnwell was chairman of the committee of the Commons House which proposed an address to the home government, in June, 1722, for grants of land for townships to be set out on the Savannah and the Altamaha Rivers.[3] But without waiting for proprietary consent or royal aid, the province had

[1] C.O. 5:387, f. 68.
[2] C.O. 5:359, B 103, 104.
[3] JCHA, June 19, 1722.

already attempted a beginning of the novel policy, novel, that is, upon the southern border, though customary in New England and already adopted by Virginia. In July, 1721, a law was enacted 'for preventing the Desertion of Insolvent Debtors, and for the better settling of the Frontiers of this Province.'[4] For seven years debtors were granted protection from civil suits for less than £30, provided they should reside beyond Three Runs, about twenty miles east of Fort Moore. Near that garrison the Indian commissioners were directed to lay out a town and common, with three hundred half-acre lots, the lands to be purchased by the public and distributed among those who would settle there. Though the township project seems to have originated with the assembly, it was warmly championed by Nicholson, who appealed in vain to Lord Carteret to permit at least the settlement of 'the Farthest Frontiers.' 'My Lord,' he wrote, 'as Old as I am yet I hope God willing to live to see this Province when the Frontiers are well Secured the most flourishing of this Continent.'[5]

The most striking illustration of the proprietary blight was the collapse of the first attempt of the Swiss *entrepreneur,* Jean Pierre Purry, to settle a Swiss colony upon the southern margins of South Carolina.

In 1722 Lord Carteret received a memorial[6] from M. Fischer de Reichenbach, a member of the council of Berne, on behalf of a company of well-to-do Bernese citizens. They asked for a grant of a considerable tract in Carolina, with full rights of government, the land to be held upon a military tenure. A military barrier colony was foreshadowed, peopled by 'les meilleurs milices de l'Europe.' Two years later appeared upon the scene one of the most persistent and ambitious colonial promoters of that era.

A biographer, writing in 1746, recalled that Purry was born at Neuchâtel, *circa* 1670, and that he had engaged for a time in the wine trade. But meeting misfortune, about 1713 he had gone out to Batavia, under contract with the chamber of Amsterdam for the East Indies. From this period dated his

[4] Cooper (ed.), *Statutes,* III. 122-4.
[5] C.O. 5 :387, f. 51.
[6] Ibid., ff. 51, 52, 53.

first colonial project, for the settlement of the Terre de Nuyts near Java. On his return voyage to Europe he was so struck with the prosperity of the colony at the Cape that he also proposed to the Dutch East India Company the colonization of the 'Pays des Cafres,' in South Africa. In two memorials in support of these schemes, published at Amsterdam in 1718, he expounded for the first time his pseudo-scientific theory that the ideal climate throughout the world, in both hemispheres, exists at or near the parallel of 33°. His proposals rejected in the Netherlands, he removed to France, where, soon after, the collapse of the Mississippi Bubble swept away the earnings of his Batavian plantations, but not his zeal for colonization. Instead, by the same account, 'his former Scheme reviv'd and having modell'd it to the French Settlements he presented it to some of the Prime Ministers, who refer'd it to the Royal Academy of Sciences.'[7] But again his hopes faded; then, in 1724, he turned to the English ambassador at Paris, Horatio Walpole. Apparently to escape his importunities, Walpole at length agreed to forward his memorial to the English court. Newcastle in due course referred it to the Board of Trade. In this first, brief document, Purry proposed to carry over to Carolina a colony of six hundred Swiss, organized in a regiment under his command, to be settled near the parallel of 33° 'en qualité de soldats ouvriers.'[8]

The larger bearings of his project Purry soon revealed in a striking contribution to the promotion literature of the southern frontier. This was his *Memorial presented to his Grace the Duke of Newcastle,* printed in London in 1724 in both English and French editions. Accepting as true the current descriptions of Carolina as one of the richest countries in the world—in this vein Montgomery had excelled—Purry expounded again

[7] See pp. [3]-4 ('Advertisement') of J. P. Purry, *A Method for Determining the Best Climate of the Earth,* London, 1744. The pamphlet was a translation of Purry's *Mémoire sur le Pais des Cafres, et la Terre de Nuyts,* Amsterdam, 1718. Apropos of Purry's climate theory the anonymous biographer remarked 'that Sir Isaac Newton, to whom I communicated it, agreed in general to the Principles of it, with a Proviso that the Nature of each Country and Soil should be first examined before Settlements were attempted.'

[8] C.O. 5:359, B 7. See also Purry to Walpole, Paris, June 6, 1724, and Walpole to Newcastle, Paris, June 7, 1724, in B.M. Add. MSS 32,739 (Newcastle Papers, LIV), ff. 39, 41f.

his theory of the ideal climate. The English, he proposed, should secure control of the 33° zone in North America by a scheme of systematic colonization. The Carolina which Purry defined as the American paradise and the appointed theatre of Anglo-French conflict embraced both Azilia and most of the region claimed by Coxe as Carolana-Florida. For this vast domain Purry now suggested a more appropriate name, *Georgia*, or *Georgina*. Year by year the English frontiers should be advanced from the Carolina settlements to the Mississippi. Circumstances in Europe, he demonstrated, were favorable. In Switzerland the depression following the wars, and elsewhere among the Protestants of the Continent religious disabilities as well, made it possible to draw great numbers of settlers to America, by judicious advertising, generous grants of land, and the offer of transportation in the King's ships. Purry did not ignore the international aspect of the scheme. The Compagnie des Indes, by its recent activities in sending colonists to Louisiana, had made counter-action by the English imperative. The French, indeed, might shut the mouth of the Mississippi to the 'Georgians,' but the English in turn could cut off the trade of the upper valley and make Louisiana more than ever a sink of French revenues. Seated on the Mississippi the English would be in a position to defend themselves against the growing French peril, and if necessary, to attack their rivals.

Chimerical though it was, Purry's scheme had this interest, that it was conceived in the prevailing spirit of Anglo-French rivalry, which was quite as much the atmosphere of the decade that produced Georgia as of the earlier period of the southwestern projects of Coxe and Nairne. For such spacious programs of western expansion the temper of the England of Walpole and Newcastle was not, of course, propitious.

Even the modest beginnings proposed by Purry encountered formidable obstacles. The Board of Trade commended the Swiss colony plan to the Proprietors;[9] it was frustrated by their fickleness when they repeatedly altered their terms of assistance. In January, 1725, Purry appeared before the Carolina board, arguing that his projected settlement 'would not

[9] C.O. 5:401, p. 33: Board of Trade report to committee of Privy Council, May 26, 1732, containing history of Purry grant.

only strengthen that province but be a Barrier to the rest of his Majesties Colonies upon the Continent of America.'[10] At this time the Proprietors agreed to find transportation for six hundred colonists, and their secretary was ordered to treat with the merchants. Two months later they sought to modify the agreement, offering Purry instead a barony of 12,000 acres, on or near the Savannah River, if he would himself carry over 300 people within a year, and promising him another barony as soon as 1200 colonists should be transported.[11] But Purry demurred, and at length the Proprietors arranged with his agent, Jean Watt, to assume the charge of transporting the first 600 colonists, upon condition of the payment after three years of a 3d. quit-rent.[12]

Purry was already in Switzerland, recruiting his colony. Soon, indeed, the activities of 'Purry et Cie.' of Neuchâtel in distributing advertisements which painted Carolina as 'one of the finest countries of the universe,' brought concern to the authorities of Berne, anxious to check the emigration fever.[13] By such propaganda during 1725-1726 Purry succeeded, however, in attracting numerous colonists, and in securing promises of financial support from several Swiss capitalists. Two hundred would-be Carolinians were assembled near Geneva by M. Vernet. In September, 1726, more than a hundred made their way to the rendezvous at Neuchâtel. Popular interest was growing, and Watt believed that six hundred volunteers could readily have been obtained. But once more the Proprietors had changed their minds about the contract. Withdrawing their pledge to transport the first detachment, they had granted instead to two London merchants, Stephen Godin and Jacob Satur, a patent of 12,000 acres in trust for Purry, on condition that he convey two hundred colonists at his own expense. When this latest tergiversation became known, Purry's backers at once withdrew their support. With success in sight, the enter-

[10] C.O. 5:292, p. 149.

[11] Ibid., p. 151.

[12] Shelton to Popple, June 8, 1725, in C.O. 5:359, B 104; Jean Watt, memorial, July 9, 1725, in C.O. 5:383, no. 10; Purry, memorial, 1730, in C.O. 5:361, C 80.

[13] *AHR*, XXII. 25 f., 131 f.; Purry, *Memorial*, Augusta, 1880, pp. 4 f.; A. B. Faust, *Guide to Materials for American History in Swiss and Austrian Archives*, 1916, p. 42.

prise collapsed. 'For want of one hundred pounds Sterling,' declared an agent, Purry had to desert his penniless and rioting colonists in Neuchâtel.[14] To this ignominious issue had come the grand design to drive a wedge of Protestant settlement into the heart of Louisiana.

But Purry's first project did not altogether fail. With the earlier promotion pamphlets his advertisements perhaps helped to direct English attention to the southern frontier. Purry's own interest was firmly fixed in Carolina; several years later he planted Purrysburgh as a feeble sister-colony of Georgia. Meanwhile Purry and Watt had won valuable friends in England for their proposals to colonize foreign Protestants upon the southern frontier. In particular, they had established contacts with a notable group of earnest and philanthropic clergymen and reformers, Hales, Hodges, Newman, and others who made up the circle of the famous Dr. Thomas Bray. Bray and his friends played a noteworthy part a little later in initiating the events which led to the establishment of Georgia, a colony designed as a refuge for continental Protestants as well as poor debtors. Upon opinion in Carolina the episode had produced a confused impression. Though the prospect of Swiss reinforcements for their frontiers was apparently welcomed, one anonymous pamphleteer denounced the plan, absurdly, as evidence of a proprietary conspiracy 'to sell us to the Swiss Cantons.'[15]

Another proof had been furnished, at all events, of the incapacity of the Lords Proprietors, whose failures as wardens of the southern marches had been persistently exploited in the Carolinian propaganda of the past decade. Though 1721 had seen the establishment of a provisional royal government and the building of Fort King George, the provincial government, through its agents, continued its twofold campaign in England in opposition to the Proprietors, and in support of a complete assumption by the Crown of the imperial defense problem on the southern frontier. The instructions of 1721 to Francis

---

[14] C.O. 5:387, ff. 119, 120. C.O. 5:383, no. 31 (petition of Jean Watt, 1726 or 1727) ; C.O. 5:361, C 80. For the Proprietors' version, which ignored the breach of faith, see C.O. 5:290, pp. 261f. See B.M. Add. MSS 22680 for 'A Short Abstract of the Contract for Transporting a Number of Swiss to South Carolina.'

[15] *The Liberty and Property of British Subjects Asserted*, London, 1726, pp. 32 f.

Yonge and John Lloyd, the first regular .agents maintained by the assembly, repeatedly recurred to settlement and defense.[16] The frontiers, they were reminded, could not be settled until the soil was vested in the Crown, when it would still be necessary 'to have three or four Regiments sent here to secure the Frontiers.' Meanwhile, arrears of quit-rents should be applied to fortifications. Land should be assigned each officer and soldier near Altamaha Fort, as Barnwell had proposed; and another fort such as he suggested should be built on St. Simon's Island. Port Royal was recommended as a port of entry 'for the greater Conveniency of Trade and Support and Settlement of the Southern Fronteirs.' 'You are also to Represent the dangerous Consequence of the French and Spaniards encroaching on Our Frontiers and getting the Indians into their Interest Especially the Creeks and Cherakees which in Time of War may be Fatall to this Province.' In August, 1722, both houses agreed to pay the passage to England of one William Tempest, who had first-hand knowledge of the new French settlement at New Orleans, and of 'the dayly encroachments they make upon the Continent.' In December, Yonge was charged to make use of Tempest's testimony. The Commons further directed that the agent 'apply to the Government that in case Gibraltar and Port Mahon be delivered up, that the continent as far as the Mississippi and St. Augustine be delivered up to the English as part of the equivalent.'[17] In succeeding years these themes were repeated and elaborated, as opportunities were furnished by the Anglo-Spanish boundary disputes and by the attempts of the Lords Proprietors to recover their government.[18]

For half a dozen years after the revolution of 1719 the Lords Proprietors, as a corporate body, had practically ceased to function; from July, 1719, until January, 1725, indeed, no

[16] C.O. 5:358, A 48, 49. The act of September 21, 1721, appointing agents and establishing a committee of correspondence is in C.O. 5:412.

[17] JC, August 4, 1722; JCHA, December 7, 8, 1722. Representation of governor and council, September 4, 1724, in C.O. 5:359, B 103. See also memorials from the 'inhabitants of Carolina' and from the 'inhabitants of the parish of St. Thomas and St. Dennis,' transmitted in 1727, in C.O. 5:360, C 6, 15.

[18] JC, June 9, 1724: the speech of Nicholson on death of John Barnwell referred to the expectation that Barnwell would go again to England as agent.

minutes were kept in their journals.[19] Then for a few years they were stirred to feeble and ineffectual activity. It had become evident that the veteran Nicholson would not return to his post at Charles Town. In August, 1724, Mr. Bertie sought the support of the President of the Council, Lord Carlton, for the Proprietors' plan to recover their powers of government. The revolution he described as the act of 'some needy Tumultuous Persons,' and he charged Nicholson with obstructing the payment of quit-rents and other dues.[20] A caveat was prepared against the appointment of a new governor without notice to the Proprietors. Colonel Horsey was presented as the proprietary nominee for the place.[21] But this appointment was opposed by the colony agent, Yonge, who offered a petition for the continuance of the royal government. The issue was joined before the committee of the Privy Council. Yonge fought successfully for delay on the ground of Lord Carteret's absence in Ireland; he sent the papers, including Shelton's representation of the Proprietors' case, to South Carolina.[22] In May, 1726, the assembly in special session moved again for the continuance of the province under a royal governor 'as the only effectual way to secure the same to his Majesty in case of an invasion by any Foreign Power.'[23] The provincial cause was vigorously espoused by an anonymous pamphleteer in a tract entitled *The Liberty and Property of British Subjects Asserted* (London, 1726). The provincial revolution he justified on the familiar ground of the failure of the Proprietors to protect the colony against the French, Spaniards, and Indians. This, he asserted, constituted a forfeiture of the charter. Quit-rents, incidentally, he described as payments for protection only. 'I won't venture to say how far *Compact* is concern'd in all Governments,' he wrote, 'but certainly it is the sole Foundation of such as owe their Powers to Patents only.'[24]

[19] C.O. 5:292 (minute book, 1707-1727). There is a similar gap, Sept., 1719-April, 1724, in the Proprietors' book of orders and instructions, C.O. 5:290.
[20] Ibid., pp. 165, 166.
[21] Ibid., pp. 167, 170.
[22] Ibid., pp. 172, 173; C.O. 5:387, ff. 100, 124; C.O. 5:383, no. 28 (11), 'The Case of the Lords Proprietors'; ibid., (12), 'The Humble Representation of Richard Shelton.'
[23] JC, May 10, 17, 18, 1726.
[24] See pp. 24 f., 27-31. On pp. 22 f. the colonial assembly was eloquently defended against proprietary aspersions, as a body 'which, however it may

Balked in their attempt to resume the government, the Proprietors were shortly drawn into those protracted negotiations which culminated, in 1729, in the surrender of Carolina to the Crown. These parleys were initiated in 1727 by the Earl of Westmoreland, of the Board of Trade, who acted, avowedly, upon the Board's well-established policy towards charter colonies. At first, no more than the surrender of sovereignty was contemplated, though Westmoreland hoped that the Proprietors might be persuaded to commute their quit-rents in Carolina for hereditary duties as 'a Meanes of its spedier Peopleing.' But difficulties arose over procedure, Carteret refused to join in the petition, and the project languished.[25] In March, 1728, again through the medium of Westmoreland, six of the Proprietors renewed and extended their proposals, offering to surrender the soil in return for £2500 per share. Carteret still held aloof.[26] There was a long delay, due, apparently, to the slowness of Parliament in passing the requisite act. At this stage appeared among the promoters of the surrender the eccentric Thomas Lowndes, who later claimed more credit in the affair than Westmoreland would allow. Lowndes claimed to be the author of a memorial presented to the Speaker and other members of the House of Commons when the demand was made for the purchase money. This paper voiced an eloquent appeal to the imperial interests involved in the acquisition of Carolina, and advocated the vigorous colonization of its borders. It urged not merely a good settlement at Port Royal, and its development as a naval base, to overlook the Gulf of Florida, but also the planting of 'the most fertile and healthy Part of all America,' 'the Tract of Land lying between Port Royal in South Carolina and Florida.'[27]

be regarded by you in England, with us in Carolina is our little Senate; and every Scoff which you think fit to throw upon this small and inconsiderable Assembly (being three thousand Miles distant) is no less to us than so many Threats of the entire Subversion of our Liberties, which we, as Englishmen, cannot in the least relish.' This pamphleteer's defense of the antiproprietary revolution is an interesting anticipation of certain features of the American case two generations later.

[25] C.O. 5:290, pp. 181-4; 292, p. 158; 387, ff. 149-51 (Westmoreland's 'Narrative of the affair of Carolina,' addressed to Newcastle, June 17, 1717) ; see also ibid., ff. 153 f.

[26] C.O. 5:290, pp. 257f., 279; Historical MSS Commission, *Eleventh Report*, part IV, pp. 256 f. (Townshend Papers).

[27] Ibid., pp. 257 f. C.O. 5:361, C 48, C 50; 306, no. 11. See article on Thomas Lowndes in *Dictionary of National Biography*, XXXIV. 208-10. His chief distinction was as founder of the professorship of astronomy in Cambridge University.

The surrender of the Carolina charter[28] was a notable event in the history of the southern frontier, for it removed the most serious obstacle to an advance of settlement into a region long marked for English occupation.

Even before the title passed to the Crown the Board of Trade was bombarded by Thomas Lowndes with a series of proposals for the exploitation of South Carolina. They ranged from a scheme for cutting off the Spanish plate fleet and another for fortifying Port Royal and the Bahamas, to projects for producing potash and extracting oil from sesamum seed.[29] The most seriously considered was his enterprise for diverting Palatine emigration from Pennsylvania to Carolina.[30] This the Board approved, in principle, as 'strengthening in so effectual a manner their Southern Frontier.' In his letters and memorials Lowndes foreshadowed important features of the Georgia project. Associated with him was Thomas Missing, of Portsmouth, formerly a contractor for victualling the garrisons of Gibraltar, Annapolis, and Placentia, who claimed experience in transporting emigrants to America, and Benjamin de la Fontaine, a shipping contractor in the Pennsylvania emigrant business. It appears that Missing had agents in Holland recruiting Carolina colonists, and that the Palatines actually sent commissioners to view the Port Royal region. The promoters were anxious that the government defray the charges of the first shiploads, apparently hoping to finance the scheme thereafter from the sale of lands. Negotiations were still in progress, in 1730, when the Palatine project was eclipsed by the revival of Purry's scheme and the emergence of the Georgia enterprise. Meanwhile Lowndes had kept constantly before the Board of Trade the importance of having 'South Carolina, the Frontier of his Majesties American Dominions, well settled by an industrious Race of People,' and in particular, that 'vast Tract of uncultivated land to the Southward.'[31]

In November, 1729, the Board of Trade was duly notified

---

[28] See C. C. Crittenden, 'The Surrender of the Charter of Carolina,' in *North Carolina Historical Review*, I. 383-402.
[29] C.O. 5:361, C 50, C 71, C 93, C 94, C 110.
[30] C.O. 5:360, C 26, C 27, C 45, C 46, C 47; 361, C 56, C 58, C 72, C 73, C 74, C 92; 400, p. 239; *Calendar of Treasury Papers, 1720-1728*, p. 166.
[31] C.O. 5:360, C 26; 361, C 73.

by Secretary Townshend that Robert Johnson, Esq., had been appointed royal governor of South Carolina.[32] The son of Sir Nathaniel Johnson, the new appointee had himself been displaced as proprietary governor by the revolution of 1719. But he had retained the respect of the colonists who had ousted him. Consequently his candidacy to succeed Nicholson had been opposed by the Proprietors. In any disinterested view Johnson was exceptionally equipped for his post. The Board of Trade took more than usual account of his suggestions when they framed his instructions. Upon this task they were engaged between December, 1729, and June, 1730, a period crowded with significant developments in the history of the southern frontier.

In a long letter of suggestions to the Board, December 19, 1729,[33] Colonel Johnson revealed his preoccupation with problems of defense and settlement in South Carolina. A present to the Cherokee Indians in acknowledgement of one which they had sent over by the trader, John Savy, 'would very much attach these people to the English'; another independent company was much needed for the security of the frontiers; and especially, he insisted, 'nothing is so much wanted in Carolina as white Inhabitants.' The Crown, he advised, might well be at the charge of transporting two hundred families of Swiss or other foreigners, for thereby great numbers more would be attracted to Carolina without additional expense. Johnson was aware, perhaps, that Purry was preparing to revive his proposals of royal aid to Swiss colonization; these he later specifically endorsed.[34] In other memorials the new governor addressed himself exhaustively to the crucial problem of encouraging settlement. Johnson had remained in South Carolina for a number of years after the revolution and must have been thoroughly familiar with Barnwell's township scheme, so strongly supported by Governor Nicholson and the assembly. This he now revived and elaborated, requesting particular instructions upon this head.[35] In March and April he submitted

[32] Ibid., C 59. See also C.O. 5:400, p. 245.
[33] C.O. 5:361, C 60.
[34] Ibid., C 101.
[35] Johnson to secretary of the Board of Trade, January 2, 1729/30, in ibid., C 62. Besides his township scheme, which developed into Georgia, Johnson advocated sending a second independent company, and additional ordnance (C.O. 5:383, nos. 40, 41, 42).

three important papers: 'A Proposal for Improving and the better Settling of South Carolina,' 'Reasons against reserving a Quit Rent of a Penny an Acre,' and an 'Explanation of My scheem given the Lords of Trade for Settling Townships.'[86] Therein he proposed to erect ten frontier townships, comprising two hundred thousand acres of crown lands, on the seven principal rivers of the province—three on the Savannah, two on the Santee, one at the head of Pon Pon River, the others on Wateree, Black River, Pedee and Waccamaw. In the middle of each square tract of twenty thousand acres would be placed, for convenience in defense, 'a little town of 250 Lotts, not exceeding 1/4 Part of an Acre to each Lott, which Town and Commons is computed will take up but 350 Acres.' The remainder of the township lands would be allotted to inhabitants in two hundred parcels of seventy-five to one hundred acres each. Since a principal object was to attract poor people to the province the quit-rents should not exceed 2s 6d per hundred acres. A special inducement for foreigners was suggested in the grant to them of the franchise for the choice of deputies. The system, he argued, would furnish such protection of the frontier in time of war as was 'almost fatally wanting during the Yamasee revolt.' 'Carolina being the Southernmost of his Majestys Dominions on the Continent of America, and the most Exposed to the Spaniard att St. Augustin, and the French att Moville, and Great Numbers of Indians about us, who are often Induced by the French and Spaniard to Cutt off our Out-Settlements; these things well Considered, I am of opinion,' Johnson declared, 'that Great Encouragement should be Given to new Commers to settle in Townships.'

This scheme, elaborating as it did the earlier suggestions from South Carolina, won enthusiastic endorsement. When the Board of Trade submitted to the Privy Council its draft of instructions for Johnson on June 10, 1730, it incorporated the essentials of Johnson's plan, and the instructions as a whole were approved by the Privy Council in September. In the future, the Board urged in its representation, all grants of land in the province should be proportioned in amount to the ability of the grantee to cultivate them. The township scheme was

[86] C.O. 5:361, C 76, C 78, C 85.

strongly supported by reference to the experience of Massachusetts and New Hampshire. In a few minor details the official project differed from that of Johnson. Thus Johnson was directed that the towns should be contiguous to the rivers, that each inhabitant should have fifty acres of land for each member of his family, to be augmented later in proportion to his abilities, and that the land within a distance of six miles from the townships should be reserved for future grants to the township inhabitants. The only significant alteration, but that one of real importance, since it represented a notable step towards the establishment of Georgia, was in the number and location of the new frontier settlements. With all convenient speed the governor was instructed to set out *eleven* townships, seven of these, as in Johnson's proposals, on rivers north of the Savannah, two on the Savannah River, and also '2 *Townships upon the River Alatamahama.'*[37]

Thus by June, 1730, the Board had determined to project colonization southward into the debatable border region where no permanent English settlement had yet been made. Was this decision prompted by Johnson, or did it represent the initiative of the Board? The instructions spoke of the new townships as located 'at Sixty Miles distance from Charles Town,' whereas the Altamaha lies some one hundred and thirty miles away. This item of the settlement scheme thus appears to have been a late interpolation in the draft. No doubt it was closely linked with the further orders, contained in the same instructions, for the rebuilding and re-garrisoning of the Altamaha fort. The Board had at length reverted to the full Barnwell program of 1720, so far as concerned that segment of the southern frontier.

But now other forces were converging upon the development of British frontier policy to transform the garrison-colonies of the revived Barnwell scheme into a full-fledged barrier province. The elaboration of Johnson's instructions had occupied the Board during a period of singular moment for southern history. Public interest in South Carolina and its hinterland was stimulated by the arrival in England, early in

---

[37] C.O. 5:400, pp. 283-376, especially pp. 290, 324-8, 357 f., 364. These instructions were approved by the Privy Council, September 17, 1730. C.O. 5:362, D 1. The same day the council referred to the Board of Trade the petition for the charter of Georgia.

June, of Sir Alexander Cuming and the seven Cherokee Indians. Already, the investigations of the prisons by the gaols committees of the House of Commons in 1729 and 1730, under the chairmanship of Oglethorpe, had raised in his mind, and in the minds of a group of philanthropists in Parliament and outside, the grave social problems of the English unemployed. From several sources had come the suggestion of colonization as the remedy. While this charitable movement was evolving an organization to establish debtor colonies somewhere in America, its leaders were in contact, in Parliament and especially in the gaols committee, with active members of the Board of Trade, now thoroughly awakened to the needs of strengthening the southern frontier.

With the arrival of Sir Alexander Cuming and the Indians whom he brought back from his self-appointed mission to the Cherokee country,[38] there was displayed in England such a pageant of the American wilderness as had not been seen since 1710, when the visit of the four 'Indian Kings' of the Iroquois had piqued the curiosity of Addison and Steele, and set the ballad-mongerers scribbling.[39] The Cherokee, though they created no such literary furore, enjoyed a remarkable popular and journalistic vogue. Two results their visit had, certainly. It projected Carolina and its frontiers into the forefront of public attention when, for the first time in two generations, a practical scheme of English colonization on the mainland was afoot. And it afforded the Board of Trade an opportunity for a rare stroke of frontier policy, in negotiating at Westminster a treaty with the Cherokee under conditions which for years to come exalted English prestige, an essential ingredient in Indian alliances, among a tribe whose friendship was indispensable to buttress the English colonies in the south.

From Deptfort the Indians were promptly conveyed to Windsor, to attend the King and the Court. Not only were they presented to his Majesty, but they also attended in St. George's Chapel at the installation of Prince William and Lord Chester-

---

[38] They landed at Deptford on June 5, 1730; London *Daily Journal,* June 12, 1730.
[39] See W. T. Morgan, 'The Five Nations and Queen Anne,' in *MVHR,* XIII. 178-82; *Tatler,* no. 171 (May 13, 1710); *Spectator,* no. 50 (April 27, 1711); *The Four Indian Kings,* broadside, *circa* 1710 (JCB).

field in the Order of the Garter. They 'stood near the King when at Dinner,' said a London newspaper, 'being dressed in their Country Habits, having in their Hands, one a Bow, another a Musqueton, etc.' Throughout these scenes, it was observed that 'the Pomp and Splendour of the Court, and the Grandeur, not only of the Ceremony as well of the Place . . . Struck them with infinite Surprize and Wonder. . . .' At Windsor, they were lodged at the Mermaid Tavern, and there they became objects of great popular curiosity, 'daily visited by a great many people, who resort from all parts adjacent.'[40] Early in August they were brought to see the sights of the town, and themselves to furnish a new London sensation. Lodgings were provided for them in King Street, Covent Garden, in the house of the upholsterer, Mr. Arne, celebrated by Steele and Addison, who had been host twenty years before to the Iroquois chiefs.[41] Under royal sign manual the Lords of the Treasury paid out £400 for their maintenance in England and the expenses of their return to America.[42] Scarcely a day passed during their stay but the journals gave space to news of their excursions. They were carried 'to all places of Note and Curiosity': to the Tower, of course, but also to Sadler's Wells, and Tottenham Court Fair, and to Christ Church Hospital to see the Blue Coat Boys at supper, and to the Artillery Ground 'to see the Performance of the White Regiment of Trained Bands.' 'Attended by a great number of the populace,' they visited Bedlam where the lunatics chained to the walls furnished a characteristic eighteenth-century spectacle.[43]

Numerous dinners[44] were given them in the taverns of the town. On two occasions they were feasted by the merchants

[40] *Daily Journal,* June 20, August 1, 1730; Isaac Basire, engraving of the seven Cherokee, with inscription, *circa* 1730; London *Daily Courant,* August 1, 1730. The latter newspaper denied the report of a brawl among the Cherokee at the Mermaid, but the landlord wrote to Cuming, July 15, demanding the removal of his quarrelsome guests (C.O. 5:4, no. 47).
[41] *Daily Journal,* August 3, 1730; Austin Dobson, *Eighteenth Century Vignettes,* third series, p. 328.
[42] *Calendar of Treasury Books and Papers, 1729-1730,* p. 590. See also ibid., pp. 411, 414, 430.
[43] *Daily Journal,* August 13, 14, 16, 1730; *Daily Courant,* August 12, 18, 26, 1730.
[44] Ibid., August 14, 21, 1730; *Daily Journal,* September 4, 23, 1730; London *Daily Post,* August 3, 20, 28, 1730; Henry B. Wheatley, *Hogarth's London,* 1909, p. 274 (Pontack's).

trading to Carolina: at the Carolina Coffee House, and at the famous Pontack's eating-house, resort of epicures. At another dinner, appropriately, the Society of Archers were their hosts. Robert Hucks was one of the philanthropists who were engaged during that summer in planning the establishment of the debtor colony in Georgia. Recognising, no doubt, the value to the intended colony of the amity of the Cherokee, he 'treated the seven Indians with a splendid supper at his House in Great Russell Street, Bloomsbury.'A ball at the Long Room at Richmond-Wells was contrived for their pleasure; and they were taken to a variety of theatrical performances. To advertise the presence of the Cherokee 'kings' at the theatre was apparently a stock device of the managers to attract an audience, so much so that it was satirized in the journals.[45] While in London their pictures were painted for the Duke of Montagu. A contemporary print showed them garbed in uniforms presented to them by George II.[46] Everywhere they were objects of curious interest. When they 'took the Air in St. James Park, habited in rich Garments laced with gold, presented to them by his Majesty, . . . accompanied by several Persons of Quality and Distinction' they were followed by crowds of spectators. 'Their Levees are very great every Day,' continued the writer in the *Daily Courant*, 'Persons of all Ranks and Distinction being admitted to see them that behave with Decency and good Manners.'[47] The decorum of the Indians themselves was greatly admired. One observer, perhaps under the spell of the 'noble savage' tradition, declared that 'they were remarkably Strict in their Probity and Morality; their Behaviour easy and courteous.'[48]

Some part of the publicity which attended the Cherokee visits should, perhaps, be attributed to press-agent activities of their eccentric but enterprising patron, Sir Alexander Cuming. Cuming apparently had ready access to the London journals, but he found the colonial authorities less susceptible to his sug-

[45] *Daily Journal,* October 1, 2, 1730; *Daily Post,* August 18, 19, 21, 1730.
[46] *Daily Journal,* August 6, 7, 1730. See cover for Isaac Basire's print (copies in British Museum and in University of South Carolina Library), engraved from a painting by Markham. On Basire and his family of engravers see *Dictionary of National Biography,* III. 358-60.
[47] *Daily Courant,* August 7, 1730.
[48] Descriptive text on Basire print.

gestions. Besides pressing his pet project for a bank in South Carolina to check the evils of colonial paper issues,[49] he memorialized Newcastle for recognition by the Crown of his over-lordship, which he claimed by virtue of the action of the Indian council at Nequasse.[50] The powers which the council had conferred at his bidding upon Moytoy were subject to their obedience to him, and he alone was directly answerable for them to the King. Now in England he sought to have his powers confirmed by the Crown for a period of three years, during which he promised to live among the Indians and to promote the royal service in such manner as to render it easy for his successor in the proposed vice-royalty of the Cherokee.

The Board of Trade sought to ignore Cuming's extraordinary pretensions, but they saw in the unexpected incident of the Indian visit an opportunity to put the Cherokee upon the same footing in the South as that long occupied in the North by the Iroquois, through their alliance and their recognition of English sovereignty. Following an interview with Robert Johnson, who may, indeed, have suggested the exploit, the Board proposed to Newcastle, August 20, 1730, that a treaty be entered upon with this 'so solemn an Ambassy.' Not only would such a treaty cement British friendship with a numerous and warlike people, but also, it was urged, the 'Agreement remaining upon Record in our Office would upon future Disputes, with any European Nation, greatly strengthen our Title in those parts even to all the Lands which those People now possess.'[51]

Already, indeed, the Board had secured from Sir William Keith, former deputy-governor of Pennsylvania, a form of the proposed agreement. The departure of Johnson and the Indians was postponed, and preparations were made for the most picturesque incident in the long and useful, but usually humdrum existence of the Board of Trade and Plantations. From Johnson and Keith and from the interpreter, Bunning, the Lords of Trade sought information of the proper manner of negotiating with savages, and to good purpose, for the treaty was accomplished in the best tradition of the Ameri-

[49] C.O. 5:361, C 99; *Daily Journal,* August 4, October 3, 1730.
[50] C.O. 4, no. 48; 5:361, C 102.
[51] JBT, August 18, 19, 20, 1730; C.O. 5:400, pp. 384-6.

can wilderness, with such added parade of Britannic splendor as was calculated to impress the Indians. To this end the secretary applied to the War Office for a detail of two sergeants and twelve grenadiers to attend at the parleys in the Plantation Office in Whitehall.[52]

On September 7, in the presence of three members of the Board, and of Colonel Johnson, Sir William Keith and several other gentlemen, the treaty[53] was read, and samples of the intended presents displayed. A preamble recited the occasion of the treaty and the desire of the King that the 'chain of friendship' now established should never more be broken or made loose. Trade was, of course, the solid basis of all Indian alliances; and so the King had 'ordered his People . . . in Carolina to Trade with the Indians, and to furnish them with all manner of Goods that they want.' There followed a curious reference to the policy of western expansion which was hardly calculated, one might think, to strengthen the league. The King had also ordered the Carolinians to 'make hast to build Houses, and to plant Corn from Charles Town towards the Town of the Cherrokees, behind the Great Mountains; for he desires that the Indians and English may live together as the Children of one Family.' Then came the crucial assertion of English sovereignty: 'As the King has given his Land on both Sides of the Great Mountains to his own Children the English, so he now gives to the Cherokee Indians the priviledge of living where they please.' To balance these somewhat questionable 'favors,' several very real services were required of the Indians as consequences of the alliance. As 'Children of the Great King' and brethren of the English they 'must be always ready at the Governor's Command, to fight against any Nation, whether they be White Men or Indians, who shall dare to Molest them, or hurt the English.' The trading path must be kept clean; this guarantee extended to the English trade with tribes at war with the Cherokee. Further, the Cherokee were pledged not to 'suffer their People to trade with the White Men of any other Nation but the English,' nor permit them 'to build any Forts, Cabins

[52] C.O. 5:361, C 109, 111; JBT, August 19, 20, 25, September 1, 1730; *Daily Journal,* September 7, 1730.
[53] JBT, September 7, 1730; C.O. 4, no. 46, i; 5:400, pp. 388-94. Text of treaty is also in *Daily Journal,* October 7, 1730.

or Plant Corn amongst them, . . . or upon the Lands which belong to the Great King.' The Indians were bound to return fugitive negro slaves, for a reward specified, and English justice was prescribed for Indian murderers of whites, and white murderers of Indians.

The scene was repeated on September 9, when the Indian reply was made.[54] The speech of the Ketagustah had the authentic ring of aboriginal eloquence:

We are come hither from a dark Mountainous Place, where nothing but Darkness is to be found; but [we] are now in a place where there is light.

There was a Person in our Country with us, he gave us a Yellow token of Warlike Honour, that is left with Moytoy of Telliko, and as Warriours we received it; he came to us like a Warriour from you; a Man he was, his talk was upright, and the token he left preserves his Memory amongst us.

We look upon you as if the Great King George was present: and We love you, as representing the Great King, and shall Dye in the same Way of Thinking.

The Crown of our Nation is different from that which the Great King George wears, and from that which we saw in the Tower, but to us it is all one, and the Chain of Friendship shall be carried to our People.

We look upon the Great King George as the Sun, and as our Father, and upon ourselves as his Children; for tho' we are Red, and you are white, yet our Hands and Hearts are join'd together.

When we shall have acqainted our People with what we have seen, our Children from Generation to Generation will always remember it.

In War we shall always be as one with you, the Great King George's Enemies shall be our Enemies, his People and ours shall be always one, and [shall] dye together.

We came hither naked and poor, as the Worm of the Earth, but you have everything: and we that have nothing must love you, and can never break the Chain of Friendship which is between us.

Here stands the Governor of Carolina, whom we know; this small Rope which we shew you, is all we have to bind our slaves with, and may be broken, but you have Iron Chains for yours; however, if we catch your Slaves, we shall bind them as well as we can, and deliver them to our Friends again, and have no pay for it.

We have looked round for the Person that was in our Country, he is not here, however, we must say, that he talked uprightly to us, and we shall never forget him.

[54] Ibid., October 7, 1730; C.O. 5:4, no. 46 ii; JBT, September 8, 9, 1730.

Your White People may very safely build Houses near us, we shall hurt nothing that belongs to them, for we are the Children of one Father, the Great King, and shall live and Dye together.

Then laying the feathers upon the table, he added,

This is our Way of Talking, which is the same thing to us, as your letters in the Book are to you; and to you, beloved Men, we deliver these Feathers, in Confirmation of all that we have said.

The Cherokee reply had pointedly objected to the exclusion of Cuming from the negotiations, and had omitted all mention of three articles of the pact. In a memorial[55] submitted to the Board on September 15, Cuming asserted that these omissions were intentional and the result of his absence, but the Indians had requested him to convey their answer on these points. They had come to England not to enter into any agreement for themselves, but solely as his friends, to give evidence that they had submitted themselves to the King at the memorialist's command. Thus Cuming demanded that the negotiation pass through his hands. Although the printed text of the treaty indicated that it was signed for the Board by the secretary, Popple, on September 9, and bore the initials of the Indians, there is some doubt as to when they gave their full consent. In an account printed in the *Daily Journal,* on information probably derived from Cuming himself, it was asserted that on September 29 Cuming gave the Board his approbation on behalf of the Cherokee Indians, and that in the evening 'the said Articles were signed by the Chiefs, at Sir Alexander's Lodgings in Spring Garden, Westminster, in the Presence of the Governor of Carolina, and the Secretary of that Board,' when the Indians 'in Token of their Satisfaction, sung and danced after a Warlike Manner, in their Way, all the evening.'[56] It is a fact that it was not until September 30, the day following this alleged triumph of Cuming's intervention, that the Board informed Newcastle that the Cherokee had given their full consent to the treaty.

Whatever concessions may have been made perforce to the vanity of Cuming, the Board was well pleased with the affair, and expected from it important imperial consequences. To Newcastle they emphasized 'that there is a full Acknowledgement in

[55] C.O. 5:361, C 112; 4, no. 46, ii.
[56] *Daily Journal,* October 1, 1730.

this Agreement of their Subjection to His Majesty.'[57] To the public the mystery 'of bringing over a Set of Savages here, whom they call Chiefs, and some will have them be called Kings, . . . and making a formal Treaty of Peace with them' was explained by a writer in the *Political State of Great Britain* of October, 1730, who stressed the importance of the Cherokee alliance in the Indian warfare of America, and in the event of future war with France.[58]

The treaty had more than the usual success of Indian alliances. Moreover, the colorful circumstances which had surrounded its negotiation had helped to place Carolina, that year, in the centre of the imperial stage. No other mainland colony was so much the topic of discussion at home. And an impression was abroad that this border province, after all its vicissitudes, was about to achieve safety and prosperity.[59]

[57] C.O. 5:401, pp. 2 f.

[58] *Political State of Great Britain*, XL. 380-7. The Indians sailed with Johnson early in October, and reached South Carolina by the middle of the next month. JC, December 18, 1730. A curious aftermath of the visit was a memorial to the Board of Trade in 1731 from one John Slater, of Cow Cross, West Smithfield, suggesting the employment of the Cherokee in silk culture. Ever since the visit of the 'chiefs,' he said, he had thought that the Indians might be brought to work at some useful manufacture (C.O. 323:9, M 28).

[59] *Political State of Great Britain*, XXXIX. 341, 345, 582 f.; Joshua Gee, *Trade and Navigation*, 1729, pp. 23, 60 f., *et passim;* [F. Hall], *The Importance of the British Plantations in America*, 1731, p. 62.

CHAPTER XIII

The Philanthropists and the Genesis
of Georgia

By 1730 a forward movement of settlement upon the south-ern frontier was clearly impending. English occupation of the Savannah-Altamaha region, so long advocated from South Carolina, had been proclaimed in instructions to Governor Johnson. But this decision of the colonial authorities, though important, was not of itself sufficient to supply the needed colonists or to win national support.

The failure of all earlier projects for southern colonization since 1670 had been due, in part, to specific weaknesses: they were visionary Edens, or mere speculators' 'bubbles,' or they were cast in the discredited mold of proprietary provinces. But in addition there had hitherto lacked any such effective impulse towards transplanting colonists as the religious and political controversies of an earlier time had furnished. Now, at last, such an impulse was provided by the organized forces of piety and philanthropy so characteristic of this epoch. To the 'imperialism' of the Carolinians and the Board of Trade, anti-Spanish, but even more aggressively anti-French, there were added the strong currents of English social reform and of that 'ecclesiastical imperialism' of which Dr. Thomas Bray had been for many years the indefatigable leader.[1] Strategy dictated that the next English seaboard colony should be planted on the exposed southern border. But it was the force of English piety and practical benevolence that furnished colonists from the unemployed of England and from the foreign Protestants, and prescribed the social character and even the organization of the new march colony, with its otherwise inexplicable reversion to the out-moded proprietorship. Institutionally, as well as in its spirit of charity, Georgia was the product of the religious-philanthropic movements of the early eighteenth century.

One of the main channels through which the rising tide of English humanitarianism was flowing consisted of the numer-

[1] E. B. Greene, 'The Anglican Outlook on the American Colonies,' *AHR*, XX. 65.

ous religious or quasi-religious societies which came into existence at the end of the seventeenth and at the beginning of the eighteenth centuries. These were formed for a variety of purposes, from the reformation of manners to the founding of charity schools.[2] If certain of their activities represented merely the resurgence of the old negative Puritan morality, others gave evidence of a more humane temper and a new social earnestness in England. To a remarkable degree the movement drew its inspiration from a clergyman of the Church of England famous neither for learning nor for high preferment, the Reverend Dr. Thomas Bray, rector of St. Botolph Without, Aldgate. A contemporary eulogist declared: 'His Memory shou'd be ever reverenced in the Religious Societies of this Place of whatever Denomination, of which he was either a Founder or principal Improver.'[3] After particular mention of his labors as a founder of the societies for the reformation of manners, for setting up charity schools, and for the relief of poor proselytes, his official biographer went on to assert that 'most of the Religious Societies in London owe . . . grateful acknowledgements to his memory and are in great measure formed on the plans he projected.'[4] The chief monuments to the zeal and organizing genius of Dr. Bray were, of course, the two great propagandist bodies in the Anglican Church, the Society for Promoting Christian Knowledge, and the Society for the Propagation of the Gospel in Foreign Parts. Another smaller church society, also created by Bray, became, shortly after his death in 1730, the parent organization of the Georgia Trust.[5]

Though Bray's colonial interests antedated his brief visit to America in 1700, they were no doubt greatly stimulated by his service in Maryland as commissary of the Bishop of London.

[2] B. K. Gray, *A History of English Philanthropy*, 1905, especially chapters iv-ix; G. V. Portus, *Caritas Anglicana*, 1912; J. H. Overton, *Life in the English Church, 1660-1714*, 1885, chapter v, *et passim*; C. F. Pascoe, *Two Hundred Years of the S.P.G.*, 1901.

[3] John Burton, *Sermon preach'd before the Trustees . . . March 15, 1732*, London, 1733, p. 31.

[4] [Samuel Smith], 'A Short Historical Account,' Maryland Historical Society, *Fund Publication*, no. 37 (1901), pp. 11-50, especially p. 48. On the authorship of this memoir, and of *Publick Spirit, illustrated in the Life and Designs of Thomas Bray*, London, 1746, see my short article in *AHR*, XXVII. 63 note 3.

[5] I have discussed this subject briefly in 'The Philanthropists and the Genesis of Georgia,' *AHR*, XXVII. 63-9.

Two benevolences which he cherished to the end of his days were designed, directly or indirectly, to ameliorate colonial society. One was the establishment of libraries for the parish clergy at home and abroad, the other the conversion and Christian education of negro slaves. For the founding of parochial libraries Bray won the patronage of several 'worthy and noble personages,' the Earl of Thanet, Lord Viscount Weymouth, Lord Digby, and Robert Nelson.[6] Nelson may well be taken as the type of the reformers of the Bray school. A supporter of Anthony Horneck's Societies for the Reformation of Manners, he was also a member of the S.P.C.K., and an active promoter of charity schools.[7] Nelson and Bray, with several of their friends, were constituted Trustees of the Parochial Libraries under an act of Parliament of 1709. From the religious societies and other sources they received contributions which they employed to lift the reproach against the Church of an ignorant clergy. Between 1710 and 1723 they had distributed from their Repository in Holborn some sixty-two libraries. Two were established thus early in the colonies, in Montserrat and at Manikin Town in Virginia. In 1716 they also presented 'a packet of Books . . . to the Honble. Col. Shute Governor of New England.' Another link with a variety of pious and colonial interests was in the person of their secretary, Henry Newman, who was secretary also of the S.P.C.K., and active in movements for the relief of poor proselytes and the establishment of charity schools. In 1720 he was appointed agent for New Hampshire. It was to Newman that Thomas Coram later appealed to revise his account for the newspapers of the sailing of the first Georgia settlers; he may have had a further hand in the great campaign of publicity which heralded the creation of the new colony.[8]

For his other work, among negroes, Bray had received a

[6] *An Account of the Designs of the Associates of the late Dr. Bray*, 1762, p. 15.

[7] C. F. Secretan, *Memoirs of the Life and Times of the pious Robert Nelson* (1860) ; Leslie Stephen, 'Robert Nelson,' in *Dictionary of National Biography*, XL. 211.

[8] Rawlinson MSS D 834 is a volume of papers relating to the parochial library trust (see especially folios 2, 7, 9, 15, 19, 38f., 41, 46, 52, 56, 59). Rawlinson MSS D 839 contains papers of Henry Newman bearing upon his pious and charitable activities (see especially folios 23, 24, 29, 42, 64, 67, 76, 98, 130). On Bray and the colonial libraries see B. C. Steiner in *AHR*, II. 59-75.

bequest of £900 from M. Abel Tassin D'Allone, of the Hague, one of the secretaries of William III, whom he had interested in the cause during a visit to Holland in 1697.[9] For this charity another trust was eventually formed. In 1723 Dr. Bray fell seriously ill. Lord Palmerston, the custodian of the D'Allone legacy, suggested to him that it was now 'requisite he should nominate and appoint, by Deed, such as he should desire to have Associates with him in the Disposition of the Legacy.' Such, by an authoritative account,[10] was the origin of the little charitable group known as the Associates of Dr. Bray, which, founded in 1723 or 1724, still exists as a Church society under the wing of the S.P.G.[11] The original Associates were but four in number besides Bray, the Reverend Stephen Hales, D.D., F.R.S., the distinguished plant-physiologist, his brother Robert Hales, William Belitha, and John Lord Viscount Percival, afterwards first Earl of Egmont.[12] Percival was an Irish peer, often at court. In the House of Commons he was a moderate supporter of Walpole, in private life, a patron of music, pious and charitable, and a diligent diarist.[13] Percival, Belitha, and Dr. Stephen Hales became charter trustees of Georgia. In that enterprise, indeed, Percival was for several years the chief collaborator of Oglethorpe.

Until 1730 the Associates seem not to have been active, nor, indeed, in agreement as to the best use of the D'Allone fund. Percival later declared frankly that he had accepted his trusteeship 'in order to assist Dean Berkeley's Bermuda scheme, by erecting a Fellowship in his college for instructing negroes; that in so doing the charity would be rendered perpetual, whereas to dribble it away in sums of five or ten pounds to missioners in the plantations, the money would be lost without any effect.'[14] His attempt to merge the D'Allone charity with Berke-

[9] Thomas Bray, *Missionalia* (1727), p. 3. [Samuel Smith], *Publick Spirit,* 1746, p. 43.
[10] Ibid., pp. 43-6.
[11] *Report for the Year 1920 of the Association Established by the late Rev. Dr. Bray and his Associates,* 1921.
[12] [Samuel Smith], 'A Short Historical Account,' *loc. cit.,* p. 41; *Dictionary of National Biography,* XXIV. 32-6 (Stephen Hales).
[13] *Diary of Viscount Percival, afterwards first Earl of Egmont.* Vol. I, 1730-1733, Vol. II, 1734-1738, Vol. III, 1739-1747. Historical Manuscripts Commission, 1920, 1923. See sketch of Percival by B. A. Roberts in his introduction to volume I, pp. v-ix.
[14] Percival, *Diary,* I. 45.

ley's famous project, so fashionable in 1725-1726, had the support also of Palmerston. Berkeley believed that a majority of the Associates were friendly.[15] Percival certainly was strongly attracted by the Dean of Derry's 'refined enthusiasm.' He subscribed £200[16] and perhaps aided in securing the royal charter for St. Paul's College and the grant from Parliament. The essence of Berkeley's scheme was the establishment of a colonial college to educate youths from the English plantations for the ministry, and to train Indians as missionaries to their own people. He had fixed upon Bermuda as the site for a characteristic reason, the 'innocence and simplicity of manners' of its inhabitants. The Indians he regarded as peculiarly open to conversion since, 'if they are in a state purely natural, and unimproved by education, they are also unincumbered with all that rubbish of superstition and prejudice, which is the effect of a wrong one.'[17] Berkeley's dream was soon dissipated, but its passing glamour had served to fix the interest of Lord Percival in America. He even toyed with the idea of emigration. To Berkeley in Rhode Island he wrote: 'Almost you persuade me to be a Rhodian.'[18] From the outset, however, Berkeley had met with ridicule from men who had first-hand knowledge of America, and who knew that Bermuda was an impossible seat for a college to train North American Indians. William Byrd of Virginia in correspondence,[19] Oglethorpe in conversation,[20] assured Percival that the idea was fantastic. None was more vigorous in his opposition than Thomas Bray.

Bray's criticism was embodied in 'A memorial relating to the Conversion as well of the American Indians, as of the

[15] Benjamin Rand, *Berkeley and Percival*, 1914, p. 229; see also pp. 203-6, 223-5, 230 f., 245.

[16] J. S. Anderson, *History of the Church of England in the Colonies*, III. 476.

[17] [George Berkeley], *A Proposal for the better Supplying of Churches in our Foreign Plantations*, London, 1725, especially pp. 8, 16.

[18] Rand, *Berkeley and Percival*, p. 248. Apropos of the vogue of Berkeley's scheme Edward Eggleston aptly described this as the 'bubble period' in philanthropy (*Century Magazine*, XXXVI. 117).

[19] Rand, *Berkeley and Percival*, pp. 243-7: Byrd to Percival, June 10, 1729. The writer described enthusiastically the back-country he had recently visited in running the Virginia-North Carolina boundary. 'Did the poor people in the old world, that groan under tyranny and priesthood, know how happy a retreat they might find here, it would not long lie uninhabited.'

[20] Percival, *Diary*, I. 45.

African Negroes.' This was printed, in 1727, as one item in his *Missionalia: or, a Collection of Missionary Pieces relating to the Conversion of the Heathen; both the African Negroes and American Indians*.[21] In these tracts Bray revealed his own concern for the extension of missionary activities among the American Indians. This, he declared, was a valid secondary object of the D'Allone trustees, though the conversion of negroes had been the chief interest of the benefactors. But Berkeley's scheme was vetoed as impractical. Instead, Bray advocated the unique expedient of establishing artisan-mission colonies on the frontiers of the settlements. Under the supervision of the parish clergy his artisan-missionaries would labor to Christianize and at the same time to civilize the natives. Since his method would operate gradually to build up a barrier against the barbarous Indians, Bray believed that it would be supported by the governors as a means of extending their territories. In this frontier mission scheme, it is possible to see one of the obscure springs of the Georgia enterprise. Certainly the seriousness with which the Trustees of Georgia later approached their responsibilities for the Indians was part of their inheritance from Bray.

There is evidence, too, that Bray and his group were in sympathetic contact with other projects which pointed more definitely towards actual colonization in America. Analysis of the personnel of the various pious, philanthropic, and colonizing movements which converged to produce Georgia will reveal the interlocking membership of the Board of Trade and the Parliamentary gaols committees of 1729 and 1730; of the gaols committees and the Associates of Dr. Bray; of the enlarged Associates and the Georgia Trust. But the personal connections were even more involved. In 1726 Purry's agent, Jean Watt, named Dr. Bray with 'Messieurs Hales, Hodges, Newman' as among 'our friends' in England, and suggested an application to Hales to procure aid in Holland for the unfortunate remnant of the Swiss 'Carolinians' who had persisted in their purpose to emigrate.[22] Thus the appeal that Georgia made to foreign

---

[21] Copy in the British Museum. See B. C. Steiner, 'Two Eighteenth Century Missionary Plans,' in *Sewanee Review*, XI. 289-305.

[22] C.O. 5:387, f. 20. In his will Thomas Bray left to Mr. John Vatt a small sum of money. P.C.C., 55 Auber (Somerset House, London).

Protestants was quite in keeping with the Bray tradition. Even more significant was Bray's contact with the colonial scheme of his parishioner and close friend, Thomas Coram. Coram, who is chiefly famous as the founder of the great London Foundling Hospital, was a former mariner and ship-builder at Taunton, Massachusetts. At this time, however, he was a London merchant engaged in colonial commerce and in promoting a project for planting 'the lands lying wast and derelict between New England and Nova Scotia.'[23] Contemporary records of Coram's conversations with his rector are lacking, but in 1734 he wrote a striking account of them in a letter to Benjamin Colman of Boston.[24] Bray, he said, had 'often lamented the great pains I had for many years took' in the plan for colonizing the northern frontier of New England. Shortly before Christmas, 1729, Coram recalled, Bray had predicted that he could not survive the winter, 'yet he would before he dyed find out a way to have a Settlement made for the Releife of such honest poor Distressed Famelies from hence as by Losses, want of Employment or otherwise are reduced to poverty and such who were persecuted for their professing the protestant Religion abroad, to be happy by their Labour and Industry in some part of His Majesties Dominions in America.' The eastern border of Maine, however, he thought too northerly and bleak a place for this asylum. Coram's narrative is in line with a persistent tradition among the friends of Bray and the executors of his pious plans that it was Bray who first moved to organize the project of a debtor colony in America.

Certain it is that Bray was deeply concerned with the con-

[23] H. F. B. Compston, *Thomas Coram*, London, 1918, is a brief biography, inadequate in its treatment of Coram's colonial interests. These I expect to discuss in an article based upon a mass of memorials, etc., in the P.R.O., which were composed by Coram, between 1713 and 1743, in his rôle of promoter of a succession of schemes to colonize lands on the Maine border, in Nova Scotia, and Cat Island (Bahamas). At different times he proposed as settlers retired officers and soldiers, French Protestants, convicts, Irish, Palatines, unemployed artisans, and the 'graduates' of his Foundling Hospital. Coram bitterly contested the eastern claims of Massachusetts and of the other pretenders to the Sagadahoc region. His ideas of colonial government were strikingly liberal, within the limits of effective mercantilism. After his break with his fellow Trustees he sought to develop Nova Scotia as a rival to Georgia, purged of the latter's military and paternalistic features.

[24] W. C. Ford (ed.), 'Letters of Thomas Coram,' Massachusetts Historical Society, *Proceedings*, LVI. 15-56, especially pp. 20 f.

dition of the poor, and especially of imprisoned debtors, prior to the memorable inquiry of the parliamentary committee which turned Oglethorpe's mind toward his great enterprise. As early as 1702 Bray took a prominent part in an investigation of the prisons by the S.P.C.K.[25] Around 1727, when he was proposing his artisan-mission scheme, his interest in poor prisoners was revived, and he undertook to raise funds for their relief. To train his missionary-probationers in 'the more distasteful part of their office,' he sent them to read and preach to the wretches in Whitechapel and the Borough Compter. Besides spiritual sustenance, they dispensed bread, beef, and broth on Sundays and sometimes on week-days. 'On this occasion,' asserted Bray's biographer, 'the sore was first opened and that scene of inhumanity imperfectly discover'd, which afterwards some worthy Patriots of the House of Commons took so much pains tc enquire into and redress.'[26]

Those 'worthy Patriots' were, of course,

the generous band
Who, touch'd with human woe, redressive search'd
Into the horrors of the gloomy jail.

Such was James Thomson's famous characterization[27] of the committee appointed from the House of Commons 'to enquire into the State of the Gaols of the Kingdom' (February 25, 1729).[28] Another poet close to the philanthropic movement of the day was the brother of John and Charles Wesley. In *The Prisons Open'd*,[29] dedicated to the committee, the Rev. Samuel Wesley etched vignettes in verse of several of the earnest re-

[25] Anderson, *History of the Church in the Colonies,* IV. 74-6; Secretan, *Nelson,* p. 102. 'A charitable visit to prisons' was a tract listed in the papers of Bray's Trustees of the Parochial Libraries (Rawlinson MSS D, 834, f. 52).

[26] [Samuel Smith], *Publick Spirit,* 1746, p. 51. By a codicil to his will, dated February 1, 1729[/30], Thomas Bray left £5 and his chancel and pulpit mourning to Thomas Grove 'in consideration of the trouble he has had in inspecting the prisons and enquiring into the Necessitous as well as sick Condition of the poor prisoners' (P.C.C., 55 Auber).

[27] From *Winter.* The first edition appeared in 1726; the thirty lines in praise of the gaols committee were interpolated in the 1730 edition. There is internal evidence that they were written before the revival of the committee in February, 1730.

[28] *Journals of the House of Commons,* February 25, 1728/9.

[29] I have used the text of the first edition, 1729, but supplied the names, there indicated by initials, from *Poems on Several Occasions* (second edition, 1743).

formers who exposed the oppressions of the notorious Bambridge, keeper of the Fleet:

> Yet, Britain cease thy Captives' Woes to mourn,
> To break their Chains, see *Oglethorpe* was born!
> *Vernon,* whose steady Truth no Threats can bend!
> And *Hughes,* the Sailor's never-failing Friend!
> *Towers,* whose rich Youth can Ease and Pleasure fly,
> And *Percival* renown'd for Piety!
> *Cornewall,* to aid the Friendless never slow,
> Whose gen'rous Breast still melts at Humane Woe!
> These dare the Tyrants long secure oppose;
> Thus gracious Heav'n its Benefits bestows,
> The Antidote is found there where the Poison grows.

James Edward Oglethorpe was chairman: it was he who had
moved for the appointment of the committee and who supplied
much of the driving force behind its work and that of the
revived committee at the next session. 'A young gentleman of
very public spirit,' Percival described him to Berkeley.[30] In
Parliament he was a frequent speaker in opposition to Sir Robert Walpole. A member of the S.P.G., and later deputy-governor of the Royal African Company, his interests ran as
strongly towards the development of the colonies as towards
social reform in England. Of the six committeemen named in
Wesley's poem, four—Oglethorpe, Percival, Edward Hughes,
and Thomas Towers—were later joined as founders of
Georgia. Among

> the rest for ardent Goodness fam'd
> Unam'd, tho' greatly worthy to be nam'd,

were several others who at one stage or another coöperated in
the colonial scheme that grew out of the committee's labors:
Major Charles Selwyn, John Laroche, Robert Hucks, Erasmus
Phillips and Rogers Holland. This committee and its successor
also included several members of the Board of Trade and
Plantations. Martin Bladen ('Trade' Bladen) served in both
investigations of 1729 and 1730.[31]

[30] Rand, *Berkeley and Percival,* p. 270.
[31] Ninety-six members were listed in the *Journals,* February 25, 1728/9,
though many were not active. Wesley named twenty-six 'acting members'
in the dedication of his poem, as follows: Oglethorpe, Percival, Sir Thomas
Lowther, Sir Humphrey Howarth, Robert Byng, Charles Selwyn, Erasmus
Phillips, Stamp Brooksbank, John La Roche, Charles Withers, John Crosse,
Velters Cornwall, Robert Huckes, Sir Robert Clifton, Sir Archibald Grant,

After holding numerous hearings the committee in its reports exposed gross abuses by brutal keepers at the Fleet and Marshalsea prisons. Popular interest was strongly aroused. Hogarth painted the scene of Bambridge's examination,[32] and poets eulogized the social reformers of the House of Commons. Parliament, in 1729, passed ameliorative laws.[33] But opposition had also appeared, in high quarters. The courts were charged by Hughes and others with obstructing reform, and the ministry was regarded as hostile. Other prisons of the Kingdom had not yet been probed. Thomson voiced the appeal of earnest men:

> Ye sons of mercy! yet resume the search;
> . . . .
> Much still untouch'd remains; in this rank age,
> Much is the patriot's weeding hand requir'd.

To finish their work and to vindicate their reputations, 'being villified in the world for proceeding so zealously last year,' Oglethorpe and the more earnest members, in February, 1730, pressed successfully for the revival of the committee.[34] Among the reformers now added were William Sloper, Captain Francis Eyles, Alderman George Heathcote, and Bray's patron, Lord Palmerston. It is significant that the second gaols committee included substantially the whole parliamentary group later named as Trustees in the Georgia charter.

The actual connecting link between the committee and the Georgia Trust was supplied, however, by the enlarged Associates of Dr. Bray. While the reforming element in the committee was being recruited, Oglethorpe and Percival were en-

Mr. Alderman Parsons, Edward Vernon, John Campbel, Rogers Holland, James Tuffnell, Thomas Lewis of Radnor, Robert More, John Norris, Edward Hughes, Thomas Towers, Sir Abraham Elton. Of these the names of Withers, More, Norris, and Towers do not appear in the *Journals* list for 1729, though all were members of the revived committee. Besides Bladen, the first committee included Sir Thomas Frankland and possibly Thomas Pelham of the Board of Trade; the second committee, Edward Ashe.

[32] Original in National Portrait Gallery, London; reproduced in Wheatley's *Hogarth's London,* opposite p. 389, and elsewhere.

[33] 2 George II, c. xx, c. xxii, c. xxxii.

[34] Percival, Diary, I. 46, 49 f.; *Journals of the House of Commons,* February 17, 1729/30. Eighty-eight members were listed, more than half of whom had served on the earlier committee. Percival's *Diary* named several others not listed as attending meetings. For proceedings see *Diary,* I. 55, 78, 90, 95.

gaged in a parallel reconstruction of the closely affiliated charitable trusts for parochial libraries and the conversion of blacks. Their object was to associate the reformers in the House with philanthropists outside in a constructive effort on behalf of the English poor. For it was now evident that the partial success of the 1729 committee had created a social problem as serious, perhaps, as the evils redressed. The act of 2 George II, cap. xxii for the relief of insolvent debtors, had released from confinement great numbers of poor prisoners—as many as ten thousand, Oglethorpe told Percival in April, 1730, adding that three hundred others had already returned from Prussia to take the benefit of the act. Another contemporary estimate set a much higher total.[35] The immediate result was a great increase of unemployment in London. One obvious remedy was colonization overseas.

On February 13, 1730, Oglethorpe and Percival met at the House of Commons, and the former unfolded his plans for pressing the prison investigation and at the same time promoting charitable colonies in America. The conversation, as recorded in Percival's *Diary*,[36] described the immediate inception of the Georgia enterprise:

I met Mr. Oglethorp, who informed me that he had found out a very considerable charity, even fifteen thousand pounds, which lay in trustees' hands, and was like to have been lost, because the heir of the testator being one of the trustees, refused to concur with the other two, in any methods for disposing the money, in hopes, as they were seventy years old, each of them, they would die soon, and he should remain only surviving trustee, and then might apply it all to his own use. That the two old men were very honest and desirous to be discharged of their burthen, and had concurred with him to get the money lodged in a Master of Chancery's hands till new trustees should be appointed to dispose thereof in a way that should be approved of by them in conjunction with the Lord Chancellor. That the heir of the testator had opposed this, and there had been a lawsuit thereupon, which Oglethorp had carried against the heir, who appealed against the decree; but my Lord Chancellor had confirmed it, and it was a pleasure to him to have been able in one year's time to be able at

---

[35] *Diary*, I. 90. Compare the assertion that this act released 97,248 prisoners, from news-letter cited by I. S. Leadam, *History of England from the Accession of Anne to the Death of George II*, 1909, p. 342.

[36] *Diary*, I. 44-6. In Chancery Entry Book, 1729 B, ff. 3, 12 bis, are references to the case of Oglethorpe *vs*. Cottin.

law to settle this affair. That the trustees had consented to this on condition that the trust should be annexed to some trusteeship already in being, and that being informed that I was a trustee for Mr. Dalone's legacy, who left about a thousand pounds to convert negroes, he had proposed me and my associates as proper persons to be made trustees of this new affair; that the old gentlemen approved of us, and he hoped I would accept it in conjunction with himself and several of our Committee of Gaols, as Mr. Towers, Mr. Hughes, Mr. Holland, Major Selwyn, and some other gentlemen of worth, as Mr. Sloper and Mr. Vernon, Commissioner of the Excise.

Percival complimented Oglethorpe warmly upon his industry in recovering so great a charity, and expressed his pleasure in being joined with gentlemen of so much worth. But he indicated that he had been thinking of quitting the trusteeship of D'Allone's legacy, which he had only accepted in the interest of Berkeley's college. Oglethorpe, after expressing his belief that nothing would now come of the Irish dean's college, returned to the new trusteeship. The old trustees of King the haberdasher's legacy would as yet only set aside £5000 for the new project, but this, he thought, would answer. The scheme, he continued,

is to procure a quantity of acres either from the Government or by gift or purchase in the West Indies [i.e., America], and to plant thereon a hundred miserable wretches who being let out of gaol by the last year's Act, are now starving about the town for want of employment; that they should be settled all together by way of colony, and be subject to subordinate rulers, who should inspect their behaviour and labour under one chief head; that in time they with their families would increase so fast as to become a security and defence of our possessions against the French and Indians of those parts; that they should be employed in cultivating flax and hemp, which being allowed to make into yarn, would be returned to England and Ireland, and greatly promote our manufactures. All which I approved.

Was Oglethorpe, as this interview with Percival implies, the originator of the debtor colony scheme? Perhaps; but the idea was in the air, and other such projects had already been broached.[37]

[37] For a tantalizing clue to one such scheme of this period see my reference in *Promotion Literature of Georgia*, 1925, p. 8.

In 1729, when the surrender of the Carolina charter to the Crown was pending, there had been published in London the first edition of Joshua Gee's *The Trade and Navigation of Great Britain Considered,* one of the most widely read of the commercial tracts of the century.[38] A merchant in the West India trade, in 1718 Gee had been one of the promoters, with Coram, of the project for settling soldiers in Nova Scotia and on the Maine border to raise hemp and produce naval stores.[39] But by 1729 his interest had turned from the northern towards the southern frontier. Repeatedly he insisted upon the value of the southern colonies, of Virginia, and especially of Carolina, 'the most improveable, in my Appprehension, of any of our Colonies; yet because it is the Property of particular Persons, supplies us with little more than one Commodity of Rice (tho' it is capable of many other valuable ones) and is liable to be overrun by the French, Spaniards, and Indians, for want of a sufficient Protection.' Pointing to the line of French forts from the St. Lawrence to the Gulf, Gee proposed that the English build posts of their own along the Appalachians, to secure 'the Mines contained in them, to protect the Indian and Skin Trade, and to preserve the Navigation' of the rivers of Maryland, Virginia, and Carolina. This suggestion somewhat vaguely recalled the Barnwell proposals for frontier forts which had been endorsed by the Board of Trade in 1720. Elsewhere Gee clearly anticipated the settlement schemes of Johnson and Oglethorpe. In view of the impending surrender of Carolina, he demonstrated that the southern piedmont was a country 'large enough to canton out into distinct Lots [i.e., townships?] all the Inhabitants we shall be capable of sending . . . , which would also be a Security to our Frontiers against the Incroachments of the French who lie on the other Side those Mountains.' But from this point of view the most significant passages in his pamphlet were contained in chapter xxvii. There he set forth proposals for transporting and colonizing the poor which were almost verbally reproduced in Oglethorpe's first recorded exposition of his charitable colony plan. Indeed, one might suppose

[38] Later editions appeared in rapid sequence, 1730, 1731, 1738, 1750, 1760, 1767. The quotations are from pp. 23, 60 f. and 'conclusion,' pp. 12-13, of the first edition.
[39] *Acts of the Privy Council, Colonial, 1680-1720,* pp. 393, 744, *et seq.*

that Oglethorpe, when he met Percival in February, 1730, had just come from a reading of Gee. Recalling that the French had lately sent over great numbers of vagrants to the settlements on the Mississippi, Gee urged that the methods used by the English for transporting convicts be employed as well 'for all Persons . . . that cannot find Methods of Subsistence at home.' These should be settled on tracts of one hundred acres or more on the exposed southern borders, their quit-rents to be paid after several years from the produce of their lands, that is, in hemp and flax. Such colonists, marrying young, would multiply rapidly, 'by which Means those vast Tracts of Land now waste will be planted, and secured from the Danger we apprehend of the French over-running them.' Both Gee and Oglethorpe expected that silk culture would also develop. Though Gee hardly suggested a new colony, under separate government, in other respects the resemblances between Oglethorpe's ideas and his own were so close as to raise the presumption of derivation, or a common origin. Oglethorpe, it is likely, envisaged his first modest scheme in terms of Gee's published suggestions.

Oglethorpe, moreover, when he approached Percival, said that he had already discussed American colonization with the Speaker of the House of Commons and 'some other considerable persons.' One of these, there is strong reason to believe, was the invalid Dr. Bray. The latter, in a codicil to his will drawn February 1, 1729[/30], recalled that he had 'from time to time negociated for these several years last past and . . . been at the trouble of drawing and expence of fair copyes of various Memorials and Proposalls for the proper Application of the late Mr. King of Milk Street Bequest for the Information of the severall Trustees according to the Testators Intention and other expences about the same to the amount of at least £50.' Since this was the trust that Oglethorpe had fought for in Chancery it is likely that the two reformers were in communication, and that it was Bray who suggested his own Associates for the supervision of the charitable colony scheme in which both were interested. That a conference occurred, and that Bray proposed the enlargement of the Associates to embrace the new cause, was positively affirmed in 1731 by the

Rev. Samuel Smith. The assistant rector of St. Botolph's, and with Belitha and the Rev. Stephen Hales one of the over-seers of Bray's will, Smith became in 1730 a secretary of the Associates and in 1732 a Trustee of Georgia; it was he who drew up in 1731 the official biography of Bray. The 'zeal and compassion' of the prison reformers, he wrote, 'could not but procure for them the largest measure of esteem from one dis-tinguished by such an extensive benevolence as Dr. Bray.' As his years pressed upon him Bray 'was desirous of enlarging the number of his Associates and adding such to them in whose zeal and integrity he might repose entire confidence. The Inquiry into the State of the Gaols was an event which at this juncture appeard to have in it something providential, as it gave occasion to an interview between the doctor and Mr. Oglethorpe. This worthy gentleman, when it was proposed, wanted no arguments to prevail on him to accept the Trust, and engaged several others, some of the first rank and distinction, to act with him and the former Associates in it. All the under-takings indeed were of such a nature, as it well became the character of great and generous minds to support. For to these two designs of founding Libraries, and instructing the Negroes, a third was now added, which tho' at first view appears to be of a different nature, has a perfect coincidence with them. . . . As the doctor was concern'd with getting this undertaking on foot, I can't justly be charged with a digression for taking notice of it.'[40] In 1734 Thomas Coram went even further in claiming credit for Bray as the author of the Georgia enter-prise.[41] He wrote that after Bray had rejected the Maine border as the site for the charitable colony which he hoped to see planted before he died, 'he sent for Mr. James Vernon, the Reverend Dr. Hales, Ld. Percival and Mr. Oglethorpe and 2 or 3 more and proposed their entering into an association with

[40] 'A Short Historical Account,' *loc. cit.*, pp. 46-8. Compare *Publick Spirit*, 1746, pp. 52-4. The will is in P.C.C., 55 Auber. The tradition of Bray's prime agency in the colony scheme was later supported by Edward Ben-tham in a Latin memoir of one of the Associates: *De vitâ et moribus Johan-nis Burtoni*, 1771, pp. 17 f. Cf. *Gentleman's Magazine*, XLI (1771), 305-8.
[41] Coram to Benjamin Colman, April 30, 1734, in Massachusetts His-torical Society *Proceedings*, LXI, 20 f. Coram himself was named as the one 'who first projected the Colony' in Thomas Stephens' historical novel, *The Castle-Builders* (second edition, 1759), p. 66.

him for the Carrying on his Design of a Colony, and two Designs of his own.' Coram, to be sure, belonged to a religious-minded faction of the Trustees, who soon came to reprobate the more worldly aims of the 'Oglethorpians.' Not unnaturally the tradition of Bray's prime agency in all three charities was cherished, and possibly exaggerated, by this group. Whatever his personal rôle, Bray died February 15, 1730, when the project was still in embryo. 'He was a great Small man,' declared Coram, 'and had done Great good things in his life Time.'[42]

From Oglethorpe's references to the French and Indians it is evident that from the first a continental, and a frontier location for the charitable colony was intended. The earliest specific mention of Carolina was in the record of a conference between Oglethorpe and Percival at the nobleman's seat of Charlton, June 26, 1730.[43] It was probably more than a coincidence that this was the first interview between two projectors since the Board of Trade had instructed Johnson to extend the settlement of South Carolina as far as the river Altamaha (June 10, 1730). When it is recalled that, from February to May, Bladen and Edward Ashe of the Board of Trade had been collaborating with Oglethorpe and his circle in the prisons investigation, the process whereby the charitable colony came to be fixed in that segment of the frontier, and assimilated for a time to the Barnwell-Johnson township scheme, becomes fairly obvious. It was almost certainly the long-maturing policy of the colonial administration to occupy and protect the exposed southern border that determined the precise *locale* of the colony of Georgia.

By feoffment, confirmed by the terms of his last will, Bray had devolved upon the Associates the D'Allone trust and also his parochial library charity. Their authority was confirmed by a decree of Chancery in 1731.[44] Meanwhile, the enlargement

---

[42] Reference in note 41.

[43] Percival, *Diary*, I. 98.

[44] *An Account of the Designs*, 1764, p. 7; 'The designs [of] . . . the Associates,' in Samuel Smith, *Sermon* (1733), p. 38. On account, presumably, of the inadequacies of the Chancery indexes for this period I have not discovered the decree. In his will Bray referred at times to his 'Associates as well for disposing of Mr. D'Allone's Bequest as Parochial Libraries' as if they were merged, though elsewhere he named them separately. To them he

of the Associates in scope and personnel had been effected. In April, 1730, Percival took legal counsel as to the method, and was informed that it could not be done by the original trustees, but only by the Master of the Rolls, by bill and answer. By July, apparently, the reorganization was completed. On July 1 Percival recorded that he 'Went to town to a meeting of the new Society for fulfilling Mr. Dalone's will in the conversion of negroes, and disposing of five thousand pounds . . . in settling some hundred of families in Carolina, who came necessitous out of gaols by virtue of our late debtors Act.' In 1737 an advertisement of 'The Associates of the late Dr. Bray' referred to their activities 'since July, 1730.'[45]

The various names by which the 'new society' was described by Percival in his *Diary* possibly indicated the varying character of the business transacted at their successive meetings. Thus, on July 15, 1730, 'Went to town to the meeting of our Society for converting negroes, and returned to dinner'; on July 18, 'Colonel Schutz gave me out of the Prince's charity money ten guineas for conversion of the blacks and promoting the settlement of a colony in the West Indies'; and on July 30, 'Went to town to the Society of Associates for Mr. Dalone's Legacy to convert blacks in America, and settle a colony in America.'[46] Little attempt was made prior to the granting of the Georgia charter, and even for some time thereafter, to

left without distinction a residuary legacy of £300; the income from certain of his books, subject to a life-interest in a one-half share thereof; four and a quarter shares in the Mine Adventure; and also, subject to the life interest of his son, the residue of his personal estate. There were also small legacies for libraries for chaplains on men-of-war, for the probationary missionaries, and for individuals who had aided him in his philanthropies.

[45] Percival, *Diary*, I. 93, 98; Nichols, *Literary Anecdotes*, II. 119. The minutes of the society at this period have not been discovered. But in the Sloane MSS 4051, f. 311, is a copy, transmitted to Sir Hans Sloane, 'of a Minute of the General Meeting of the Gentlemen associated for executing Mr. D'Allone's Will; by Instructing the Negroes of the British Plantations in the Christian Religion: And also for settling parochial Libraries in Great Britain & Ireland; and for establishing a Charitable Colony in America, on the 12th. of August 1731.' Anderson had acquainted the meeting that Sloane was desirous of obtaining materials relating to missionary enterprises among the heathen, and was ordered to acquaint him that 'they will speedily prepare & present him with a Manuscript Copy of a Work, intended to be published, Giving an Account of the Life of the late Dr. Thomas Bray. . . Together with Some Account of the Proceedings and Designs of the Gentlemen associated as above named.' See above, note 4, and references.

[46] *Diary*, I. 98, 99, 273, 276.

differentiate the administration of the three kindred charities. The long series of Bray 'anniversary sermons,'[47] provided for by a fund left in his will, was inaugurated February 23, 1731, when the Rev. Samuel Smith preached, as the *Gentleman's Magazine* reported, before 'the associates of Dr. Bray, deceased, at the Church of St. Augustine, near St. Paul's.' He spoke in praise of all three charities. 'A Recital of the diffusive Advantages, arising from each Design,' he declared, 'will be a recital of your Praises, who support All.'[48] At the meetings of this conglomerate trust, between 1730 and 1732, the colonizing enterprise took shape. It was at a meeting of the 'Society of Associates' on July 30, 1730, that the petition to the King and Council 'for obtaining a grant of lands on the south-west of Carolina for settling poor persons of London,' was agreed upon and partly signed by the 'Associates.' At the same time the campaign for public subscriptions was inaugurated, and that remarkable program of publicity was begun which gave Georgia for a season a popular vogue unexampled in the earlier record of English colonization. On that day the London *Daily Journal* announced: 'We hear there is a noble Settlement going to be made upon Savanna River in South Carolina, and that Gentlemen of great Honour and Worth are at the Head of that Affair.'[49]

The roster of the society amply confirms the other evidence that the enlarged Associates of Dr. Bray formed the nidus of the Georgia Board.[50] The Associates included some eight indi-

[47] See my *Promotion Literature of Georgia,* 1925, p. 5 note.

[48] *Gentleman's Magazine,* I. 80 (February, 1731); Samuel Smith, *Sermon* (1733), p. 27. See also Burton, *Sermon* (1733), and Percival, *Diary,* I. 224-6.

[49] Percival, *Diary,* I. 99; see also pp. 98, 120, 127, 128 f., 154, 155, 157, 164, 165, 167, 172, 193, 204, 209, 214-20, 223, 226, 230-2, 235, 254, 260, 265, 266, 273, 276, 285 f.; London *Daily Journal,* July 30, 1730. On the publicity campaign and the vogue of Georgia, see my *Promotion Literature of Georgia,* 1925.

[50] The list in *Publick Spirit,* 1746, follows: 'John Lord Viscount Percival, now Earl of Egmont; the Reverend Mr. (now Dr.) Stephen Hales; William Belitha, Esq.; the Honourable Edward Digby, Esq.; the Honourable George Carpenter, Esq., now Lord Carpenter; James Oglethorpe, Esq., now Major-General; Edward Harley, Esq.; the Honourable James Vernon, Esq.; Edward Hughes, Esq.; Robert Hucks, Esq.; Thomas Tower, Esq.; Rogers Holland, Esq.; John Laroche, Esq.; Major Charles Selwyn; Robert More, Esq.; William Sloper, Esq.; Oliver St. John, Esq.; Henry Hastings, Esq.; George Heathcote, Esq.; Francis Eyles, Esq.; Mr. Adam Anderson; Sir James Lowther; Captain Thomas Coram; the Reverend Mr. Digby

viduals who never served as Georgia Trustees, but no one was named in the royal charter from outside that composite society. The list of thirty members was headed by three of the original Associates: Lord Percival, the Rev. Dr. Stephen Hales, and William Belitha. Exactly half of the Associates were members of Parliament, and all but two or three of these—the Hon. Edward Digby, Sir James Lowther, and possibly Edward Harley—had served on one or other gaols committee. Harley, brother of the Earl of Oxford, was a well-known philanthropist who in 1725 had become chairman of the trustees of the charity-schools of London.[51] He was one of the four parliamentary members who were later omitted from the Georgia Trust.[52] Digby was probably drawn in as the nephew of the pious Lord Digby who had been a lifelong friend and patron of Dr. Bray. The Bray tradition was further represented by the group of seven clergymen, five of whom continued as Trustees. Of these the most famous, after Hales, was John Burton, D.D., theologian and classical scholar, who later achieved a great reputation as an Oxford don.[53] Burton and Oglethorpe were contemporaries at Corpus Christi, but according to Burton's Latin memoirist it was Bray who drew him into this circle. The Rev. Richard Bundy[54] was a chaplain-in-ordinary at court, while the Rev. Arthur Bedford had won some note as a fellow-crusader with Collier against the stage.[55] The pious and philanthropic groups outside of Parliament were represented by these clergymen, and by several other worthy persons, two of whom also qualified as authorities on commerce and plantations. Adam Anderson, secretary of the Scottish Corporation of London, was second accountant at the South Sea House, and was acquiring that reputation as a trade expert which his authorship of the *Origin of Commerce* (1764) has perpetuated.[56] Captain Thomas Coram imported the salty dialect of the sea into dis-

Cotes; the Reverend Mr. Arthur Bedford; the Reverend Mr. Samuel Smith; the Reverend Mr. Richard Bundy; the Reverend Mr. John Burton; the Reverend Mr. Daniel Somerscald.'

[51] *Dictionary of National Biography,* XXIV. 394.
[52] Overton, *Life in the English Church,* p. 123.
[53] Bentham's memoir, cited in note 40, and *Dictionary of National Biography,* VIII. 8.
[54] Ibid., VII. 268; Percival, *Diary,* III. 349 (memorandum by Percival).
[55] *Dictionary of National Bibliography,* IV. 109.
[56] Ibid., I. 371; Nichols, *Literary Anecdotes,* IX. 491.

cussions of charity and colonization. Percival remarked that 'he knew the West Indies well,' and the elder Horace Walpole declared that he was 'the honestest, the most disinterested, and the most knowing person about the plantations, I have ever talked with.' Already Coram was deeply concerned in his plan for a colony in the Maine-Nova Scotia region which later, when he fell out with the 'Oglethorpians,' he sought to develop into a rival to Georgia. Already, too, he was agitating for the great Foundling Hospital which became and remains his monument. It was significant of the ramifications of the Georgia scheme in contemporary philanthropy that the three charities singled out for special praise by James Thomson, the social poet, *par excellence,* of the period, were Oglethorpe's prison reforms, the founding of Georgia, and the creation of the Foundling Hospital by Thomas Coram, Associate and Trustee.[57]

During the first year after the enlargement of the Associates the chairman was Oglethorpe, the secretaries were the clergymen Smith and Bedford.[58] But in the second year it appears that a dual organization was evolving. Lord Percival presided at the stated monthly meetings 'of the trustees for executing the purposes of Dr. Bray's and Mr. Dalone's wills.'[59] At other meetings apparently Vernon was in the chair. But there was not yet a clear separation. Even after the Georgia charter had passed the seals (June 9, 1732) the business of the Associates and the Trustees was for some time jointly transacted. At the first official meeting of the Trustees on July 20, 1732, the oaths were administered, and laws for the colony considered; and Mr. Purry attending, the Trustees presented him, with 'a small library out of Dr. Bray's books, of which we are trustees.'[60] May 23, 1733, the Trustees 'ordered a distinct meeting of the trustees of Dr. Bray's legacy to-morrow sennit at four aclock, to consider of making that part of our trust a separate care

[57] See references in note 23, and the following: *Dictionary of National Biography,* XII. 194; Percival, *Diary,* I. 261; Coxe, *Walpole* (1798), III. 243; C. A. Moore in *Publications* of the Modern Language Association, 1916, pp. 281f.

[58] Percival, *Diary,* I. 98. The index incorrectly interprets this passage to mean that Bundy and Hales were secretaries.

[59] Ibid., p. 273.

[60] Ibid., p. 286. See also *Colonial Records of Georgia,* II. 9, for action on the accounts of the Trustees and Associates in the Common Council, November 1, 1732.

from the Georgia affair, our charter taking no notice of it.'[61]
This meeting of May 31 was attended by 'that part of the
trustees who are concerned in the trust of Monsr. Dalone's
legacy for instructing negroes in the Christian religion, and in
executing the purposes of Dr. Bray's will for settling parochial
libraries'; they applied to the Trustees for the payment of the
balance due to the religious trusts, and agreed to seek further
aid from the Earl of Thanet's legacy. The memorial to the
trustees of this fund, however, was signed at a meeting of the
Georgia Trustees on June 6.[62] Formal separation soon followed. But for a long time the Associates and the Trustees
were closely linked in personnel.[63] The Associates held their
monthly meetings at the Georgia Office;[64] annually down to
1750 they attended, with the Trustees, the anniversary sermons
in honor of Dr. Bray; and in 1752, when the Trustees took an
inventory of their effects, books belonging to the Associates
were found intermingled with those of the Georgia Trust.[65]

The separation of these charities was not accomplished
without protest, and helped to split the Trustees into two ill-
assorted factions. In 1734 Captain Coram asserted that 'there
are not many'of those associates [i.e., Trustees] who gives
themselves any Trouble about the other two Matters, but I believe I may venture to say the better sort of them do.'[66] Vernon
also was critical of the behavior of several of the younger
Trustees. Heathcote, White, Towers, Hucks, and More, he
complained to Percival, had 'too little regard to the religious
part of our designs. . . . He took it ill that they separated the
Colony affairs and the members of it from the care of Mr.
Dalon's legacy for converting the blacks, and Dr. Bray's improvement of that design, of which the others of the Trustees
for Georgia are Trustees; with these he put Mr. Martin, our
secretary, who he thinks leads the gentlemen I have men-

[61] Percival, *Diary*, I. 378-82.
[62] Ibid., p. 384.
[63] In 1762 the thirty-two Associates included Oglethorpe, Rogers Holland, Robert More, George Heathcote, Adam Anderson, Dr. Burton, all
former Trustees; and among others, Benjamin Franklin, Esq., LL.D., and
Samuel Johnson, M. A. *An Account of the Designs* (1762), pp. 31, 32, 37.
[64] Percival, *Diary*, III. 256.
[65] *Colonial Records of Georgia*, I. 576.
[66] Reference in note 24.

tioned.'[67] But the secularization of the Georgia enterprise went on apace. At a later time practically all tradition of its origins in the activities of a religious society was lost.

By such converging paths did English benevolence and a nascent Anglo-American 'imperialism' combine, between 1730 and 1732, for the establishment of the colony of Georgia. Oglethorpe, of course, was the real founder, in the sense that it was he who mobilized the forces of piety and charity, already well developed in England in the pre-Wesleyan epoch, to accomplish a task of strategic as well as philanthropic concern.

Georgia, however, promised to realize the dreams of many men; hence, in part, its extraordinary vogue in its early years. For several decades before the Trustees and their literary secretary summoned the propaganda forces of press, pamphlet, and poetry to extol their charitable and patriotic scheme, the region had been advertised to the English public by a succession of enthusiastic promoters. A larger significance attaches to the work of the Carolina expansionists. From the time of Henry Woodward provincial explorers and traders had faced southward and westward, more than half-conscious of their rôle as advance agents of English dominion. For half-a-century Georgia soil had been traversed by the branching trading-paths from the inland entrepôt at Savannah Town. The Spanish mission system had crumbled; Guale and Tama had fallen easy conquests to English trade. From its centres in the Savannah-Altamaha region the traffic for peltry and slaves had been projected rapidly westward to the Mississippi, southwestward to the Gulf. Too rashly the Carolinians had aimed at the seizure from France of the whole fur trade of the Mississippi valley. The great Indian revolt of 1715 had checked their first western offensives, and had initiated a stiffer three-cornered competition for primacy in the South. It had given new point to fears of French encirclement in North America, a danger which southern leaders, at the end of the seventeenth century, had been among the first to envisage. Their successors had now made the French menace the theme of a persistent, and, at length, a successful propaganda for royal government and for a British frontier policy of forts and settlements upon the southern bor-

[67] *Diary*, II. 41.

ders, indeed along the whole western margin of the sea-board colonies. The Indian retreat from the Georgia region had cleared the way for the next advance of colonization. In 1721 the building of Fort King George had staked out the limits of that advance. By 1730 the disappearance of the last vestige of proprietary control had made possible at length the fulfillment of the Carolinian policy of expansion, adopted a decade earlier by the Board of Trade. Of that policy, anti-Spanish, to be sure, but basically anti-French, Georgia became, after 1732, the concrete embodiment.

APPENDIX A

Exports of Peltry, 1698-1765

Table I

Imports into Great Britain of beaver and deerskins from Carolina and Virginia, Christmas, 1698, to Christmas, 1715.[1]

		From Virginia		From Carolina	
		Beaver (number)	Deerskins (number)	Beaver (number)	Deerskins (number)
From Christmas, 1698,	to Christmas, 1699	2390	22678	1436	64488
1699	1700	2104	24900	1486	22133
1700	1701	1476	15107	451	51086
1701	1702	1063	18937	2724	49646
1702	1703	71	849	489	57881
1703	1704	2481	34387	540	61541
1704	1705	401	1958	25	10289
1705	1706	2679	24393	258	32954
1706	1707	526	12037	436	121355
1707	1708	590	2349	[no entry]	31939
1708	1709	1621	28511	52	52014
1709	1710	491	7521	125	68432
1710	1711	8050	22927	36	33409
1711	1712	4800	16230	314	80324
1712	1713	357	3019	242	60451
1713	1714	407	4952	533	50781
1714	1715	404	6843	694	55806

[1] Based on tables received by the Board of Trade from the Inspector General's office, Custom House, on June 19, 1716. The Carolina table is in C.O. 5:1265, Q 75; the Virginia table in C.O. 5:1317, P 69. Ibid., P 74, contains an inaccurate account of peltry imported from Virginia, 1706-1715, furnished by Mr. Cary.

TABLE II

Exports of deerskins from South Carolina, Christmas, 1715, to Christmas, 1724.[1]

	Deerskins (number)
From Christmas, 1715, to Christmas, 1716, ...	4702
" " 1716 " " 1717	21713
" " 1717 " " 1718	17073
" " 1718 " " 1719	24355
" " 1719 " " 1720	35171
" " 1720 " " 1721	33939
" " 1721 " " 1722	59827 [2]
" " 1722 " " 1723	64315
" " 1723 " " 1724	61124

[1] From table of South Carolina exports sent by Governor Nicholson to Arthur Middleton, July 23, 1726 (copy of paper furnished by Commissioners of Customs); C.O. 5:387, f. 112.

[2] From JCHA, January 31, 1724, it appears that the duties arising on skins exported January 1, 1722 to January 1, 1723 were £1564 9s. 10½d. (Carolina currency). At 6d. per skin these duties represented approximately 60,000 deerskins exported.

TABLE III

Exports of deerskins from Charles Town, November 1, 1724 to November 1, 1739.[1]

From November 1,	—	to November 1,	Chests	Hogsheads	Tierces	Loose Skins
1724	—	1725	139	6		349
1725	—	1726	162	8		2390
1726	—	1727 [2]	115	21		1912
1727	—	1728 [3]	105	29		790
1728	—	1729	119	46		1260
1729	—	1730	126	59		2356
1730	—	1731	185	116		400
1731	—	1732	40	240		580
1732	—	1733	29	385		428
1733	—	1734	20	312		1140
1734	—	1735	11	359		398
1735	—	1736	24	451		2009
1736	—	1737	5	339	7	1050
1737	—	1738		441	15	1465
1738	—	1739		559		856

	Deerskins (number)	Duties (currency)
September 29, 1726 to March 25, 1731	[79753][4]	£8972 5s 3d[5]
March 25, 1731 to March 25, 1732	[86771]	£2169 5s 9d
March 25, 1732 to March 25, 1733	[74483]	£1862 1s 9d
March 25, 1733 to March 25, 1734	[96523]	£2413 1s 6d
March 25, 1734 to March 25, 1735	[84958]	£2123 19s 0d
March 25, 1735 to March 25, 1736....	[81017]	£2025 8s 9d

[1] These statistics are taken from *Port of Charles-Town in South Carolina, November 1, 1737. An account of sundry goods imported, and of sundry goods this province exported, from the year 1724, to the year 1735.* Charles Town: Lewis Timothy, 1736, (broadside, BM); and from similar broadsides of 1737, [1738], [1739]. Unfortunately the accounts were kept by chests, hogsheads, etc.; but approximate totals for slightly different periods (March 25 to March 25) may be deduced from the records of duties collected. These are drawn from JCHA, September 20, 1733; May 22, 1736; and January 21, 1737.

[2] JC, February 8, 1728/9: Report of state of the province shows exports for 1726-1727 of 67247 heavy deerskins, 13218 light deerskins.

[3] Ibid., 1727-1728: 59260 heavy deerskins, 12103 light deerskins.

[4] Average annual export.

[5] Gross duties for whole period.

TABLE IV

Exports of deerskins from Charles Town, 1739-1765.[1]

Stuart From Christmas,	To Christmas,	Deerskins (pounds)	Hogsheads	*Gazette* From November 1,	To November 1,	Hogsheads	Tierces	Barrels	Bundles	Loose Skins
1739 —	1740	229500	450	1739 —	1740	432				
1740 —	1741	153180	298	1740 —	1741	330				
1741 —	1742	257952	506	1741 —	1742	426				
1742 —	1743	264844	519	1742 —	1743	536				
1743 —	1744	130884	257	1743 —	1744	347				
1744 —	1745	305717	661	1744 —	1745	657				
1745 —	1746	277728	602	1745 —	1746	574				
1746 —	1747	277545	607	1746 —	1747	589				
1747 —	1748	214956	427	1747 —	1748	720				
1748 —	1749	227363	618	1748 —	1749	535				
1749 —	1750	143948	299	1749 —	1750	392				
1750 —	1751	186916	444	1750 —	1751	468				
1751 —	1752	157489	342	1751 —	1752	370				
1752 —	1753	206990	424	1752 —	1753	438				
1753 —	1754	237858	477	1753 —	1754	493				
1754 —	1755	263586	512	1754 —	1755	449				
1755 —	1756	210434	408	1755 —	1756	[559][2]				
1756 —	1757	239817	450	1756 —	1757	[411][2]				
1757 —	1758	260433	476	1757 —	1758	[542][2]				
1758 —	1759	355207	609	1758 —	1759	527	1	7	18	8253
1759 —	1760	303610	514	1759 —	1760	449			335	2863
1760 —	1761	155902	276	1760 —	1761	397	1	1	358	
1761 —	1762	177491	350[3]	1761 —	1762	349			205	1143
				1762 —	1763	633		3	745	301
				1763 —	1764	413		2	381	3781
				1764 —	1765	259		1	841	1972 (& 19 packs)

[1] The statistics in the left-hand columns—of hogsheads and *pounds* of deerskins exported from Christmas to Christmas—are from a table (based on the Charles Town customs books) transmitted by John Stuart to the Board of Trade, March 9, 1764 (C.O. 323:17 R 74, ff. 499-501). The other figures were published from week to week in the *South Carolina Gazette*.

[2] The figures in brackets are supplied from Stuart's table.

[3] From this table it appears that a hogshead of deerskins ordinarily weighed from 500 lbs. to 515 lbs., according to the size of the skins and the method of packing. The skins exported to Great Britain probably averaged about 1½ lbs.

APPENDIX B
Prices of Indian Trading Goods (1716-1718).

GOODS	Savannah Town (1716)[1] Quantity	Buck Skins (number)	Cherokee (1716)[2] Quantity	Skins (number)
Gun	1	30	1	35
Pistol	1	20	1	20
Powder	1 lb.	"as you can"		
Bullets	50	1	30	1
Flints	18	1	12	1
Steel	1	1	1	1
Hatchet	1	2	1	3
Cutlass	1	8		
Sword			1	10
Knife	1	1	1	1
Hanger				
Scissors	1 pair	1	1 pair	1
Axe	1	4	1	5
Hoe (narrow)	1	2	1	3
Hoe (broad)	1	4	1	5
Kettles (brass)		"as you can"		
Looking glasses		"as you can"		
Pipes				
Rum				
Rum "mixed with 1-3 water"	1 bottle	1		
Beads	3 strings	1	2 strings	1
Salt		"as you can"		
Vermilion		3		
Red lead		3		
Strouds	1 yd.	7 [4]	1 yd.	8 [5]
Plains or half-thicks	1 yd.	3	1 yd.	3
Duffel blankets (white)	1	14 [6]	1	16
Duffel blankets (blue or red)				
Duffel blankets (striped)				
Double striped cloth				
Shirt	1	4	1	5
Coat (broadcloth, laced)			1	30
Coat (strouds, laced)				
Coat (half-thicks, laced)			1	20
Coat (double-striped cloth, laced)				
Coat (strouds, plain)				
Coat (half-thicks, plain)				
Hat (laced)	1	8		
Hat (plain)				
Calico (flowered)				
Petticoats (calico)	1	12	1	14
Scarlet caddice	1 yd.	1		
Red girdle	1	2	1	2

[1] JIC, August 11, 1716: 'A Schedule of the stated prices of the Goods, as they are to be disposed of to the Indians in barter.'

[2] Ibid., July 24, 1716: 'An Account of the prices of goods settled between Collo. James Moore and the Conjurer, the 30th day of April 1716 as they are allways to be sold to his people' ('all skins to be taken one with another').

[3] Ibid., November 29, 1716: 'Allowed to mix vermilion and red lead equally.'

[4] Ibid., reduced to 6 skins.

[5] Ibid., November 6, 1716, reduced to 7 skins.

[6] Ibid., September 10, 1717: on complaint of the Indians lowered to 2 skins per yard. Other abatements at the same time were: hatchets, 1 skin; caddice, 2 skins for 3 yards; 'likewise in the mixture with Rum, a convenient proportion.'

331

Prices of Indian Trading Goods (1716-1718).

Settlements (1718)[7]		Creeks (1718)[8]			
Quantity	"Heavy drest deer skins" (pounds)	Quantity	"Heavy drest Skins" (number)	Quantity	"Light" (number)
1	16	1	25	1	35
		1	12	1	18
1 lb.	1	1 lb.	1		"in proportion"
4 lbs.	1	40	1	30	1
50	1	20	1	15	1
1	2				
2	1				
		1	7	1	10
		1	4	1	6
		1	2	1	3
1	3	1	4	1	6
1 lb.	2½				
24	1				
1 gal.	4				
1 lb.	3				
1 lb. 2 lbs. } Mixed	20				
1 yd.	4	1 yd.	6	1 yd.	9
1 yd.	2	1 yd.	2	1 yd.	3
1	8				
2 yds.	7	1	6	1	9
		1	6	1	9
1 yd.	3				
1	3				
		[Listed, no price]			
		1	20	1	30
1	14	1	14	1	21
1	16				
		1	18	1	27
1	12	1	12	1	18
1	3	[Listed, no price]			
1	2	[Listed, no price]			
1 yd.	4				
3 yds.	1				

[7] Ibid., April 23, 1718: 'A Table of rates to barter by.'
[8] Ibid., June 3, 1718: Agreement with 'the Esqr. and several head Men of the Indians (commonly called Creeks).' Established as 'fixed rule' by resolution of same date.

INDEX

Abeca, Abecau. See *Abihka*

Abihka (or Coosa) Indians (Upper Creeks), 23, 39, 46, 82, 83 *n.*, 104, 169, 257, 268; numbers and location, 135

Abihkutci, Upper Creek town, 135

Achitia, 164 *n.*

Acolapissa Indians, 46, 67, 105

Adair, James, Indian trader and historiographer, 124; quoted, 125-6, 127, 135, 261

Adrian, Apalache chief, 258

Aëquité, 164 *n.*

Africa, 4, 215, 219

Agents, colonial, 177, 198, 210, 213; and western policy, 208-9, 218-20, 228-34; instructions to, 287-8. *See also* Barnwell, Berresford, Boone, Kettleby, Yonge

Agents, Indian, 89, 92, 95, 98, 201-2, 267, 271-2; functions, 150-2; jurisdiction, 166

Agrarian Laws, 139

Alabama Fort. *See* Fort Toulouse

Alabama Indians (Upper Creeks), relations with French, 23, 70, 78, 82, 83, 85, 95, 97, 104, 255-6; relations with English, 46, 82, 85, 88, 96, 104-5, 151, 169, 259, 265, 268; numbers and location, 135; and Chickasaw, 136, 273

Alabama River, 46, 102, 135, 257, 261

Albany, fur trade of, 50, 63, 109, 136; councils, 177

Albemarle Sound, 3, 5

Albemarle, Duke of, Proprietor, 118

Alford, James, Chickasaw trader, 181

Alibamons. *See* Alabama

Allen, Andrew, merchant, 121

Altamaha, Yamasee chief, 25

Altamaha, Yamasee town, 151, 164 *and n.*, 255

Altamaha Fort. *See* Fort King George

Altamaha River, Indians of, 36, 133, 178, 190; as boundary (of Carolana), 58, (of Azilia), 210, (of Carolina), 252; fortification of, 191, 230, 232-3, 245, 248, 251, 261; French designs on, 227, 229, 261; Anglo-Spanish disputes over, 236, 238-45, 249, 251-3; proposed settlement of, 264, 282, 294

Alvord, Clarence W., viii

Amelia Island, 26

Amy, Thomas, Proprietor, 142

Anderson, Adam, Associate and Trustee, 320 *n.*, 321, 323 *n.*

Andrews, C. M., on Azilia, 210 *n.*

Anglo-French rivalry, ix, 4, 22, 47, 63-107, 167, 185-6, 206-9, 211-12, 220-34, 238, 254-76, 281-2, 285, 303, 324-5; continental phase, 60, 63, 67, 71

Anglo-Spanish rivalry, 3, 7-11, 17-18, 22-6, 30-3, 64-5, 73-81, 86-8, 167, 185, 217-8, 222-3, 227, 238-53, 257-61, 265, 267-72, 288, 324; in the Caribbean, 5, 11; subordinate to Anglo-French rivalry, 71, 75, 77-8, 212, 233-4, 303, 325

Annapolis Royal, 235, 291

Annarea, projected colony of, 103

Anne, Queen, 83, 92, 101, 103 *n.*

Apalache, mission province, 7, 8-9, 24, 35, 73-5, 133, 179, 258; campaigns in, 75, 78-82, 86, 133; English occupation proposed, 94, 223.

Apalache Bay, 55, 230, 255

Apalache Indians, 8-9, 70; Spanish allies, 73, 74, 78, 86; conquest, 79-81; near Mobile, 86; in South Carolina, 88, 128, 187; in Yamasee War, 170, 173, 180-1; dispersion, 254-5; at San Marcos, 258

Apalache River, 9, 212

Apalachicola, Spanish province of, 34-6, 38, 45, 244, 254, 258; Lower Creek town, 134, 255, 268, 269, 271. *See also* Cherokeeleechee; Palachacola Old Town

Apalachicola Indians. *See* Creeks, Lower

Apalachicola River, 17, 23, 55, 56

Appalachian Mountains, 3, 15, 16, 30, 40, 44, 135, 206, 225

Apple Tree Creek, 129

Appomatox Indians, 21

Arachi, Cherokee town, 131

Aranguiz, governor of Florida, 6

Archdale, John, Proprietor, governor of Carolina, 37-9, 45, 109, 143 n., 145

Argoud, Sieur, 48

Argüelles, Captain Alanso, 6

Peter H. Wood

Dr. Wood lives in Hillsborough, North Carolina, and teaches colonial American history at Duke. He is the author of *Black Majority: Negroes in Colonial South Carolina from 1670 through the Stono Rebellion* (Norton paperback), which received the Beveridge Prize of the American Historical Association.

COLONIAL AND REVOLUTIONARY AMERICAN HISTORY IN NORTON PAPERBACK

Michael G. Hall, Lawrence H. Leder, and Michael G. Kammen (Eds.) *The Glorious Revolution in America: Documents on the Colonial Crisis of 1689* 9398

Christopher M. Jedrey *The World of John Cleaveland: Family and Community in Eighteenth-Century New England* 95199

Thomas Jefferson *Notes on the State of Virginia* N647

Francis Jennings *The Invasion of America: Indians, Colonialism, and the Cant of Conquest* N830

Winthrop D. Jordan *White Over Black: American Attitudes Toward the Negro, 1550–1812* N841

Stephen G. Kurtz and James Hutson (Eds.) *Essays on the American Revolution* 9419

Stanley I. Kutler (Ed.) *Looking for America: The People's History* (2d Ed.) (Vol. I) 95007

Benjamin W. Labaree *America's Nation-Time: 1607–1789* N821

Benjamin W. Labaree *Patriots and Partisans: The Merchants of Newburyport 1764–1815* N786

Douglas Edward Leach *Flintlock and Tomahawk: New England in King Philip's War* N340

James T. Lemon *The Best Poor Man's Country: A Geographical Study of Early Southeastern Pennsylvania* N804

Seymour Martin Lipset *The First New Nation: The United States in Historical and Comparative Perspective* 911

Kenneth Lockridge *Literacy in Colonial New England* 9263

Kenneth Lockridge *A New England Town: The First 100 Years* 9984

John McCardell *The Idea of a Southern Nation: Southern Nationalists and Southern Nationalism, 1830–1860* 95203

Forrest McDonald *The Presidency of George Washington* N773

Alan Macfarlane *The Family Life of Ralph Josselin, a Seventeenth-Century Clergyman: An Essay in Historical Anthropology* N849

James Madison *Notes of Debates in the Federal Convention of 1787 Reported by James Madison* N485

Jackson Turner Main *The Antifederalists: Critics of the Constitution, 1781–1788* N760

Jackson Turner Main *Political Parties Before the Constitution* N718

Edmund S. Morgan *American Slavery—American Freedom: The Ordeal of Colonial Virginia* 9156

Edmund S. Morgan *The Challenge of the American Revolution* 876

Edmund S. Morgan *The Meaning of Independence: John Adams, George Washington, and Thomas Jefferson* 896

Edmund S. Morgan (Ed.) *Prologue to Revolution* 9424